Analecta Gregoriana

Cura Pontificiae Universitatis Gregorianae edita
Vol. 242, Series Facultatis Theologiae: sectio A, n. 26

WILLIAM A. VAN ROO, S.J.

TELLING ABOUT GOD

Volume I.

PROMISE AND FULFILLMENT

EDITRICE PONTIFICIA UNIVERSITÀ GREGORIANA
ROMA 1986

IMPRIMI POTEST

Romae die 6 dec. 1985

R. P. Urbanus Navarrete, S.J.
Rector Universitatis

Con approvazione del Vicariato di Roma
in data 9 dicembre 1985

Editrice Pontificia Università Gregoriana
Editrice Pontificio Istituto Biblico
Piazza della Pilotta 35 - 00187 Roma, Italia

PREFACE

I insert this preface to forestall some possible bewilderment concerning at least two matters: (1) the length, content, and purpose of the Introduction; (2) the apparent paradox of this first volume.

First, then, my Introduction was conceived as an opening upon the whole of what is now projected as a three-volume work. Surely it is long. Yet it presents reflections which bear on the whole work, and it could hardly have been presented as a part or a chapter of this volume. All of the elements treated bear on the whole work, not on the first or second volume alone. I trust that the order will appear rational, and that this Introduction will indeed contribute to the preparation for the thought elaborated in the whole work.

Second, this first volume is paradoxical in more than one way. When I elaborated the Introduction, I did not intend to write what now constitutes this volume. As has been the case with my three preceding works,[1] I was driven by my own further questions to write books which I had not intended originally. A brief account of the origin and evolution of those works can help to clarify the purpose and function of those earlier works and of this volume of *Telling*.

Over seventeen years ago I intended to write two works, one in each of the fields of theology in which I had specialized: the general theology of the Christian sacrament, and the basic theological treatment of God. What I originally projected as an introduction to a work to be called *The Christian Sacrament* evolved into *The Mystery*. Work on a first draft of the work on the sacrament called for further reflection on symbolizing and symbols, and resulted some years later in *Man the Symbolizer*. Then I decided to do my work on God first. As I elaborated my thought, I reflected on many basic questions which could not be inserted into a work on God. Consequently I wrote *Basics of a Roman Catholic Theology*.

---

[1] *The Mystery* (Rome: Gregorian University Press, 1971); *Man the Symbolizer* (*Analecta Gregoriana*, vol. 222, Rome: Gregorian University Press, 1981); *Basics of a Roman Catholic Theology* (*Analecta Gregoriana*, vol. 226, Rome: Gregorian University Press, 1982).

The result was a series of three basic books. *The Mystery* is a personal reworking of the whole Bible, tracing the themes of salvation history and the mystery of Christ. It is my introduction to Christian life and theology. *Man the Symbolizer* presents the elaboration of some of my basic philosophical thought. *Basics* is a companion volume, presenting some basic theological thought.

When I began my work on *Telling About God*, I intended to do two volumes: *The God of Christian Experience* (in two parts: experiencing God, and The God whom we experience); and *The Search for Further Understanding*. As I planned a chapter on experiencing God in history, I thought that it would be helpful to begin with a section on what I called the dialectic of promise and fulfillment. What I projected first as a section of a chapter became what I thought would be Part I of the volume, and then it developed to proportions which make it my present first volume.

Obviously this first volume has a distinctive scope and nature. Clearly it is not a volume on Christian experience. Rather it contains a series of essays in biblical theology, developing the theme "promise and fulfillment." My purpose in developing this series of essays, for the most part concerned with the fulfillment revealed in the New Testament, is to set forth the revelation of the potential of Christian experience. Only as we come to grasp more fully what God has done in Christ, and what He has revealed concerning our potential fulness of life in Him, in Them, fully revealed as Father, Son, and Holy Spirit, can we envision what our life can be, what we can experience of God, and what we can know of the God whom we experience.

This volume of biblical theology, therefore, is a preparation for what must be said of experience of God. I set forth its relationships to the subsequent volumes below, pp. 48-53; and I shall make the matter clearer in the introduction to my second volume.

TABLE OF CONTENTS

INTRODUCTION

TELLING

First, a reflection on the key word in the title of the whole work, *telling*. It was occasioned by reflections on a verse of John's prologue, which I translate thus: "No one has ever seen God: the only Son, who is in the bosom of the Father, *he has told us about him*" (Jn 1.18). I have italicized the words in which I differ from the translation of the RSV, NEB, and JB: "*he has made him known*". Eventually my choice of translation here suggested the title of the whole book.

Why, then, do I translate as I do? The Greek verb is ἐξηγέομαι. BAG give the meanings *explain, interpret, tell, report, describe*; and for its sense in Jn 1.18 they suggest *he has made known* or *brought news of* (the invisible God). I prefer the simplicity, strength, and pregnancy of the Anglo-Saxon verb. To *tell* is to mention one by one, relate in detail, make known or manifest, disclose, divulge, reveal, inform, report to. *Telling* suggests all of the mystery of the revelation by which God told us of himself, and Jesus told us of the Father. It suggests too the mystery and the frustration of all subsequent telling about God, as the message is passed on. It suggests the limitations, the eternal inadequacy of all divine-human symbolizing. God can tell us about himself only by some sort of human symbolizing; and evidently we can pass on the word only by symbolizing which, though it is taken up into the divine self-manifestation, is always human[1]. Jesus *told about* the Father. He did so gradually by the words with which he spelled out the message. He did so by all of the human actions, and the whole of the human life which he lived. In both word and action, and by the whole of his human reality, he could reveal only bit by bit. Though as man he is the Prime Symbol, Prime Sacrament, most complete revelation

---

[1] For my treatment of divine symbolizing and symbols see *Basics*, pp. 41-70; divine-human symbolizing in the continuing process of God's self-manifestation, pp. 71-220; and theology in particular as a form of divine-human symbolizing, pp. 256-257.

of the Father, still as such he is an imperfect image of the full Reality. Only as the eternal divine Son is he the perfect natural image of the Father.

All telling, all symbolizing, bears the mark of human diffusion, limitation, movement. Whether it be prevalently intuitive or conceptual[2], all symbolizing is discursive in the primitive, etymological sense of the word *discourse*: dis-currere, to run in different directions. From the center of his personal sphere[3], symbolizing man can thrust out in an infinity of directions, in the ever inadequate effort to image the full reality of the world which he encounters and of himself. If this is true of all human symbolizing, how much more is it true of human attempts to pass on the message about God. To the end of time we shall never finish telling.

Telling, then, is very apt to express the total process in which we shall be engaged in the whole of this work. Whether we gather the intuitive symbols by which God has revealed something of himself, and by which men and women have continued to witness to the God whom they have experienced, or attempt in prevalently conceptual symbols to work out some further understanding of God, we shall be telling about him.

EXPERIENCE

The second volume of this work will be entitled *Experience*. In it I shall deal with Christian experience of God, and briefly sum up what can be said of the God whom we experience. I am fully aware at the outset of a number of problems suggested by the title, and I wish to spell them out briefly and make clear what I am attempting to do in this work. Taking them in the order of intelligibility, I shall deal with experience, experience of God, Christian experience of God, and the God of Christian experience.

First, then, what do I mean by experience? This is the basic question, for the others arise in turn from my notion of experience.

I take *experience* in the limited sense which concerns me here and in my preceding works, *Man the Symbolizer* and *Basics of a*

---

[2] For the basic treatment of conceptual and intuitive symbolizing and symbols see especially MS, pp. 186-194.

[3] For the notion of sphere see MS, pp. 105-142.

Roman Catholic Theology: I am considering *human experience*. Whatever could be developed regarding an analogous phenomenon in lower forms of life, or treated by a theologian dealing with suprahuman beings, I am concerned with human experience. Moreover I am concerned principally with fully conscious experience: in full waking consciousness, as opposed, for example, to dream consciousness. The reason for this concern is the conviction that the structures of such experience are most accessible to our reflection, and that such structures enable us best to understand the properly human way of being.

Experience, then, is a small segment of total process in the universe of bodily being. Like all that is bodily, man is involved constantly in the infinite interplay of forces and agents in the continual process of the universe. Like all living things, man has a specific range of susceptibility to stimulus which evokes a properly human response. That specific mode of susceptibility and response is a function of the organization which is characteristic of the highly complex human way of being and operating. Because man is in a bodily way, there is a bodily, "physical" element in both stimulus and response as they figure in all human experience. At the higher levels of human operation, both stimulus and response are within the realm of human consciousness: awareness. As man undergoes influence, and as he responds, he is aware of the "other" which somehow acts upon him. He is aware too both of his operation regarding the other, and of himself operating. His awareness, or consciousness, of the other is objective: it regards the other, not in the fulness of its being, but in the manner and to the extent to which it affects him and is the object of his conscious, "intentional" operation. His awareness of his own operation regarding the other, and of himself "caught" in his operation regarding the other, is subjective. In turn, he may stand back and reflect on his operation, and then on himself the operator. In doing so he objectifies his operation and himself, making them in turn the object which he considers. Even in such objectification, however, he is aware of the operations by which he performs it, and of himself operating. He never catches up with subjective consciousness, for it is at the core of all objectifying, of all conscious, intentional operation.

The mystery of consciousness is part of the mystery of knowledge, and intellect permeates all conscious operation, all experience: cognitive, emotive-volitional, and motor. I have dealt with all of these matters at considerable length in earlier works, and I must be content here with the basics which I have mentioned, referring to other works for further treatment[4].

One aspect of human experience, however, calls for emphasis here, since it occasions the further questions which we must consider. It is the bodily, "physical" dimension of all of the forces and agents which affect us, and to which we respond in cognitive and emotive-volitional-motor operations which are bodily, whatever they are beyond that. Our knowledge begins with the senses: with what we somehow perceive, or remember or imagine, in operations which are somehow derivative from original perception. What we know to be good or bad for us, to the extent to which it attracts or repels by reason of its perceptible, remembered, or imagined qualities, somehow involves a response which is emotive and motor: reverberating in our humanly bodily being. All experience begins somehow with perception, though it be permeated from the outset by intellect.

What we have considered thus far, however, does not suffice to bring out the uniquely human way of being. Man is unique not only in his personal structure, his specific organization, and his patterns of stimulus and response, but also, and especially, in the distinctly human way in which persons interact in the interpersonal world in which men and women live most fully. We are involved not merely in a world of impersonal things and forces, but also in the higher world of human interpersonal action and response. We act upon one another, and react to one another. We do so normally not by buffeting one another and pushing one another about bodily, but by the vast gamut of our uniquely human symbolizing. We affect one another by communicating through symbols, sharing our thought and feeling and will, and evoking responses and effects in worlds of meaning.

Here we touch the properly human dimension of the sensuous and the sensibly perceptible factor of all direct human experience—indeed of all human experience. We symbolize in all of our conscious intentional operations. All of our symbols,

---

[4] The whole of MS is concerned with structures of human experience. The first part of the work discerns and differentiates conscious, intentional operations, their blend, and their permeation by intellect. For my treatment of consciousness and knowledge, see especially MS, p. 111-132. The second part, dealing with symbolizing and symbols, continues a reflection on the uniquely human way of being and operating, personal and interpersonal. Many of these developments are presupposed in *Basics*. One section of that work, however, gives further development to the notions of process and human experience, pp. 122-127.

sensuous as they are, are meaningful, with varying blends of a manifold meaning, cognitive, emotive, volitional, and motor.

Whether we consider human encounter with things and impersonal forces, or with human persons, all of our human experience involves what is sensuous. It begins in awareness of what is somehow sensibly perceptible, in perception which is external or internal. One can affirm therefore that all human experience is somehow confined to the world of the sensuous. Yet, what we grasp, and the patterns of our response, have meaning which itself is not sensibly perceptible. So we rise somehow above the level of the sensuous. Yet we do so in operations all of which have their sensuous element. Our most profound—or loftiest—worlds of meaning are real and meaningful only for men and women, with cognitive, emotive, volitional, and motor meaning which makes sense only to human persons. Yet we elaborate and share those worlds of meaning by symbols in which we give meaning to the sensuous[5].

These reflections on characteristics of human experience must suffice here to suggest difficulties and questions concerning any alleged human experience of God. To those questions we must now turn.

EXPERIENCE OF GOD

How can we *experience* God? All human experience begins with the senses, with what is somehow sensibly perceptible. Within that perceptual experience, penetrated and permeated by intellect, we grasp relationships and elaborate intelligible worlds which are not themselves sensibly perceptible. Our total experience, cognitive and emotive-volitional-motor, therefore, transcends the merely perceptible factor in our experience. Yet the fact remains: all experience begins somehow with the senses, and is marked for ever, through all of its highest development, by its sensuous origins. God simply does not fall within the realm of the bodily, the sensibly perceptible. How, then, do men and women come to know him, and to respond to him as their known good?

---

[5] For further treatment of the sensuous factor in symbols, see MS, pp. 215-219; for meaning and meaningful, pp. 216, 220-222, 311-317; for the real and reality, pp. 135-140, 281-282.

We do not come to know God by somehow going "beyond" the universe of bodily being, to discover the "transcendent". Rather, we probe the world which does fall within the range of our direct knowledge. Because that probing leads to the grasp and understanding of something of the mystery of bodily things and persons, we somehow transcend the realm of the purely sensible by penetrating it. What we come to understand raises further questions. However much we understand and correlate relationships, eventually we face further questions which go to the very heart of persons and things: how and why *are* they? What is the ground of their very being? What is the ultimate goal of their endless, insatiable desires and strivings?

As we read something of the mystery of things and something of their manner of operating and of being, we may come to at least intimations of the answers to those further questions. In all times and in all places, as far as we can trace human experience, men and women have come to such intimations of a Transcendent: something or Someone who grounds the very being of the universe, and especially human life in all its mystery. Comparative religion traces such experience in all of its varieties.

The visible world, and human life, lead inquiring men and women to some answers to their deepest questions and concerns. Within the mystery of the visible world they come to some knowledge of a Transcendent. We call that Transcendent *God*.

I am concerned here in this section only with such intimations, with what can be achieved universally by men and women seeking to probe the mystery of the world and of themselves. All that they experience somehow symbolizes the Transcendent. By all of the visible universe we are led to affirm what we have come to call God.

How, then, does man experience God? By probing the sensibly perceptible world and himself. That is an answer to the question, but, as we shall reflect, it is a partial, severely abstractive answer. It is given in terms of what men and women can achieve by the power of human reason. God lies somehow within the range of human reason. There is a natural knowledge of God—at least within a larger knowledge in a human life elevated and transformed by the gift of a higher life, a share in the divine. All of the persons and things which we know are symbols, and the Reality which they image imperfectly is the full reality of God the Symbolizer. The natural knowledge of God corresponds to the universal revelation of God in all that he has made. That is the answer in brief[6].

Hypothetically such knowledge of God, and the total experience which it would initiate, is within the power and range of pure human reason. Hypothetically, by the pure power of human reason a man or woman could not only attain intimations of the existence of a god or God, but also elaborate a highly philosophical argument which would ground the certain affirmation that God *is*. I say *hypothetically*: all this lies within the power and range of human intellect. The hypothesis is twofold: first, that men and women would live in a state of "pure nature"; second, that the power of their intellect and will were not impaired as a result of sin. Actually neither hypothesis is verified. What we affirm in accordance with our faith is that no man or woman has ever lived except in the one world process in which all human process is taken up into the mystery of God's plan for a more than human life for us. All come under the influence of divine grace: no one lives in a state of pure nature. Moreover, allowing for the exceptions which we also affirm by faith regarding the God-man, and in some respects concerning his Mother, no man or woman has remained untouched by the effects of sin. The so-called "demonstration" grounding the certain affirmation of God's existence is possible, and it is a work of pure reason operating in the most difficult of all philosophical efforts. It is accomplished now. But to my knowledge no philosopher has ever accomplished it except within some religious experience, under the influence of grace. All this I merely assert here, for the matter calls for mention at this point. I reserve my own grounding of these assertions to my treatment of the role of natural reason within a life of faith, in the third volume of this work.

What I have said must suffice for now in answer to the general question regarding the possibility of a human experience of God. A further question remains, and I turn to consider it now.

---

[6] I have developed these notions elsewhere, and I shall have to return to a much more profound reflection in the projected third volume of this work. For now I can only refer to what I have elaborated. See my treatment of God the Symbolizer in *Basics*, pp. 41-70; for the transcendent world, MS, pp. 134-135; for universal and special revelation, *Basics*, pp. 43-49, 64, 71-93.

CHRISTIAN EXPERIENCE OF GOD

Christian experience of God is unique. It makes far greater demands than finding God somehow within the world about us by probing its mystery and coming at least to intimations of Someone or something which grounds its being and makes it somehow intelligible. That, as we have seen, is a work of human reason, and it can discover a certain intelligibility immanent in the visible world. For most men and women it is achieved sufficiently in the discovery of such intimations both of the existence of God and of its consequences for their way of life.

(1) *Greater demands: the "leap of faith"*. Christian experience of God is grounded on something more arduous and more demanding. It presupposes a certain sense that there is a God, and that we depend on him, seek him as our good, and must live according to our judgment of what is right and wrong in order to reach that good. Beyond this it calls for a "leap of faith": we must firmly believe and affirm what has been revealed by One who claims to be our God, tells us of himself and of his plan for us, and demands our faith as the absolutely indispensable beginning of all Christian life. What he tells us goes far beyond anything which we could discover by our own powers, probing the mystery of the visible universe and of ourselves. Such probing could never open to us the mystery of *who* he is, what he offers to us, and how we are to come to a fulfillment which transcends all human conception and imagination. We must *believe* in the full biblical sense: affirm as true what he has affirmed, trust in him to fulfill his promises, and entrust ourselves entirely to him. We can read the many signs that he has given, be convinced that he is good and truthful and that it is good for us to take his word, that he offers us an enrichment far greater than we could achieve by our own human powers. Still what he tells us goes beyond all evidence. We affirm unhesitatingly what is not and cannot be evident to human reason. We cling to him, commit ourselves to him, in the basic act of faith which combines a vague cognitive element and a strong impulse of the will toward what we sense somehow to be our supreme good.

By our act of faith we enter into the shared experience of a multitude of fellow-believers, present and long-past. We are in continuity with a living tradition which goes back to Abraham and all who received God's gradual revelation, responded in faith, and bore witness to their experience. We are in continuity with the experience of those who heard Jesus tell of the Father, and tell too who he himself is. More directly we are in continuity with all who did not themselves hear the words of God revealing himself in the Old Testament, nor the words of Jesus; who did not themselves see the signs, the works performed by God and then by Jesus; but who believed taking the word, the witness, of those who had. Moved by the Holy Spirit teaching us interiorly and drawing us, we believe even though we ourselves have not received the Word nor seen the signs. We are in the living community of believers through the centuries and spread around the world.

In a sense our faith is more arduous and more demanding. Yet we are at no disadvantage. Those who saw the signs did not believe fully until they had received the Holy Spirit: then, when the signs were no longer visible, then alone did they fully believe, taught and moved by the Spirit within them. We have the consolation of sensing that we are among those of whom Jesus spoke to Thomas: "Have you believed because you have seen me? [or, with JB: You believe because you can see me ...] Blessed are those who have not seen and yet believe" (Jn 20.29: RSV). Essentially the demands of faith are made upon all: seeing and hearing is *not* believing. Thomas *saw*, but he still had to *believe*. He saw a sign. He professed his faith in an invisible reality: "My Lord and my God!" (Jn 20.28). One cannot believe without making the leap of faith beyond the visible and intelligible, beyond the evident [7].

(2) *I-Thou relationship with the revealing God.* In a relatively full sense, Christian experience of God involves much more than a leap of faith. We come to a relative fulness in our experience of God only when, as the beginning of a total response to him, we turn to him and address him in a full I-Thou relationship. What do I mean?

It is not enough to read or hear about God, to read or hear God's words about himself, as for example in the text of Isaiah: "I am the first and I am the last; besides me there is no other God" (Is 44.6). In a sense, to hear such words is somehow to experience God: to come under the influence of his divine-human symbolizing through the prophet. Yet, I contend, more is required for a full Christian experience of God.

---

[7] For further reflections on the role of faith see *Basics*, pp. 137-142.

Nor is it enough to make a corresponding affirmation *about him*, or even a profession of faith *in him*, such as: "Yahweh, the God of Abraham, Isaac, and Jacob, is the first and the last"; or "I believe that Yahweh, the God of Israel, is the first and the last, the only God"; or to recite one of the many Christian professions of faith: "I believe in one God.... and in Jesus Christ...." To hear the word of God and either silently or in spoken words to believe or affirm *this about him* is somehow to make the leap of faith: I *believe* this about him. Yet Christian experience of God in faith comes to a relative fulness only in direct I-Thou relationship. What does this involve?

When I hear his words about himself, or the witness of others concerning him, he speaks to me, and I respond directly to him. Penetrating somehow the meaning of his words, affected personally by him through his words, aware of One who in a personal mode is addressing me personally, I respond to him in direct I-Thou relationship. With or without words, I address him directly: "*You* are my God. *You* are the first and the last. *You* are the Father of our Lord Jesus Christ, and our Father. *You* are love."

There is an analogy here with merely human interpersonal relationship. I can know much about a person. I can recognize his or her qualities, feel admiration and attraction and eventually love. But until I respond to such knowledge and attraction, until I turn to him or her in direct interpersonal relationship, and say: "*You are* wise and gentle, affectionate and considerate, loving and lovable. *I love you*", or make some other similar direct I-Thou response, recognition, and act of love—until then I have not responded fully to him or her as a person. And until two persons make such mutual affirmation, act of love and mutual gift of self, they do not fully experience each other. They do not begin fully to know each other. For only in the unique I-Thou experience of mutual knowledge and love can both come to a deeper, connatural knowledge of themselves and of the unique fulfillment which they have reached together. Only within such direct I-Thou relationships do two persons come to an increasingly full experience of themselves and of each other, to a deeper sense of their mystery in their massive connatural knowledge of the very shape of their experience of each other.

There is something analogous, and far more wonderful, in a relatively full and continually developing Christian experience of Father, Jesus, and Holy Spirit. Beyond all acceptance of propositions *about* them, and all professions of faith *in* them, beyond all such acts which are *third-personal,* we are moved to break the barrier of the unseen and unfelt, and address them person to person. Only in the ensuing, deepening experience of them do we come to a relatively full experience of them, including a knowledge of them which can be acquired in no other way. Only in a life in which we live in I-Thou relationship with them, and address them habitually in *full second-personal acts*[8], can we realize something of the potential of Christian experience, something of the deepening knowledge of the revealing and saving God. If, as I contend, religious experience in a life of faith is the matrix of theology[9], then without doubt such an I-Thou relationship with Father, Son, and Holy Spirit is indispensable as the living context within which a rich, authentic Christian theology can develop. I shall say more of this later.

(3) *Four ways.* How can we come to know God better, and be enriched by an ever increasing experience of God? I should indicate four ways, not the only ones which could be suggested, but surely important. I shall only mention them here, since I have treated them elsewhere[10]. Regarding the first of the four, I shall make some further suggestions later, in a section on Christian reading of the Bible. The four ways are these: (a) a Christian reading of the Bible; (b) the Eucharist; (c) experience of union with Father, Jesus, and Holy Spirit, and gradually increasing connatural knowledge (to which I have alluded also in the preceding paragraphs on I-Thou relationships); (d) learning from one another as we share our life in the Church.

In the second volume of this work, tracing ways of coming to know God, I shall be reflecting on structures of experience along these four ways.

FACTORS IN CHRISTIAN EXPERIENCE OF GOD

Christian experience of God is unique. To approach some understanding of it, and of what is involved in the attempt to discern it, and to determine aspects of the God whom we experience, I think that it is necessary to set forth the principal factors which are at work in it. I shall enumerate them, and give some brief account of them here. In my earlier work, *Basics,* I

---

[8] For my treatment of first-, second-, and third-personal acts, see MS, pp. 126-132.

[9] For the matrix of theology, see *Basics,* pp. 221-239.

[10] See especially *Basics,* pp. 212-220.

have treated many of them from a different point of view. At appropriate places I shall refer to more ample consideration proposed in that work.

I confess from the outset that, in my judgment, no single order can be established, according to which these factors should be considered. Consequently I make no claim for the exclusive advantage of the order in which I shall enumerate them. As I develop them, I shall point out some of the perplexities which beset anyone who would attempt to fix a single order of intelligibility.

(1) *Father, Son, and Holy Spirit.* Any analysis of factors must begin with the absolute primacy of the Divine Persons. For us, God has revealed himself as Father, Son, and Holy Spirit, one God in three Persons. All Christian experience is grounded in them, and is under their massive impact. Their operation in us penetrates all other factors which somehow mediate our experience of God, and which affect us with the power and efficacy of God acting upon us through them. All of our own acts of response are themselves borne by divine grace, by that heightening of our powers which is the mystery of their gift. They are present and acting within us. They are acting in and through all that affects us. Thus, the total effect of the divine word in Scripture far exceeds that of ordinary human words. As we read the Scripture, taking it as God's word, the Holy Spirit dwelling within us illumines us, teaches interiorly, gives us a sense of the deeper meaning of the word, gives us too a sense of the shape of our experience of reception and response, and guides us in the discernment of our experience. The total meaning of the word goes beyond the apparent meaning of any text. Our total experience of response exceeds any possible account in any of the modes of symbolizing which are within our power.

I have said that we must begin with Father, Son, and Holy Spirit as "factors" in Christian experience of God. Yet the first perplexity regarding order occurs here. Note the proportions of the problem. At times, in the search for an intelligible order, we can distinguish different bases on which the order is elaborated. Thus, at times, philosophers or theologians will distinguish two orders of priority in intelligibility: that of the elements in themselves, in their natural or causal order; and that of elements considered in the order in which we advance towards understanding. Neither order would suffice, or be completely satisfactory in the matter which we are considering. We are reflecting on factors in a mode of human experience. Since any such experience involves a multiple interplay, objective and subjective, of persons and things or events, personal and interpersonal, we cannot proceed simply considering either the order of elements "in themselves" or that of our knowledge and total experience of them.

Thus, regarding God, we can say that "in Himself" he is undoubtedly absolutely first. Yet we come to know him, and are able to think and speak of him, only as we ground a natural knowledge of God by probing the mystery of the world about us and ourselves. And, more to the point, God as he *is* is Father, Son, and Holy Spirit. That we can know only by his revelation and the faith which is his gift. So in a sense revelation and faith precede our affirming that God is Father, Son, and Holy Spirit. In our *experience* of God which, then, is prior: Father, Son, and Holy Spirit, or revelation and faith? This is only the beginning of our difficulties, for we are attempting to consider as far as possible all of the most significant factors in the Christian experience of God. As we shall see, they are many and extremely complicated, as far as any human knowledge of them is concerned. As in a living organism, everything is somehow related to everything. Thus, God's eternal plan and his original creation are prior to revelation and to our knowledge of them as they are illumined by faith. Yet we can speak of their significance for us, and of the manner in which they figure in our *experience* of God, only in the light of revelation. Creation itself somehow is the beginning of salvation history: it is part of God's eternal plan to bring all things to fulfillment in Christ. This we know only by revelation and faith.

Let this suffice to set forth the perplexity of our present problem. I renounce any claim to establishing *the* order of priority in intelligibility. We must hold all of the elements, and consider their interrelationships in a continuing contemplation of the whole Reality which is our concern: objective and subjective, personal and interpersonal.

(2) *Revelation and faith.* I couple these two, precisely because we are considering factors in Christian experience of God. Revelation really figures fully in that experience only when it evokes the human response of faith. Together, revelation and faith transform the world of the believer, or rather open up more of a Reality which was hidden. We find God, experience God, to the extent to which we come to know the whole of his revelation, in the Old Testament and in the New, and respond with faith. Only in the light of revelation do we come to know more of

ourselves and of God, respond to him, and come to something of our full potential in the share of the divine life [11].

(3) *God's eternal plan.* "In itself" obviously it is "prior". It figures in Christian experience of God only to the extent to which it has been revealed and we affirm it and continue to contemplate it in a life of faith.

(4) *Creation* from the "outset" is salvific: it is the beginning of the realization of the one divine plan for all of his creation, to be brought to fulfillment in Christ. We know of God as creator and lord, not as the conclusion reached by probing the world by the light of reason, but as he has revealed himself; and we attribute creation to Father, Son, and Holy Spirit. Our sense of his lordship and of our complete dependence is grounded on what we know of him by revelation and faith.

(5) *Salvation history.* Since creation itself is "salvific", God's saving action begins with creation. In a special sense we regard it as beginning with God's revelation to Abraham, and his action on behalf of Abraham in fulfillment of his promise. It reaches its culmination in Jesus Christ. In him revelation is complete, our salvation is radically accomplished. Jesus, the glorified Christ, is forever present and active in us and in all who will live to the end of time, as salvation history is fulfilled. We understand ourselves and our saving God in the light of revelation and faith which illumine all history. We locate ourselves, as did the Israelites and the early Christians, in that process of saving action. In that history we somehow define ourselves. As we contemplate saving action, we *know* our God, not only as he has acted in the lives of others, but as he is acting now in us.

(6) *The Church.* Part of the mystery of Jesus Christ, and of fulfillment of salvation in and through him, is the unique function of the Apostles and of the Church. Their vocation, and their total experience of Christ, figure in the very constitution of the Church. Their experience is normative for all times, and their witness is precious. We have in *Acts* and in the letters their testimony to first-generation post-pentecostal experience of living in Christ, and of knowing God as he has revealed himself fully, and as he continues to act in the lives of the community of believers. The Church itself is the unfailing mediator of Christ's word, will, and sanctifying action to the end of time. In the Church, in the endlessly varying interplay of all members according to their

---

[11] On revelation see *Basics*, pp. 71-93; on faith, *ibid.*, pp. 137-142; and on the "leap of faith", above, pp. 8-9.

proper charisms, we live and learn from one another more of the mystery of our saving God and of ourselves [12].

(7) *The Word mediated by the Church.* In the total role of the Church, it is fitting to single out a special factor: its mediation of God's revelation. As the Old Testament was gradually formed and recognized as God's word in the people of Israel, and handed on in the living tradition, so it was within the Church that the New Testament was formed and the whole of the Bible was recognized as God's word. That word is preserved and passed on in the living tradition of the Church, and its interpretation is secured from error by the unfailing teaching power and authority of the Church. The Bible plays a unique and indispensable role in our lives, and in our Christian experience of God. We shall reflect on Christian reading of the Bible, and its role in that experience.

(8) *Sacraments and sacrifice.* As Father, Son, and Holy Spirit continue to have a massive impact upon us through their word, preserved in the Bible; so too they influence us powerfully in and through the public worship of the Church, principally the sacraments and the Eucharistic sacrifice. Every such act of public worship is a complex peak experience in the life of the Church. It is a symbolic action in which Father, Son, and Holy Spirit continue in a special way to show forth and to accomplish in us their saving action: *They* are acting. In the human frame within which such action is accomplished, sacraments and sacrifice are the principal acts in which Christ continues to offer his worship of the Father in and through the Church, the ministers, and the symbolic actions in which that worship reaches its term. He honors the Father by an act which consecrates and sanctifies his sons and daughters. But the role of the Church and members is not merely instrumental, mediating a descending, sanctifying divine action. In the total celebration of public worship the Church, in the Spirit, honors Christ her Spouse and the Father; and all participants are taken up into that action.

Sacraments and Eucharistic sacrifice mediate our experience of God in a unique way. Approaching with faith, with a deep sense of the symbolism of those acts, we encounter God in privileged moments of our life, experience his saving and sanctifying action, come to deeper union in faith and love, and realize a massive connatural knowledge of God. In the sensibly perceptible aspects of these acts we show forth the mystery of

---

[12] For an ample treatment of living in the Church, and its role in the continuing process of God's self-manifestation, see *Basics*, pp. 119-220.

what we are.   In the invisible reverberation of his grace within us we come to a deeper knowledge of what we are, and of what kind of God he *is*—They *are*.

(9) *Total personal response.*   In sacraments and sacrifice we are active, responding in faith and love and pledge of fidelity. Our action in public worship rises from the ground of a total personal worship, a life of personal prayer, of faith, love, and covenant fidelity.   His saving action comes to its relative term in our response. We come to a greater realization of our potential of life in Father, Son, and Spirit.   As we do so we come to a deeper massive connatural knowledge of Them and of ourselves living in Them.

(10) *Interplay of human persons.*   As men and women, we live most significantly in the human interpersonal world, and what counts in that world—or those many worlds—is most real to us.   As Christians we live most fully in the transcendent human interpersonal world of the Christian community of believers, and in the larger fellowship of all men and women who are living according to their consciences, whatever their explicit profession of belief, disbelief, or ignorance of the revealing God.   To the extent to which we live in God, and especially to the extent to which we live explicitly Christian lives and show forth something of the unique Christian mystery, we symbolize to one another, teach one another, mediate to one another the knowledge and love of the God in whom we believe.

At any moment in the experience of a Christian all of these factors are somehow operative.   Through all of the factors which are somehow mediatory, Father, Son, and Holy Spirit are acting upon us.   We experience Their impact in all of the other factors. They are present and operating in all, and symbolizing in and through all.   They are continuing the divine process of self-manifestation.   They are evoking our total response.   To the extent to which we respond, we experience God in a connatural knowledge, a dimension of our life of faith, love, and fidelity.   All of these factors, therefore, function in our experience of God.   It is within that total Christian experience that we may hope to come to deeper explicit knowledge.   Within such experience alone a Christian theological account of God can be elaborated.

CHRISTIAN READING OF THE BIBLE

My purpose here is twofold: to recall some of the elements which I have developed at length in *Basics,* and to add some complementary reflections.

(1) *General principles.* The Bible is the inspired word of God. It is a single complex written linguistic symbol, elaborated by men moved by God, term of a divine-human symbolizing. God properly is the Author, the Symbolizer. The meaning of this complex symbol is *His*: going beyond the meaning and intention of the individual authors. The Bible images the total Reality which God revealed: God himself, eventually fully revealed as Father, Son, and Holy Spirit; his eternal plan; its gradual revelation and realization in saving action which culminates in Jesus Christ and continues in the life of the Church to the end of time; and the final consummation. The efficacy of the Bible is divine: beyond all human efficacy which could be measured in terms of literary excellence or of the depth of the human experience of the individual human symbolizers. Consequently the Bible is to be read with faith, reverence, prayer for illumination, response of faith and love. Reading the Bible in this way, Christians in the Church come to a deepening insight and a deepening of their full response to the divine word, bearer of the divine grace. In our very response, personal and interpersonal, we somehow continue to show part of the meaning of the Bible: salvation history coming to its term in us. The Word was given once for all. Its meaning in part is shown forth continually in the gradual realization of salvation history in the lives of men and women [13].

I should like to make some further suggestions regarding a Christian reading of the Bible. They concern what I should call *prologues* and *flashes.*

(2) *Prologues.* First, in my judgment one can regard at least four passages of the New Testament as prologues, not just to the individual books which they serve to introduce, but to the Bible as a whole. Differing greatly among themselves in literary form, somehow they have in common the function of profound theological introductions which are meant to guide the reader in the interpretation of what follows in the individual books, and—in my view—of the whole Bible.

To me it seems that there is a basic question running through the gospels, sometimes explicitly formulated, always somehow implicit: who *is* he? The question, of course, regards Jesus. True to what we can judge to have been the strategy of Jesus himself, the gospels present him in such a way as to make a gradual

---

[13] For the development of these elements, see *Basics*, pp. 94-118, 130-137, 213-217, 304-315, 343-351.

revelation, a "veiled unveiling", of the answer to that question. The letters contain earliest Christian witness to the experience of who he really is. What I call prologues stand out as markedly different from the rest. I regard them as theological formulations of deep insights into the mystery of Jesus. If I read correctly the intention of the individual human authors, and of the Prime Symbolizer, God the author of the whole, these prologues suggest what we are to keep in mind as we read the rest. They provide the theological ground for the gospel narrative and for the development of the arguments of the letters. They are "theological", not like later conceptual theology which is developed in the subsequent life of the Church, but formulations of deep insights into the Mystery. They are the fruit of illumination and perhaps some further revelation by the Holy Spirit, and of reflection on a rich Christian life in the apostolic community.

What passages do I have in mind? There are four, two in the gospels, and two in the letters. I shall not go into a detailed commentary on them. In themselves they are well-known. For my present purpose it is enough to cite the passages, and to explain why I consider them to be "prologues" to the whole Bible, every one in its own way.

First, Lk 1-2 is much more than a unique nativity-childhood gospel, with a skillful, highly artistic parallelism bringing out John's greatness and the incomparably greater dignity and role of Jesus. This finely worked narrative, somewhat like that of the Yahwist in the Old Testament, in its own way, by a unique intuitive symbolism, proposes an implicit theology. If we ponder its meaning, and keep it in mind as we read the remainder of the gospel, we come to a deeper insight into the meaning of the veiled unveiling of Jesus in the gospel narrative. Holding the profound theological insight of the prologue, we contemplate Jesus with a sense of the answer to the tantalizing question: Who *is* he really? Beyond that, such a reading of the whole of Luke in the light of the meaning of the prologue contributes in turn to our deeper insight into the full Reality which is imaged in the symbolic elements of the whole of the New Testament, and indeed of the whole Bible.

Second, Eph 1.3-14, whatever one may hold with one or other group of critics in the matter of Pauline authorship[14], is one

---

[14] For the matter of Pauline authorship and Pauline thought, see J. A. GRASSI, M. M., "The Letter to the Ephesians", JBC, II, 56:4-9, pp. 341-342; and J. A. FITZMYER, S.J., "Pauline Theology", JBC, II, 79:8-9, p. 802.

of the most profound New Testament texts. It is a theological prologue (not in temporal order of composition, but in the order of intelligibility of a whole body of thought) not only to *Ephesians*, but immediately to the whole of Pauline thought, then to the rest of the New Testament, and finally for the Christian to the whole Bible. It formulates the most profound Pauline insight and understanding of the mystery of Christ, his place in God's plan, and our relation to him. Thus, in its own way it presents a Pauline counterpart to recitals of salvation history culminating in fulfillment in Christ and his role in our regard, such as Luke presents as the apostolic preaching, for example in Acts 2-3. What we come to understand by prayerful reading and reflection upon Eph 1.3-14 contributes to our Christian reading of the whole Bible.

Third, Heb 1.1–4.13. Most perhaps would wonder at my taking so much of the opening of the letter and calling it a "prologue": more commonly commentators would regard 1.1-4 as the prologue or introduction [15]. Granting that their view is preferable for anyone seeking to understand and present the structure of the letter, still, in the special sense in which I am considering "prologue", I take 1.1–4.13 as a unit which spells out the unique dignity, excellence, and role of the Son, Jesus, in comparison with both angels and Moses. Again, if we ponder its meaning and keep it in mind, it illumines in turn the whole letter, the New Testament, and the Bible.

Finally, Jn 1.1-18 is the prologue par excellence. It is the deepest of all, and the most profound theological prologue to John's gospel and, for us, to the whole Bible. No one who has grasped something of the mystery announced in these verses should ever forget it, in subsequent contemplation of Jesus as he is portrayed on any page of the gospel, or in reflection on the witness given to early Christian experience in the letters of the New Testament, or in seeking to understand the whole Bible as somehow preparing for the supreme revelation in Jesus. In the gospel of John itself, when one keeps in mind this deep insight, there is a special poignancy to the recurring questions, "Who is he?" and "Where does he come from?"

Fitzmyer bases his study on ten letters, including Eph. Marcus Barth, *Ephesians*, AB, vol. 34 (Garden City, N.Y.: Doubleday, 1974), after weighing the arguments, concludes that "...it is advisable for the time being to still consider Paul its author" (p. 49). See below, p. 105.

[15] As examples which many readers can find near at hand, I cite the editors of the Oxford Annotated Bible, and Myles M. Bourke, "The Epistle to the Hebrews", JBC, II, 61:6-9, pp. 382-384.

So much for what I have called "prologues". What, then, do I mean to refer to with the other word, "flashes"?

(3) *Flashes.* I use the image *flash* to suggest a momentary brilliant illumination, which for an instant illumines all which before and after is wrapped in darkness. I have in mind isolated texts, or in one case a symbolic element which recurs. Every one of them stands in stark contrast to its context. In that sense they are like flashes in the dark. Yet, if we reflect for a moment, the figure "flash" is utterly inadequate. The light of these texts is never extinguished. They are momentary and passing only in the sense that the reader passes on. Perhaps most readers never notice the brilliance of these elements in the text, or notice but do not pause to reflect sufficiently, and so do not gain the insight which these texts can occasion: they have only the vaguest notion of their meaning but do not probe it, grasp it, and retain it. These are texts on which we should pause, and to which we should return often. What we can come to understand should become part of us, and affect our reading of the whole Bible. They image in very special ways that Reality which in most of the Bible is only darkly portrayed. Far beyond what they meant perhaps to the individual human authors who contributed them to the total complex symbol, they can give us precious clues to the meaning of the Principal Symbolizer: God's meaning, which *is* the meaning of the Bible.

What texts, or elements of texts, do I have in mind? I propose six, claiming neither that the list is complete, nor that all are of equal brilliance and profundity of meaning.

(a) Ex 3.14: the single word EHYEH, translated simply I AM. In the form of the first-person singular, in which God speaks of himself and gives his name as I AM, the name appears only in this verse. Then the name is given in the third-person singular, YAHWEH, in which it is locked for ever in the Hebrew text: even when in later texts God is speaking of himself, ironically only the form YAHWEH is retained where he identifies himself. In Israelite tradition the name is petrified in reverent awe, so much so that normally Israelites were not permitted to pronounce it. It stands in the written consonantal text, but is pronounced with the vowels of the Hebrew LORD, and eventually the written text is vocalized with those vowels. In such a tradition one could scarcely expect to find any reflection on the deeper meaning of the name. Exegetes by scientific efforts in modern times have differed concerning the meaning of the name in the original revelation. We are not even certain of its correct pronunciation, of which there is not a trace. Here perhaps more than in any other word of the whole Bible we may look for deeper insight only in the effort to find the deeper, richer meaning (the *sensus plenior*) [16].

(b) The theophany at Jesus' baptism by John: Mk 1.9-11; Mt 3.13-17; Lk 3.21-22; Jn 1.29-34. I am not concerned here with obvious differences in the texts of the Synoptics, and between them and the text of John; nor with the endless discussions of exegetes regarding the original experience behind the accounts given by the evangelists: who saw the Spirit, to whom were the words addressed, who heard them, etc. Taking the texts as they stand, one must face the question now: what do they tell of the answer to our recurrent implicit question, "Who is he really?" Taking the texts as varying readings on the reality of Jesus and the manner in which he was revealed, we must ponder these texts, seek their deeper meaning, and hold it as we contemplate Jesus in any scene of the gospels, or as we reflect on early Christian experience of him, recorded in the letters especially.

(c) The Transfiguration: Mk 9.2-8; Mt 17.1-8; Lk 9.28-36; and for a reverberation in what is presented as Peter's experience, 2 Pet 1.16-19. Parallel in part is Jn 12.28-30. For our present concern, two elements of the account of the transfiguration are significant: the vision of the transfigured Jesus, and the words spoken from the cloud. Together they constitute a symbol revealing in yet another moment who and what Jesus really is.

(d) Jesus' prayer to the Father in the Synoptics: Mt 11.25-27; Lk 10.21-22. So sharply does this text contrast with the rest of the Synoptics that at times it has been called the "Johannine passage in the Synoptics". It is remarkable both for the prayer which reveals suddenly something of the mystery of Jesus' personal relationship to the Father, and for the affirmation of the exclusive mutual knowledge of Father and Son. In their versions of the latter Mt and Lk differ, and it seems to me that Lk gives the more striking and more radical claim: " ... no one knows *who the Son is* except the Father, or *who the Father is* except the Son and any one to whom the Son chooses to reveal him" (Lk 10.22).

(e) Jesus' absolute affirmation: "I am": Jn 8.24, 28, 58; 13.19. Most probably echoing the divine name in the Old Testament, Jesus seems by the use of this absolute affirmation to claim to be God [17]. Though this sense of the affirmation seems

---

[16] See *Basics*, pp. 308-311. For a summary of exegetes' interpretations of the name Yahweh see DNTTh, "God", vol. II, pp. 67-70.

[17] R. Brown, in his *The Gospel according to John* I-XII (Garden City,

clearest in the four Johannine texts indicated, it resonates too in others where a predicate is supposed: 6.20; 18.5. Moreover, as Brown holds quite reasonably in my judgment, three synoptic texts suggest something of the absolute sense of the Johannine texts: Mk 14.62 and Lk 22.70; Mt 14.27 (Mk 6.50); Lk 24.36; and one "...approaches close to the absolute Johannine usage...."[18]: Mk 13.6; Lk 21.8.

(f) Jesus' "priestly prayer": Jn 17. This long prayer is a revelation both of Jesus' intimate relationship with his Father, and of his special love for his disciples, and the place reserved for them.

How, then, do these prologues and flashes bear upon our consideration of a Christian reading of the Bible? Immediately they may occasion insights into the mystery of Jesus. Gradually they should help us to gain deeper insights into the whole Bible. As a single complex symbol, God's word enshrining his revelation, every part bears somehow upon the full revelation which only gradually is communicated. Beyond the literal sense of Old Testament texts, there is a deeper meaning, an intimation of something of God's full meaning, brought out only in the course of a process of revelation which reaches its completion in Jesus Christ, and in the continuing process of illumination by the Holy Spirit and deepening insight and understanding in the life of the Church. The old Christian view that the whole Bible is somehow about Jesus Christ is right. In a unique way, then, our prologues and flashes, giving deeper insights into the mystery of Jesus, in turn enable us to reach a deeper meaning of the Bible as a whole.

DISCERNING CHRISTIAN EXPERIENCE

In dealing with this matter I should like to avoid or dispel two possible misunderstandings of what I shall be attempting in the second volume of this work, dealing with a Christian experience of God. The first is likely to be formulated explicitly: it is that of the critical reader. The second is likely to remain undetected, but to condition the manner in which my thought is received.

N.Y., 1966), pp. 533-538, gives an excellent concise exposition of uses of "I am" in Greek, and of the classes of meanings which are most probable in a number of Johannine passages.

[18] *Ibid.*, p. 538.

First, some critics may suspect that I have a naive conviction that I can "read my feelings" and discern in them what really cannot be discerned. Such suspicion, misunderstanding, and objection could come from one who has a more or less explicitly behavioristic notion of human experience. According to such conceptions, emotion and thought are illusory, unreal, and consequently there can be no question of a meaningful discernment of them. For such thinkers, what we call "feeling", or emotion, and thought too, are to be reduced to what is empirically observable and measurable: the bodily factors or dimensions in such experience. Such empirically observable bodily factors do not provide a base for any such discernment as I shall be attempting.

Second, more readers may be rather uncritical, and simply unaware of what I am really trying to do. They themselves perhaps have only what may be termed an "experience of experience", and "feelings about feeling". The whole matter has been simply unexamined, and is not at all problematic. Such readers would simply approach my work without a sense that the whole notion of experience and its discernment presents many problems. If indeed they would read this work, they could only suppose that I share their state of mind.

Both hypothetical types of readers, each in its own way, would miss what I am really trying to do, and miss my concern with the difficulty and the delicacy of the operation. I shall try to anticipate both of the misunderstandings by explaining as briefly as possible how I conceive human experience in general and Christian experience in particular, and how I conceive discernment to be possible.

I have dealt above with Christian experience of God (pp. 8-11). Let me attempt to make clear here what I think is involved in discerning such experience, and in giving an account of aspects of the God whom we experience in various ways.

Discerning our experience of God is not a matter of "reading" and discerning and differentiating our "feelings", and then subsequently giving an account of aspects of God which correspond to such feelings. I am concerned not with "feelings", but with the concrete whole of human experience, and in particular with a Christian experience of the God in whom we believe. Human experience is complex, with cognitive, emotive, volitional, and motor factors which are blended in a concrete whole. As I have set forth at length in *Man the Symbolizer*, such factors can be discerned and differentiated. That is what I did in developing the first half of the book, which is a re-thinking and re-elaboration of a basic philosophy of the human way of being. After an initial discernment and differentiation, however, I found it necessary to consider the blend, and to focus on the many roles of intellect which permeates all conscious experience. Within the operations which are properly emotive, volitional, and motor, there is a function of intellect which is indispensable. We cannot know what is good or bad for us, and respond to it appropriately, on the basis of mere sense knowledge. In all human discernment of the good and bad, and in all human response to both, intellect plays an important role, varying as it permeates operations which are emotional, volitional, and motor [19].

With regard to human experience generally, I should distinguish three aspects of the involvement of intellect. First, we are concerned with modes of conscious operation, and all consciousness is part of the mystery of knowledge. Our awareness itself is a function of intellect, permeating all of our sense awareness. Second, intellect plays a role in the discerning of the objects of our emotive, volitional, and motor operations, and in monitoring all such operations [20]. Third, obviously the discernment and differentiation of operations and objects in a reflection on structures of experience is the work of intellect.

Christian experience, being human, is characterized by the same basic human structure, the same blend of cognitive, emotive, volitional, and motor operations. It is unique because it is taken up into a far richer, more complicated world, opened by revelation and faith and the heightening of our human powers by God's free gift. We know now, not with our purely natural power of intellect, but with an intellect illumined by faith. We love Father, Son, and Holy Spirit, and we love one another in them, because we know by faith that they are lovable beyond all merely natural, merely human good. To the extent to which we respond emotively, we resonate to a good which is not sensibly perceptible; we sense joy and hope and desire which are themselves gifts of the Spirit, fruits of the Spirit within us.

When Paul witnessed to his sense of union with Christ, he wrote of an experience which was wonderfully real to him; yet it was an experience to which he came only in response to God's revelation of the life offered to him, of the gift given. Similarly

---

[19] For my extensive treatment of these matters, see *Man the Symbolizer*, pp. 17-181.

[20] See especially *ibid.*, pp. 143-181.

he tells of his sense of the Spirit within him, as he lives fully the life opened to him by faith and all of God's gifts to him. When he writes of the role of the Spirit in our lives, he is witnessing to a reality which he knows from experience. Surely the letters of Paul are full of emotion, of passion, and of strong drive. He is aware of all this, with an intellect enlightened by faith. He has a connatural knowledge of Father, Son, and Spirit: of the shape of the very experience of living in them, and of loving his fellow Christians in them. In all of Paul's rich and eloquent testimony to a life of Christian experience we can sense the influence of the many factors which I have enumerated above: factors of Christian experience [21].

Discerning Christian experience, then, is not a matter of merely "reading our feelings". Like all discernment of human experience, it involves a multiple role of intellect. Beyond all merely human experience, it involves intellect illumined by faith and the gifts of the Spirit. Because we know now by faith, we know all of the factors which I have enumerated in Christian experience. We are aware with the awareness of an intellect guided by faith. Similarly we know what is good for us as we discern with an intellect enlightened by faith. We discern and differentiate elements of our total Christian experience by the operations of intellect enlightened by faith.

Of all the factors which I have indicated above, the most important for our present consideration are these: revelation and faith, and the operation of Father, Son, and Holy Spirit within us. They are the Word: the external word spoken or written, and the inner word by which God enlightens us. Our Christian experience is a total response to that Word. All of our cognitive, emotive, volitional, and motor operations regard "objects" which we know only because we have received the Word, and live under its influence. All of our discernment of Christian experience is possible only in the light of revelation and faith and the interior teaching of Father, Son, and Spirit dwelling in us. It is a properly theological work, a work of intellect enlightened by faith, discerning and differentiating and elaborating intelligible structures within a life of faith, whose shape is vaguely known in massive connatural knowledge by all who share that life.

---

[21] See, for examples, Phil 3.3-14; 2 Cor 4.1,5-12; 5.13-21; 1 Cor 2.6-16; Rom 8. I have dealt with these texts among others which bear witness to the fulness of Christian life in *The Mystery*, esp. pp. 247-284.

Christian experience is unique. Theology is unique. Neither is intelligible except for those who share the same faith, the same experience. If anything should be obvious from all that I have said, it is this: we are concerned here not with a "god of the philosophers", but with the God of Christian experience.

The God of Christian Experience

I am concerned here with the God whom we encounter in Christian experience: what kind of God is He? In terms of my theory of symbolism, applied to the whole process of God's self-manifestation, what is the Reality which is imaged in all of the divine-human symbolizing and symbols by which God has revealed himself and continues the total process to the end of time? In the whole of his creation and continuing operation in all persons and things, by all that he has made and sustains in being and operation, God symbolizes. Imperfectly even in the whole of his creation, nonetheless in and through it all, he images himself: shows forth something of his infinite perfection. Whether by the intimations which men and women have had in all times and all places, or by the rigorous philosophical reasoning which few have achieved—and, as I have affirmed, only within a religious experience—it is possible for men and women to read the divine symbols in creation, to penetrate the mystery of the universe and especially their own human lives, to come to some knowledge of God. They can spell out something of their conception of God. In doing so, they themselves symbolize about God, and their symbols image both their own personal experience and the transcendent reality which they have encountered in their probing. In knowing God to any degree, and in responding to what they recognize somehow to be their supreme good, they are somehow experiencing God. It is not their *experience* of God which is God, but the *God* whom they experience: the Reality which they find imaged in the world and in themselves, and which in turn they image in all of the symbols by which they elaborate and portray their knowledge and total response to God. At any level of human experience of God, we must distinguish similarly between the experience of God and the God who is experienced. What *is* the invisible Reality which men and women discover, and to which they respond, as they probe the mystery of the visible universe and of themselves?

We have reflected on what is unique in Christian experience of God. We must ask now about the God whom Christians experience, and about whom they tell.

We may answer that question by distinguishing three levels of experience which for the Christian have a certain continuity. The first is that which I have just recalled: the experience which lies within the range of the power of human intellect, and which has been had by men and women in a variety of ways throughout the ages, as far as we are able to read the record of human thought and feeling. It corresponds to God's universal revelation of himself in all that he has made. The second and third are unique, proper to Israelite and Christian experience of God. Both are possible only in response to God's special revelation, by which historically at given times and in given places he somehow "spoke" to chosen men and women, telling of himself and his plan for man. Moreover, only by his gift of faith could the men and women who received his word believe: affirm what he said as true, trust in his promise, and entrust themselves to him. They had to make the leap of faith. Knowing roughly, as others did, what they meant by "God", they accepted the revealer as *their* God. Though they could not see the evidence of what he affirmed, they believed.

There are two clearly distinct phases in this unique Israelite and Christian experience of God. The second phase, however, is *real* and valid only for a Christian. Keeping that in mind, let us reflect on what they involve.

First, Israelite experience of God, faith, knowledge of God and total response to him, presupposes what is possible for men and women universally: the knowledge corresponding to God's universal revelation. All that the Israelite could *know* about God by probing the mystery of the universe and human life, he or she now attributes to the God of Abraham, Isaac, and Jacob in whom they believe. I regard Psalm 104 as a striking illustration of what I mean. It is a hymn to God the creator. All that is sung in his praise could be attributed to God discovered in probing the mystery of heaven and earth, and all of the wonders especially among the living things and man. Since the Israelite acknowledges Yahweh alone to be *his* God, and his reflection on the dominion displayed by Yahweh in the course of salvation history has made him realize that Yahweh, his God, is the creator and lord of all, creation and dominion are attributed by the Psalmist to Yahweh. Whatever is true of *God* is true of Yahweh: he alone is truly God.

Beyond such knowledge of God, Israel knows about Yahweh from the whole course of his special revelation in word and action. Far more than the creator and lord who could be discovered by the power of human intellect probing the visible universe, the God of Israel is *Yahweh*: he has revealed his name, he has formed a people of his choice and entered into covenant with them, he has shown all of the personal qualities which could never have been known except by his revelation in word and action. World process, as a consequence of Yahweh's promise and fulfillment, merciful forgiveness and renewed promise, has a unique meaning and direction for the Israelite.

Israelite experience of God, then, involves knowing and acknowledging God on two levels: as the God of all that is created, who reveals himself universally through his creatures; and as the God who has revealed more of himself by his special revelation to Israel. The first is taken up into the second.

The God of Israelite experience, therefore, is the universal God, creator and lord of all, but to Israel he has revealed more of himself, and to this extent he can be known only by faith. This is what I have termed the first phase of the unique Israelite and Christian experience of God.

The second phase is Christian experience. For the Christian this experience is in continuity with that of Israel. It too takes up all that can be known of God by probing the visible universe: our God is the creator and lord of all. He is also the God of Abraham, Isaac, and Jacob. But further, for us, he is the Father of our Lord Jesus Christ, in whom and through whom he has made his final revelation of himself. For us, God fulfilled his promises to Israel by raising Jesus from the dead. He is all that we know him to be by believing the words of Jesus, whose revelation in word and in the whole of his life as man is illumined by the Holy Spirit, sent by the Father and Jesus. He continues to manifest himself in the life of the Church till the end of time. Our God, Father, Son, and Holy Spirit, is the one God whom we encounter in the whole of Christian experience. It is this one God who is revealed in part by his universal revelation, but far more wonderfully by his special revelation to Israel and then to us in Jesus Christ. He is the great Reality imaged imperfectly in all of the divine-human symbolizing and symbols. He is the one whom we encounter, whom we contemplate, and about whom we tell.

DISCERNING ASPECTS OF THE EXPERIENCED GOD

Our experience of God is not God: we cannot stand back to contemplate our experience, and have the illusion that we are contemplating God. Yet it is only in experience that we know God and respond fully to him in faith, love, and fidelity. In such acts we are not reflecting on ourselves and on the structure of our operations. Rather we are directly concerned with him, with Them: Father, Son, and Holy Spirit.

In our effort to tell of God, to give an account of the God whom we experience, we proceed by discerning aspects of our experience, and discerning accordingly aspects of the God whom we experience. In the elaboration of this work I shall consider many such aspects of our experience, and aspects of the experienced God. With regard to such discernment, I should like to make clear what is involved, and how such a procedure is possible and fruitful. Here, as above in my treatment of discerning Christian experience, I seek to avoid a possible misunderstanding.

One might object that discerning aspects of God is like carving water: we do not really discern or divide, but come again and again to a few basic notions of God's power, love, truth. So as a matter of fact, in the course of our investigation, it may seem that we come repeatedly to affirm a few attributes of God.

There is an element of truth in the objection. Yet from many different experiences of God we come to know different facets of God's love, lordship, and so on. In the fulness of his being God is simple. We come to know him only gradually as we discover more and more fully the kind of God he is. Every limited experience of him brings deeper insight, some further truth and understanding. What is simple in God can be approached and grasped imperfectly only as we continue to find him and to contemplate him in an experience which is manifold and varied. I trust that the whole course of our consideration will make my meaning clear by continual illustration.

I AM. YOU ARE. HE IS.

(1) *A peak experience.* I begin by recounting again an experience, quoting the account with which I concluded *Man the Symbolizer*:

One last bit about man the symbolizer. It is something which struck me a few years ago, and which I have shared with many. As I prayed the thirty-fifth Psalm one day, I was struck by verse ten: "O LORD, who is like thee..." I stopped and reflected: what would be the effect if we replaced the capitalized "LORD" with the name for which it stood? But in what form? If God, speaking of himself, said that his name is "I AM", and if the sacred writers, writing of him in the third person, wrote the name 6000 times as "HE IS", then, when I address him directly the name should be "YOU ARE". It is a simple, two-syllable linguistic symbol. How it transforms that prayer! "O You ARE! Who is like you?" "YOU ARE!" It is a massive affirmation of the fulness of being of the Beloved. All else that I can say of him or to him merely retails the wonder of that name. It is a massive affirmation, full of wonder, love, joy. It expresses the full thrust of symbolizing man, who would burst the bonds of language, who tends toward a knowledge and love which will not terminate in any image fashioned by man. He stretches for a moment and yearns to fly—and still is standing on his toes [22].

For me personally, and for some with whom I have shared it, that insight into the implications of the divine name, as God is recorded as revealing it (Ex 3.14), was a memorable experience. It remains a part of me, and has affected my own religious experience of God. More recently, as I planned this work, it served to challenge me as a theologian, and to force me to bring into focus the nature of my task, the method which I must employ, the kind of *telling* which is properly theological.

Before I undertake to explain the theological challenge, I should like to say what I think is involved in the insight and conception regarding the divine name. What I have suggested concerning the sense of the name in its original form, and the shift to the third-person singular throughout the Hebrew Bible, has nothing to do with scientific exegesis aiming to establish the literal sense of the text [23]. Nor, on the other hand, do I regard it as a mere "bright idea". It is a theological reflection, and I think that it may qualify as a bit of theological exegesis. In my own experience it continues to resonate in the dialectic of religious and theological experience.

---

[22] MS, p. 340.

[23] I have cited a representative summary of exegetes' views above, in note 16, following my brief treatment of Ex 3.14 as one of the "flashes" which illumine the whole Bible.

(2) *Three ways of telling.* How does this reflection set problems regarding the properly theological manner of *telling*? By the title of this section I intended to suggest three kinds of telling. "I am", "You are", and "He is" are three massive existential affirmations. Each is in a sense the model of a kind of telling. Each is also the massive initial affirmation whose implications are unfolded in all subsequent telling according to that model. The question is, first, what are the three kinds of telling; and then, what kind is proper to theology?

Our whole reflection regards revealed truth and the ways in which it can be affirmed. "I am" is a massive existential affirmation in the first-person singular. It is the way in which God speaks of himself, and in which later Jesus too will speak of himself. It is the properly divine way of telling. Since it is a massive existential affirmation, it is not only the model of all subsequent particular affirmations by which God/Jesus tells of himself, but is also the affirmation which contains eminently and inexhaustibly all that can be spelled out in detail. It is absolutely original in the realm of revealed truth, the absolute beginning of the telling in which God will reveal himself and his plan for us, and invite us to share in his own divine life. It is exclusively the model and the manner of God's telling about himself. Both in its interpersonal structure and in its meaning it is unique and proper to God himself, and to Jesus, speaking to us about himself. No one else can affirm absolutely: "I am". No one else can speak thus in the first-person about God. Obviously, then, there is no question here of a possible way of the theologian's telling about God.

"You are!" is the radical personal response made directly to God/Jesus in a massive, full second-personal act: in full I-Thou relationship. It is the immediate massive response to God's radical "I am". Full of wonder and of love, it is the model and the matrix of all subsequent particular affirmation directed to him in I-Thou relationship. It not only sets the pattern, but holds eminently all that can be affirmed in this mode: all else that we affirm to him concerning what we believe he is merely spells out inadequately what is held in this radical massive affirmation and acknowledgment. It is the way in which we speak to him/them alone, telling what we believe about him/them. It is an expression of the deepest religious experience of God/Jesus. Whether in the uttered words or in silent wordless response, it is in this full second-personal response to God/Jesus that we encounter him in an act which is at once faith and love and full commitment—and all that we can spell out regarding the full implications of our response. In it we can come to a fulness and richness of religious experience, in which we have not only a sense of the shape of the experience, but our deepest knowledge of God. He is a personal God. We respond to him only in a full second-personal act, and only in the union with him in that act do we come to our deepest knowledge of him, the God whom we experience. It is a connatural knowledge, massive, implicit, relatively "primordial". Within that knowledge, in a life of prayer we tell him what we believe of him. From that knowledge we turn to tell others about him.

"He is" is first the massive affirmation which Jesus could make to his hearers about the Father and the Holy Spirit. There is no record of his having done so in this form, but I allow for this as a possibility in considering *who* could use this model in telling *whom* about *whom* or *what*. More to our immediate purpose, it is the model for all of our telling one another about God. It too is massive, absolute, indeterminate, unlimited. It is richer than the sum of all particular statements which we could make about God.

(3) *The theologian's way.* I have set forth briefly three models of telling about God. Which is proper to the theologian as such? Until recently I should not have considered the question. It seemed perfectly obvious that his telling about God follows the third model: he tells others about God, sharing with them what he is able to elaborate as he comes to some understanding within a life of faith. If he has come to some understanding of the mystery of the divine name, he knows that the affirmation "He is" holds eminently all that he may be able to formulate in explicit conceptual symbols. What doubt could there be about his model? Obviously it is not "I am", for the reasons which we have considered. Nor could it be "You are": for theology is not prayer. But is the matter so obvious here? I think not: there are reasons for serious consideration of the question.

First, let me approach the matter by sharing an experience which admittedly is personal, and therefore of little significance as a solitary witness; but which can hardly be unique. I use it to approach my question, not to ground any conclusion regarding my reply.

Long ago, in my first months of attempting to meditate as a Jesuit novice, I experienced difficulty with the "method" of meditation which we had been taught to use, and I found it necessary to modify that method in order to yield to what seemed clearly to me to be the movement of grace. My difficulty came with the process of reasoning *about* God or some aspect of our life in relation to him, and then moving on to a "colloquy" with God. In the colloquy one made the appropriate volitional and affective responses to what had been the object of the meditation. After a short time I had two difficulties with this method. The first was that I found less and less need to "meditate", to reason: often a word or phrase of Scripture, or the mere thought of the Father, or Jesus, or some aspect of my conduct, sufficed to evoke the volitional and affective response. This was normal: gradually our meditation should yield to a form of prayer in which volitional and affective acts prevail; and indeed our prayer is simplified as such acts tend to fuse in a sustained dwelling upon the object or Subject. At this stage they are hardly distinguishable as acts.

My second difficulty was more significant for my present concern, and perhaps it was less "normal". Gradually it seemed to me to be wrong to "turn away" from a conscious sense of God's presence, in order to reason *about* him as a sort of object. I followed what seemed to be the solution of this difficulty. What little reasoning I did in prayer took the form of colloquy: I reasoned as I spoke inwardly *to* him.

What was happening? My experience in prayer was becoming more and more second-personal in structure. More and more I attended to him in direct I-Thou relationship. Less and less room was given to reasoning of a third-personal, objective type: *about* him, or about my life in relation to him. I am convinced that more and more I was coming to a truly religious experience: occurring within the structure of a transcendent interpersonal I-Thou relationship.

So much for the personal experience, recounted as an approach to our question here about the theologian's way of telling about God. The question is this: should the theologian's symbolizing take the form of colloquy? Should he turn to God and address him in a full second-personal mode? Should theological reasoning be taken up into prayer, as a continuation and intensification of the theologian's personal experience of God in his most profound religious experience? Or should he follow what has been the common way of theologizing: turning from his direct personal experience of God, to address others, telling them about God? Basically the question regards the relationship of theological symbolizing to the whole of the theologian's personal religious experience.

I have maintained that the theologian's religious experience within a life of faith in a community of believers is the matrix of theology[24]. That remains my conviction. Theology is the effort to understand within a life of faith, a life which can be lived only in a community of believers. Without personal religious experience in such an interpersonal setting, no would-be theologian could have the faintest notion of the reality which he or she seeks to understand. If we measure any theologian's potential, then we must affirm that, all other things being equal (for example: intelligence, freedom for the long effort, vocation to this role in the Church, and diligent application to theological labor), the richer the theologian's personal religious experience, the greater the hope that he or she will produce a creative theological work which will enrich the Church.

But, if we consider the structure of such personal religious experience, sooner or later we must face the question: what is the way of telling about God which is best suited to the theologian's task: "colloquy" in which he continues to address God, and spells out as well as he can what he understands of the God whom he contemplates and with whom he is intimately united; or objective, discourse, in which he turns for the moment from absorption in God, and addresses others, telling them about God?

Why must the question arise? Basically the reason is this: like any other Christian, the theologian has his most profound religious experience, and comes to his deepest knowledge of God, in direct I-Thou relationship. Our God is personal: Father, Son, and Holy Spirit. On the analogy of human interpersonal experience, we come to our deepest knowledge of persons in full second-personal acts, in mutual knowledge and love. If the whole question of the proper way of theologizing could be reduced to the question of the way in which the theologian comes to his or her deepest knowledge of God, then the answer would be simply that the theologian should remain in direct I-Thou relationship, in union with Father, Son, and Holy Spirit. Within that union, not turning from God to speak to others *about* him, the theologian would speak directly *to* God, spelling out his or her sense of wonder. Thus theology would be reduced to a form of prayer, with the theologian speaking to God aloud, so to speak, for the benefit of those who listen in. Driving this line of thought to its inevitable conclusion, I think that we set forth the basic illusion from which it begins.

Before I point out that basic illusion, I think that it is worth while to note that any effort to reduce theology to colloquy would

---

[24] See *Basics*, pp. 221-239.

result only in harm to both prayer and theology. First of all, we should not make personal prayer a public spectacle. Our most profound personal and interpersonal experience of God is most intimate: it is not to be displayed for the "enrichment" of listeners-in. If the curious casual listener-in had any sense, he or she would turn quickly from any such spectacle, regarding it as spurious prayer. Second, there is a radical opposition between the demands and the dynamism of prayer and theology. Prayer tends to more and more intimate interpersonal union, to a more and more profound personal knowledge, but a knowledge which is connatural, massive, ineffable. We know God most intimately as we come to a knowledge within a life of love, a knowledge which is beyond explicit symbolizing, linguistic or other. On the contrary, the theologian is driven to symbolize explicitly, to conceptualize, to work out as well as possible the intelligible structure of both the experience of God and the experienced Reality. The theologian is driven to find answers to his or her own insistent questions, and to the questions which crowd in from all sides. Only relatively few have the vocation to creative theology. They do not respond to their vocation by remaining fixed in ecstatic union, while the world waits in vain for answers, and their own questions no longer compel them. I am not saying that theology is the nobler vocation. I say simply that it is different. Prayer and theologizing can be confused only to the detriment of both.

What, then, is the basic illusion to which I have referred? It is the confusion of the indispensable prerequisite for theology and the nature of the theologian's task. The prerequisite is a profound personal experience of God in a total response to the revealing and saving God. It is massive, a response of knowledge, acknowledgment, and love. Fully conscious, it is permeated by intellect. Fully second-personal in structure, it is on the model of "You are!" Within that massive personal response to Father, Son, and Holy Spirit, the theologian has an ever deepening connatural knowledge. Only within that experience does the theologian, like any other Christian, know the shape of the experience, and have a massive, implicit, "primordial" knowledge of the God who is experienced. Without that experience, on the model of "You are!", the theologian could not perform his or her task—no one could *be* a theologian. Without continual return to prayer, to the contemplation of God, to the ever-deepening "You are!", theology would wither and die: cut off from its source, its fountainhead, from which it draws all of its vitality, and within which it is continually challenged and impelled to seek to understand, and to communicate what has been understood, for the enrichment of the Church, and mysteriously for the continuing personal growth and enrichment of the theologian. The prerequisite, then, is a life of prayer, of contemplation, of full response on the model of "You are!" This the theologian shares with all Christians who come to mature life in conscious interpersonal relationship with Father, Son, and Holy Spirit.

The task is something quite different. It is not demanded of all mature Christians to be theologians, at least creative theologians. It is a labor of love within the Church, a particular way of life which calls for particular gifts and a particular vocation. It is an arduous work of human reason within a life of faith, a work to which some are impelled by the very drive to understand which characterizes all human life, but which is intense in those men and women who by personal talent and vocation are driven to a highly intellectual way of life, and correspondingly to a highly conceptual mode of symbolizing. The gifts are a charism for the good of the Body, but like all charisms they set the pattern and the particular challenge of a personal way of love and holiness of the theologian. If I am called to be a theologian, then theology is my work of love. I am not called simply to rest in contemplation, in loving silent union. To that I must return continually to keep alive. But for the good of the Church, and for the accomplishment of my work in the Church, my work of love, I must endure the agony and labor of a uniquely difficult search for understanding and of the elaboration of the intelligible structure of what has been understood. Woe to me if I don't!

That task is performed in telling others about God. It is on the model of "He is!" It objectifies God, but so do all of the ways of telling. When God says of himself, "I am", even in that massive affirmation he is objectifying himself as he "descends" to employ a human type of symbolizing; more obviously he is doing so when he affirms, "I am the first and the last", or "I alone am the God of Israel". In some circles, *objectify* and *objectification* are pejorative terms: all of the virtue is on the side of the subject, and of subjectivity analysis. Ironically, in circles dominated by philosophies of another brand, *subjective* and *subjectifying* are pejorative: all of the excellence is that of "objective" science. Both views are myopic. They call for further reflection. Moreover, when we attempt to speak of God or of the divine mode of being and operating, both the *objective* and the *subjective* must undergo a purification, teased into analogous meanings, as human intellect grapples with understanding the God who is beyond all human grasp[25]. All human conscious intentional operations regard an *object*, whether in our direct encounter with others in our many worlds, or in our turning in reflection upon our operations and ourselves. All of our impact and response in our many worlds involves others—and ourselves—in so far as they terminate our conscious intentional operations, not in the fulness of their being in themselves. The three models, "I am", "You are", and "He is" do not, therefore, differ in objectifying or not objectifying, but rather in the mode of objectifying, and in the interpersonal structure of the operations and the objects which they regard.

When the theologian turns from the intensity of personal experience in the pattern of a massive "You are!" and reflects upon what he has experienced, and what he can determine of the God whom he has experienced, he begins to think of *him*; and all of the symbolizing and symbols by which he will reach further understanding and a communicable formulation of the intelligible pattern of what he has understood will necessarily be on the model "He is". All that he elaborates will be an unfolding of what "He is" affirms eminently.

So much for the model of telling: "He is". We shall have to note in the next section that theological telling on this model is not the only one: it is differentiated from others by its mode of symbolizing and symbols.

With regard to our present concern, I suggest two other comparisons which may help to understand better the theological mode of telling. One regards mystical experience and writing; the other, philosophy.

What I have said in distinguishing sharply between the theologian's personal religious experience on the model "You are" and his theological symbolizing on the model "He is" suggests a helpful comparison with another distinction which I have worked out elsewhere, between mystical experience and mystical writing[26]. The most intense mystical experience is in a massive, wordless "You are" in the overwhelming presence of the ineffable. Mystical writing may be cast in the form of "You are" or "He is", depending on the literary form, the symbol, which the mystic employs when he or she turns to writing—or recounting

---

[25] For my treatment of *objective, objectify,* and *subject, subjective, subjectify,* see MS, pp. 173-176.

[26] See *Basics*, pp. 293-298.

orally—to record the experience. In either case, mystical writing is but the shadow of mystical experience, a complex symbol which may be excellent as such writings go, but which is utterly inadequate—as are all human symbols—to image the full experience and experienced Reality. Mystical writing calls for another talent. It is once removed from mystical experience. Its excellence depends as much on the symbolizing talents of the writer as on the quality of the experience. We cannot judge that the greatest mystical writer is the greatest mystic. So too theology is once removed from the most intense personal religious experience of the theologian. It too calls for different talents. It operates on a different model. It is utterly inadequate as a complex conceptual symbol imaging both the original experience and the experienced Reality [27].

The second comparison is of theology and philosophy. They are analogous, with two sets of similarities and sharp contrasts which are relevant to our present consideration. First, there is a similarity and contrast in the structure of experience and search for understanding. Both reflect upon intelligible relationships and seek to deepen understanding of "ultimate causes", and to elaborate the intelligible structure of what they have understood of a world which they have encountered, and within which they reflect upon both their experience and the world experienced. Yet they are literally "worlds apart": they are concerned with diverse worlds of human experience, and with ultimate causes—more properly, in each case *an* ultimate cause—which are diverse, at least in so far as they fall within the range of each of the two intellectual pursuits. The philosopher ponders the mystery of the world about him, as it falls within the range of human experience, and is intelligible by the power of human intellect. He may find the being and intelligibility of that world grounded in a transcendent, which we call God, intelligible as it/he falls within the range of human experience. The theologian ponders the mystery of a world accessible only to human intellect whose natural power is heightened by the gift of faith. The world which he contemplates is accessible only as a consequence of special revelation and the "leap of faith". He reaches his deepest or loftiest experience not in ecstatic wonder at the beauty and

---

[27] I do not wish to deviate here to consider the question of relative values: of mystical writings compared with mystical experience; or of theology compared with the theologian's religious experience. What I should have to say may be surmised from my treatment of the relative value of theology, in *Basics*, pp. 288-302.

mystery of the universe, but in full second-personal acts, in a transcendent contemplation and massive response which is at once cognitive, volitional, emotive, and motor. His most profound knowledge of the mystery of the world in which he lives is a connatural knowledge of One God, Father, Son, and Holy Spirit, a massive, "primordial", implicit knowledge of the shape of his experience and of the God experienced. Within the matrix of that total experience, the theologian works out intelligible relationships and the intelligible structure of the whole.

Second, despite a superficial similarity in the terminologies of philosophies of some schools and highly conceptual theologies, especially classic "scholastic" theologies, there are deep differences in meaning. Conceptual theologians take over philosophical concepts, but if they work with careful attention to the exigencies of their own unique task, they must perform an inner transformation of those concepts in the elaboration of some understanding of the mysteries of revealed truth[28]. Most of the concepts which the theologian takes over are analogous. He uses the same words as some philosophers. Yet if he truly works at his task, his words function differently as they play their part in the whole of a conceptual world developed in response to the challenge of the Christian Mystery. If we wish to understand his words, his symbolic elements, we too must attend to the meaning which can be gathered only as they function in a whole, and contribute to imaging a unique world, subjective and objective.

So much for theological telling. Quite definitely it is on the model of "He is": the theologian tells others about God. It is not the only such telling of the Christian Mystery, and I reserve to the following section a brief comparison of theology and a cluster of other sorts of telling in which Christians spell out something of the revealed truth.

RELIGIOUS AND THEOLOGICAL TELLING

Understandably, I hope, I have treated theological telling rather fully in the preceding section: after all, that is my task, and I must clarify it for myself as well as for my eventual readers. What I have to say here briefly is intended simply to set such

---

[28] I have treated this matter in *Basics*, pp. 274-280, 284-285, and 355-359. I hope that the thought which I propose to undertake in the third volume of this work will illustrate what I mean.

telling in its place within the fulness and rich variety of Christian telling, which I call simply *religious*. I do not suggest a judgment of the relative values of the two sorts of telling. Rather I call attention to the obvious fact that theological telling is only one kind of religious telling, and a rather rare one, with a special function in the life of the Church.

In general, all Christian witness to experience of God is telling about God. All such telling, mostly by word, is on the model of "He is": rarely taking the form of the massive affirmation, but rather the endless variations on particular telling about the God whom we encounter, in whom we live. Christian religious telling varies according to both the kinds of religious experience and the kinds and quality of the symbols employed. The range of experience is from the peak of mystical union, through all of the degrees of "normal" Christian life, to the highly specialized telling which is proper to the theologian. The kinds of symbols range from richly intuitive to highly conceptual. Most symbolizing in normal Christian witness lies in the vast regions between the two extremes. The quality of symbols, both intuitive and conceptual, can vary greatly in the three broadly designated areas: mystical, normal, and theological. One example of outstanding excellence within the realm of normal religious experience is an outstanding work of sacred art in any form: it may be the supreme achievement in intuitive symbolizing, superior in symbolic quality and efficacy to either mystical or theological telling; yet it may be the work of an artist who is neither mystic nor theologian.

I have dealt sufficiently with the proper mode of theological symbolizing: it must be prevalently conceptual as it approaches its goal of understanding and elaboration of an intelligible structure[29]. Yet I maintain that the theologian can and should elaborate his own mature, most personal, and most creative thought in a discourse which is free from both pedantry and esoteric philosophico-theological terminology. I have qualified my affirmation deliberately. There is room for highly specialized, technical exposition and critique of the works of other theologians—and often philosophers, whose thought has served, or may serve, to contribute to the elaboration of theological conceptualization. For most of my own years devoted to philosophy and theology I myself have done that sort of work. It is necessarily scholarly, with careful documentation of details, faithful exposition retaining highly technical, conceptual symbols.

---

[29] See *Basics*, esp. pp. 240-257, 274-280.

Ideally it makes some personal contribution in the form of critical evaluation and raising further questions. But, in my judgment, some theologians should aspire to more than this.

Ideally, as further questions are formulated, so too are answers beginning to multiply; and the structure of the critic's personal thought begins to emerge. Then the time is ripe for what should be the richest of all of the theologian's work: elaboration of a personal, creative thought. Works in which such thought is developed need no longer be either jammed with endless name-dropping and footnotes sending the reader off on countless unending side-trips, or encumbered from the outset with a highly developed conceptual system which is inaccessible and unintelligible for most readers. Theological works are not for "Everyman". Yet they should be intelligible for intelligent Christians who have had a relatively rich religious experience, and who desire to come to a deeper understanding within their life of faith. Certainly, if my notion of theology is correct, the symbolism must be conceptual. But the terminology and concepts can be accessible if they are generated within the movement of a developing thought. The theologian should not attempt the utterly impossible and absurd undertaking of bringing his or her readers through the thirty or forty or more years of historical and critical studies which have been necessary for the theologian's development to this point. I am convinced that it is possible to develop a rich, personal, creative theology which is accessible to mature, intelligent Christians; and that such theology can contribute most to enriching the life of the Church—in so far as enrichment comes from theology. It is my aim to elaborate such theology as far as I am able in the work which remains for me to do.

TELLING, NOT DEMONSTRATING

I have entitled this whole work *Telling About God*. Besides the implications of the word *telling* which I indicated in the first section of this introduction, I should like to make clear that in the whole work I am engaged in telling, not demonstrating. In the second volume I shall be concerned with giving an account of Christian experience of God, and of the God experienced. What I am proposing is simply such an account: *this* is the way Christians have experienced God, and *this* is the kind of God experienced. In the third volume I shall be concerned with elaborating an intelligible account of such a God. The second volume will concern witness to experience within a life of faith. In the third I shall seek to set forth a further understanding. Though that will include a rational grounding of the affirmation that *God is*, such "demonstration" is taken up to function within a life of faith, within a theology concerned with what is believed. I am convinced that I can "demonstrate" that God is. I know that I cannot demonstrate that the God of Abraham, Isaac, Jacob, the God and Father of Jesus Christ and our Father *is* the one true God. I believe that. I cannot demonstrate it, nor can anyone else.

What then is the *evidence* that I propose, and on which I ground my account? Strictly speaking, there is no *evidence*: this is an account of what is believed, an account of experience which can be had only within a life of faith. True, there is a sort of historical evidence: the fact that some men and women have given such witness. But what they witness to is never evident.

How, then, do I intend to establish my account? One cannot probe all Christians, and establish that all of them, always, are involved in such experience. There is a question rather of reporting accounts of peak experiences, of one man or woman at a given moment, or a series of moments of intense religious experience. Such peak experiences illumine the whole life of the man or woman in question. Since they share their experience with us, as far as that is possible and reasonable, we too are illumined. What they experienced gives meaning to their whole life, gathers up the whole of their past, thrusts them into the future with a new sense of their potential, a new direction, a new purpose, a life of richer faith and love and fidelity. When we read or hear of their account, we may never have had such experience. Yet we come to know more of the Christian mystery, of the potential of a life in Christ; and as we receive such an account with human faith in the teller, the word can mediate God's grace in us, open us to our own possibilities, evoke in us a response of faith and desire, and the beginnings of a greater fulness of life.

Clearly such an account depends on the witness of the teller, and can be meaningful only to one who with human faith receives what is told, ponders it, and comes under the influence of God's grace. In the Christian mystery God permeates and penetrates our actions, and in his providence we mediate grace to one another.

Some of the witnesses are the great men and women in the long history of Israelite and Christian experience: Abraham, Isaiah, Jeremiah, Paul, John. Unique among all is the God-man

Jesus Christ, who tells what he has seen with the Father from all eternity. Their word comes to us as God's word. It evokes a response of divine faith. Others in the long life of the Church bear witness which calls for our human faith in their testimony, and our willingness to open ourselves to the action of grace which can make some variation of experience possible for us.

In the whole process of life in the Church, the theologian bears witness according to his or her own charism. In part that witness concerns intelligible patterns discovered in the long record of Israelite and Christian experience. In part it may share what the theologian has experienced in his or her own intrapersonal dialectic: what has been understood in the experience of others has mediated a personal experience which is itself shared as part of the record. Theological experience itself is part of the Christian mystery, one of the ways of living in the Church. Obviously I write as a theologian. I propose my account of certain intelligible patterns of experience of God, and aspects of the God experienced. All that I hope for is this: that my account may ring true, that it may resonate in the experience of those who share my faith, living in the same community of believers, and that it may mediate a richer life of faith in them.

THE DIALECTIC

All telling about God plays its role in the highly complex, multiple dialectic, personal and interpersonal, which characterizes Christian life.

I mention it only briefly, since I have developed it at length in *Basics*[30]. Religious telling generally, and theological telling for those called to develop theology and also those who can read and reflect profitably on theological works, function in the total dialectic. Each in its own way contributes to the development of the teller and of those who hear or read the word which is told. Each occurs only in the matrix of a deep religious experience. Each is a kind of symbolizing in which the teller is actualized, and the word told can evoke a total religious response in the recipient[31]. Ideally theology is integrated into the whole personal

---

[30] For personal and interpersonal dialectic, pp. 126-127, 198-212.

[31] For the notion of actualization of the symbolizer, and possible effect of symbols in the human world, personal and interpersonal, see MS, pp. 269-290.

life of the theologian as a believer. Every discovery of an
intelligible aspect of the Mystery can and should stimulate the
theologian's own deeper faith and love and total personal
response to God. If theology is developed as it can be, accessible
and intelligible for many mature Christians, it mediates in them a
deeper wonder and total response. The theologian's contribution
to the life of the Church is especially understanding; and the better
he or she and their fellow believers understand, the more they are
drawn to what they know to be their supreme good. We move
from faith and love to deeper faith and love.

PARTICIPATION AND APPROPRIATION

One important aspect of the dialectic which I have just treated
calls for particular notice. Perhaps the best way to make clear
what I have in mind is to recall the contrast between philosophy
and theology, and to note the difference in the functions of their
respective symbols. I have pointed out the differences in the
worlds of the philosopher and of the theologian, and I have
indicated what is unique in a theologian's experience (above,
pp. 38-39). The theologian, unlike the philosopher who may
come to affirm the existence of a god, knows his God only as a
consequence of his "leap of faith", and he comes to his most
profound knowledge of God in full second-personal acts, in a total
response in an I-Thou relationship: a response which is at once
cognitive, volitional, emotive, and motor. To do his work as a
theologian he must turn from such explicit acts in the I-Thou
relationship, and fashion his symbols on the model of the
third-personal "He is." There is no such similar experience in the
life of the philosopher: he does not come by philosophy to a
personal knowledge of God and to an intimate connatural
knowledge in an I-Thou relationship with the god whom he
affirms to be.

There is, as a consequence, a great difference in the functions
of the symbols elaborated by philosopher and theologian. The
philosopher's symbols mediate knowledge. When we read a
philosopher's work and understand it, we too can affirm that
there is a god. We may, like the philosopher perhaps, sense too
a wonder at the beauty and mystery of the universe, a joy in the
truth we have attained, and a further rich emotional experience.
So in a sense a philosopher's symbols may mediate more than a
merely cognitive experience in us. Of themselves, however, they

do not evoke a response which leads us to an intimate I-Thou relationship with God. I say "of themselves", for I recognize that for a believer, philosophical experience is inseparable from religious and theological experience: philosophical contemplation of god is taken up into a religious and theological contemplation of the God in whom we believe. Of themselves, philosophical symbols are third-personal. They mediate a third-personal knowledge. When we understand them and are convinced of the force of the philosopher's reasoning, we can affirm as he does: "This is so."

Theological symbols, cast in the form "He is", do not mediate directly the full experience of the theologian, not even in its cognitive dimensions. The theologian reaches his deepest knowledge in I-Thou relationship, in which he symbolizes in the form "You are"—if he symbolizes at all, and does not simply hold to a wordless contemplation and union of love. His deepest knowledge is connatural, within his total experience of God. It is ineffable. When he symbolizes in the form "He is", his symbols have a unique function. They are intended—or should be, in my judgment—not just to mediate to others the propositional truth cast in the form "He is". Beyond that, hopefully, they may function by evoking in the reader or hearer a total response similar to that of the theologian, and in many cases much richer. If theology is to function fully in the dialectic of which I have written, it should occasion in the reader or hearer a full personal response to God in an I-Thou relationship. Only in that full response will the reader or hearer realize his or her own full personal potential. Theological symbols should mediate a full response, cognitive, emotive, volitional, and motor. And only within that full response, in a massive connatural knowledge of the shape of the full experience, will others come to their deepest theological knowledge.

Hence the title of this section. The man or woman who reads or hears the work of a theologian and understands what he or she is communicating in the form "He is" must go on to participate in an experience similar to the theologian's, to appropriate it. A theological work, therefore, is meant to mediate much more than knowledge cast in a third-personal form. Theological symbols, as a consequence of the manner of telling which the theologian must use, are uniquely inadequate to communicate the theologian's own richest experience. They stand between theologian and reader. They are a humble yet necessary type of symbol. They function fully in the life of the community of believers only when providentially they mediate that participation and appropriation which is possible. They mediate as divine-human symbols, bearers of grace.

PRINCIPLES GOVERNING THE ELABORATION OF THIS WORK

(1) *The matrix of theology.* Theology as an activity is the search for understanding within a life of faith in a community of believers. The matrix within which theology develops, therefore, is the theologian's own experience of God, and of Christian life, in that setting[32].

(2) *The role of the Bible.* In a unique way the Bible mediates our experience of God. The Bible is the total complex written linguistic symbol—God's own divine-human symbol—of the Reality, the Mystery. Far more powerfully, extensively, and profoundly than any other symbol or set of symbols, it mediates our encounter with the revealing God whose word it enshrines. Yet the Bible itself is a symbol, an image of the Reality: once removed from the Reality, which is God, Father, Son, and Holy Spirit, his eternal plan for man's fulness of life in a share of the divine, his total revelation and saving action culminating in Jesus Christ, and his continuing action in the Church to the end of time. First and foremost the Reality which the theologian seeks to understand is God: all else interests him in relation to God. Though the Bible itself is an inadequate image, its meaning is inexhaustible, and Christians never finish the prayerful reading and reflection which continues, with the illumination of the Holy Spirit, to unfold its meaning.

(3) *Exegesis and biblical theology.* The works of exegetes and biblical theologians are among the other data which the theologian must consider, but which obviously can never be regarded as the total resources of theology at any given stage of development in the life of the Church. The exegete serves the important yet humble purpose of mediating the impact of a text upon a reader seeking to understand its meaning. Exegetical works themselves are symbols, helps to the understanding of elements of the one great principal symbol, the Bible. They never substitute for the Bible. Usually they are read once, or consulted occasionally, and then, with what help they have given, the reader goes on to contemplate the primary symbol, to gather more of its

---

[32] See *Basics*, pp. 221-239.

whole meaning and undergo its total efficacy: cognitive, emotive, volitional, and motor.

Biblical theology in a sense is one step farther removed from the primary symbol, yet in its own way it contributes helpful guides to intelligible structures within the total meaning of a portion of the Bible: a book, a tradition (for example, the Yahwist or the Priestly in the Old Testament), the human author of several books (Paul most conspicuously in the New Testament). Like works of exegetes, those of biblical theologians mediate the impact of the Bible upon readers. They make their limited contribution, and then return to their places on the shelf, to be taken down again when they are needed for further help. No theologian, therefore, can make an exhaustive study of exegetes and biblical theologians, gather their contributions, rely further on the rich data gathered in dictionaries of the Bible and of biblical theology, and feel that he has all that he needs, all that he must reflect upon in order to do his own work. They are only some of the important secondary data: readings taken, not on the Reality, but on the primary symbol, the Bible. Like all other secondary data, they serve to mediate the experience in which, under the influence of grace, a believer senses more of the total meaning of the Bible: more of the Reality, the Mystery.

(4) *Dogma, theology, and further Christian witness.* There are other data, other symbols, which afford readings upon the Reality. I group here three of them, simply to recall their importance. Every dogma fixed by the Church in the exercise of its supreme unfailing teaching authority is a symbol: a particular reading on an aspect of the Mystery. It has a truth which must be determined by its total context. That particular affirmation of revealed truth is true and will remain true to the end of time, when neither dogmas nor any other symbols will be needed. Every such dogma is a fixed point of reference which the theologian must never disregard. It has a place in the analogy of faith, the total intelligible structure of revealed truth. All authentic theological development must be achieved in harmony with that structure. Dogma, taken collectively for all such particular solemn affirmations of the magisterium, has a unique value. Yet it too is limited, and no theologian does his or her full work simply by faithfully setting forth dogma. Most revealed truth is undefined, and the work of probing the intelligibility of the Mystery will remain to challenge the theologian for all time.

Theology is itself a sort of witness, the body of symbols elaborated by theologians to date, often suggestive of further insights into the full meaning of the revealed truth.

What I refer to broadly as further Christian witness embraces all that individual believers have formulated of their own deep religious experience, their own readings on the Mystery, taken as they reflect on aspects of their life in community: public worship, personal prayer, and the infinitely complex interplay of a transcendent interpersonal world in which we teach one another and learn from one another something of the deeper meaning of the Mystery.

All of these data, symbols, are readings on the total Reality, God and the whole of the transcendent interpersonal world in which we encounter him and seek to understand him. All are pertinent to the theologian's search to know the God of Christian experience, and his subsequent search for further understanding.

Since it is only within a life of faith in a community of believers that theology can develop, one important final witness is that of the theologian to his or her own personal experience.

(5) *Gathering meaning.* In a sense one could say that in the continuing life of the Church the Bible continues to gather meaning. Yet obviously that is an improper way of stating the truth. Rather, the community of believers can continue to gather richer and deeper meaning, without ever coming to the full meaning: God's meaning, beyond our comprehension and even the eventual vision for which we hope [33]. We may hope and strive to gather ever richer, deeper meaning, as we read the Bible prayerfully, reflect on dynamic structures within it, and reflect on structures of our own shared personal religious experience. For part of the Mystery is the continuing divine saving action to the end of time: saving action which comes to its term continually in unique personal realizations of the Christian potential. Every such realization is a further manifestation of God, and an unfolding of the full meaning of the Word which he revealed once for all. Reflection on shared Christian experience is very much part of what should be the theologian's total concern: it is within that total experience that he or she may hope to find more and more of the God who is experienced.

(6) *Three stages, three volumes.* In the light of my past experience, it may still be hazardous to indicate the three volumes of this work as I now project it. Still, at this stage of the

---

[33] Compare *Basics*, pp. 102-103, 137, 213-217, 307-311.

elaboration of my thought on God, I feel safe in indicating three stages for certain, which probably will call for no more than three volumes. These, then, are the stages:

(a) Essays in biblical theology. I have worked out what could be called essays in biblical theology, on the general theme of promise and fulfillment. My purpose is to provide patterns of the development of a theme which I consider of greatest importance as a guide to the reading of the Bible which can contribute most to mediating our experience of God. We can come to such experience only as we recognize and respond to God's plan for us, as we come to understand our full potential for life in Christ, in the transcendent interpersonal world, in that share of the divine life to which God calls us. We can locate ourselves, understand our potential, as we situate ourselves in the history of salvation, in the Mystery which is being realized. God's promise to Abraham opened the prospect of an utterly new beginning, of blessings undreamt of. Only gradually was the full meaning of the promise revealed. For Christians, that full revelation came only in the revelation in Christ and the illumination by the Holy Spirit. In the gradual development of the meaning of the promise as it was revealed in its ever-unexpected fulfillments, and especially in the Gospels which offer the project of a new fulness of life, and even more in the early Christian writings in which the inspired authors witness to the experienced reality of the fulfillment, and the further promise of final fulfillment—only in a continuing prayerful reading and reflection upon the whole of this revelation can we come to a sense of our potential for an experience of God, and a sense of the invitation, the urging, to respond fully to God's offer. Only in such response can we come to that connatural knowledge of God, that knowledge of God within experience, that massive ineffable knowledge sensed in the very shape of the experience of living in and loving Father, Jesus, and the Holy Spirit, responding to Their love of us.

(b) Experience of God, mediated in great part by a Christian reading of the Bible, but also by many other factors which mediate our experience of God in our own community of believers.

(c) Search for deeper understanding. This is the kind of search which has resulted in the gradual development of a prevalently conceptual theology. Marveling at the God whom we experience, we are driven to ask: how can such a God be intelligible? And if it is our personal charism in the life of the Church, we are driven to seek to work out ever inadequate answers to that question.

Hence this work is projected as a single *Telling About God* in three stages: *Promise and Fulfillment, Experience,* and *Understanding.*

(7) *Characteristics of this first volume.* Though the title is simply *Promise and Fulfillment,* the theme could be called more adequately *The Dialectic of Promise and Fulfillment.* What do I mean?

Salvation history, as it is understood commonly, begins with God's word to Abraham: a command, and a promise. Abraham obeys the command, and God gradually fulfills the promise, and unfolds further details of the blessings which he has promised. It is not a simple process, but extremely complex. There is a succession of promises, and a varying pattern of human response. The whole process is that of salvation history. The written records of portions of the process preserve successive insights into the process, and formulations of the pattern of its development. It is in the course of human process that God gradually revealed his plan for man, and gradually realized that plan. He formed a people which was to be his very own, and which was—beyond its understanding of its role—to mediate blessings to all nations. It was by recognition of its place in salvation history that Israel came to a sense of its identity as a people. It is by recognition of our place in the further process of revelation and realization that we find our own identity as Christians, and come to a deeper sense of our potential as persons in community: our own personal fulness of life, and our role in mediating the fulness of life to others.

The Dialectic of Promise and Fulfillment suggests the complexity and interplay of many factors in the total process. Yet that title is too simple. If we were concerned only with a succession of promises and fulfillments, the title would be adequate. The fact, however, is that human failure complicates the process. Through the centuries the human response has been at times one of faith and obedience, rewarded by the promised blessings. Too often, however, it has been one of unbelief and disobedience. Knowing what is in man, God not only promises, but threatens; he not only rewards, but punishes. What is involved, then, is not a simple dialectic, but a sort of contrapuntal dialectic: of promise and fulfillment, and of threat and punishment. Moreover, the former involves faith, love, and fidelity; and the latter involves sin and diverse patterns of repentance and forgiveness or of obdurate rebellion. In the great contrapuntal dialectic the two great themes are continually intertwined through the whole course of human history. The final resolution will come in the definitive judgment and its execution: victory and fulness of life and blessing for the servants of God; and final punishment of the obdurate wicked (cf. Ap 20.11–22.15).

The dialectic runs through the whole Bible. Here we can only trace some lines and mark significant moments in the whole process. Much of their significance can be grasped only gradually later, as we seek to penetrate other particular themes of the whole Mystery. In the brief account which I can give here, especially of Old Testament witness, I shall emphasize the theme of promise and fulfillment, and shall give only occasional indications of the pattern of threat, sin, and punishment. Repentance and forgiveness themselves are God's gift, further gifts from the God who first promised his blessings to the Fathers, and who continually shows what kind of God he is.

Like my last two works especially, *Man the Symbolizer* and *Basics of a Roman Catholic Theology*, this is a work of personal thought, not of erudition. This volume is a sort of "theologian's biblical theology". I am not a professional biblical scholar. I make no pretence of covering the field of biblical scholarship concerning every portion of the Bible which I consider. Yet, with deep respect for the work of biblical scholars, I have attempted to maintain contact with them by trusting one or more reputable experts in every field, considering their contributions as representative of at least one respectable line of thought, and referring to their indications of principal bibliography and of the range of exegetical opinions on some highly controverted matters.

Exegetes and biblical theologians themselves present their works for the benefit of theologians and others seeking to understand the Bible. Their work, like that of any other thinker, is open to critical examination. Where I have differed with one or more of them, I have indicated my difference, and I have not hesitated to make my own suggestions regarding exegesis, translation, and biblical theology in the vast majority of this volume devoted to New Testament exegesis and theology.

My work, then, is personal, and I take full responsibility for it. I make only one observation, one counsel, regarding eventual criticism of my work. Like any other who elaborates a personal thought, I make only one request of my potential critic, completely consistent with the laws for any responsible interpretation and critique: respect for the context of the thought which is being judged. The context of my thought is the whole movement of a single developing thought in my last three volumes: a full theory of symbolizing and symbol set against the ground of a rather full philosophy of human being, the application of that theory to all of the phases of a total theological enterprise, including exegesis, and its continual application in the elaboration of this volume. One who may have found it too much to ponder that context would do well to ponder the prudence of judging without knowing the context.

The proportions of this volume may seem strange. The chapter on the Old Testament is scanty in comparison with the proportions of the treatment of the New Testament. Frankly I am concerned principally with fulfillment, which for the Christian is revealed in the New Testament. In the project of life offered in the Gospels, and in the ample witness to experience of that life in Acts and the letters, we have God's word concerning the full potential of the life to which we are called, and within which we can experience God, Father, Jesus, and Holy Spirit.

I am fully aware that the ''chapter'' on Paul is a book within a book. That, too, I think, is consistent with the difference between Gospel as revelation of a call to a way of life, and Paul's ample witness to the experience of that life lived. I can only trust that the clear divisions of the matter make it accessible, and that the movement of thought is such that it would have been a mistake to divide it into chapters. In any case, division into chapters would not change the proportions of my treatment of Paul in relation to other New Testament writers.

I do not deal with all of the books of the New Testament, and my grouping of *Peter, Hebrews,* and *Apocalypse* may seem strange. I propose essays in biblical theology, not a complete biblical theology or set of biblical theologies. I regard it as sufficient for my purposes to set forth only complementary witness which contributes important aspects of full Christian life. I trust that, taken together, the various New Testament witnesses will provide an adequate guide to that reading and reflection upon the Bible which will mediate a rich Christian experience of God.

Finally, in the light of what I have written above concerning Christian reading of the Bible, and its role in mediating experience of God, one may wonder what relation my work in this volume has to such a Christian reading. The answer calls for some distinctions. First, basically this is a biblical theology, or more accurately a series of biblical theologies, with a considerable amount of exegesis where I judged that it was called for. I should say that my chapter on the Old Testament is entirely biblical theology, tracing the development of the central theme which I consider supremely important. Similarly, my chapters IV-VIII are a series of distinct essays in biblical theology, in which I have confined my effort to the thought conveyed in the Apostolic preaching, and then in Matthew, John, Paul, Peter, Hebrews, and Apocalypse.

Second, there is inevitably a considerable amount of Christian reading of the "Scripture"—the Old Testament—in the thought of the authors of the New Testament: they read a deeper, richer meaning of the Old Testament, in the light of the new revelation in Christ and of the illumination of the Holy Spirit in the early Christian communities.

Third, Chapter III, on the uniqueness of New Testament Witness, clearly prepares for the Christian reading of the whole Bible, which I shall be concerned with in the next volume.

As for Chapter IV, the substance of my treatment of what I call prologues and flashes is exegesis and biblical theology, though I consider that the function of the texts regards the whole Bible, and my treatment of these texts would be an essay toward a general biblical theology. The closing reflections, however, clearly point to the implications of these texts for a Christian reading of the whole Bible.

Basically, then, this volume is devoted to essays in exegesis and biblical theology, concentrating on the thought of the individual authors. In the portions which I have just indicated, however, the orientation and purpose of this volume is clear: it is a preparation for that Christian reading of the whole Bible which in a unique way mediates the Christian experience of God with which I shall be concerned in Volume II.

CHAPTER I

OLD TESTAMENT WITNESS

THE PROMISE TO ABRAHAM AND THE FATHERS

The promise to Abraham, repeated with personal applications
to Isaac and to Jacob, is the basic, radical promise. Though it is
not the first (the implicit promise of man's victory over the
serpent in Gen 3.15, and the covenant with Noah and his
descendants in Gen 9.8-17 precede) still it is considered reasonably
to be the beginning of salvation history. For those who, like
Abraham, believe, it is decisive, unrepented, everlasting [1].

God promised Abraham a land, defined in Gen 15.18-20,
with many bewildering variations in the course of subsequent
revelations in the history of the people. He was to be [father of]
a great nation: his descendants would be as numerous as the dust
of the earth (13.16), the stars of the heaven (15.5), the sand which
is on the seashore (22.17). Since he was to be the father of a
multitude of nations, God changed his name from Abram to
Abraham, popularly understood to mean "father of a multitude"
(17.5). God would bless him so greatly that he would be the
exemplar of a man blessed by God [2]. Though his wife was old
and barren, God would give Abraham a son by her (15.4;
17.15-21; 18.14). He would deliver Abraham's descendants from
slavery in a foreign land and give them great possessions
(15.13-14). He would establish his covenant between himself and
Abraham and his descendants: an everlasting covenant, to be God
to them (17.3-8) [3].

---

[1] The texts are Gn 12.2-3, 7; 13.14-17; 15.1-5, 13-21; 17.1-21; 18.
14; 22.15-18.

[2] The meaning of Gn 12.2-3 is obscure. For a brief discussion see *The
Mystery*, pp. 44-46.

[3] "... As the text stands 'Covenant' seems to be used in three different
senses: (1) a series of promises; (2) a basic relationship between
Abraham-and-descendants and Yahweh their God; (3) circumcision, which is
both a covenant obligation and a sign of the Covenant with Yahweh. Rather
than three different senses, these seem to be the three elements which constitute
the covenant ...." (*The Mystery*, p. 13).

Abraham "...believed the LORD; and he reckoned it to him as righteousness" (15.6).   His faith is decisive: all subsequent fulfillment depends on it.   Moreover, two conditions appear in the texts.   One is implicit as a condition: "...walk before me, and be blameless" (17.1): fulfillment of the promises would seem to call for such conduct on Abraham's part.   The other too may be said to be implicit: after Abraham showed his obedience even to the point of being ready to sacrifice Isaac, God said: "By myself I have sworn, says the LORD, because you have done this, and have not withheld your son, your only son, I will indeed bless you...." (22.16-17).

Initial fulfillment of the promises are the son born of Sarah (21.1-3) and the blessings which Abraham received (24.1, 35). God makes his promises also to Isaac (26.2-5, 24), and fulfills them in part (26.12-13, 28); and to Jacob (28.13-15; 35.9-12; 46.2-4).   The deliverance of Israel from Egypt is in fulfillment of God's promise to Abraham (cf. Ex 3.6-22).

I have said that the promise to Abraham and the Fathers is the basic, radical promise.   When Israel has sinned, and has broken its covenant, there would be little ground for pleading for the blessings which God promised as the reward for their fidelity to him.   They have been unfaithful, and they are suffering the curses threatened in the covenant.   Their only hope rests in the prior promise, the oath which God swore to Abraham and the Fathers.   Thus, when God has declared his intention of consuming his people for their sin of idolatry, Moses pleads: "'...Turn from thy fierce wrath, and repent of this evil against thy people.   Remember Abraham, Isaac, and Israel, thy servants, to whom thou didst swear by thine own self, and didst say to them, "I will multiply your descendants as the stars of the heaven, and all this land that I have promised I will give to your descendants, and they shall inherit it for ever"'.   And the LORD repented of the evil which he thought to do to his people" (Ex 32.12-14).   Repeatedly in the Old Testament forgiveness is motivated by this promise (cf. Lv 26.40-45; Nm 14.20-23; Dt 9.26-27; Bar 2.34; Dn 3.34-36 [JB; in the RSV, among the *Apocrypha*, "Song of the Three Young Men", vv. 11-13]).

It is this promise too which is cited as the reason for God's actions in favor of his people:

"Do not say in your heart, after the LORD your God has thrust them out before you, 'It is because of my righteousness that the LORD has brought me in to possess this land'; whereas it is because of the wickedness of these nations that the LORD is driving them

out before you. Not because of your righteousness or the uprightness of your heart are you going in to possess their land; but
because of the wickedness of these nations the LORD your God is
driving them out from before you, and that he may confirm the
word which the LORD swore to your fathers, to Abraham, to Isaac,
and to Jacob" (Dt 9.4-5)[4].

With regard to the fulfillment of the promise, one may be
struck as I have been by the pathos of the conclusion of the
account of the occupation of the land in *Joshua*:

> Thus the LORD gave to Israel all the land which he swore to give to
> their fathers; and having taken possession of it, they settled there.
> And the LORD gave them rest on every side just as he had sworn to
> their fathers; not one of all their enemies had withstood them, for
> the LORD had given all their enemies into their hands. Not one of
> all the good promises which the LORD had made to the house of
> Israel had failed; all came to pass (Jos 21.43-45; cf. 23.14.16,
> with a significant addition of warning)[5].

Whoever finally wrote those words must have done so with
mixed feelings, knowing much of the subsequent history of
infidelity and punishment. Much more realistic are the pleas for
forgiveness after Israel's sins, appealing to the promise to
Abraham.

We shall consider later the role of the promise to Abraham in
the New Testament, and the sharply different conceptions of the
manner of fulfillment.

BLESSINGS AND CURSES IN THE MOSAIC COVENANT

I am not concerned here with a consideration of the covenant
formula, the elements involved in establishing the covenant, and
the relationship which results. Within the limits of our theme, I
am concentrating on the blessings promised to the people for
fidelity to the covenant, and the curses threatened for infidelity[6].

---

[4] See also Ex 33.1-3; Jos 21.45; Neh 9.6-37; 2 Mc 1.2; Ps 105. 6, 8-11,
and the long recital of God's deeds in vv. 12-45; and Bar 2.27-35.

[5] For an introduction to the complicated matter of the literary history of the
book of Joshua, and the plausible attribution of this conclusion to Deuteronomist
editors, see PETER J. KEARNEY, "Joshua", JBC I, 7:2, pp. 123-124; 62 pp.
145-146, who interprets the promises as those of blessings in the Covenant.

[6] The basic texts on the Mosaic covenant are Ex 19.1–24-18; 34.1-35 (a

Exodus gives a short formula of promises and warnings (Ex 23.20-23, 32-33). *Leviticus* has a rather long list of blessings (26.3-12), concluding with the motive for Israel's embracing the covenant relationship (13); then there is a series of successive sets of curses for eventual successive infidelities (14-39). The ultimate hope of repentance and forgiveness is grounded not on their fidelity, but on God's covenant with Jacob, Isaac, and Abraham (40-45). Most of the promised blessings are all sorts of abundance and the fruitfulness and multiplication of the people. There is, however, a notable "qualitative leap": "... [I] will confirm my convenant with you.... And I will make my abode among you, and my soul shall not abhor you. And I will walk among you, and *will be your God, and you shall be my people*" (9, 11-12). I have italicized the words which are one of the variations on the formulation of the classic covenant relationship. What is significant here, in my judgment, is the shift from temporal, material blessings to the richest of "spiritual" blessings: that intimate union with God which is the essence of the covenant relationship. There is a curious doubling here, which I have noticed elsewhere reflecting on a text of Ezekiel[7]. First, the exclusive union of God and people is the ground for fidelity. Then, the principal reward for fidelity is a confirmation and deepening of the same union. There is in the covenant relationship itself a mysterious dialectic: a process in which fidelity is blessed most of all by a deepening and enrichment, a confirmation, of the covenant union.

Deuteronomy reflects the greater urgency of the times. After the long history of Israel's sin, of which the author is painfully aware, the list of curses is greatly lengthened. In an earlier list the blessings are not mentioned explicitly: they are implicit in the charge of some of the tribes to bless the people from Mount Gerizim (Dt 27.12). Others are to stand on Mount Ebal for the curse, and the curses are to be pronounced, and to every curse the people are to say "Amen" (13-26). Finally, in the conclusion of Moses' second address, both blessings and curses are expanded, the latter with astonishing fulness (Dt 28). Here again, among

---

parallel account in the form of a covenant renewal); Dt 4-5; and Jos 24. For introductions to the problems concerning hypothetical structure of the covenant ritual and formula, and traces of elements of such a covenant formula in the present text, see especially JOHN E. HUESMAN, S.J., "Exodus", in JBC, I, 3: 44-68, pp. 6-61; JOHN L. MCKENZIE, "Aspects of Old Testament Thought", JBC, II, 77: 74-98, pp. 749-753.

[7] See *The Mystery*, on Ez 36.28, p. 53.

the blessings, there is the qualitative difference which I noted in Lv 26. Most of the blessings concern what we might call—in non-biblical terms—temporal and material goods. Yet here too, in the very midst of them there is a difference: "The LORD will establish you as a people holy to himself, as he has sworn to you, if you keep the commandments of the LORD your God, and walk in his ways. And all the peoples of the earth shall see that you are called by the name of the LORD; and they shall be afraid of you" (9-10). Here again, in different words, what is promised as a reward for covenant fidelity is the essential covenant relationship itself.

What bearing do the Mosaic covenant blessings have upon our theme: the dialectic of promise and fulfillment? Very little in the long run. A people which has multiplied its sins, has shattered its covenant, can have little hope of blessings promised for fidelity. Its only hope is grounded on the basic promise to Abraham.

I should point out one important element in these promises. What I have noted as a qualitative difference among the blessings is significant for the gradual development and enrichment of the conception of the blessings which are to be hoped for. I shall return to this in dealing with the promises through the prophets.

The Promise to David

Through the prophet Nathan God promised David many blessings: a great name, a land for his people Israel, rest from his enemies, a «house» [dynasty], a son who would be king and who would build a house for God's name [the temple], a throne which would last for ever, a father-son relationship between David's son and God. Moreover, if the son should commit iniquity, God would punish him, but David's house, kingdom, and throne would be established for ever [8].

Indications of a sense of the fulfillment of details of the promise are given in 1 *Kings*: "... [in the reign of Solomon] Judah and Israel were as many as the sand by the sea...." (4.20). David's son was on the throne, and he had built the temple (8.15-21). At the conclusion of the dedication of the temple,

---

[8] 2 Sm 7.9-16; cf. 1 Chr 17.18-14 and Ps 89.1-4, 19-37.

Solomon pronounced this blessing: "Blessed be the LORD who has given rest to his people Israel, according to all that he promised; not one word has failed of all his good promises, which he uttered by Moses his servant...." (8.56).

Yet portions of the text attributed to the Deuteronomist editors add conditions which make the simple everlasting covenant problematic. Thus Solomon prays for the fulfillment of the promise, which he formulates thus: "There shall never fail you a man before me to sit upon the throne of Israel, if only your sons take heed to their way, to walk before me as you have walked before me" (1 Kgs 8.25). In a vision God tells Solomon "...if you walk before me, as David your father walked, with integrity of heart and uprightness, ... then I will establish your royal throne over Israel for ever.... But if you turn aside from following me, you or your children, and do not keep my commandments and my statutes which I have set before you, but go to serve other gods and worship them, then I will cut off Israel from the land which I have given them; and the house which I have consecrated for my name I will cast out of my sight; and Israel will become a proverb and a byword among all peoples. And this house will become a heap of ruins...." (9.3-9) [9]. When that text was written, the temple was already in ruins. There is a tension between a theological conviction and even an article of Israelite faith on the one hand, and the reality of the historical situation after the destruction of the dynasty on the other hand [10].

PROPHETIC AND APOCALYPTIC PROMISES

"Write the vision; make it plain upon tablets, so he may run who reads it. For still the vision awaits its time; it hastens to the end—it will not lie. If it seems slow, wait for it; it will surely come, it will not delay" (Hab 2.2-3). I set these words of the LORD to Habakkuk at the head of this brief treatment of the new promises announced by the prophets and apocalyptists, for they seem to me to sum up what can be said of all of the promises. All are thrusts into a vaguely conceived future. All gather meaning as time passes and previous interpretations become manifestly

---

[9] Cf. 2 Chr 7.17-22.
[10] On the theological foundations of Deuteronomic history, see PETER F. ELLIS, C.SS.R., "1-2 Kings", JBC, I, 10:4-5, pp. 179-180.

irrelevant. I couple prophetic and apocalyptic because many of the texts which I shall cite are judged by exegetes to be late insertions into collections of pre-exilic or exilic prophets. More than any other elements in the Bible, these texts have their meaning as they are set in the whole of a single complex written linguistic symbol: the Bible as it now stands. For Christians they have a deeper, richer meaning in the light of later, New Testament revelation. Yet for us too they veil as much as they reveal, and in rich, often exuberant, highly imaginative symbolism they stir wonder. We come to a sense of their deeper meaning in so far as they are fulfilled in Jesus and in continuing life of the Church. Their full meaning is that of the Prime Symbolizer, God alone.[11] Exegetes, by the methods of scientific exegesis, can enlighten us concerning hypothetical dates of portions of the text, and the process of literary composition. The fact remains that the texts as they are stand in the Bible, that the whole Bible is the inspired Word of God, and that we can progress in our grasp of its meaning as we hold steadily to the task of understanding all elements as they are set in the whole.

The title, and the material, of this section would be more than enough for a long book. I can devote only some pages to it. I shall proceed by listing what seem to me to be important elements of the promises, by some brief comment and the quotation of a few texts, and by citing what may seem to be maddeningly long lists of texts. I am fully aware that portions of this section will read like notes in a fairly fully annotated edition of the Bible. I am aware too that reading this exposition and glancing at the lists of texts will not occasion an experience of God. Why, then, do I proceed thus? Because the relevant biblical texts are numerous, and we can come to an experience of God mediated by prayerful reading of the Word only gradually. I have considered all of the texts which I regard as most significant for our theme. I believe that by distinguishing elements of the prophetic and apocalyptic promises, and by listing texts for reflective, prayerful reading, I am performing a service, providing a program for reading and reflection which hopefully will mediate the experience which is desired.

---

[11] On the meaning of the Bible, and on the senses of the Bible (literal, fuller/richer/deeper, and full), see *Basics*, pp. 103-118, 308-311. For the distinction between prophetic and apocalyptic, and the characteristics of each, see Bruce Vawter, C. M., "Introduction to Prophetic Literature", JBC, I, 12, pp. 223-237; and Carroll Stuhlmueller, C. P., "Post-exilic Period: Spirit, Apocalyptic", JBC, I, 20, pp. 337-343.

(1) *Return of the exiles and restoration of Zion.* This is the
most prominent of the promises, and it may be found in texts
ranging from pre-exilic prophets to post-exilic apocalyptic.[12]
The texts in Is 24—27 are in the so-called "Isaiah Apocalypse",
one of the additions made later by Isaiah's "spiritual
descendants" (JB, pp. 1124-1125). Chapter 35, with its
paradisiac description of the restored Zion, may have been part of
Second Isaiah (40-55) originally. After the LORD's threat of
exile, delivered by Jeremiah, come the words of the promise of a
new Exodus:

> "Therefore, behold, the days are coming, says the LORD, when it
> shall no longer be said, 'As the LORD lives who brought up the
> people of Israel out of the land of Egypt,' but 'As the LORD lives
> who brought up the people of Israel out of the north country and
> out of all the countries where he had driven them.' For I will
> bring them back to their own land which I gave to their fathers...."
> (Jer 16.14-15; cf. 23.3-8).

One of the most striking prophecies of the new deliverance and of
the restoration of Zion is the beautiful thirty-first chapter of
Jeremiah, to which we shall return later for other elements of the
prophetic promise. Of the many texts of Ezekiel I should single
out chapter thirty-six, many elements of which I shall cite later.
From Second Isaiah note especially 43.1—44.8, and the second
Servant Song: the Servant's task will be to gather and restore
Israel:

> And now the LORD says,
>   who formed me from the womb to be his servant,
> to bring Jacob back to him,
>   and that Israel might be gathered to him,
> for I am honored in the eyes of the LORD,
>   and my God has become my strength—
> he says:

---

[12] See Am 9.11-15; Hos 1.10–2.1; 5.15–6.3; 11.8-12; 12.6; 14.1-7; Is
4.2-6; 11.10-16, 14.1-2; 25.6-10; 26.1-6; 27.6, 12-13; 29.1-8; 35.
1-10; Mi 4.1–5,15; 7.8-20; Hab 2.23; Jer 16.14-15; 23.3-8; 24.1-7; 30.
8-22; 31.2-40; 32.37-44; Ez 11.17-20; 20.33-38, 40-44; 28. 24-26;
34.11-24; 36.1–39.29; 39.25; 40.1–48.35; Is 40.1-11; 41.8-20; 43.1–44.8;
46; 49.1-6 (second Servant Song), 7-26; 50.4-11 (third Servant Song);
51.1-16; 52.1-12; 52.13–53.12 (fourth Servant Song); 54; 55; 56.1-8;
57.14-21; 60–62; 65.8-10, 13-16, 17-25; 66.7-16, 18-23; Zech
8.1-17; 10.3-12.

"It is too light a thing that you should be
   my servant
to raise up the tribes of Jacob
and to restore the preserved of Israel;
I will give you as a light to the nations,
   that my salvation may reach to the end of the earth."

(Is 49.5-6)

As time passes, and the hoped-for deliverance is projected into an ever more distant future, the description of Zion's future glory becomes more splendid, as does the description of the mission of a future prophet, reminiscent of the Servant (Is 60-61, and on to the end of the book).

"For behold, I create new heavens and a new earth;
and the former things shall not be remembered
   or come into mind.
But be glad and rejoice for ever
   in that which I create;
for behold, I create Jerusalem a rejoicing,
   and her people a joy..." (Is 65.17-18).

And the prophecy goes on with details of a new paradise (19-25).

We may return to Ezekiel for one last note. At the end of his account of the visions of the restored city, temple, and land, the prophet concludes: "And the name of the city henceforth shall be, The LORD is there" (48.35).[13]

(2) *The new age of righteousness and justice.* "... And I will betroth you to me for ever; I will betroth you to me in righteousness and in justice, in steadfast love, and in mercy. I will betroth you to me in faithfulness; and you shall know the LORD" (Hos 2.19-20). "Zion shall be redeemed by justice, and those in her who repent, by righteousness" (Is 1.27). "Behold, a king will reign in righteousness, and princes will rule in justice" (Is 32.1). When "... the Spirit is poured upon us from on high,

---

[13] The prophets announce other names of the restored Jerusalem. "At that time Jerusalem shall be called the throne of the Lord" (Jer 3.17). "... Jerusalem shall be called the faithful city, and the mountain of the LORD of hosts, the holy mountain" (Zech 8.3). "Afterward you shall be called the city of righteousness, the faithful city" (Is 1.26). It will be called "... the City of the LORD, the Zion of the Holy One of Israel" (Is 60.14). Compare the name by which Judah and Israel will be called: "The LORD is our righteousness" (Jer 23.6; cf. 33.16). Cf. Is 62.1-5.

... justice will dwell in the wilderness, and righteousness abide in the fruitful field. And the effect of righteousness will be peace, and the result of righteousness, quietness and trust for ever" (Is 32.15-17). "Behold, he whose soul is not upright in him shall fail, but the righteous shall live by his faith" (Hab 2.4). The Servant of Yahweh will bring forth justice to the nations (Is 42.1-3). Righteousness is the condition of restoration (cf. Is 58.6-14).[14]

(3) *The future king.* While the Davidic dynasty endured, each new king was hailed with hope as the savior of his people. When the dynasty had ended, prophetic texts which originally most probably celebrated the coming of a particular monarch were understood in terms of a future, ideal king, a messianic king. Two classic texts of Isaiah stand out:

> The people who walked in darkness
>   have seen a great light;
> those who dwelt in a land of deep darkness,
>   on them light has shined....
> For to us a child is born,
>   to us a son is given;
> and the government will be upon his shoulder,
>   and his name will be called
> "Wonderful Counselor, Mighty God,
>   Everlasting Father, Prince of Peace."
> Of the increase of his government and of peace
>   there will be no end,
> upon the throne of David, and over his kingdom,
>   to establish it, and to uphold it
> with justice and with righteousness
>   from this time forth and for evermore.
> The zeal of the LORD of hosts will do this (Is 9.2-7).
>
> There shall come forth a shoot
>   from the stump of Jesse,
> and a branch shall grow out of his roots.
> And the Spirit of the LORD shall rest upon him,
>   the spirit of wisdom and understanding,
>   the spirit of counsel and might,
>   the spirit of knowledge and the fear of the LORD.
> He shall not judge by what his eyes see,
>   or decide by what his ears hear;
> but with righteousness he shall judge the poor,

---

[14] Compare Is 1.16-19; 2.2-5; 26.2, 7-9; 51.1-8; 57.14-21; 61; 62. 12; 66.2.

> and decide with equity for the meek of the earth;
> and he shall smite the earth with the rod of his mouth,
> and with the breath of his lips he shall slay the wicked.
> Righteousness shall be the girdle of his waist,
> and faithfulness the girdle of his loins.... (Is 11.1-5).

The text continues with a description of the paradise of the age to come.[15]

Finally, in the apocalyptic vision of *Daniel*, expectation shifts from a messianic king in a restored line of David to the everlasting kingdom given by God, the Ancient of Days, to one like a son of man, coming with the clouds of heaven (Dn 7.13-14). "The saints of the Most High shall receive the kingdom, and possess the kingdom for ever, for ever and ever" (7.18; cf. v. 27). "Seventy weeks of years are decreed concerning your people and your holy city, to finish the transgression, to put an end to sin, and to atone for iniquity, to bring in everlasting righteousness, to seal both vision and prophet, and to anoint a most holy place" (9.24).

(4) *Peace and abundance.* As in the blessings of the Mosaic covenant, so in the prophetic and apocalyptic promises, peace and abundance figure prominently. "O LORD, thou wilt ordain peace for us, thou hast wrought for us all our works" (Is 26.12).

> "I will make with them a covenant of peace and banish wild beasts from the land, so that they may dwell securely in the wilderness and sleep in the woods. And I will make them and the places round about my hill a blessing; and I will send down the showers in their season; they shall be showers of blessing. And the trees shall yield their fruit, and the earth shall yield its increase, and they shall be secure in their land; and they shall know that I am the LORD, when I break the bars of their yoke, and deliver them from the hand of those who enslaved them. They shall no more be a prey to the nations, nor shall the beasts of the land devour them; they shall dwell securely, and none shall make them afraid. And I will provide for them prosperous plantations so that they shall no more be consumed with hunger in the land, and no longer suffer the reproach of the nations. And they shall know that I, the LORD their God, am with them, and they, the house of Israel, are my people, says the LORD God. And you are my sheep, the sheep of my pasture, and I am your God, says the LORD God" (Ez 34.25-31).

---

[15] On the future king, see Mi 5.2-4; Jer 23.5-6; 30.9, 33.14-26; Ez 34.23-24; 37.24-25; Is 55.3-4.

"Behold, the days are coming," says the LORD,
  "when the plowman shall overtake the reaper
   and the treader of grapes him who sows the seed;
the mountains shall drip sweet wine,
   and the hills shall flow with it.
I will restore the fortunes of my people Israel,
   and they shall rebuild the ruined cities
    and inhabit them;
they shall plant vineyards and drink their wine,
   and they shall make gardens and eat their fruit.
I will plant them upon their land,
   and they shall never again be plucked up
   out of the land which I have given them,"
   says the LORD your God (Am 9.13-15).[16]

(5) *The Spirit.* When the Spirit is poured out upon Israel from on high, then there will be justice, righteousness, peace, quietness, and trust (Is 32.15-18).

A new heart I will give you, and a new spirit I will put within you; and I will take out of your flesh the heart of stone and give you a heart of flesh. And I will put my spirit within you, and cause you to walk in my statutes and be careful to observe my ordinances. You shall dwell in the land which I gave to your fathers; and you shall be my people, and I will be your God.... (Ez 36.26-28; cf. 11.19; 39.29).

"And as for me, this is my covenant with them, says the LORD: my spirit which is upon you, and my words which I have put in your mouth, shall not depart out of your mouth, or out of the mouth of your children, or out of the mouth of your children's children, says the LORD, from this time forth and for evermore" (Is 59.21).

"And it shall come to pass afterward,
   that I will pour out my spirit on all flesh;
your sons and your daughters shall prophesy,
   your old men shall dream dreams,
   and your young men shall see visions.
Even upon the menservants and maidservants
   in those days, I will pour out my spirit...." (Jl 2.28-29)[17]

(6) *A new heart.* "I will give them a heart to know that I am the LORD; and they shall be my people and I will be their God, for

---

[16] Compare Is 30.23-26; Hos 2.21-23; Jer 31.12-14; Ez 36.8-11, 29; Is 65.17-25; Zech 8.10-13.

[17] Compare Is 44.3; 61.1.

they shall return to me with their whole heart" (Jer 24.7). In the promised new covenant, God will put his law within them, and write it upon their hearts: then they will know him (Jer 31.33-34). God will give them one [18] heart; replace their heart of stone with a heart of flesh: then they will obey; they will be his people, and he will be their God. "... But as for those whose heart goes after their detestable things and their abominations, I will requite their deeds upon their own heads, says the LORD God" (Ez 11.19-21). At one point God exhorts: "... Repent and turn from all your transgressions, lest iniquity be your ruin. Cast away from you all the transgressions which you have committed against me, and get yourselves a new heart and a new spirit!..." (Ez 18.30-31). Twice he promises the heart as his gift.

Heart in Hebrew thought is a broad-ranging term, designating both the physical heart and a wide range of figurative senses. It is both mind, and intelligence, and will, in particular moral and ethical disposition toward God. Thus, a change of heart is a moral transformation, of mind and of will. The man with a new heart given by God will *know* God in the full sense: know and acknowledge and accept him as God in his life.[19]

(7) *Forgiveness*. In the great promise of the new covenant, the difference between the new and old is this: they will not break this covenant; they will know the Lord. Two factors seem to be operative to bring about this change: God will put his law within them, writing it upon their hearts; and "... I will forgive their iniquity, and I will remember their sin no more" (Jer 31.34). Despite Jerusalem's harlotries, God will establish an everlasting covenant with her, and she will be ashamed: "I will establish my covenant with you, and you shall know that I am the LORD, that you may remember and be confounded, and never open your mouth again because of your shame, when I forgive you all that you have done, says the LORD God" (Ez 16.62-63). To vindicate his holy name, God will gather Israel from among the nations, and he will cleanse her of the profanations of his holiness: "I will sprinkle clean water upon you, and you shall be clean from all your uncleannesses, and from all your idols I will cleanse you" (Ez 36.25). When Israel will return to the Lord

---

[18] Thus the RSV. JB translates "a single heart". Both editors cite another reading: a *new* heart.

[19] Compare the Psalmist's prayer: "Create in me a clean heart, O God, and put a new and right spirit within me" (Ps 51.10).

their God and beg him take away all iniquity, he responds: "I will heal their faithlessness; I will love them freely, for my anger has turned from them" (Hos 14.4).[20]

(8) *A new covenant.* God promises variations of a new covenant, and by other figures promises an intimate bond of union between himself and his people. A single text of Hoseah suffices to present some of the complexity of the promise:

> "And in that day, says the LORD, you will call me 'My husband,' and no longer will you call me, 'My Baal.' For I will remove the names of the Baals from her mouth, and they shall be mentioned by name no more. And I will make for you a covenant on that day with the beasts of the field, the birds of the air, and the creeping things of the ground; and I will abolish the bow, the sword, and war from the land; and I will make you lie down in safety. And I will betroth you to me for ever; I will betroth you to me in righteousness and in justice, in steadfast love, and in mercy. I will betroth you to me in faithfulness; and you shall know the LORD....
> And I will have pity on Not pitied,
>   and I will say to Not my people, 'You are my people';
>   and he shall say, 'Thou art my God'" (Hos 2.16-23).

The promise is of a renewed spousal union. The covenant, as the word is used here, does not signify directly the intimate exclusive union of God and people. Seemingly it is used in a derived sense: the "covenant" with the beasts, birds, and creeping things seems rather to suggest the blessings of the promised union, which itself could be called properly a covenant, a covenanted spousal union. Though the term *covenant* is not used to designate directly the union, still the prophetic word closes with a variation on the classic covenant formula: "You are my people" and "Thou art my God".[21]

Ezekiel exhibits a breadth of application of the word *covenant* which could confirm the interpretation which I have given of its sense in Hoseah. First, there is the primary sense of union of God and people: "I will establish my covenant with you, and you shall know that I am the LORD" (16.62). Second, "I will make a covenant of peace with them; it shall be an everlasting covenant with them; and I will bless them and multiply them, and

---

[20] Compare Is 1.16-18.

[21] Compare Jer 24.7; 30.22; 31.1; 32.38; Ez 36.28. The use of covenant in this text of Hos may, of course, be simply an instance of a broad sense, such as that in which God speaks of his "covenant" with day and night, comparable with the "ordinances" of heaven and earth (Jer 34.20, 25).

will set my sanctuary in the midst of them for evermore. My dwelling place shall be with them; and I will be their God, and they shall be my people" (38.26-28). Here *peace* would seem to suggest both peace between God and people after their infidelities, and that peace which is one of the blessings of the covenant. Finally, in a promise which concludes with the classic covenant formula (God and people), God speaks of a "covenant of peace" in a manner which is reminiscent of Hoseah, but which goes on to make explicit the many blessings which are to be the effects of the basic covenant (Ez 34.25-31).

The intertwining of covenant and spousal union is apparent in the classic text of *Jeremiah*, where God speaks of the former covenant which they broke, "...though I was their husband...." (31.32). *Covenant* is intertwined with another figure which expresses the intimate union of God and people: that of shepherd and sheep. The text which I have quoted above, Ez 34.25-31, comes in a context in which God is speaking of himself as the shepherd of his people, and it is followed immediately by the verse which closes the "word": "And you are my sheep, the sheep of my pasture, and I am your God, says the LORD God" (34.31).[22]

The promised covenant is in continuity with that with David: "Incline your ear, and come to me; hear, that your soul may live; and I will make with you an everlasting covenant,[23] my steadfast, sure love for David" (Is 55.3). Moreover, foreigners who join themselves to the LORD and hold to the covenant will be part of God's community (cf. Is 56.3-8).

In a text which we have considered regarding the spirit, the covenant is a solemn promise of the spirit (Is 59.21).

(9) *Salvation open to all nations.* Israel, as the exemplar of a nation blessed by God, is to mediate salvation to those of other nations. So it was in instances of the earlier history of the people.[24] So, much more effectively, will the glory of Israel and Jerusalem draw other nations to the worship of Yahweh.[25]

---

[22] On the spousal union of God and people see also Is 54.5-8; 62.2-5.

[23] On the covenant as *everlasting,* see Is 61.8; cf. 54.4-10, where again the covenant and spousal themes are intertwined.

[24] Compare the effect which Yahweh's blessings on Israel had on Abimelek (Gn 26.28-29); Laban (Gn 30.27-30); the Egyptian Potiphar (Gn 39.1-6); the Midianite Hobab (Nm 10.29-32); Balaam (Nm 24.9); Rahab (Jos 2.8-24; 6.22-25); the Gibeonites (Jos 9); and note Solomon's prayer for foreigners who will have heard of Yahweh's great deeds and will have come to the temple to pray (1 Kgs 8.41-43).

[25] See Isaiah's word concerning the future conversion of the nations (Is

Finally, there is the oracle of the Lord to Malachi: "...from the rising of the sun to its setting my name is great among the nations, and in every place incense is offered to my name, and a pure offering; for my name is great among the nations, says the Lord of hosts" (Mal 1.11).

(10) *The consummation.* Before the coming of the Lord, he will send a messenger to prepare his way (Mal 3.1): Elijah the prophet. Before the great and terrible day of the Lord, Elijah "...will turn the hearts of fathers to their children and the hearts of children to their fathers, lest I come and smite the land with a curse" (Mal 4.5-6: RSV; 3.23-24 in JB, following the numbering of the Hebrew text). Then the Lord will suddenly come to his temple, the messenger [angel: JB] of the covenant,[26] "...in whom you delight, ...But who can endure the day of his coming...?" (3.1-2). He will purify the sons of Levi (the priesthood), and then will judge. Those who worship him as they should will be blessed (3.6-12). The righteous will be blessed; the wicked will be burnt like stubble (3.16—4.3: RSV; 3.16-21: JB).

The apocalyptic visions of *Daniel* give a highly imaginative symbolic account of the passing of the four kingdoms (Babylon, the Medes, the Persians, and the Greeks), the divine judgment, the conferring of an everlasting kingdom on the Son of man, the seventy weeks of years, and the consummation.

Before God, the "Ancient of days", the books of judgment are opened (Dn 7.9-10).

> I saw in the night visions,
> and behold, with the clouds of heaven
>   there came one like a son of man,
> and he came to the Ancient of Days
>   and was presented before him.
> And to him was given dominion
>   and glory and kingdom,
> that all peoples, nations, and languages
>   should serve him;
> his dominion is an everlasting dominion,
>   which shall not pass away,
> and his kingdom one
>   that shall not be destroyed (13-14).[27]

2.2-5; 14.1-2; 18.7; 19.16-25); Mi 4.1-4; Zeph 3.9-10; Jer 4.2; 12.14-17; Is 66.18-23; Zech 8.12-13, 20-23. On Israel as a mediator of salvation, see *The Mystery,* pp. 44-49.

[26] According to the editors of JB, the angel, whose coming is simultaneous with that of Yahweh, obscurely designates Yahweh himself.

[27] Compare 7.18, 22, 27: the kingdom of the saints of the Most High.

Seventy weeks of years are decreed before the end (9.24-27). Daniel's last vision concerns the final cosmic conflict and the end (10.1—12.13).

> "At that time shall arise Michael, the great prince, who has charge of your people. And there shall be a time of trouble, such as never has been since there was a nation till that time; but at that time your people shall be delivered, every one whose name shall be found written in the book. And many of those who sleep in the dust of the earth shall awake, some to everlasting life, and some to shame and everlasting contempt. and those who are wise shall shine like the brightness of the firmament; and those who turn many to righteousness, like the stars for ever and ever...." (12.1-3).

Finally I simply note another apocalyptic account of the consummation: Zech 12-14.

Reflecting upon the qualitative difference which I noted above in the blessings promised in the Mosaic covenant, we may see clearly how the "spiritual" blessings have come to prevail in the prophetic promises. Surely the material, temporal blessings remain, and often they are described in paradisiac terms. Yet there is a strong emphasis on "spiritual" blessings: those pertaining to intimate union with God and interior transformation and enrichment of man.[28]

ESCHATOLOGICAL AND MESSIANIC PSALMS

I merely cite three groups of Psalms which reflect some of the elements of the prophetic and apocalyptic promises. The Songs of Zion (Pss 46, 48, 76, 84, 87, 122) celebrate the future glory of the city when God will have established his kingdom. The Psalms of the kingship of Yahweh (47, 93, 95, 96, 97, 98, 99) look to the reign of Yahweh himself as King. The royal and messianic Psalms (2, 18, 20, 21, 28, 45, 61, 63, 72, 84, 89, 101, 110, 132, 144), originally dating from the Davidic monarchy, came to be understood as messianic after the fall of the monarchy. They look to a future not yet realized within the Old Testament.

---

[28] On the gradual shift in emphasis in the promised blessings, see the treatment of salvation in *The Mystery*, pp. 51-58.

Resurrection and Immortality

I put together here two elements of promise which are not of the same derivation or meaning. The first is a development of Hebrew thought. The second reflects Greek influence upon the wisdom literature.

Three passages of 2 *Maccabees* witness clearly to a belief in resurrection after death. Most striking is the testimony of the mother and sons put to death as martyrs by Antiochus. The second son affirmed: "... you dismiss us from this present life, but the King of the universe will raise us up to an everlasting renewal of life, because we have died for his laws" (7.9). The third, putting out his tongue and stretching forth his hands as he was ordered, said: "I got these from Heaven, and because of his laws I disdain them, and from him I hope to get them back again" (7.11). Exhorting her sons, the mother said, "I do not know how you came into being in my womb. It was not I who gave you life and breath, nor I who set in order the elements within each of you. Therefore the Creator of the world, who shaped the beginning of man and devised the origin of all things, will in his mercy give life and breath back to you again, since you now forget yourselves for the sake of his laws" (7.22-23). And she pleaded with her youngest son: "... Accept death, so that in God's mercy I may get you back again with your brothers" (29). Defiantly the youngest scorned his tormentor: "... You have not escaped the judgment of the almighty, all-seeing God. For our brothers after enduring a brief suffering have drunk of everflowing life under God's covenant; but you, by judgment of God, will receive just punishment for your arrogance...." (35-36).[29]

The book of *Wisdom* witnesses to faith in the immortality and blessedness of the righteous after death:

> But the souls of the righteous are in the hand of God,
> and no torment will ever touch them.
> In the eyes of the foolish they seemed to have died,
> and their departure was thought to be an affliction,
> and their going from us to be their destruction;
> but they are at peace.
> For though in the sight of men they were punished,
> their hope is full of immortality.... (Wis 3.1-4).

---

[29] The other two brief passages are 12.43-45 and 14.46.

But the righteous live for ever,
and their reward is with the Lord;
the Most High takes care of them.
Therefore they will receive a glorious crown
and a beautiful diadem from the hand of the Lord....
    (5.15-16).[30]

A Transitional note

I conclude thus my presentation of elements from the Old Testament. Before passing on to treat New Testament witness, I should acknowledge two apparent disproportions in my consideration of the Old Testament. The first is a matter of my own choice. I have stressed the positive theme, promise and fulfillment, and have said little about threat and punishment. I feel that the darker theme, in what I have called at the outset a contrapuntal dialectic, is sufficiently evident. It is enough to consider—beyond the covenant curses which we have noted—the prominence of threat in the books of the prophets, and the ample witness to punishment in the historical books, as well as in prophets and Psalms. The second is due to the very nature of Israel's revelation and experience: there is far more promise than fulfillment. I shall reflect on this later.

---

[30] Compare Wis 4.7-15; 5.1-5; 6.17-20. For approaches to the conception of retribution after death, see Sir 11.26-28; 1.13; 7.36; 28.6; and Dn 12.2.

Chapter II

THE UNIQUENESS OF NEW TESTAMENT WITNESS

All of the human authors of the Bible participated in a transcendent, Divine-human symbolizing.[1] All of them, therefore, differ from all other human writers. Their whole effort, and the works they produced, were taken up into the constitution of a single complex written linguistic symbol, of which God is the Prime Symbolizer, the Author. The meaning of their works, consequently, transcends that which they themselves understood and intended. The whole of their work, and every portion of it, has its full meaning as it is set in the whole of which it is a part. That whole is the Bible. The interpretation of their works differs from that of any other human works of literature. The task of the interpreter is not merely that of determining as accurately as possible the full meaning of the human author: that is an important part, the determination of the "literal sense", as the word *literal* is commonly used in discussions of biblical exegesis. The human authors were taken up into a process which they could not possibly comprehend, and what they wrote had a meaning which they could not know. The further, more important, work of interpretation regards the determination of that meaning as far as that is possible. The full meaning of the Bible, and of any portion of it, is God's meaning. No interpreter can comprehend that meaning, just as he or she cannot comprehend God. Yet we can come to a deeper, richer understanding of the Bible and of its parts as we succeed in setting the part in the whole complex Symbol, in which alone it can be understood. The efficacy of the Bible exceeds that of any merely human work, and it cannot be measured by judging it in terms of literary excellence, of the relative adequacy of the symbol which the human authors elaborated. The Bible is the Word of God, vehicle of grace for any man or woman who reads it with the reverence and prayerful disposition which it deserves. All of this is true of

---

[1] For divine symbolizing and symbols, see *Basics*, pp. 41-70; on the Bible as a divine-human symbol, pp. 94-118.

the whole Bible, and of all of its human authors and their works. Yet there is something unique in the role of the New Testament writers.

THREE ASPECTS

I should say that New Testament writers are unique for at least these three aspects of their work as inspired writers: (1) the total world, subjective and objective, in which their symbols are set: the total Reality which they image; (2) the importance of their work for the understanding of the Bible as a whole; (3) the manner in which they they affect us—or rather, in which God affects us—through the works which God inspired.

(1) *World and reality*. What I have to say here, in the whole of this chapter, involves an application of my theory of symbolizing and symbol. I have defined *symbol* in this way: a sensuous image which terminates a human intentional operation, represents the imaged reality, and may affect the human world with a manifold efficacy.[2] My concern in this section is with the reality which the new Testament writers image. Their symbols, like all human symbols, represent the whole world of the symbolizer, subjective and objective.[3] With varying degrees and blends, they represent the total subjective world of which they are a sensibly perceptible part: the whole of the experience from which they proceed, and in which they are elaborated. That experience in its totality is at once cognitive, and emotive-volitional-motor. They represent too the objective world which the symbolizer has encountered, and to which he is responding. In the case of the divine-human symbolizing and symbols involved in the New Testament, the total world, objective and subjective, and the total Reality, transcend those of all other biblical writers. The difference is based on this: God has now made his full revelation in and through Jesus Christ, and by the gift of the promised Spirit he is teaching the meaning of Jesus' words, and of the whole of the mystery of his human being as the revelation of the Father. The promise has been fulfilled in the glorification of Jesus and the gift of the Spirit. The Church, the new Israel, has been established, and the New Testament writers live the full reality of life in Christ in the community of believers. By the whole of the Paschal Mystery salvation has been

---

[2] *Man the Symbolizer*, p. 294.
[3] *Ibid.*, pp. 278-280, 300, 302.

accomplished in Jesus, and is open to all who believe, repent, and turn to receive the gift of life in Him. That is the difference in the objective world: the transcendent Reality which men and women now encounter.

Their total subjective world has been transformed proportionately. They have been given the Spirit, illumining them and moving them to a full response of faith, love, and fidelity. They believe now, for the Spirit has taught them the meaning of Jesus' words, and the meaning of the full reality of Jesus, the Prime Sacrament. Many of them had responded to Jesus and had received his word with an imperfect faith during his public life. Now they understand, and respond fully. In most cases we can only conjecture the depth of that response: cognitive, emotive, volitional, and moter. In some cases, especially in the letters of Paul, we have beautiful revelations of some of his feelings, as well as of the truth, the gospel, which he preaches.

In every inspired writer of the New Testament both worlds, subjective and objective, are unique. For every man who is moved by God to write, to contribute a portion of the total symbol, is unique. He has a unique personal point of view, unique personal gifts, a unique share in the gifts of the Spirit, and a total personal response to the grace which is uniquely his. Every one writes from the whole of his personal world. Every one gives a fragmentary account, symbolizes inadequately both his own experience and the Reality which he has experienced. All of them write with a symbolism which is prevalently intuitive: sharpening of conceptual symbolism will come later, much later, in the life of the Church. Yet every writer has his own personal stamp, his own personal symbolizing power and style. Every one witnesses to the Reality as he has experienced it, within the limits of his own powers to symbolize.

Consequently all of the New Testament writers are mutually complementary in their function as inspired writers. It is not that they influence one another, except in some cases in which it is clear from personal witness that one is familiar with the writing of another, or where internal evidence makes a degree of dependence clear. An instance of the former is the mention of Paul's letters by the author of 2 Pt (3.15-16). The latter is clear in the case of Mark's influence upon both Matthew and Luke, according to varying theories concerning the Synoptic problem.[4]

---

[4] For a brief introduction to the problem, see FREDERICK GAST, O.C.D., "Synoptic Problem", JBC, II, 40, pp. 1-6.

What is more to the point is their complementarity which transcends their awareness. In God's plan they are contributing their shares to his work, and in the continuing life of the Church they are serving in complementarity as they affect us as God's instruments. They serve to mediate our insight into the one great Reality to which all of them bear witness. Their works form a book which they themselves do not know in its fulness. Their individual readings on the one great Reality mediate an experience of God, and an insight into the fulness of his plan for us, whose unity is held in the living faith of the community of believers.

The unity of the Bible, then, does not depend on the awareness and conscious collaboration of the human authors. It is grounded in God, who alone is the Author, who alone moves all to write their shares in his single complex symbol. It is held in the faith of the community of believers, the Church.[5]

I have mentioned both the subjective and the objective worlds of the New Testament writers. Both are unique, in comparison with all other biblical authors, for the reasons which I have indicated. Which is the more important? I should say without hesitation that it is their objective world. What contributes most to the life of the Church is the Reality which the writers have experienced. Paul's affectivity, and other aspects of his distinct subjective world in his own personal response to Father, Jesus, and the Spirit, are precious. We know more of the human potential for full, rich life in Them through Paul's witness to his own personal experience. But what is most precious to us is the Reality to which Paul and all of the New Testament writers witness: the Reality which they experienced. In God's plan they serve to evoke in us a personal response to the same Reality. We are to respond to what God has accomplished in Jesus, to the full revelation of the entire Paschal Mystery and of the gift of the Spirit. *What* Peter and Paul and John believe and witnessed to is more important for the life of the Church, and for every one of us personally, than how they felt about it. What happened in the transcendent events of the fulfillment of God's saving action in Christ is all-important to us. It is, then, above all the transcendent objective world of the New Testament writers which is important for us.

What do I mean by "transcendent objective world"? The answer to this question is extremely important, for it goes to the

---

[5] On the unity of the Bible see *Basics*, pp. 130-131.

heart of the matter of the objectivity and value of the New
Testament writers' witness. Beyond that immediate issue, the
answer is all-important for the interpretation of the New
Testament immediately, and of the whole Bible as it is understood
in the light of New Testament revelation.

The possible challenge, of course, would be provoked by the
very fact that I am insisting on the value and importance of the
witness which is given from within the community of believers,
after the Easter and Pentecost experience, within a full life of faith
and experience of living in the glorified Christ. Some could claim
that such witness is not "objective": It is colored by subjective
faith, and it is not a reliable witness to the reality of Jesus, the
"historical Jesus".

I have gone into the whole matter of "objective" and
"subjective" elsewhere, as well as that of "historical" and
"real",[6] and I shall not go over the same ground again. To get to
the essential, let us begin with the notion of the real, and of
reality. Whatever *is* is real. The world which I encounter is real:
it *is*, quite independently of my encountering it. When I
encounter it, my knowledge is real, and so are all of my other
conscious, intentional operations which in any way regard the real
world. These conscious operations are real because they are very
much a part of me, very much a part of the way I *am* in my
human mode of being. Intentional being—the heightened
manner of being which we attain in our conscious, intentional
operations, and the terms of our operations—is *real* being. It is
part of the mystery of a universe of being in which human
persons *are* and operate in these ways. Yet we distinguish clearly
the modes of intentional being and the being which persons and
things in the universe have independently of our knowing, loving,
desiring, or fearing them, or acting upon them in any way.

The pair of terms *objective* and *subjective* have sense only in
so far as they refer to human subjects, persons who are conscious
of the world in which they are, and of their own operations by
which they somehow regard that world, and of themselves. The
objective is not the person or thing "outside" us, in the fulness of
its being. Rather it is that person or thing in so far as it is the
term of one or more of our conscious, intentional operations. We
attain them only in such acts, and, in every case, what we attain

---

[6] For my treatment of *objective* and *subjective*, see MS, pp. 173-176. On
the *real* and *reality*, see MS, pp. 135-140, 281-282; and *Basics*, pp. 30,
232-237; 67; 103, 107-108, 131-135, 343-351.

we *objectify*. Both *objective* and *subjective* pertain to the realm
of the human conscious, intentional world: the persons and things
which we objectify as we encounter them and respond to their
impact by a manifold symbolization. The whole terminology is
clouded by philosophical movements in which terms are used in
quite different contexts. For my own thought, the context within
which alone all that I say or write has its meaning, I can only refer
to *Man the Symbolizer*. Suffice it to say that we *objectify* only by
symbolizing, that all objectification is the work of a symbolizing
subject, and that all objective "fact" is pitifully abstractive and
limited, as all symbolizing and symbols are pitifully inadequate.
Whether we are regarding persons and things distinct from us, or
our own conscious operations upon which we turn in reflection, or
ourselves, which we know only as we catch ourselves in acts
regarding others, we are objectifying, and we are attaining
something which in its own way is *real.*

Apart from questions about *objective* and *subjective*, the
essential question regards what is *real.* Who and what *was* the
real Jesus? Is he real now, and if so in what state? What really
happened in the Easter "event" and in the three accounts of a
Pentecostal experience.[7] What is the reality, if any, which
corresponds to the account of religious experience in the early
Christian Church?

I used the phrase "transcendent objective world". Let us call
it instead the "transcendent real world", or the "fully real
world". All of the questions which I suggested concerning Jesus,
Easter, Pentecost, and early Christian life regard simply what is
real, what truly *is.*

First, it is the *real* world: it really *is.* Events which have
transpired in it truly *were,* and persons who existed in the past
really *were* in the fulness of their reality. Second, it is
transcendent in a particular sense. All that truly is or was is
transcendent in the broad sense that in the fulness of its reality it
exceeds all that we can know of it, or could have known of it, all
that can be captured in human concepts and projected in human
symbols. We never exhaust the fulness of being, the mystery, of
anything that is. Our knowledge is always abstractive,
fragmentary. When I say transcendent in a particular sense, I
refer to aspects of the real world, of persons and events and levels
of being, which simply lie beyond the powers of human

---

[7] The "Lucan" Pentecost, Acts 2, esp. vv. 1-4; the "Johannine", Jn
20.19-23; and the "Pentecost of the Gentiles", Acts 10.44-48.

perception. The transcendent in this sense can be known and affirmed only as a consequence of God's special revelation, and of his gift of the power of faith by which a man or woman makes the "leap of faith", and affirms what is in no sense evident, and what could never be evident or accessible to purely human powers of knowledge.[8]

To avoid confusion, I point out the distinction of two sorts of knowledge of the transcendent, of God. The first is a knowledge of the transcendent "ground" of all being. It is attained by probing the mystery of the universe and especially of human life. It is within the range of the power of human intellect, without revelation or the gift of faith. Most men and women come to intimations of the transcendent, God, and such knowledge is enough to ground their conviction that there is a God, and that they should live their lives in conscious relation to him. It is enough, too, to provide the natural factor which enters into their act of faith in response to special revelation. Knowing at least vaguely what they mean by "God", convinced that God *is*, they do not yet know *who* he is, or how they can come into interpersonal relationship with him. Beyond such intimations of God, there is also the possibility of a philosophical affirmation of God, and some knowledge of what must be affirmed about God consistently with the basic affirmation that he *is*. That is the most difficult of all natural human knowledges.[9] There is, then, a natural knowledge of God, ranging from universally attainable intimations to a rare philosophical achievement.

The second sort of knowledge of God, the transcendent, is beyond all mere human knowledge. It is attainable only by revelation on God's part, and by an act of faith which itself is possible only by the gift of God. Such knowledge regards truth about God, and about the potential of human life offered as pure gift, which could never be affirmed without special revelation, and which can never be understood completely even after revelation and the affirmation of faith. It concerns aspects of reality which are simply beyond the reach of natural human powers of intellect. Only when men and women are confronted with the message of a

---

[8] On the inadequacy of all human concepts, see MS, pp. 70-72. Further, on the inadequacy of all human symbols, see pp. 294, 300-301. On special revelation, see *Basics*, pp. 71-75; on the leap of faith, see *Basics*, pp. 137-142, and above in this work, pp. 9-10.

[9] On intimations of God as the transcendent ground of the universe and of human life in particular, see MS, pp. 134-135; on the natural knowledge of God attainable by philosophy, pp. 208-213, esp. p. 213.

special revelation by which God makes himself known and offers a way to a greater fulness of life, they respond: *"You* are my God".

The "transcendent objective world", or "transcendent real world", or "fully real world" is *real*, but it lies beyond the range of any merely natural human knowledge. What is affirmed about this world can be affirmed only by the light of God's special revelation, and by the power of faith which is his gift.

New Testament witness is precious above all for its account of *what* the Apostles and the other early Christians believed about God and Christ and the Holy Spirit, and about their life in Them. The apostolic preaching, and the New Testament in which alone portions of that preaching are preserved, is normative for all Christians. What the New Testament writers, inspired by God, have written about Christ and God's saving action in Christ and in us is our most reliable witness to the transcendent world in which they lived, and in which we live now. Yet it is a witness which has full value only for those who share the faith which we have in common with the Apostles. Here is the crucial truth. Here is the great divide.

For those who do not share our Christian faith, and our acceptance of the New Testament—and the whole Bible—as God's Word, or for those who believe, but who are dedicated to a purely empirical, "scientifically historical" search for a knowledge of Christ and of the real world corresponding to Christian religious experience, the New Testament as it stands in its entirety is not a reliable witness. Only the empirically verifiable, scientifically historical data which can be established "behind" the New Testament, and which hypothetically would be unaffected by faith in the transcendent events of Easter and Pentecost, could be regarded as reliable. For those who share our faith, and who are not inhibited by an exclusively scientific, empiricist approach to the Bible, the New Testament witness is fully reliable, precisely because it is grounded on the special revelation, the gift of the Spirit, and the illumination and faith which are God's gift. The two positions are simply contrary, beyond reconciliation.

Without special revelation and the gift of faith, we could never know what we now affirm by faith to be most *real* and most precious in the world in which we live. Only within a life of faith in our community of believers is a Christian theology possible. And for some aspects of our faith and the reality which we affirm, it is only within the Roman Catholic Church that I can elaborate my theological work. I have explained my ground for this conviction in *Basics*,[10] and I work as a theologian consistently with that conviction.

(2) *Understanding the Bible.* The New Testament writers are uniquely important for their contribution to the understanding of the Bible as a whole. I should distinguish two aspects of this contribution. One runs through the whole of the New Testament: it is a Christian reading of the Old Testament. The other is found in certain texts which stand out as peaks in the New Testament.

First, by their Christian reading of the Old Testament, the New Testament writers contribute to an understanding of the deeper, richer meaning of the Old Testament.[11] In this it is reasonable to conjecture that they follow the example of Jesus himself. To the disciples on the road to Emmaus, downcast after Jesus' death and the report of the empty tomb and of his being alive, Jesus said: " 'O foolish men, and slow of heart to believe all that the prophets have spoken! Was it not necessary that the Christ should suffer these things and enter into his glory?' And beginning with Moses and all the prophets, he interpreted to them in all the scriptures the things concerning himself" (Lk 24.25-27). Again, in an apparition in Jerusalem, he said: " 'These are my words which I spoke to you, while I was still with you, that everything written about me in the law of Moses and the prophets and psalms must be fulfilled'. Then he opened their minds to understand the scriptures...." (Lk 24.44-45). In his confrontation with the Jews, as reported by John, Jesus told them, "You search the scriptures, because you think that in them you have eternal life; and it is they that bear witness to me;..." (Jn 5.39). And again: "If you believed Moses, you would believe me, for he wrote of me" (Jn 5.46). We have no record of the details of what Jesus refers to in his interpretation of texts of the scriptures (the "Old Testament" for us). It is reasonable to suppose that the apostolic preaching and the Christian reading of the Old Testament throughout the New is grounded in the type of interpretation which Jesus himself had used during his life, and which he gave after his resurrection.

What is the value of such a reading of the Old Testament? On what is it grounded? It is not mere artifice, not a merely

---

[10] For my reasons for writing *Basics of a Roman Catholic Theology*, in particular for the qualification "Roman Catholic", see *Basics*, pp. 9, 221-239.

[11] On the senses of the Bible: literal, fuller/richer/deeper, and full, see *Basics*, pp. 308-311.

traditional type of exegesis such as that which could have prevailed among Jews. It is grounded in a new revelation and an illumination by the Holy Spirit. Before Pentecost no Jew—except Jesus himself, and the few men and women who according to the gospel narrative were inspired to see in Jesus a fulfillment of the scriptures (Elizabeth, Mary, Zechariah, Simeon, and Anna: Lk 1-2)—would understand the scriptures as they were understood by the Apostles and in the early Church. Only the new revelation, faith, and the continuing illumination by the Holy Spirit could make possible such an interpretation of scripture.

The Bible is a single complex written linguistic symbol. Its meaning is God's meaning, for he alone is the Prime Symbolizer, the Author. Every symbolic element has its full meaning only as it is set in the whole. Only when special revelation has been completed, and the New testament has been written within the Christian community under the inspiration of the Holy Spirit, can earlier texts be understood in their deeper, richer sense.

Unique among the human authors of the Bible, then, the New Testament writers witness to early Christian reading of the Bible, and contribute to our understanding of the whole Bible.

I do not say that every New Testament allusion to a fulfillment of the scriptures opens us to the deeper, richer meaning of the Old Testament text in question. Indeed, at times we do not know to what text allusion is made, for example in Jn 7.38: "Out of his heart shall flow rivers of living water". Often, however, the citation or quotation is clear, and a deeper, richer meaning is given. Individual instances of such allusion to fulfillment must be pondered and evaluated soberly. Yet the important truth remains: Jesus himself interpreted scriptures in ways which he alone understood, and which others could understand only in the light of full revelation and illumination by the Holy Spirit. The New Testament contributes to understanding the deeper, richer meaning of the Old.

Thus far I have been concerned with the first of two aspects to which I referred at the beginning of this section. The second is the role of those texts which I have already proposed as "prologues" and "flashes".[12] They are peaks in the New Testament, revealing profound insight into the Mystery, contributing to our understanding not only of the individual books in which they are found, but of the whole Bible. In particular,

---

[12] See above, pp. 17-22.

they give profound answers to the question concerning Jesus: "Who *is* he?" They should affect our reading of every page of the New Testament and much of the Old. They should affect too our continuing contemplation of Jesus and our sense of him as we experience him in the Eucharist, dwelling within us, and somehow symbolized in every man and woman whom we meet.

If we reflect on what we have considered in these two sections (1) and (2), and on the New Testament symbols as they can be understood in terms of the functions of symbols,[13] and of the definition which I have given above (p. 75), both refer to the second function of symbols, and the second part of the definition. The second function of a symbol is to reveal the symbolizer and his or her world. The second part of the definition corresponds: "represents the imaged reality". The imaged reality is the whole world, subjective and objective, of the symbolizer. The whole world of the human symbolizers taken up into the divine process of inspiration, is both subjective (the whole symbolizing person, and the whole complex intentional, conscious operation which terminates in the symbol) and objective: the Reality which the symbolizer has encountered, and to which he is responding. I have insisted on the relative importance for us of the objective world, the Reality which is experienced. For the New Testament writers that Reality was immediately the person of Jesus Christ and the transcendent events in which God's saving action culminated in him and in the gift of the Spirit, the establishing of the Church, and the full human response of the early Christians. But it was also the Reality obscurely represented by the whole of the Old Testament, and now illumined and more clearly understood in the light of the new revelation and illumination.

The third of the aspects which I regard as unique in New Testament witness pertains to the third part of the definition of a symbol, and the third function: affecting the human world by a manifold efficacy.

(3) *Affecting us.* We cannot consider the efficacy of the New Testament without recalling that the human writers were moved by God, the principal Symbolizer, the Author of the whole Bible. All of the human powers of the writers, all of their personal religious experience, all of their symbolizing and symbols are taken up into the total process of the divine-human symbolizing.

---

[13] See MS, pp. 269-290.

The individual writers had their own purposes in writing, as some of them make clear: to set forth the truth, to exhort, to reprove, to share fellowship with the Father and with his Son Jesus Christ and so come to complete joy [14]. All communicate what they have understood of the Mystery, every one from his own point of view. All share with us what they have grasped in their many complementary readings upon one great Reality. All of their efforts and contributions are taken up into the one process by which God influences us through his written word.

Though all of the symbolic elements of the Old Testament and the New have their meaning and efficacy as they are set in the whole, and though through all of them instrumentally God illumines and moves us to a full response, still the New Testament witness has a special role, a special efficacy. In complementarity all of the new Testament writers communicate a knowledge of fulfillment in Christ, and of the further new promises which are part of Christ's message. By illumining the Old Testament they contribute to the greater efficacy of Old Testament witness: early promises, early longings for deliverance, take on new meaning for us as we now read the Old Testament. We shall have occasion to note this in the course of our reflections on the many aspects of our experience of God, in volume II of this work.

The New Testament witness influences us directly in our prayerful reading of the whole Bible. It affects us too repeatedly in the other ways in which we experience God. When we take part in the Church's worship, it is the Word which illumines us, gives a sense of what we are doing. As we live together in our community of believers, and in the broader fellowship of all men and women, it is the Word, especially as it is held in the New Testament, which teaches us the deeper meaning and value of our lives, and which enables us to mediate God to one another. Finally, in the intimacy of our personal lives, in our personal union with Father, Jesus, and Holy Spirit, in our personal prayer, in our longings, in our joys and sufferings, it is the New Testament witness most of all which helps us to understand the meaning of it all.

Thus far I have indicated a multiple efficacy of the New Testament witness in communicating a knowledge of the Mystery, the one great Reality which the Bible represents. Through the New Testment, however, and the whole Bible illumined by it,

---

[14] Compare Lk 1.1-4; the repeated exhortation and reproof in Paul's letters and in *Hebrews*; and John's desire (1 Jn 1.1-4).

God does much more than communicate knowledge. He evokes a total personal response: emotive, volitional, and motor in response to the known good and evil which we come to know. Prayerful reading and hearing of the Bible, especially of the New Testament, is one of the greatest occasions and vehicles of grace. As we come to know Jesus and the Father and the Spirit more profoundly through such reading and hearing, we should respond with a deeper love and commitment, and desire of full fidelity to the God who has made us his own in the new Covenant.

OUR ROLE

We have a threefold role to play in the continuing efficacy of the New Testament. All are involved in the multiple dialectic of charisms, personal and interpersonal, which characterizes Christian life[15].

First, by faith, as the living community of believers, we hold the unity of the Bible. That unity, as I have affirmed, is grounded in God, in his eternal plan. In its realization in history, however, that unity is to be found not in a bound book, not in the many complementary witnesses of human authors set down in print one after another. It is held only in the living community of believers, in the Church which to the end of time is guided by the Holy Spirit. Under that guidance, it is the Church which has decreed which books are part of the Bible. Beyond that, it is in the living faith of the Church, in the consciousness of the living, believing community, that the many witnesses are held in unity, and that we believe in the one great Reality to which the many human authors bore their fragmentary witness.

It is in the whole Church that the Holy Spirit dwells. It is the whole Church which is illumined by the Spirit. It is the whole Church which reads and hears the many words and holds together the Word which represents the whole Reality. Though we live in a hierarchical Church in which decisive judgment is exercized by those privileged members empowered by God, in the ordinary life of the Church it is not only the magisterium which reads the Bible and holds its unity. You and I, to the extent to which we live full lives of faith, and read the Bible prayerfully, and ponder the dynamic unity of its great themes, and contemplate lovingly God, Father, Jesus, and Holy Spirit, and

---

[15] On the dialectic of charisms see *Basics*, pp. 198-212.

their plan for our fulness of life in Them—*we* share in the role of perceiving and holding the unity of the Bible.   To the extent to which any one of us reaches deeper insight into the unity of the one great Reality, he or she is enriched personally and stimulated to a deeper full response in his or her personal dialectic of charisms.   To the extent to which we share our insights, we mediate to one another our sense of the unity of the Bible, and of the Reality which it represents: together we hold that unity, as we influence one another in the great interpersonal dialectic of charisms.

Second, individually we have a role which pertains to our own personal dialectic, a process in which there is a continual interplay of knowledge and love.   More intimate knowledge of Jesus and of the Father and of the Holy Spirit evokes a response of love.   Such knowledge is mediated especially by prayerful reading of the Bible, and most of all the New Testament.   Yet we are not passive.   We must approach reading or hearing the Word with that reverence which is due to God who speaks, with a prayer for enlightenment and for the grace of a full response. More intimate knowledge evokes a response of love.   Living in loving union with Them, we have a vague sense of the shape of the experience of loving, that connatural knowledge which is part of the mystery of love.   When we have come to a deeper love of Jesus, then hearing or reading the gospel or a letter of Paul, means more to us.   It resonates in us.   We have a deeper, more intimate knowledge of Jesus.   And so the process, the dialectical interplay of knowledge and love continues.

Two texts of the New testament suffice to illustrate what I mean.   Both are from John.   It would be easy to cite many from Paul.

When the Jews marveled at Jesus' teaching, and wondered how he had such learning, since he had never studied, he answered, "My teaching is not mine, but his who sent me; if any man's will is to do his will, he shall know whether the teaching is from God or whether I am speaking on my own authority...."(Jn 7.16-17).   How will such a man *know* that the teaching is from God?   Knowing and loving God, knowing and doing his will, he will have a connatural knowledge of God, and will recognize that what Jesus is teaching is in harmony with God's will.   And he will believe in Jesus, and receive the gift of a deeper knowledge and love.

In one of many passages from John's first letter, a rule of discernment is given, one of many rules all of which involve somehow a connatural knowledge: "... And by this we may be

sure that we know him, if we keep his commandments. He who
says 'I know him' but disobeys his commandments is a liar, and
the truth is not in him; but whoever keeps his word, in him truly
love for God is perfected. By this we may be sure that we are in
him: he who says he abides in him ought to walk in the same way
in which he walked'' (1 Jn 2.4-6). Typical of the spiralling
thought of John, there is a dialectical interplay of knowing Christ,
keeping his commandments, loving God, being in him, walking in
the way in which he [Christ] walked.

I shall have occasion later to return to John's complicated
series of criteria for discernment. For the present, we may be
content to note the first of two aspects of our role in the continuing
efficacy of the New Testament: it concerns our own personal
growth in knowledge and love, our personal dialectic of charisms.

The second concerns our part in the interpersonal dialectic of
life in the community of believers. It is manifold. There is first
an obvious mutual influence in sharing our understanding of the
Bible: this is an experience which is more and more common in
the enrichment of Christian life in our time. There is, beyond this
conscious, explicit sharing of knowledge, a subtle mediation of the
meaning of the Word by the whole of our lives, in so far as we
show forth in them something of the meaning of living in Christ.
God's revelation, his special revelation, is complete. The Word
has been spoken. For the most part, that Word is preserved in
the Bible, the great divine-human symbol. Part of the Reality
which is represented by the Bible, part of the Mystery revealed
once for all, is the life of the Church, our continuing life in Christ.
The Mystery regards both God himself, Father, Son, and Holy
Spirit, and the whole of his revelation and saving action which
comes to its term in every one of us, in our personal response.
Christians will continue to show one another something of the
meaning of the Word as they show in the whole of a truly
Christian life God's action coming to term in their personal
response. Most of all by a life of love, and in the mystery of
mutual love in Christ, we show one another more of the fulness
of John's simple statement, "God is love", and more of the
meaning of that mutual love which is the sign that the Father has
sent the Son. As the saving action comes to term in us, we show
one another the meaning of the word; we continue the process of
God's self-manifestation; we mediate God to one another [16].

New Testament witness is unique, and we have a share in it.

---

[16] Compare what I have written on the imaged reality in *Basics,* pp.
131-135; and on universal sacramentality, pp. 189-191.

Chapter III

PROLOGUES AND FLASHES

It is wholesome to be forced to settle for being human. This is what I must do as I attempt to devise the most effective strategy for the elaboration of this theme—as indeed it is what all theologians must do in whatever work they are attempting.

My problem here is set by the demands—or apparent demands—of the very theory of symbolizing in general, and of divine-human symbolizing, which I have elaborated. Every symbolic element has its full meaning as it is set in the whole of which it is a part, the full reality which it inadequately images and represents. The whole in this case is the full Reality: God, Father, Son, and Holy Spirit, their eternal plan, and their gradual revelation and execution of that plan for our fulness of life in Them. If it were possible to project that whole Reality, then every symbolic element, in whatever order the elements were presented, could be set against the ground in which it can be understood. It is impossible. We are not God. He is present to himself; his "mind", his "plan" are identical with him eternally. He needs no inadequate symbols except because from all eternity he decrees to manifest himself and his plan to us. From all eternity the Son is the perfect image, the perfect Symbol of the Father. Since God wills to manifest himself, and eventually reveal himself fully as Father, Son, and Holy Spirit, he must do so by a divine condescension. He must use human symbols in the total process of his divine-human self-manifestation and execution of his plan. And so historically God has gradually revealed himself in a process culminating in Jesus Christ and in the gift of the Spirit who illumines us, teaches us interiorly the very meaning of Jesus and his words.

I have said that the unity of the Bible is grounded in God: the one full reality which it images is God and his plan. I have said too that the unity of the Bible is held in the living community of believers, the Church. What should be said, to refine that statement, is that in the continuing process of illumination and understanding in the life of the Church, the whole Church holds

as far as it is possible humanly that degree of insight into the
unity of the Reality which it has attained. To the extent to which
the Church has reached insight into that unity, it reads every
symbolic element and understands it as it is set in the whole. To
the extent that the individual believer participates personally in
that insight and understanding, he or she should attempt to do
the same.

God's condescension involved using sensuous images and
submitting, so to speak, to the laws of human being and
symbolizing: he took men, with all of their powers and
limitations, and spoke through them, and wrote through them.
So the divine revelation proceeds according to the exigencies and
limitations of human symbolizing. Though God could reveal
aspects of the truth in visions which portrayed in a flash a whole
message projected in a visual intuitive symbol, when he moved
men to write the vision, they could do so only word by word in
the linear projection which characterizes all human linguistic
symbolizing. To no man or woman could God reveal the whole.
Through no human writer could he write the Bible except bit by
bit, in poor divine-human symbols which gradually communicated parts of the message.

How, then, is the theologian to proceed? I have insisted on
the importance of the *sensus plenior*: the deeper, richer meaning
of the Bible, the meaning which any symbolic element has as it is
set in the whole. I should like to be able to present the whole,
and then situate the symbolic elements against that ground. That
is impossible. Yet there is something which I can do, and which I
shall attempt to do as successfully as possible. I can begin with
those passages or books of the New Testament which I judge to
be the richest, and which mediate our deepest insight into the
Mystery. All of the writers, and all of their books, in the New
Testament are limited in their insight and in their symbolizing
powers. All are complementary. In the normal course of
reading of the Bible we read them in the order which seems best,
and we read all of them—ideally—several times. In that process
we come to hold a fulness of truth which is more than can be
attained through the reading of any one. As I read the Bible
again and again, the richest, most profound texts illumine all the
rest. What I know of Jesus from the richest New Testament texts
affects my grasp of him as I contemplate him in the reading of any
page of the gospel. I cannot take my readers through any such
long process. For every one it is a unique personal experience,
and it develops within every one's unique personal history. What

I can do is to begin with what I regard as the richest of all. These texts I shall consider in this chapter. Then in the following chapters I shall consider further New Testament witness. My purpose is to foster as well as I can insight into the richer, deeper meaning of all of the texts of the New Testament and of the whole Bible. As I have insisted on other occasions, I am not supposing or suggesting that Mark understood and meant what John or Paul wrote. The deeper, richer sense is *not* what the human author himself knew and meant: it goes far beyond what he grasped from his personal point of view, and what he symbolized as best he could. The deeper, richer sense is what *we* have as the fruit of repeated readings of the whole Bible, retaining the unity which we have found by holding many complementary bits of God's word.

Without holding rigidly to my distinction between "prologues" and "flashes", I deal with these key texts in the order of their importance as I evaluate it.

JOHN'S PROLOGUE (Jn 1.1-18)

I regard this text as the most profoundly theological answer to the question "Who and what *is* Jesus?" It is one of the most difficult texts in the New Testament, the occasion of controversies among editors of the Greek text, translators, and exegetes and commentators [1]. I make no pretence of having considered and evaluated all of the positions. Of the translations and exegetical interpretations which I have pondered, I do not find one which is satisfying in every respect. Since I am not a qualified exegete, some may consider my judgment rash. Yet exegetes do communicate their understanding of the text, and it is reasonable to judge whether or not such accounts are coherent and intelligible, and whether or not they do what the exegete is qualified to do, without introducing a conceptualization which is alien to the text, and which involves the exegetes in ventures into conceptualization for which perhaps they are not qualified. I shall quote the translation of the RSV, not because it is the best in my judgment, but because it is an acceptable translation based on

---

[1] For a good idea of the range and difficulty of the problems, see RAYMOND E. BROWN, S.S., *The Gospel according to John* (i-xii), AB, 26 (Garden City, N.Y.: Doubleday & Co., 1966): translation, notes, comment, and bibliography, pp. 3-37; and appendix, "The 'Word'", pp. 519-524.

an option at a crucial point in the text. It has the disadvantage of
not dividing the text and presenting it typographically in such a
way as to indicate what belongs to a probable original hymn, and
what represents the prose additions of the one who wrote the text
as it stands. But, as one can quickly gather from reading Brown
in the work which I have cited, the lines of division themselves are
a matter of controversy, and any one presentation of the text
results from one man's options in this matter. My concern, it
should be unnecessary to state, is not to resolve any of the
controversies. Rather it is this: to find elements of the essential
truth to which the text witnesses, elements which I judge to be
clear enough despite the controversies.

> [1] In the beginning was the Word, and the Word was with God, and
> the Word was God. [2] He was in the beginning with God; [3] all
> things were made through him, and without him was not anything
> made that was made. [4] In him was life, and the life was the light
> of men. [5] The light shines in the darkness, and the darkness has
> not overcome it.
>
> [6] There was a man sent from God, whose name was John. [7] He
> came for testimony, to bear witness to the light, that all might
> believe through him. [8] He was not the light, but came to bear
> witness to the light.
>
> [9] The true light that enlightens every man was coming into the
> world. [10] He was in the world, and the world was made through
> him, yet the world knew him not. [11] He came to his own home,
> and his own people received him not. [12] But to all who received
> him, who believed in his name, he gave the power to become
> children of God; [13] who were born, not of blood nor of the will of
> the flesh nor of the will of man, but of God.
>
> [14] And the Word became flesh and dwelt among us, full of grace
> and truth; we have beheld his glory, glory as of the only Son from
> the Father. [15] (John bore witness to him, and cried, "This was he
> of whom I said, 'he who comes after me ranks before me, for he
> was before me.'") [16] And from his fulness we have all received,
> grace upon grace. [17] For the law was given through Moses; grace
> and truth came through Jesus Christ. [18] No one has ever seen
> God; the only Son, who is in the bosom of the Father, he has
> made him known.

"In the *beginning was* ..." (v. 1). The "beginning" here is
not the beginning of creation, as in the opening word of *Genesis*.
Even the beginning of creation and of time eludes adequate
conception. What John is grappling with here is even a greater
challenge to human thought and language. He is trying to
express the vaguely conceived eternity of the Word. Later in the

life of the Church theologians will attempt to fashion conceptual symbols which reflect the difficulties of the task, and which are themselves subject to a severe critique which makes clear their inadequacy. John's resources are simply not adequate for the effort. There is no way of expressing the theologically conceived eternity in biblical language. Both "beginning" and "was" are saturated with the successive being and time in which we are immersed. There is no "beginning" in eternity, and it does no good to affirm that the imperfect verb *was* denotes "...continuous, timeless existence...." [2] First, I know of no grounds for the assertion that the imperfect tense denotes timeless existence [3], and none are given in the context of the phrase which I have cited. Second, *continuous existence* is alien to the very notion of eternity. John is attempting to express the mystery which later will be formulated in term of eternity, but he is not aware of the inadequacy of his words, and it is better to leave them in their condition. Later, in one of the "I am" texts, there is a clue to how Jesus' "pre-existence" (a term which itself is inept) is expressed in words which shatter normal human speech and thought: "...before Abraham *was*, I am" (Jn 8.58). If one were to venture far beyond John—and far beyond exegesis—one might suggest an approach to the problem of expressing the mystery: "Without beginning the Word is ... is with God ... is God ... is with God without beginning."

"All things were made [or: came to be] *through* him" (3). Again, it is better to leave John's expression in all of its indeterminacy. It is no service to John or to others to say that John's meaning is that the Word is the instrumental or mediative cause of creation, and that this does not imply subordination but a logical order [4]. John says nothing of the kind, and his statement is far preferable to his interpreter's.

The crucial portion of the text is verses 3-4, and the issue depends on the division of the text in verse 3. The words "that was made" (a relative clause: ὃ γέγονεν) is taken in many ancient versions of the text as belonging to the following, as subject of the next sentence. Many recent translators have taken this option. Here are some specimens:

---

[2] Cf. Bruce Vawter, C.M., in JBC, II, 63:40, p. 421.
[3] No trace of such sense appears in BDF, §§ 325-330.
[4] Cf. Vawter, *ibid.*, 41, p. 422.

That which had come to be in him was life,
and this life was the light of men (Brown, AB).

All that came to be had life in him
and that life was the light of men (JB).

All that came to be was alive with his life,
and that life was the light of men (NEB).

Whatever came to be in him, found life,
life for the light of men (NAB).

The text, with this division, runs thus: ὃ γέγονεν ἐν αὐτῷ ζωὴ ἦν, καὶ ἡ ζωὴ ἦν τὸ φῶς τῶν ἀνθρώπων. I suggest that a simple, direct translation would be this:

What came [or: had come] to be in him was life,
and the life was the light of men.

In the first line, "was life" is surely the simplest rendition of the Greek: not "has life", nor "had life", nor "found life". Brown apparently translates thus directly: "was life", but there is a difficulty in his rendition of the whole verse, as I shall point out. Of the translations which I have quoted, only NEB comes close to what I think is the sense, but it does so in an unnecessarily roundabout way. If the author (supposing that it was not John himself, but one of his disciples, who, however regarded the revised hymn as an apt introduction to the whole gospel) had intended to convey the meaning "had life", the obvious wording would be such as that in Jn 6.40, 47, 54: ἔχῃ ζωὴν αἰώνιον — has eternal life.

What is my objection to Brown's translation? Brown himself invokes a structural rule to support the division of the text: "...the poetry of the Prologue favors our division, for the climactic or 'staircase' parallelism of the lines requires that the end of one line should match the beginning of the next. In our division the 'came to be' at the end of vs. 3 matches the 'had come to be' at the beginning of 4...."[5] Brown takes "That-which-had-come-to-be-in-him was life" as a statement which moves beyond the statement in v. 3. Verse 3 regarded all creation. Verse 4 has sense only with regard to men who come to eternal life in the Word[6]. Thus there is a verbal parallelism

---

[5] *Ibid.*, p. 6.
[6] *Ibid.*, pp. 6-7.

between "came to be" at the end of verse 3 and "had come to be" at the beginning of verse 4; but the thought moves to a higher level, regarding another influence of the Word on men alone.

According to the same rule, there should be a parallelism between "life" at the end of 4a and "life" at the beginning of 4b. Superficially Brown's translation preserves the parallelism, but his verbal parallelism of "life... life" does not preserve the sense of the text in my judgment. What *was* life, according to Brown's version of 4a? Brown makes that clear: it is "That-which-had-come-to-be-in-him". Then 4b begins: "and this life", clearly referring back to the end of 4a, and by "this" emphasizing that the predicate "life" of 4a and the subject "life" of 4b are the very same. There is no movement to a higher level, another stage of thought. I contend that this is unintelligible. The [eternal] life which is the predicate in 4a cannot be the life which was the light of men. What came to be *in him* was life, in the sense that it had *life*, participated in the life of the Word. That participated life, or participation in life, was not itself the light of men. Only the Life which is in the Word can be the light of men: not that limited life which others were. Put it another way. What is the Life which is the Light of men? Not "what I have come to be in him", but the Life in which [or in whom] I have come to be.

For this reason I say that the NEB version, though awkward, preserves the sense which alone is intelligible. What came to be was alive with *his life*, and *that life (his)* was the light of men.

One clear advantage of the other division of the text is that it offers a sense which is beyond question: "In him was life, and the life [in him] was the light of men."[7]

---

[7] Is there any way of preserving both the more ancient division and a direct translation in which "life" means the same at the end of 4a and the beginning of 4b? I do not know the history of all proposals in the matter: this is not my field. I see one interpretation which calls for a "harder reading" and yields a somewhat obscure meaning, but one which is intelligible. Take what I have proposed as a simple direct translation: "What came to be in him was life, and the life was the light of men." Instead of understanding the subject as Brown does, take it as simply "What came [or: had come] to be". Take "in him" as modifying "was". Take, further, a hint from a variant reading of the Greek with wide support: not "was" but "is". Then the meaning is this: what came to be was [or: is] life *in him*. All that came to be *is* eternally life in the Word. That does not involve foisting a notion of the "divine ideas". It does involve settling with an obscure text which gives a vague insight into a relationship of Word, knowledge, wisdom, and life in the God who is the ground of all being. At least I am being sportsmanlike. Having shot down some other interpretations, I offer one which is fair game and an easy mark for the exegetes.

With regard to the central portion of the text, vv. 5-13, exegetes differ about the stages of salvation history which are involved: all men prior to and outside Israel, Israel under the action of the eternal Word, and the epoch of the Word Incarnate.

What is to the point for us is this: Jesus (for the whole prologue is an introduction to what the gospel will tell us of him) is the Word, intimately united with God, yet distinct from him; he is God; in him is life, the light of men, the true light that enlightens every man, the light which shines in a darkness which has not mastered it[8]; to all who received him, who believed in him ["believe in his name" = "believe in him"] he gave the power to become children of God, begotten [or: born] of God.

The Word became flesh, and dwelt ["tented"] among us. Even as the Incarnate Word, he was resplendent with glory, the glory of the only Son, coming from the Father[9]. He is full of grace and truth: very probably an echo of God's attributes in the Old Testament: love/steadfast love/loving kindness and faithfulness (in keeping his promises). From his fulness we have all received, grace upon grace[10]. The law was given through Moses; grace and truth came through Jesus Christ. He, the only Son, who is in the bosom of the Father, has made known [told about] God, whom no one has ever seen.

This, then, is the first answer to the question, "Who and what is Jesus?"

"I Am"

I am treating together here what I have indicated separately in the introduction as "flashes": the "I am " of Ex 3.14, and a group of "I am" texts in John and in the Synoptics[11]. In doing so, I am dealing only in part with the question of the divine name

---

[8] Knox translates: "And the light shines in darkness, a darkness which was not able to master it." For the aptness of "master" to hold the full sense of the rich Greek original, see *Basics*, pp. 114-115.

[9] "Coming" is not in the Greek, which has only "from the Father". This phrase may be taken to modify either "glory" or "Son".

[10] For various translations of this text, revealing different interpretations, see Brown, *ibid.*, pp. 15-16: "Love in place of love" (Brown's translation, with the idea of the New Covenant love replacing that of Sinai); "grace upon grace" (suggesting accumulation); "grace for grace" or "grace matching grace" (suggesting the correspondence of the grace given to us to the grace of the Word. Compare JB: "grace in return for grace", and note "q").

[11] Above, pp. 17-22.

in the Old Testament: to the extent to which it is bound up with our understanding of some of Jesus' statements in the New Testament. For the rest, I shall return in Volume III of this work, to consider further the matter of the meaning of the name in the Old Testament.

First, then, I wish to indicate what I consider to be most significant in the revelation of the name in *Exodus*.

> Then Moses said to God, "If I come to the people of Israel and say to them, 'The God of your fathers has sent me to you,' and they ask me, 'What is his name?' what shall I say to them?" God said to Moses, "I AM WHO I AM." And he said, "Say this to the people of Israel, 'I AM has sent me to you' ". God also said to Moses, "Say this to the people of Israel, 'The LORD, the God of your fathers, the God of Abraham, the God of Isaac, and the God of Jacob, has sent me to you: this is my name for ever, and thus I am to be remembered throughout all generations...' " (Ex 3.13-15).

What is the *name*? I think that the most direct answer is given in the second part of verse 14: "I AM". The first answer, which could be translated simply "I am who am" seems to give the name in a relative clause which functions as the predicate. It is the equivalent of the reply: "I am I AM," where "I AM" is the name. Thus, it would be like a man's response: "I am *John Jones.*" The name LORD is YAHWEH, most probably an archaic third-person singular form of a variant form of the verb *to be*. As a response given by God, speaking of himself, "I am" surely seems to be the simplest, direct form of the name. YAHWEH (He is, or He will be, or other variations which have been suggested) is the form which is apt for giving the name in speaking about God. Ironically, however, in the Hebrew text the name is locked for ever in the form YAHWEH. Even where God is speaking of himself, he is represented as saying: "I am YAHWEH.": a strange identification: "I am HE IS."

Taking the name to be simply "I AM", I do not suggest any philosophical sense of "absolute being" or "abstract existence" or any other such spectres which some exegetes conjure up when they reject the suggestion that the name means simply "I am". It is "absolute" in the sense that it is a simple affirmation of existence, without qualification. To one exegete who objected that such an interpretation of the name was too "abstract", I asked, "What is *abstract* about 'I am'?" There was no answer. God is giving a name in human words, and any name which he gives must be inadequate. Neither an "abstract" name nor a "concrete" name is apt, for God transcends the difference between abstract and concrete, which make sense only concerning creatures, composite in their being. Saying simply "I AM" is responding in what humanly speaking is a concrete manner. The name is a simple affirmation of existence. It is as full of meaning as a name could be, and all else which which we can say about God merely affirms aspects of the fulness of his being. Later reflection will make more explicit the fulness of the name. As it is given, it supposes no philosophical or theological reflection on *being* or *to be*.

Beyond this first direct indication of what seems to me to be the name in its primitive form, I should like to add two lines of reflection given by Brown, one in reporting elements of what has been proposed by H. Zimmermann [12].

Many times in the Old Testament God says "I [am] Yahweh" or "I [am] God" or "I [am] he". I have bracketed the verb, since the Hebrew expression is without a verb, and the Greek translation too usually is simply "I Lord" or "I God"; sometimes in the Greek the verb "am" (εἰμί) is expressed. Such statements, to reassure the people, or to assert the authority which sanctions a law or command, or points to an action as a sign that He is Yahweh or God, are what Zimmermann and Brown mean by absolute statements. I shall have occasion to return to consider them more generally when I treat of God in Volume III of this work. For the present, two sets of such texts are significant for the study of the Old Testament background of John's use of the absolute "I AM"—or rather, Jesus' use, as reported by John.

First, there are texts which stress that Yahweh is the *only* God, the only Yahweh: six in Second Isaiah, and two others: Hos 13.4 and Jl 2.27. In one of them, Is 45.18, "I Yahweh" is translated in the Septuagint by "I am" (Ἐγώ εἰμι). Other texts stressing the unicity of Yahweh take the form "I [am] he" in Hebrew. All of them are translated by "I am". The tendency of the Greek translators is to stress not only the unicity of Yahweh, but also his *existence*. This tendency is at work, according to Brown, in the translation of Ex 3.14: "I am the Existing One" (Ἐγώ εἰμι ὁ ὤν).

Second, there is evidence that the Greek "I am" in translation of Second Isaiah not only expresses Yahweh's unicity

---

[12] R. E. BROWN, S.S., *op. cit.*, Appendix IV, pp. 532-538. He draws in part on an article by H. ZIMMERMANN, "Das absolute 'Ego eimi' als die neutestamentliche Offenbarungsformel," BZ 4 (1960) 54-69, 266-276.

and existence, but also is a divine name. In Is 43.25 the sense of the Hebrew is "I, I [am] He who blots out your trangressions..." The Septuagint translates with a double "I am", which can mean "I am he, I am he who...". It can also mean "I am 'I AM' who blots out your transgressions". In this sense, "I AM" is a name. Similarly in Is 51.12 the Greek translation can mean "I am 'I AM' who comforts you." Further, Is 52.6 couples such usage with explicit mention of the name: "Therefore my people shall know my *name*; therefore in that day they shall know that it is 'I AM' who speak; ..." Brown cites additional evidence given by Dodd: rabbinic understanding of Is 52,6 in the sense of "In that day they shall know that 'I AM' is speaking to them." Other evidence cited by Dodd shows that not only the Greek form "I am", but also the Hebrew "I He" was used as a divine name in the liturgy. Brown cites too Daube's [13] evidence from the Passover *Haggadah* [an exposition or interpretation of Scripture] in the Mishnah, roughly contemporaneous with the New Testament and the Christian Apostolic Fathers [14]: God is emphasizing that He and no other delivered Israel: "I and not an angel ... I and not a messenger; I Yahweh—this means, I AM and no other".

Against this background of Old Testament and post-biblical Judaic usage, we may consider two aspects of Brown's treatment of John: the absolute "I AM" texts in John and the Synoptics; and the many Johannine references to the divine name which Jesus bears.

Most important are the texts in which Jesus uses "I am" in an absolute sense: without a predicate:

> Unless you come to believe that I AM, you will surely die in your
> sins (Jn 8.24).
> When you lift up the Son of Man, then you will realize that I AM
> (8.28).
> Before Abraham even came into existence, I AM (8.58).
> When it does happen, you may believe that I AM (13.19).

I have given Brown's translation. Except for 8.58, RSV and JB lose the impact of the statement by translating "I am he". NEB has the simple "I AM" also in 8.58, but needlessly encumbers the

---

[13] D. DAUBE, "The 'I am' of the Messianic Presence," *The New Testament and Rabbinic Judaism* (London: Athlone, 1956) pp. 325-329.

[14] For a brief account of Haggadah and Mishnah, see the article "Talmud" in *Dictionary of the Bible*, edited by JAMES HASTINGS... (New York: Scribner's, 1963) pp. 954-956.

translation of the other three: "I am what I am", going back arbitrarily to the first part of Ex 3.14, whereas the relevant part is the simple "I AM". The most obvious explanation of these texts is that Jesus is alluding to the Divine name in the Old Testament and in rabbinic Judaism. Jesus' hearers sense the implications of the expression: after the statement in 8.58, the Jews "... took up stones to throw at him" (8.59). They considered it blasphemy, as they did when Jesus affirmed "I and the Father are one" (10.30: cf. vv. 31-33).

Two other texts are important: in them there is no predicate, but one may be understood to be implicit. When the disciples are frightened as they see someone coming to them on the water, Jesus says: " 'I am'; do not be afraid" (6.20). In ordinary usage the expression would mean "It is I". Here, however, a transcendent sense is suggested, parallel with theophanies in the Old Testament (cf. Gn 26.24; 28.13; Ez 20.5). The second text is Jn 18.5. To the soldiers who had come to arrest him, Jesus asked, "Whom do you seek?" At their answer, "Jesus of Nazareth", he said, "I AM". The ordinary meaning would be "I am he". Here, however, the effect was that the soldiers drew back and fell to the ground. The suggestion is that this was a sort of theophany which left them terrified. Brown reasonably considers that there is a play on a twofold use of "I am".

It is reasonable to understand that in these "I am" texts Jesus is alluding to the divine name, and suggesting his own divinity. There are texts in the Synoptics which suggest a similar double sense of "I am".

Asked by the high priest, "Are you the Christ [the Messiah], the Son of the Blessed?" Jesus said, "I AM, and you will see the Son of man sitting at the right hand of Power, and coming with the clouds of heaven" (Mk 14.62; cf. Lk 22.70). He was condemned to death for blasphemy. As Brown points out, such a condemnation is more understandable if Jesus is not merely claiming to be the Messiah, but also claiming the divine name.

There is a parallel in the scene of Jesus walking across the water in John. His assurance to the disciples, "I AM; do not be afraid," evokes a profession of faith: "Truly, you are the Son of God" (Mt 14.27, 33; cf. Mk 6.50-51).

Again, after the resurrection Jesus appears to his disciples, and says, "I AM; do not be afraid" (Lk 24.36). Again, the ordinary usage would suggest the meaning "It is I", but the context in the apparition after the resurrection suggests a revelation of Jesus' Lordship.

Closest to Johannine usage is the text in which Jesus, speaking of the signs of the last days, says, "take heed that no one leads you astray. Many will come in my name, saying, 'I am!' and they will lead many astray" (Mk 13.5-6; cf. Lk 21.8). The stark "I am", linked in the context with "in my name", suggests the claim to divinity. Matthew loses the force by adding a predicate: "I am the Christ" (Mt 24.5).

Besides these "I am" texts in John and the Synoptics, there is another set of texts referring to the name which Jesus bears. They complement other texts in which Jesus refers to the Father's name. First, then, here are texts concerning the Father's name:

> I have manifested thy name to the men whom thou gavest me out of the world; ... (17.6).
> I made known to them thy name, and I will make it known, ... (17.26).
> I have come in my Father's name, ... (5.43).
> ... The works that I do in my Father's name, they bear witness to me; ... (10.25).
> ... The hour has come for the Son of man to be glorified.... Father, glorify thy name.... (12.23, 28).

These are the texts concerning Jesus' name:

> Whatever you ask in my name, I will do it, that the Father may be glorified in the Son; if you ask anything in my name, I will do it (14.13-14).
> ... so that whatever you ask the Father in my name, he may give it to you (15.16).
> ... if you ask anything of the Father, he will give it to you in my name (16.23).
> But the Counselor, the Holy Spirit, whom the Father will send in my name, he will teach you all things ... (14.26).
> ... he who does not believe is condemned already, because he has not believed in the name of the only Son of God (3.38).
> Holy Father, keep them in thy name, which thou hast given me, ... While I was with them, I kept them in thy name, which thou hast given me, ... (17.11-12).

What, Brown asks, is the divine name given to Jesus? he thinks that it is possible that John thought of "I AM" ('Εγώ εἰμι) as that name. His suggestion seems plausible. If this is the case, then there are two lines running through the texts of the Bible: (1) Yahweh, Adonai, Kyrios; (2) Ehyeh ("I am"), Ὁ ὤν (the

Existing One), Ἐγώ εἰμι ("I am"). In *Acts* and Paul (Phil 2.9), the name given to Jesus, "... at which every knee should bow, ..." is Kyrios, the Greek translation of Adonai, "Lord": the substitute in the Hebrew text for Yahweh. For John, the name would be Ἐγώ εἰμι ("I am"), and the sense of John 8.28 is clear: "When you lift up the Son of Man ["lifting up" signifying the whole Paschal mystery of death, resurrection, and glorification] [15], then you will know that 'I AM'".

What, then, is the importance of the name "I am"? Why is it a "flash", a brilliant revelation which should illumine the whole Bible, and give us our deepest insight into the mystery of both God (the Father) and Jesus? The "I am" of *Exodus* and of Jesus' statements in John and in the Synoptics, is a massive affirmation whose meaning comprehends all that we can say in particular concerning either God or Jesus. It is the first-person affirmation of simple, unqualified existence, without limit. To it we respond to either the Father or to Jesus in I-Thou relationship: "You are", and we can simply hold to that affirmation in a continuing contemplation of the wonder of their being. Speaking to others concerning either the Father or Jesus, we say all when we say: "He is".

JESUS' HIGH PRIESTLY PRAYER (Jn 17.1-26)

Continuing our consideration of Johannine texts, I propose here the prayer which concludes Jesus' last discourse in John, and which gives further revelation of the mystery of Jesus [16]. Moreover, it contributes to our understanding of the dialectic of promise and fulfillment. I shall not attempt a running commentary on the prayer, but shall present synthetically those elements which are most significant for our present purpose.

First, Jesus' prayer reveals much of the mystery of the "inner life" of the Incarnate Word, God and man. Thus it goes beyond all statements about Jesus, and beyond his massive statement in the "I am" texts in which he seems surely to reveal his name and the mystery of his divinity. We come to know more profoundly *who* and *what* Jesus is only as we penetrate more deeply the mystery of the God-man. The mysterious blend of what

---

[15] See *The Mystery*, p. 165.
[16] For detailed notes and comment on the text I recommend BROWN, *op. cit.*, vol. 29a, pp. 739-782.

theologians later will ponder as the divine and human consciousness of Jesus is revealed in great part by this prayer.

What is the interior life of Jesus as it is revealed in his prayer? Most prominent, I should say, is his sense of intimate union with the Father, whom he addresses repeatedly by name, "Father", "Holy Father" (11), "righteous Father" (25). Here we face the mystery of Jesus' twofold consciousness, revealed to us only through his human words, yet expressing the mystery of his divine and human consciousness. He is the eternal Word, the Son, who speaks of his union with the Father. Yet he is the Word Incarnate, fully human. Only as man can he function as priest. Only as man can he intercede for those whom the Father has given him, and ask for his own glorification. Yet he is one Person, utterly unique in his blend of divine and human.

He prays for his glorification (1, 5): a glorification which in part has been realized, in part is to be fulfilled. Though he speaks already from the "hour" in which the fulfillment occurs, and senses thus that already he is no more in the world (11), still he prays for his glorification. Though in a sense, from the perspective of the "hour", he has accomplished the work given him to do (4), yet an essential part—*the* essential part—of the work remains to be done: he must fulfill the Father's command; he must be lifted up [17]: lifted up on the cross, he must rise, return to the Father, come again and give the Spirit. The glorification is mutual: Father and Son glorifying each other. Again mysteriously it is partly realized (1, 4. 5, 22). Jesus *has* made known the Father's name, and he *will* make it known (26).

Jesus reveals his deep concern for those whom the Father has given him, for *his*, who are also the Father's (9). He desires that they may have eternal life, *knowing* the Father, the only true God, and Jesus Christ whom the Father has sent (3) [18]. For this Jesus has been sent, and given power over all flesh (2-3). He desires that they may be *one*: "I do not pray for these only, but also for those who believe in me through their word, that they may all be one; even as thou, Father, art in me, and I in thee, that they may also be one in us, so that the world may believe that thou hast sent me. The glory which thou hast given me I have given to them, that they may be one even as we are one, I in them and thou in me, that they may become perfectly one, so that

---

[17] On glory and the "hour", see *The Mystery*, pp. 161-168, esp. p. 165.

[18] On eternal life consisting in *knowing* the Father and Jesus Christ, see BROWN, *op. cit.*, pp. 752-753.

the world may know that thou hast sent me and hast loved them even as thou hast loved me'' (20-23). Jesus prays that they may have his joy fulfilled in themselves (13), that they may be sanctified and consecrated in truth (17-18). He has sent them into the world, as the Father sent him (18), but he desires that they may be with him where he is [will be], to behold his glory, glory given by the Father in his love for Jesus before the foundation of the world (24). Finally, he desires that the love with which the Father has loved him may be in them, and that he may be in them (26). This long prayer for his own reveals much of the desire which motivates Jesus throughout his life. In a sense one might say that this reveals much of the human love, desire, motivation of Jesus' life. Yet it is *he*, Jesus Christ, the Incarnate Word who is speaking, manifesting his human love, but also his own divine love and the Father's: for in the whole of his being in human nature he is the revelation of the Father.

Beautiful as this revelation of Jesus' desires for his own is, the deepest mystery revealed in this prayer is that of Jesus' relation to the Father. It is his priestly prayer, and so it is a revelation of his relation to the Father as the Son who has become man: only as man is he priest, only as man can he obey the Father's command, accomplish the work given him, and pray for glorification. Yet he reveals much of his relationship to the Father as the eternal Son. He need not make himself God, as the Jews accused him (Jn 10.33). He is God. He does not affirm that he is the ''equal'' of the Father. Rather he hints in many ways at the relationship. Eternal life consists in knowing the Father, the one true God *and* Jesus Christ whom the Father has sent (17.3). All that is his is the Father's (10). The Father has given him his name, and they are one (11-12). The glory which he prays for is the glory which he had with the Father before the world came into existence (5, 24). The exemplar of the unity of his disciples for which he prays is the oneness of Father and Son (21-22).

Many of these themes are developed in the whole of the gospel of John, and in his first letter; and we shall reflect on them later as we treat those works more fully concerning our theme of promise and fulfillment. I shall not, therefore, dwell here on what this text suggests on that theme. Rather, consistently with our limited scope in setting forth prologues and ''flashes'', we may rest with what we have seen to justify regarding this prayer as singularly rich for its revelation of much of the mystery of Jesus.

GOD'S FULL BLESSING ON US (Eph 1.3-14) [19]

I know of no translator who has performed the feat of rendering these twelve verses with the sentence structure—or rather complete disregard for structure—of Paul's Greek text. Words, phrases, clauses tumble out in an unbroken scramble for expression. I shall quote the AB translation, to have it as a basis for reference to the text. I shall attempt little by way of comment or attempt to indicate a structure of the thought, of the aspects of the full blessing: all such attempts seem to me to impose on the text an order which it simply does not have [20]. Surely this passage deserves consideration among the texts which I have called prologues: to an individual book, and to the whole Bible. Barth says simply: "Eph 1:3-14 is a digest of the whole epistle and replete with key terms and topics that anticipate the contents of what follows" [21]. And many regard *Ephesians* as the most sublime of Paul's writings [22]. This prologue, therefore, occasions insights which enable a Christian reader to come to a richer, deeper sense of the meaning of the Bible as a whole.

> [3] Blessed is God the Father of our Lord Jesus Christ. He has blessed us in Christ with the full spiritual blessing of the heavens.
> [4] As [we confess]
>> Before the foundation of the world he has chosen us in Christ
>> To live by love [standing] holy and blameless before him.
> [5] He has predesignated us through Jesus Christ to become his children
>> according to his favorable decision

---

[19] For an extraordinarily rich introduction, translation, annotation, and comment on the text, see MARKUS BARTH, *Ephesians*, AB, vols. 34 and 34A (Garden City, N.Y.: Doubleday, 1974). I quote the translation as it is given in the running translation of chapters 1-6 (pp. XXVII-XXXIV) and I call attention to a confusing typographical error in the section 1.3-14 as it is given on p. 76: the two lines of v. 4 are inverted.

[20] As for the shape of vv. 3-14, Barth cites E. Norden, who called it " ... the most monstrous sentence conglomeration ... that I have ever met in the Greek language" (quoting from Norden's *Agnostos Theos*, p. 253, n. 1: p. 77 in Barth).

[21] *Op. cit.*, p. 97; cf. pp. 143-144.

[22] I say "Paul's", well aware of the dispute concerning authorship. Barth, after a sober evaluation of the various views, judges: "In view of the insufficient linguistic and historical arguments, and of the prejudicial character of the theological reasons exhibited against Ephesians, it is advisable for the time being to still consider Paul its author" (*op. cit.*, p. 49; cf. his treatment of the matter, pp. 36-50).

⁶ so that the glory of his grace be praised
  which in his beloved son he has poured out upon us.
⁷ Through [the shedding of] his blood
  we possess freedom in him, forgiveness of our lapses.
Such are the riches of his grace
  ⁸ which in all wisdom and prudence he has lavished upon us.
⁹ He has made known to us the secret of his decision
  —for he has set his favor first upon Christ
  ¹⁰ that he should administer the days of fulfillment—
"All things are to be comprehended under one head, the Messiah,
  Those in heaven and upon earth—under him!"

¹¹ As resolved by him who carries out all things after his will and decision, we [Jews] were first designated and appropriated in the Messiah. ¹² We, the first to set our hope upon the Messiah, were to become a praise of God's glory. ¹³ You [Gentiles] too are [included] in him. For you have heard the true word, the message that saves you. And after you came to faith you, too, have been sealed with his seal, the promised Holy Spirit.

¹⁴ He is the guarantee of what we shall inherit [to vouch] for the
  liberation of God's own people, to the praise of his glory.

Barth, following the opinion of many, regards vv. 4-10 as a hymn or confession quoted by Paul: introduced by "As", which Barth supplements by the inserted "confess", to show that it is functioning as the introduction of a quotation. Rather than listing blessings which could be enumerated (as JB does in its notes), the text sets forth aspects of the fulness of the blessing which is ours in Christ.

Verses 4-6 regard the eternal choice and the designated grace. Verse 6 in the Greek simply begins with "to praise of the glory of his grace...". Similarly verse 12 begins: "that we might be a praise of his glory...". Finally verse 14 concludes "to praise of his glory". The three phrases mark three phases in the developing thought: (1) the eternal choice or decree; (2) its realization in the Jews who first believed in Christ; (3) fulfillment in the Gentiles: sealing with the Spirit now, as the guarantee of the [final] liberation of God's own people.

Two things are noteworthy for our general theme. First, Jesus Christ, the Beloved [Son], has a unique role in our regard. We have been chosen in him before the foundation of the world. Through him we are to become adopted children. Then, in the historical realization of the decree, it is through the shedding of

his blood that we are freed (7-8).   Again it is within history that
God has made known to us the secret, the mystery[23]: his decision
of what should be accomplished in the fulness of time: bringing all
things together under one head, Christ.

Second, we see the dialectic of promise and fulfillment.   It is
God's eternal plan which underlies, humanly speaking, his
promises.   The plan (and the promises, not mentioned here, but
prominent in Paul's thought) is fulfilled now both in the Jews who
set their hope (believed) upon the Messiah, and in the Gentiles.
Yet all look to the consummation: what has been received is a
guarantee of the final liberation.

---

[23] Barth prefers "secret" to "mystery" for two reasons principally:
"mystery" suggests the rites of the mystery religions; and a mystery which is
made known is not a mystery (op. cit., pp. 85, 123-217).   I do not see much
force in his arguments.   I have treated the matter long ago in De Sacramentis in
Genere (Rome: Gregorian University Press, 1957, 1960, 1962) pp. 3-22: O.T.
and apocalyptic backgrounds, Synoptics (Mk 4.11; Mt 13.11, Lk 8.10), Pauline
usage, Greek-hellenistic mysteries (cult mysteries, philosophical, and gnostic),
and Greek patristic usage.   For Paul's use, see 1 Cor 2,7-10; Rom 16.25-26;
Col 1.26-27; 2.3; 4.3; Eph 1.9-10; 3.3-12. Add 1 Tm 3.16.   Paul's use
depends on biblical and apocalyptic use of the word.   The classic text is Dn 2.18,
19, 27-30, 44-47: the mystery is both God's hidden purpose for the last
days, and the king's dream, which is an obscure revelation of the divine secret.
In God alone is wisdom (v. 20) and knowledge of the hidden meaning.   God
alone can reveal the meaning of the mystery (vv. 21-23, 28-29).   Jesus told
his disciples. "To you has been given the secret (μυστήριον) of the kingdom of
God, but for those outside everything is in parables; ..." (Mk 4.11).   From the
context the mystery seems to be that the messianic kingdom has come in Christ.
Some vague, general knowledge of this secret can be had from the parables, but
they cannot be understood without further revelation, which Jesus gives only to
his disciples in private.   Briefly, in Pauline usage μυστήριον means hidden, as
opposed to revealed or manifested.   The divine plan, the mystery, was hidden,
kept secret for long ages.   Even now that it has been revealed and realized in
Christ, it is a mystery, because it has been revealed only by the Spirit, and it is
communicated only in words taught by the Spirit to those who possess the Spirit:
to the unspiritual it remains hidden.   Hence in general "mystery" in Paul
indicates directly a relationship to human knowledge.   The word μυστήριον is
not used by Paul to designate baptism or the Eucharist or any other Christian
rite.   When he calls matrimony a mystery (Eph 5.32), he is hardly calling it a
mystery-sacrament in our modern sense.   Patristic usage is another matter;
but only in the fourth and fifth centuries, perhaps because of the danger of
contamination by mystery religions was considered remote, did the Fathers
adapt a full mystery terminology to Christian worship.   The outstanding
example is St. John Chrysostom (see G. FITTKAU, Der Begriff des Mysteriums bei
Johannes Chrysostomos [Bonn: 1953]).   Apart from his predominant use of
mystery for cult mysteries (baptism and especially the Eucharist) Chrysostom
retains Paul's sense of the word.

Two other points seem worthy of notice. First, the bringing together of all things under Christ as head is an interpretation which is not based on the ordinary sense of the word in the Greek text: ἀνακεφαλαιώσασθαι. The verb is linked not with κεφαλή: head, but with κεφάλαιον: main thing, main point, summary[24]. Nor is it based on a mistaken etymology of the Greek word. Rather it is a meaning which is suggested by the presence of the word κεφαλή: head, in Eph 1.22; 4.15; and 5.23, and the importance of the notion of Christ as head in Paul's doctrine.

The distinction between Jews and Gentiles, made explicit by Barth's interpolations, seems reasonable. Earlier in the text Paul speak of "us" without distinction. Here the distinction between "we" and "you" (vv. 11-14) seems to indicate the order of Jews and Gentiles in God's plan. The gospel was preached first to Jews, and some of them believed. Paul is one of them, and speaks of them and of himself in the "we". Then the message was brought to the Gentiles[25].

UNIQUENESS OF JESUS (Heb 1.1—4.13)

This long section of *Hebrews*, like the whole letter, is a blend of doctrine and exhortation. I am concerned here only with the teaching, which affords another profound answer to the question regarding Jesus: who and what is he? The answer itself is a blend of two aspects of Jesus in his full reality: the eternal Son, and Messiah. I shall consider elements of the prologue (1.1-4) and exposition of Jesus' superiority over angels and Moses[26].

> [1] In many and various ways God spoke of old to our fathers by the prophets; [2] but in these last days he has spoken to us by a Son, whom he appointed heir of all things, through whom also he created the world. [3] He reflects the glory of God and bears the very stamp of his nature, upholding the universe by his word of power. When he had made purification for sins, he sat down at

---

[24] See BAG on the words involved.

[25] JB seems to me to push the distinction too far: "the people who would put their hopes in Christ before he came". Paul's sense is preserved without taking him to mean the Jews who were to be a witness to Christ *before* he came. The Jews have a priority in that they first believed.

[26] For an introduction to the literature on *Hebrews* and a helpful brief commentary, see MYLES M. BOURKE, in JBC, II, 61, pp. 381-403. Among the major commentaries I should single out C. SPICQ, O.P., *L'Épitre aux Hébreux*, vol. I, Introduction; vol. II, Commentaire (Paris: Gabalda, 1952, 1953).

the right hand of the Majesty on high, [4] having become as much superior to angels as the name he has obtained is more excellent than theirs (1.1-4: RSV).

Even in this prologue we see the blending of what is proper to the eternal Son and what is unique in him as the divine-human Messiah. I shall synthesize, for brevity here, the elements pertaining to each aspect of Jesus, dealing first with what pertains to him as the eternal Son.

The Son reflects the glory of God and bears the very stamp of his nature: he is God, of the very nature of God. Through him God created the universe and all that it holds. The Son sustains the universe by his powerful word. "Through him" should be left with all of the indeterminacy of the biblical language. Only a trinitarian theology, gradually developed later, can come to terms with the difficult task of elaborating the conceptual symbols which hold the revealed truth with least inadequacy. Surely one should not suggest here (nor in Jn 1.3, as I have pointed out) an instrumental or mediatorial role.

Other elements of the prologue bear upon the Son's role as Messiah. Through him in these last days God has spoken. He is the appointed heir of all things: though as eternal Son he is "heir" of all things, still by his priestly role in making purification for sins he merited the exaltation at God's right hand, and as Messiah was "appointed heir".

Jesus is superior to the angels (1.5—2.18). The author proves this superiority by a series of texts from the Old Testament, taken in a messianic sense, and applied to Jesus, the Son, as they never have been addressed by God to any angel. All except one of these regard the exaltation of the Messiah, and clearly bear on the glorification of Jesus, the Incarnate Son. The exception is Ps 102.25-27 (LXX 101.26-28), quoted in Heb 2.10-12:

> Thou, Lord, didst found the earth in the beginning,
> and the heavens are the work of thy hands;
> they will perish, but thou remainest;
> they will all grow old like a garment,
> like a mantle thou wilt roll them up,
> and they will be changed.
> But thou art the same,
> and thy years will never end.

This Psalm is addressed to Yahweh, and as it is applied here to Jesus it regards his excellence as the eternal Son, the divine Son.

Continuing the theme of Jesus' superiority over angels, the author stresses Jesus' exaltation, and the subjection of the world to come (2.5), everything (2.8), to Jesus after his humiliation and suffering. At the same time, he brings out the beauty and uniqueness of his priesthood. Jesus is our brother (11-13). Since we share in flesh and blood, he partook of the same nature, to die and deliver us from the fear of death which enslaved us. His concern is with the descendants of Abraham, not with angels (14-16). "Therefore he had to be made like his brethren in every respect, so that he might become a merciful and faithful high priest in the service of God, to make expiation for the sins of the people. For because he himself has suffered and been tempted, he is able to help those who are tempted" (17-18).

Finally, Jesus, "... the apostle and high priest of our confession" (3.1) is superior to Moses, as a son is superior to a servant (3.1-6). Thus this treatment of Jesus' excellence opens upon the treatment of the excellence of his priesthood and of the New Covenant of which he is the mediator, developed through the remainder of the letter.

This opening passage of *Hebrews*, from another point of view and with a diffent symbolism, gives another contribution to the full answer to the question: who and what is Jesus? He is unique, as God, and as the God-man[27].

LUKE'S INFANCY NARRATIVE (Lk 1-2)[28]

I have proposed considering this section of Luke's Gospel as a "prologue": not in the sense of a literary prologue (which in *Luke*

---

[27] For an excellent treatment of Jesus, the Son of God, in the theology of *Hebrews*, see Spicq, *op. cit.*, vol. II, pp. 287-301. For the use of the Old Testament in *Hebrews*, see also pp. 330-350, with a special section on the hermeneutic of the letter, pp. 341-350. Given the striking use of the Old Testament in this letter, it is important to note that no exegesis relying solely on modes of rabbinical exegesis can suffice to set forth what is unique in *Hebrews*, as in the whole of the New Testament, where a deeper meaning is read in Old Testament texts. Beyond all such exegetical techniques, two unique factors are at play here: a new revelation and illumination of the Holy Spirit, and the charism of inspiration. Without full recognition of their influence on the text and its meaning, no satisfactory interpretation is possible.

[28] See Joseph A. Fitzmyer, S.J., *The Gospel According to Luke* (I-IX). Introduction, Translation, and Notes. AB, vol. 28 (Garden City, N.Y.: Doubleday, 1981). See also Raymond E. Brown, S.S., *The Birth of the Messiah: A Commentary on the Infancy Narratives in Matthew and Luke* (N.Y.: Doubleday, 1977).

is 1.1-4), but as a sort of theological prologue. It sounds many of the principal themes of the Gospel, but more importantly it gives a deep theological insight into who and what Jesus is. Written after the rest of the gospel, it provides a clue to the total subjective and objective world from which Luke wrote in his Christian community. Fitzmyer calls it an overture to the Gospel proper, and regards it as an integral factor in Lucan theology [29]. The purpose of the infancy narrative, according to the same commentator, is to make Christological affirmations about Jesus from the beginning of his earthly existence [30]. What is affirmed represents the degree of insight reached by the Christian community in which Luke lived, and the conviction that what Jesus was *recognized* to be only after his resurrection he *was* from the moment of his conception. From the point of view of Luke and his community, then, Christological affirmations are pushed back to the beginning of Jesus' earthly existence. There is here no awareness of Jesus' "preexistence" or incarnation, reached later in the Johannine community [31].

What, then, does the infancy narrative tell us? First, it establishes clearly the pattern of Old Testament promise, prophecy, and figure; transcendent fulfillment; and further promise. Zechariah and Elizabeth, Mary and Joseph, Simeon and Anna, and the many secondary characters in the double narrative, are representative of Israelite piety and expectation. John stands at the end of the period of Israel, with the role of introducing Jesus, preparing his way. Jesus is the transcendent fulfillment, and the affirmation of his Messianic role is full of further promise, beyond all Israel's hopes and understanding.

Luke accomplishes his purpose with an elaborate narrative of two beginnings, John's and Jesus'. Step by step he depicts the events regarding John, stirring wonder, and the more wonderful events and pronouncements which affirm the transcendent dignity and role of Jesus.

Several features of the narrative highlight continuity with the Old Testament. John, according to the angel, "... will go before him [the Lord: Yahweh here, most probably] in the spirit and power of Elijah, to turn the hearts of the fathers to the children, and the disobedient to the wisdom of the just, to make ready for the Lord a people prepared" (1.17). Jesus will be given "... the

---

[29] *Ibid.*, p. 163.
[30] *Ibid.*, p. 446; cf. p. 340.
[31] *Ibid.*, pp. 340, 351.

throne of his father David, and he will reign over the house of
Jacob for ever..." (1.32-33). Mary recognizes that in what he
has done in her the Lord "...has helped his servant Israel, in
remembrance of his mercy, as he spoke to our fathers, to
Abraham and to his posterity for ever" (1.54-55). At John's
naming, Zechariah, filled with the Holy Spirit, prophesied:

> Blessed be the Lord God of Israel,
> for he has visited and redeemed his people,
> and has raised up a horn of salvation for us
> in the house of his servant David,
> as he spoke by the mouth of his holy prophets from of old,
> that we should be saved from our enemies,
> and from the hand of all who hate us;
> to perform the mercy promised to our fathers,
> and to remember his holy covenant,
> the oath which he swore to our father Abraham, to grant us
> that we, being delivered from the hand of our enemies,
> might serve him without fear,
> in holiness and righteousness before him
>   all the days of our life.... (1.68-75).

Joseph is of the line of David (2.4). The angels announce to the
shepherds a child born in the city of David, a Savior, Christ
[Messiah] the Lord. Simeon, enlightened by the Spirit,
recognizes in the child Jesus the salvation which God has
prepared, "...a light for the revelation to the Gentiles, and for
glory to thy people Israel" (2.29-32). Anna spoke of him to all
who were looking for the redemption of Jerusalem (2.36-38).

Into this narrative Luke introduces the titles whose sense is
understood in his post-pentecostal Christian community. Jesus
is Son of the Most High, implicitly Son of David (1.32; cf. 1.69; for
the explicit title Son of David, 18.38, 39) and King (implicit in
1.32-33). He will be called holy, the Son of God (1.35; for the
title Holy One, 4.34 and Acts 2.27; 3.14). He is the Lord (1.43,
76[32]), Savior, Messiah, Lord (2.11). Probably too Luke intends
Jesus to be understood as the Dawn from on High[33].

---

[32] Whereas "Lord" in 1.15-17 most probably is meant to refer to
Yahweh, in 1.76, after the narration of the birth of Jesus and the recognition of
his dignity, the title is probably to be understood by Luke's readers as referring
now to Jesus. See FITZMYER, *ibid.*, p. 386.

[33] See FITZMYER, *ibid.*, p. 387. He translates 1.78-79 as follows: "In the
merciful compassion of our God, the Dawn from on High will take note of us /
and shine on *those who sit in darkness, in the shadow of death,* to guide our feet
into the *path of peace*" (p. 375, italicizing quotations from Ps 107.10 and Is 59.8).

Fitzmyer makes two other points which are significant for our present concern. Both regard the finding of Jesus in the Temple. In Fitzmyer's translation, Mary asks, "Child, why have you treated us like this? Look, your father and I have been terribly worried and have been searching for you." Jesus replies, "Why are you searching for me: Did you not know that I had to be in my Father's house?" (2.48-49). Fitzmyer considers the various interpretations of the last phrase, and concludes: "In any case, it is clear that Jesus is referring to God as his heavenly Father. He expresses disappointment that his earthly parents have not understood that his relation to his heavenly Father transcends all natural family ties ..." [34] The first point, then, is this: Jesus has a special relationship to his heavenly Father. We shall have occasion to return to this when we consider the texts concerning Jesus' baptism and his transfiguration.

The second point regards Luke's concluding statement: "But they did not understand what he was saying to them" (2.50). Fitzmyer comments: "This is Luke's way of getting across to his readers the difficulty of understanding who Jesus is or was" [35]. Despite all that had been revealed to her, Mary did not understand from the outset who and what Jesus really was. She had to ponder the words that had been spoken, and she had too to come gradually to deeper understanding. "... However, after the resurrection Mary will be depicted among the first believers in Acts 1:14" [36]. The process of penetrating the mystery of Jesus was slow for Mary. It is slow for all who believe, even after Pentecost and through the history of Christian life. We must ponder the meaning of all that is said of Jesus: the full mystery of who and what he is, partially revealed in all that he says and does and in all that is said about him by those who witness to him. We shall never finish that loving contemplation.

For the present let us simply note the theological riches of the infancy narrative, and keep in mind its contribution to the answer to our question about Jesus. What Luke has affirmed here artfully through his narrative must serve as a ground against which every succeeding scene of the Gospel will portray Jesus. These two chapters should occasion deep insights into the Reality which is so inadequately suggested in most of the Gospel events and words.

---

[34] *Ibid.*, p. 444.
[35] *Ibid.*, p. 439.
[36] *Ibid.*, p. 445.

JESUS' BAPTISM [37]

I have suggested that these parallel texts are one of the "flashes" which suddenly reveal depths of the mystery of Jesus. Without considering the details of the whole event in the varying versions of the Synoptics, I wish to stress here only the descent of the Spirit and the words of the Father.

Jesus' baptism, with the symbolic descent of the Spirit [38] and the words spoken from heaven, is an important event for the revelation of who Jesus really is: Son of the Father in a unique, transcendent sense. In the Gospel according to Mark this episode has relatively greater significance, since Mark has no infancy narrative, and this is the first event which marks Jesus' unique dignity.

The symbolism of the dove is vague [39]. What is significant in this element of the event is the visible descent of the Spirit upon Jesus, complementing—or complemented by—the Father's words, which reveal Jesus' special relation of sonship to the Father, and suggest at least that he is the Servant of Yahweh, with the connotation of obedience and suffering [40]. The allusion

---

[37] Mt 3.13-17; Mk 1.9-11; Lk 3.21-22; cf. Jo 1.29-34. For a discussion of the event and its significance in the accounts of the Synoptics, see FITZMYER, *ibid.*, pp. 479-487.

[38] The formulae vary: the Spirit (Mk, Jn), [the] Spirit of God (Mt), the Holy Spirit (Lk). Whether in English we write "spirit" or "Spirit" affects the sense of the texts. From the point of view from which the gospels were written, in the post-Pentecostal Church with a full revelation and experience of the Holy Spirit, it makes most sense to write *Spirit*.

[39] E. J. MALLY, S.J., in his brief commentary in JBC, II, p. 24, gives evidence for regarding the dove as the symbol of Israel, and of Jesus here as the representative of God's new People according to the Spirit. The dove in the text, however, symbolizes not Jesus, but the Spirit.

[40] Clearly, as Fitzmyer holds, the texts do not suggest Jesus' inner experience, much less his sense of a messianic consecration and mission (*op. cit.*, pp. 480, 482, 485-486). It seems to me, however, that he protests too much against any "clear" evidence that the titles used of Jesus in Luke have a messianic sense. His norm seems to me to be dubious, to say the least: the sense of terms in pre-Christian Judaism (cf. pp. 480, 485). His strain is obvious when he admits that although Jesus' baptism is not a "messianic consecration", still Acts 10.37-38 *interpret* it as a messianic anointing. He explains that this must be understood in terms of Lucan theology as a whole, even though the idea of messianic anointing is not clear in the baptism scene itself. Since Lucan theology is the theology of Luke in his post-Pentecostal community, and it is the theology of the "end product" [the whole of Luke and Acts] Fitzmyer's reluctance to make any but the most grudging recognition of some messianis sense, however "unclear", seems strange.

to the Servant of Yahweh is found in the words "...with thee I am well pleased" (Lk 3.22; Mk 1.11; cf. Mt 3.17: "with whom"). For the problem regarding the Greek text of Is 42.1, see Fitzmyer, *op. cit.*, p. 486.

As the text stands in the Gospel of Luke, the baptism account marks one of the events in which the Spirit has a special role in initiating phases of the life of Jesus and of the Church [41]. Though John makes no explicit mention of the baptism of Jesus, his account of John the Baptist's witness adds an important symbolism to the descent of the Spirit upon Jesus: it is Jesus, according to God's revelation to John, who will baptize with [or: in] the Holy Spirit (Jn 1.33).

THE TRANSFIGURATION (Mk 9.2-10; Mt 17.1-9; Lk 9.28-36)

It is in Luke's arrangement of events that the Transfiguration stands out most dramatically. Fitzmyer sees this chapter as central in Luke's Gospel [42]. Dominating the chapter is Herod's question: "...*who is this* about whom I hear such things?" (Lk 9.9). Herod's question sets the stage for a number of answers, implicit or explicit, which have a deep Christological purpose: the further identification of Jesus. A minor element in the account of the question is the implication of Jesus' own prophetic role, suggested by some of the reports which perplexed Herod: concerning John the Baptist (cf. Lk 7.26: a prophet and more than a prophet), Elijah, and one of the prophets of old (Lk 9.7-8). Herod's question itself is foreshadowed in Lk 5.21; 7.20, 49; and 8.25.

Luke marshals five answers to the question. The first is implicit in the feeding of the 5,000: Jesus is portrayed as a person "...in whom God's message, activity, power, and creative presence are revealed...." [43]

The second is given in Peter's confession (9.18-21). When Jesus asks Peter, "But who do you say that I am?" Peter answers:

---

[41] See FITZMYER, *op. cit.*, pp. 227-231, 481. Here Jesus is portrayed symbolically as being "fitted out" with the Spirit prior to beginning his ministry; cf. Lk 4.1, 14.

[42] For Fitzmyer's treatment of the chapter, see *op. cit.*, pp. 756-804. I present here the essential elements of his commentary.

[43] *Ibid.*, p. 763.

"The Christ of God" [or "God's Messiah"]. Peter attributes to Jesus an explicit Christological title[44].

The third answer is Jesus' own, given in his first announcement of his passion: "The Son of man must suffer many things, and be rejected by the elders and chief priests and scribes, and be killed, and on the third day be raised" (9.22). The transcendent sense of "Son of man" is suggested in Jesus' words in the following answer (9.26). In the Synoptic tradition suffering is associated with the Son of man: there is no suffering Son of man in the Old Testament[45].

The fourth answer is also Jesus', implicit in his series of sayings about what it means to follow him (9.23-27). The following of Jesus makes radical demands, and these demands further correct any mistaken conceptions of the kind of Messiah he is[46].

The fifth answer is the Father's given in the symbolic action and words in the Transfiguration (9.28-36). Three elements in the event are most significant. First, the transfiguration itself: in Luke's account, with his significant mention of the circumstance, "... as he was praying....", "... the appearance of his countenance was altered, and his raiment became dazzling white...." Second, both the presence of Moses and Elijah (and their conversing with Jesus about his "departure": his entire passage to the Father, ending in the ascension) and their disappearance before the Father speaks, function to heighten the meaning of the whole event. Moses and Elijah symbolize the Law and the prophets: the whole of the Scriptures; and they speak with Jesus of the passage which he must accomplish in Jerusalem. This element of the event should be kept in mind when we read later in Luke (24.25-27, 44-47) that Jesus' suffering, death, and resur-

---

[44] In Fitzmyer's comment, there is question of "... a messiahship that involves suffering, repudiation, death, even though it may end in resurrection...." (p. 771): all this is implicit in the revelation given in the course of the chapter. "Peter's confession has to be understood as an admission of what he at that time thought Jesus to be. *Christos* would have to be understood in the Jewish sense of an expected anointed agent sent by God in the Davidic, kingly or political tradition...." (*ibid.*, p. 775). The further answers given in the course of Luke's account suggest the necessary corrections and modifications of the conception of the Messiah which Peter himself could have had at the moment of his confession.

[45] Cf. *ibid.*, pp. 779-780; and on the Son of man in Lk 5.24: pp. 584-585.

[46] On the meaning which taking up one's cross could have meant to Jesus' hearers, see *ibid.*, pp. 784-785.

rection are the fulfillment of what Moses and the prophets and the psalms wrote about him (cf. Jo 5.39, 45-47). As their presence symbolically witnesses to him, so their departure prior to the Father's words heightens the meaning of his words. Third, the Father's words give a twofold answer to the question, and an all-important command:

> This is my beloved Son; listen to him (Mk 9.7).
> This is my beloved Son, with whom I am well pleased; listen to him (Mt 17.5).
> This is my Son, my Chosen; listen to him (Lk 9.35).

The Father's answer reveals two titles, "my Son" and "my Chosen One", and the command to listen to him, now the full spokesman, the only spokesman, for the Father: Moses and Elijah have disappeared; Jesus alone is with them. He is the Son and the Chosen One in a unique sense; he is the revealer of the Father. Jesus is far more than could have been expressed in any prior notion of the Messiah[47].

The Transfiguration, then, is intimately related to the baptism of Jesus. Two elements are added: the command, and the glimpse of Jesus' glory here anticipated. As the first announcement of the passion did not end with the prediction of Jesus' death, but included his being raised, the Transfiguration links his "departure" or "passage" and the glory of the status of the Risen Jesus[48].

JESUS' PRAYER OF THANKSGIVING (Lk 10.21-24; Mt 11.25-27)

This text gives a sudden revelation of Jesus' interior life: his conscious intimate relationship with the Father. Two elements of the parallel texts are remarkably similar to aspects of John's portrayal of Jesus: (1) "All things have been delivered to me by my Father" (cf. Jn 3.35; 17.2; 13.3); (2) the mutual, exclusive intimate knowledge of Father and Son, revealed especially in

---

[47] Fitzmyer sees in "My Chosen One" or "the Chosen One" a possible allusion to Is 42.1 in the LXX, and consequently an allusion to the Servant Song, but characteristically he insists that nothing in it is explicitly messianic (*ibid.*, p. 803).

[48] Luke, as Fitzmyer points out, [and as one could say regarding Mark and Matthew obviously] is writing from hindsight (*ibid.*, p. 794). On the reference to the event in 2 Pt 1.16-18, see *ibid.*, pp. 796-7.

Jesus' high priestly prayer (Jn 17.1-26: above, pp. 120-122).
So different from the texture of the Synoptics, and so
remarkably like John, this prayer has been regarded as the
Johannine passage in the Synoptics ("a meteor from the
Johannine heaven"). Yet it is one of the most striking instances
of a text in which Luke and Matthew differ from Mark, and have
written with almost perfect verbal correspondence. Consequently
it is one of the most striking instances cited to support the
hypothesis of an early written source used by both: the verbal
correspondence could not be explained solely by oral tradition,
with its inevitable variation of detail[49]. However one would
explain ultimately its origins, this text gives us a precious insight
into Jesus' interior, and another fragment of the answer to the
question, "Who *is* he?"

REFLECTIONS

In presenting these texts as prologues and flashes, I have
sought in every case to establish the sense of the texts as they
stand. Pondering the contributions of some representative
exegetes, and at times suggesting my own interpretation, I have
sought to determine the "literal" sense of the texts. Having done
that, I must face a further question. How do these texts, and
what we have established concerning their meaning, function in
the whole of the theological enterprise which I have undertaken?

In singling out these texts as prologues and flashes, I have
maintained that they present singularly profound theological
insights into the individual books, the whole of the New
Testament, and the whole of the Bible. Beyond that, they can
and should function in the endless dialectic of Christian experience
which is mediated in great part by prayerful reading of the Bible.
All of this involves much more than resting with the literal sense
of the texts, holding them in isolation. Like all of the parts of the
Bible, every one of them is a symbolic element which has its full
meaning only as it is held in the whole complex symbol. In that
whole, they are very rich symbolic elements which contribute
much to the meaning of the whole symbol. All of the elements
are somehow interrelated. All contribute somehow to our

---

[49] For this aspect of the text and its relevance to the sources of the
Synoptics, see FREDERICK GAST, O.C.D., "Synoptic Problem," JBC, II, 40,
pp. 1-6.

understanding of all the others. Yet these prologues and flashes play particularly important roles. By mediating an insight into the Reality of Jesus, they help us to contemplate him as we read any page of the Gospel, and to hold even relatively minor actions and words in their setting. What we learn of Jesus through these texts should affect our understanding of the whole Reality which the Bible imperfectly images.

How are we to proceed? How are we to read these texts, and hold them in mind as we read the rest of the Bible? There is no single program. We cannot program insight and understanding, much less the full reverberation which these texts and the whole Bible may have in us: the full experience, at once cognitive and emotive-volitional-motor. We cannot program the infinitely complex multiple dialectic of Christian experience, personal and interpersonal. Seeking to penetrate these texts more and more, holding their meaning as we read the rest of the Bible, we may hope that in the unique pattern of our own personal experience we shall come to an ever deeper understanding and full response. Moreover, our Christian reading of the Bible itself will be an important factor in the whole of our Christian experience.

We are interested in these texts—and in the whole of the Bible—for what they can mediate to us of God's meaning, and for what they can do to evoke in us a full response to the grace which they mediate. We are interested in a Christian reading of the Bible, seeking to advance in understanding of its richer, deeper meaning. How, then, are we to read these texts?

First, there are some obvious negative answers to that question. We are not to read them and hold them in isolation: precious as they are, they are partial, fragmentary, particular readings or sets of readings on the great Reality imaged by the whole Bible. They complement one another, and our insight into their sense deepens as we hold them together, and as we continue to live our full response to God. We are not to try to fix and dwell exclusively on the meaning which they had for John, or Paul, or Luke: what John and Paul and Luke and the other human writers of the Bible understood and intended to communicate is not the whole truth. Every one of them was moved by God to symbolize as well as he could what he had come to know. Every one of them contributed to a Symbol whose full meaning transcends all that any one of them individually, or all of them collectively, could grasp and convey in words. We are not to read Luke, for instance, endeavoring to situate ourselves in the living context—hypothetically reconstructed—of the Lucan com-

munity of believers.   It is an interesting exercise in historical
research and thought to determine such meaning, as Fitzmyer
does.   Yet we do not live in that community, nor do we read
Luke only.   We live in our own age in the life of a Church which
through long centuries has read prayerfully and pondered the
whole of the Bible.   We share in an understanding and in a
living total response to the whole of God's revelation, and we
hope to advance in understanding and to help one another in the
living dialectic of the community of believers.   Finally, we are
not to attempt some sort of blend of these prologues and flashes,
as if by doing so we might achieve an adequate synthesis. There
will never be an adequate synthesis of God's revealed truth.
There is hope of continued progress in discovering the richer,
deeper meaning of these texts and of all others in the whole
Bible.   Such progress will come only as we continue in the living
Church to ponder the Word, to sense relationships within the
total Reality imaged by the many words, to respond fully to that
Reality, to sense the shape of our experience of total response,
and to seek to symbolize what we have grasped at any stage of
our experience of Father, Jesus, and the Holy Spirit, and of our
life in Them.

In rejecting four possible answers to my question I have elaborated elements of the positive response, which is familiar to those
who have read *Basics* and the long introduction to this volume.

Why have I dealt with these prologues and flashes at this stage
of my present work?   We are concerned in this first part with the
theme which runs through the whole of salvation history, the
whole of the Bible, and the whole of the continuing life of the
Church: our own life, personal and interpersonal in our community
of believers.   Subsequent reflections on aspects of our experience of
God, and aspects of our life in relation to Him, will be illumined by
what we grasp of the intelligible pattern of promise and fulfillment.
Crucial to that theme of promise and fulfillment is the total Reality
of Jesus Christ.   In him, in the whole of the Paschal Mystery, God
has fulfilled his promise, and in turn has made further promises
which ground our hope.   The prologues and flashes should help us
to understand better who Jesus really is, to grasp better the sense
of the rest of the New Testament, and to understand his unique
role in our experience of God.   This reflection on prologues and
flashes, then, is crucial both for our present theme and for the
whole of our reflection on our experience of God and the God
whom we experience.

We turn now to consider further New Testament witness concerning promise and fulfillment.

CHAPTER IV

THE ACTS OF THE APOSTLES

INTRODUCTORY NOTE

Considering what I have called prologues and flashes in the preceding chapter, I have reflected on some of the richest texts in the New Testament. My purpose, as I have explained, was to register first the witness of those texts which contribute most to our understanding of the remainder of the New Testament, and of the whole Bible.

I have no intention now of attempting to treat all other New Testament texts in what might be called a descending order: with regard to their depth and richness of revealed truth and theological insight. Any such effort would be simply arbitrary. Rather, keeping in mind what we should hold from our reflection on key texts in Chapter III, I shall present further witness gathered from principal elements of the New Testament regarding our general theme: the dialectic of promise and fulfillment.

In presenting this New Testament witness I shall hold to this general pattern: first fulfillment, then further promise. Within each I shall further divide as follows: regarding Jesus and regarding us. Further, in treating fulfillment in us, I shall distinguish between what may be called project (in the Gospel principally) and realization (in part in the Gospels, and further in post-Pentecostal Christian experience).

In carrying out this plan I shall consider individual books or authors separately. Though this has the disadvantage of what may be a tiresome repetition of the structure of exposition, it has the overriding advantage of respecting the heterogeneity of the witness of the New Testament writers. Although in our life of faith we hold all of the elements in unity, we do not achieve that unity by stewing a hotchpotch. Every inspired writer bears his witness from his point of view, with his proper symbolization. All contribute readings on single Reality. All mediate our contact

with that Reality, and in our living contemplation of, and
response to, that Reality we reach the unity of a life of faith, love,
and fidelity.

Evidently, in my separate treatment of prologues and flashes,
I have drawn on some of the material from the books involved. In
my present synthetic treatment of themes, I shall cite some of the
elements considered in Chapter III. This involves no great
embarrassment, however, for in the following chapters I shall
deal with my themes in a manner which is at once schematic and
selective. I shall present such evidence as suffices to establish the
pattern of promise, fulfillment, and further promise. I shall not
attempt to consider all of the texts, nor shall I undertake any
extended theological reflection. If I did not respect these limits, I
should find myself expanding this chapter into a full theology. My
purpose is modest: to establish the general structure of promise
and fulfillment. Within that structure, as we are aware of it, we
experience God, and we shall be able to discern aspects of both
our experience of God and the God whom we experience. That
will be our task in Volume II of this work.

I begin with *Acts* because it is Luke's report of the primitive
apostolic preaching and of the life of the first Christians. Though
Acts does not give the record of all of the early communities, it
gives us much concerning the early life of the Church, within
which other books of the New Testament were written. It is
from within a life of Christian faith in the post-Pentecostal
Church that the Gospels took their present form. Though the
Gospels record earlier events, they give their accounts against the
ground of post-Pentecostal experience. Hence we recognize
their limitations as measured by standards of modern conceptions
of scientific history, but also the wealth of their insights into the
deeper meaning of the events which are understood after
experience of the illumination of the Spirit.

Though I am fully aware of the distiction between the
primitive apostolic preaching and the rest of Luke's account of life
in the early Church, I shall not treat them separately. As they
stand, they are all embedded in the Lucan account. Inspiration
bears upon the whole of that account as it stands, and I draw on
the Lucan book as it stands[1].

_____

[1] The following texts in Acts present Peter's basic message, his "kerygmatic
discourses": 2.14-39; 3.11-26; 4.8-12; 5.29-32; 10.34-43. Exegetes
differ regarding the extent to which these discourses as they stand represent the
original Petrine preaching on the one hand and Lucan composition on the other.

FULFILLMENT IN JESUS

Here I shall limit myself to the contents of Peter's kerygmatic discourses. What God does by raising and glorifying Jesus is the fulfillment of Old Testament prophecies, as Peter understands them[2]. Moreover, Jesus is the antitype of the Suffering Servant (Is 52.13): "The God of Abraham and of Isaac and of Jacob, the God of our Fathers, glorified his servant Jesus..." (Acts 3.13).

In the titles which he attributes to the risen Jesus, Peter gives the first post-Pentecostal answers to the question: "Who and what is he?" Having raised Jesus, exalted him at his right hand (symbolizing his authority), and given him the promise of the Holy Spirit (that is: the Holy Spirit, who *is* the promise), "... God has made him both Lord and Christ, this Jesus whom you crucified" (Act 2.36)[3]. *Christ* here is *Messiah*.

DAVID M. STANLEY, S.J. represents the view that these discourses are authentic summaries of the primitive apostolic kerygma (JBC, II, 78:4, p. 769). JOSEPH A. FITZMYER, S.J. regards them as Lucan compositions which "... reflect the missionary preaching of the first generation...." but are "... far from word-for-word reproductions of what was said by Peter...." (JBC, II, 45:5, p. 166). The difference between these two views is not sharply drawn. After all, "authentic summaries" are not "word-for-word reproductions". The question remaining would be this: who made the summaries, Luke or someone else?

[2] These are the Old Testament texts, and the texts of Acts in which their fulfillment is indicated: Ps 16.1-11: Acts 2.25-28; Ps 132.11 and 2 Sm 7.12-13: Acts 2.30; Ps 110.1: Acts 2.34-35; Dt 18.15-16, 19: Acts 3.22-24; Ps 118.22: Acts 4.11.

[3] With regard to the titles of the risen Jesus in Peter's discourses, I am following Fitzmyer's commentary on Acts 1-5, JBC, II, 45:9-34, pp. 168-181. He gives ample indication of the literature and of the variety of exegetes' views. With regard to the titles in Acts 2.36, compare "Lord of all" (10.36). Fitzmyer, *ibid.*, 21, p. 175, affirms "... the saving name (2:21) henceforth belongs to the exalted Messiah...." Yet a little farther on he holds: "... Such proclamation has not yet recognized the divine implications of the *kyrios*-title....": his reason is that the setting of v. 36 is clearly "adoptionist": "... God has made Jesus *kyrios* and *christos* by raising him and exalting him...." I do not find this convincing. The "saving name" (2.21) is clearly the name of the LORD: it occurs in the quotation of Joel. I do find one problem concerning the saving name: in Acts 4.10 Peter affirms that it is by the name of Jesus Christ of Nazareth that the cripple has been healed. To me the explanation seems to be the same as that which I should give for a similar ambiguity in Phil 2.9-11. God has "... bestowed on Christ Jesus the name which is above every name, that at the name of Jesus every knee should bow, in heaven and on earth and under the earth, and every tongue confess that Jesus

Jesus is God's *servant* (3.13): clearly the antitype of the
Suffering Servant[4]. He is the *Holy and Righteous One*, the
Leader to life[5] (3.14). He is the *prophet* promised by Moses
(3.22-23: Dt 18.15-16, 19). Finally, he is *Savior* (5.29).

It is not just Jesus' resurrection and glorification, nor just the
conferring of titles which reveal at last his real dignity, and which
pertain to the fulfillment of the promise in and through him. It is
also his continuing action as the Risen Lord which must be
recognized as an essential element of the fulfillment. *He* has
poured out the Spirit (2.33). It is *in his name* that baptism is to be
received for the forgiveness of sins and the gift of the Spirit (2.38).
Name and person are one. An action performed in the name of
Jesus Christ is done, as the very function of a name suggests, with
some invocation of the name (cf. 3.6); and by the authority and
with the power of the one who is named the act is performed and
the effects produced (cf. 3.12-16). It is he who has been sent to
bless (3.26). In his name alone there is salvation (4.12). In his
name the Apostles continue to speak and to perform signs and
wonders in defiance of human authority which would forbid them
(4.19-20; 5.27-32). With great power they gave their witness
to the resurrection of the Lord Jesus, and great grace was upon
them (4.33). Jesus is the saving Lord, and in and through his
Apostles he is present and acting in fulfillment of the promise (1.8).
He the Lord continued to add to the number of those who were
saved (cf. 2.47). Stephen saw Jesus standing at the right hand of
God, and to him he prayed: "Lord Jesus, receive my spirit" and
cried out "Lord, do not hold this sin against them" (7.56, 59-60).
Jesus is believed to be present and acting as the Lord, as God.

FULFILLMENT IN US

By "us" I mean all who receive the promise, who come to
fulness of life in and through Jesus, from the Apostles on

Christ is Lord..." The name which is above every name is *Lord*. Every knee
should bow at the name of *Jesus* because Jesus Christ *is Lord*.

[4] Cf. FITZMYER, *ibid.*, 24, p. 177: "...Is 52.13 is doubtless alluded to...."
See also *ibid.*, 30, pp. 179-180, on Acts 4.27.

[5] RSV translates *Author of life*, which Fitzmyer rejects: "...The genitive is
one of direction, in view of 26.23 and the Moses-typology (cf. 7.35; Heb
12.2;...). With Jesus' resurrection, the resurrection of all believers has its
beginning (cf. 4.2; 17.31)...." (*ibid.*). JB and NEB take basically the same line.

Pentecost to all who follow to the end of time. In the fragmentary, gradual revelation preserved in *Acts* we gather elements which somehow pertain to the total experience in which we receive the fulfillment of the promise. Some of these elements are at once our actions and God's gift. Some are simply gift. All are part of a total process and its effects, to which no single name is given, though three perhaps may be regarded as designating the whole.

The promise is the Holy Spirit, and fulfillment of the promise comes in the gift of the Spirit, in being baptized with the Holy Spirit. The Apostles were to await the promise, and to receive power when the Holy Spirit came upon them, empowering them to be Christ's witnesses (1.4-5, 8; cf. Lk 24.49). Immediately, in this instance, the gift of the Spirit is a fulfillment of Jesus' promise. Yet it is clear that it is the fulfillment of Old Testament prophecy and promise: Joel's prophecy (2.17-21) and the promise to Abraham (explicitly in 3.25-26, implicitly in 2.38-39).

The gift of the Spirit is the great moment in six accounts in Acts: 2.1-33 (the Apostles); 2.38 (the multitude who heard Peter and received his word on Pentecost); 8.14-17 (the Samaritans); 9.17 (Saul); 10.44-46 (the Gentiles; cf. 11.15-17); 19.6 (the Ephesians). Twice explicitly it is accompanied with speaking with tongues (2.4; 10.44-47). In a third account some external charismatic gift is implicit: Simon *saw* that the Spirit was given through the laying on of the Apostles hands (8.18).

Other effects follow upon the gift: boldness in witness (4.8 ff.; 4.31; 5.32); wisdom (6.3, 10); faith (6.5; 11.24); comfort (9.32); and joy (13.52).

Three acts are mentioned explicitly in some of the accounts as prerequisites to the gift: faith, repentance, and turning. In the account of the Apostles' reception of the Spirit no mention is made of faith, but Peter mentions it later (11.17). The recipients' faith is so prominent in the total experience that often later they are referred to simply as believers, or those who have believed (e.g. 2.44; 4.4, 32). Sometimes to believe is an act required prior to baptism (18.8; and 8.37 in the variant reading concerning the eunuch), or as a condition of forgiveness (11.39; 10.43) or salvation (16.31). Sometimes *to believe* expresses the whole process including the other elements which we shall point out. Implicit here, I should say, is the sense that the act of believing is the basic, decisive act, the beginning of the full human response to the signs, wonders, and preaching; hence it stands for the whole experience[6]. As for the meaning of *to believe* (πιστεύειν), one can only attempt to gather its sense from the context. Surely it includes accepting and affirming as true what the Apostles have affirmed in their preaching: without this the rest of the response of faith would be unintelligible. But it includes much more: acknowledgment of Jesus as Lord (much as the Israelites acknowledged Yahweh as their God), trust, entrusting oneself to Jesus and to God, committing oneself to a way of life. This element of commitment is closely linked with two other acts of the recipient: repentance and conversion or turning[7].

Repentance is not simply sorrow or remorse: it involves a change of mind and heart and of one's way of life. So it is intimately linked with turning, or returning, or conversion to God from a life of sin.

Faith, repentance, and turning are evidently acts of the person who responds to the call of God. Faith, expressed by the noun, πίστις, usually designates the act or disposition or virtue of the one who believes (cf. 6.5; 14.9; 14.22 (?); 15.9; 16.5). Rarely it means the object of faith: what is believed (cf. 6.7; and perhaps 14.22, 27). Repentance (cf. 2.38; 3.19; 5.31; 11.18; 20.21) and turning (3.19; 9.35; 11.21) too are acts of response. Less prominent, but equally important, is another aspect of all three: they are gifts of God, acts of God. God "... cleansed their hearts by faith...." (15.9). "... God exalted him at his right hand as Leader and Savior, to give repentance to Israel and forgiveness of sins...." (5.31; cf. 11.18). "God, having raised up his servant, sent him to you first, to bless you in turning every one of you from your wickedness" (3.26).

Obviously too faith, repentance, and turning mean more than a single act in the process of beginning a new fulness of life: they are permanent dimensions of a way of life, as the whole narrative bears out.

Besides these three acts performed by the person responding, two other acts are performed upon them to mediate the gift of the Spirit: baptism and laying on of hands of the Apostles[8]. The relation of baptism to the gift of the Spirit is obscure in *Acts*.

---

[6] Cf. 2.44; 4.4, 32; 5.14; 9.42; 11.17; 15.5; 17.12, 34; 19.2; 21.20, 25.

[7] For the range of meanings of believe and belief, see BAG on πιστεύω and πίστις; for repent and repentance, *ibid.*, μετανοέω, μετάνοια; for turning, returning, conversion, *ibid.*, ἐπιστρέφω.

[8] Baptism: e.g. 2.38, 41; 8.12, 13, 36, 38; 10.47-48; laying on of hands: 8.17; 9.17 (preceding baptism); 19.6.

... There are four different patterns in which the gift of the Spirit occurs according to *Acts*: (1) on Pentecost the disciples received the Holy Spirit, and there is no mention of their ever being baptized; (2) those to whom Peter preached and who believed were baptized and received the gift of the Spirit, and there is no mention of a further rite; (3) in Samaria those baptized by Philip are said not to have received the Holy Spirit, which subsequently was given to them through the Apostles' Peter and John laying on of hands (8.12-17); similarly at Ephesus those who had received only the baptism of John were first baptized in the name of the Lord Jesus, and then when Paul had laid his hands upon them the Holy Spirit came on them: there is no mention of a baptismal gift of the Spirit (19.1-6); (4) at Caesarea Peter preached Jesus to the Gentiles, and as he was still speaking the Holy Spirit fell on all who heard the word and they spoke in tongues; then they were baptized (10.44-48); speaking later of them Peter affirms that God cleansed their hearts by faith (15.9): apparently the remission of their sins occurred when they believed and received the Spirit, before their baptism.

No simple harmony can be effected without going far beyond the evidence of theological reflection reached by the author of *Acts*. At this stage of our study I prefer to abstain from such further reflection....[9]

The effects of this complex of divine and human action are themselves a manifold: aspects of the term of a total process, rather than so many distinct effects. We may simply enumerate these aspects, without suggesting an order of priority of any sort. First mentioned by Peter is forgiveness of sins (2.38), and it is prominent in successive accounts [10]. Implicitly the most important of all, and perhaps somehow summing up all, is the gift of the Spirit (2.1-33, 38), which we have considered. Saving or salvation seems to sum up all of the effects [11]. Two other elements are eternal life (13.46, 48) and sanctification (26.18). Finally two further aspects of the total experience call for special attention: life in community, and the "Way".

In the days of preparation for the gift of the Spirit, in various ways we are told that "they" (the Apostles [1.2-13], the women, Mary the mother of Jesus, and his brothers [1.14]) were together, devoting themselves to prayer with one accord (1.14).

---

[9] *The Mystery*, p. 201.
[10] Cf. 3.19; 5.31; 10.43; 13.38; 15.9; 26.18.
[11] Cf. save: 2.40; 4.12; 11.14; 14.9; 15.11; 16.30-31; salvation: 4.12; 13.26, 47; 16.17.

On Pentecost "... they were all together in one place" (2.1). The *setting* for the gift is a group living together. The effect of the gift obviously too is the gradual formation of community (cf. 2.41-47; 4.4, 32-37).

As for terminology, in the days of preparation, there is no term designating them as a group. They are described concretely as having come together (1.6); some of their actions together are mentioned (1.14). They were simply the brethren, the company of persons in the same place (1.15: ὄχλος ὀνομάτων ἐπὶ τὸ αὐτό). On Pentecost "... they were together in one place" (2.1). As others believed and were baptized [and received the gift], many were "added", and their life of fellowship is described (2.41-47; 4.32-37). The *number* of men, of disciples, is the vague term used (4.4; 6.7); then the "company" [12] of those who believed (4.32). Finally the assembly of believers is called a church (ἐκκλησία), a term which is used most often, in the singular or plural, for local churches, but also can designate the church as a whole [13].

I mentioned above that three of the particular terms used regarding the complex process and its effect may be taken to stand for the whole. First, *to believe*, the initial, basic act of response can stand for the whole process, the whole experience; and those who have had the experience are simply *the believers*. Second, as the principal gift, the *gift of the Spirit* can stand for the whole effect or term of the process; finally, *saving* and *salvation* can stand for the whole process and its effects.

In its own manner the term "the Way" stands for the whole manner of life to which men and women commit themselves by believing, repenting, and turning, the distinctive way of life which marks those who have received the Spirit, have believed, have been saved [14].

Before concluding my treatment of fulfillment recorded in *Acts*, I should like to add two sobering reflections: one regarding life in community, the other regarding the Way.

---

[12] πλῆθος is a number, multitude, and the term gradually comes to mean in a special sense a religious fellowship, community, or church: cf. BAG.

[13] For a local church, or several local churches, cf. 5.11; 8.1, 3; 9.31; 11.22; 12.1, 5; 13.1; 14.23, 27; 15.3, 4, 22, 41; 16.5; 18.22; 19.32, 39, 41; 20.17. For the term as designating the church as a whole, see 9.31; 20.28.

[14] For the "Way" mentioned without qualification, see 9.2; 19.9, 23; 22.4; 24.14, 22; for the way of salvation: 16.17; the way of the Lord: 18.25; the way of God: 18.26. The "Way" has Old Testament echoes (cf. 2.28: Ps 16.8-11), and echoes too of the preaching of John the Baptist in fulfillment of Isaiah's prophecy (cf. 13.10).

If one were to concentrate on two early descriptive accounts of life in the first Christian community, in 2.42-47 and 4.32-37, he or she might be tempted to see here the fulfillment of prophetic visions of a paradise in the new age of salvation. The reality was far different. First, from the outset the believers were persecuted. Second, it is enough to move on to chapter six of *Acts* to find them quarreling among themselves. Life in the first generation of Christian community was not paradise, as we learn especially from Paul's letters.

Second, two aspects of the symbol of the Way should be kept in mind. The Way is not a *state* of blessedness: it implies a journey. We must continue to *walk* along the Way. Christian fulfillment comes not in an ecstatic moment of fulfillment, but in the beginning of a process in which we advance in a new direction, with a new destination. We are a pilgrim people. Further, it is possible to deviate from the Way, and soon in the record of *Acts* we see the scandal of a deviation: the sin of Ananias and Sapphira (5.1-11). The rest of the New Testament, especially in the letters which witness to the reality of experience in the early Church, makes the reality of sin painfully apparent.

FURTHER PROMISE

Acts records remarkably little concerning further promise. With regard to Jesus himself, there is a vague suggestion of a still future fulfillment of an element of the prophecy of Joel quoted by Peter: the *day* of the Lord (2.19-21). A clearer promise concerns both Jesus and us: "...that times of refreshing may come from the presence of the Lord, and that he may send the Christ appointed for you, Jesus, whom heaven must receive until the time for establishing all that God spoke by the mouth of his holy prophets from of old...." (3.19-21). For us, there is a share in the continuing mission of the Apostles, with the assurance of power from the Holy Spirit (cf. 1.8; 9.15-17): thus through the Gentile converts "...the word of the Lord spread throughout all the region...." (13.49). Secondly, among the effects of the initial fulfillment is *eternal life* (13.46, 48). We have eternal life now, but the very notion of *eternal* life involves present and future reality, and beyond the future into eternity. The promised times of refreshment and the second sending of Jesus regard a further fulfillment (3.19-21). Beyond these scanty indications of promise of further fulfillment, we have the somewhat veiled, obscure words reported in Paul's controversy with the Jews and his defense before the Roman authorities. He speaks of the resurrection of the dead, and of future judgment (24.25). The manner in which he uses the conviction concerning resurrection of the dead suggests, however, that he is not presenting a distinctively Christian belief, but one on which Jews themselves were divided; and Paul uses it to drive a wedge between the Sadducees and the Pharisees (23.6-10; cf. 24.15, 21; 26.6-8). Nevertheless in one instance Luke reports Paul as proclaiming a distinctively Christian belief in his defense before Agrippa. Having told of his experience on the road to Damascus, Paul affirms that he has proclaimed "...nothing but what the prophets and Moses said would come to pass: that Christ must suffer, and that, by being the first to rise from the dead, he would proclaim light both to the people and to the Gentiles" (26.22-23). This sounds like a Lucan echo of an early Pauline theme: "...Christ has been raised from the dead, the first fruits of those who have fallen asleep...." (1 Cor 15.20).

Chapter V

MATTHEW

Preliminary Notes

(1) *Why Matthew?* I had intended to present here a schematic, synthetic account of elements in the Synoptic Gospels. For good reasons, in my judgment, I have preferred to consider *Matthew* only.

First, I wish to avoid giving the impression of regarding the Synoptics as homogeneous, or as a sort of trio composed in conscious concert by the three authors. There is a certain complementarity of the three, but any "trio" on the analogy of a musical composition takes its form in the reader. The three Gospels are distinct, written from different points of view by men with different insights and intentions. If it were possible within the scope of this work, it would be ideal to consider all three. I consider that impossible, and my solution is the choice of one of the three.

Second, *Matthew* seems an excellent choice. I am concerned with the dialectic of promise and fulfillment, and Matthew most of all the Synoptic writers stresses fulfillment of Old Testament promise and prophecy. Implicit in his Gospel is a distinctive, if only vaguely conceived, sense of *fulfill* and *fulfillment.* Moreover, Matthew's Gospel is the work of a theologian who fashions his narrative and Jesus' discourses in a distinctive manner, to compose a Gospel which meets the needs of what one can conjecture to have been the particular community in which he lived. His Gospel, then, is a remarkable illustration of the fruit of a personal reflection on his sources, a reflection achieved in the light of his unique personal illumination by the Holy Spirit within the Apostolic age. Consequently *Matthew,* when compared with *Mark* and *Luke,* is a striking example of the perspectivism and process which characterized the Church within the Apostolic age, and which, without further revelation and the special charism of inspiration, will mark Christian reflection and reworking of the message under the influence of the Spirit to the end of time [1].

Finally, my concentration on *Matthew* here complements the relative emphasis on Lucan theological themes in my treatment of Luke's "prologue" (infancy narrative), and of Jesus' baptism and transfiguration.

(2) *The probable setting and scope of Matthew's Gospel.* I should say that arguments advanced by modern biblical scholars give strong support to the contention that Matthew was writing in and for a non-Palestinian local church, plausibly that of Antioch, a church which had been Jewish-Christian and had become increasingly Gentile Christian. Matthew's sharp portrayal of Jesus' confrontation with the Jewish leaders, his treatment of the relationship of Gospel to Law, his account of Jesus' rejection by the Jews, of the consequent transfer of the Kingdom of God from the Jews to a people bearing its fruits (Mt 21.43), of the death and resurrection of Jesus as one great apocalyptic, eschatological event transforming salvation history, and of the final universal mission given to the Apostles by the risen Christ are intelligible in the light of such suppositions regarding Matthew's community and his purpose in writing. His Gospel reflects not simply the conflicts between Jews and Christians, but also those within the early Church between Jewish and Gentile Christians. Problems with judaizing, and with the relationship between Gospel and Law seem to have been as keen for Matthew as for Paul [2].

(3) *Matthew's interpretation of Old Testament texts.* I entitle this note thus, rather than simply "The sense of *fulfill* in Matthew". The sense of *fulfill* is only part of a larger problem, as I shall indicate.

To begin with, Matthew quotes, or vaguely refers to, the Old Testament much more frequently than Mark and Luke. Numbers here depend on who is counting what. In the text edited by Aland and others direct Old Testament quotations are printed in bold face, and the Old Testament texts are identified: sometimes

---

[1] For helpful and suggestive introductions to the book, see JOHN L. MCKENZIE, "The Gospel According to Matthew," JBC, II, 43, pp. 62-114; and JOHN P. MEIER, *The Vision of Matthew* (New York: Paulist Press, c. 1979).

[2] For a zealous, but generally plausible, presentation of arguments for such a position, see MEIER, *op. cit.*, pp. 12-39. He presents the view of some scholars that Matthew himself was not a Jew but a Gentile, adding what he regards as more precise arguments (pp. 18-23). I do not find his arguments convincing.

two or more for a single quotation, sometimes two for portions of a composite quotation[3]. My count of such quotations is 64. Some, however, involve more than one quotation of the same text (Lev 19.18 three times; Hos 6.6 twice). Moreover, Matthew makes four general references: "what was spoken by the prophets" (2.23), "as it is written" (26.24), "the scriptures" (26.54), and "the scriptures of the prophets" (26.56); for these no definite Old Testament texts can be found.

I should say that the quotations and references can be arranged in five classes. First, an event, word, or action in Matthew's account is said to *fulfill* the text quoted or referred to[4]. Second, an event, word, or action is recognized as the fulfillment of Scripture, though the word *fulfill* is not used: some equivalent formula links event and Old Testament text, such as "... prophesied" or "as it is written"[5]. Third, a text is quoted without introductory formula, to explain an action[6]. Fourth, there is a cluster of texts somehow related. One is Jesus' word to John at his baptism: "... thus it is fitting for us to *fulfill* all righteousness" (3.15). Another is Jesus' statement regarding his relation to the Law: "Think not that I have come to abolish the law and the prophets; I have come not to abolish them but to *fulfill* them" (5.17). Related to these two are several instances in which the sense of an Old Testament text is somehow enriched by its application in the Gospel[7]. Fifth, there are instances of quotations in which no deeper, richer meaning of the Old Testament text is suggested[8].

With the exception of the last class of texts, simple quotations without deepening of meaning, I should say that the whole matter of Matthew's interpretation of the Old Testament hinges on the meaning of *fulfill*. I shall begin with that.

---

[3] *The Greek New Testament*, edited by Kurt Aland and others (New York ...: United Bible Societies, c. 1966).

[4] The verb *fulfill* ($\pi\lambda\eta\rho\delta\omega$), used in a relevant sense, is found in these texts: 1.22; 2.15, 17, 23; 4.14; 8.17; 12.17; 13.35; 21.4; 26.54, 56; 27.1. Add one instance of the compound verb with the same sense ($\dot{\alpha}\nu\alpha\pi\lambda\eta\rho\delta\omega$): 13.14.

[5] These are the texts: 2.5; 3.3; 15.7; 21.13, 16, 42; 22.31; 24.15; 26.24, 31; 27.9.

[6] See 4.4, 6, 7, 10.

[7] See 5.21, 27, 31, 33, 38; 9.13; 10.35-36; 11.5, 10, 23; 12.7, 40; 15.4; 18.16; 19.4, 5; 21.9, 33; 22.32, 39-40, 44; 23.38, 39; 24.21, 29, 30; 26.15, 64; 27.34, 35, 39, 43, 46, 48. In 22.39-40, the enrichment consists in the elevation of the "second" commandment to the level of the first, something not suggested by Lev 19.18.

[8] See 5.34, 35, 43; 19.7, 18-19; 22.24, 37.

At the outset I should affirm that there is no question of determining Matthew's conception of *fulfill*. He gives us no clue to any explicit concept. Understanding his use of *fulfill*, and his further interpretation of the Old Testament, is a theological task.

McKenzie has given a helpful suggestion. "... Matthew's idea of fulfillment... is not... [that] of the fulfillment of a prediction, but of the growth of a reality to its destined fulness...."[9] "... The 'fulfillment' of Israel must be realized in the Gentile world without the people of Israel"[10]. "But the reign of God is not identified with the Church in such a way that the identifications is total. The reign of God is fulfilled only in an eschatological event...."[11] "... Jesus did not come to destroy the Law, but to fulfill it. To fulfill the law means to bring it to the fulness of which it is a developmental phase. The reign—and Jesus himself is identified with the reign—is this full reality.... Jesus is lord of the Law; he does not annul it any more than mature manhood annuls childhood, ..."[12]. Applying this notion to the interpretation of Mt 1.22, McKenzie affirms: "... The term [*fulfillment*] does not signify mere prediction and fulfillment; .... The saving event of the Gospel gives the word of the OT, which is a declaration of the power and will of God to save, a new dimension of reality.... [The LXX translation "virgin" for the Hebrew "young girl" in Is 7.14] ... gives the text of Is a new dimension of reality, and Matthew uses it to affirm the virgin birth. His emphasis, however, seems to be more on the declaration of a savior who shall be called Emmanuel, 'God with us,' than on the word *parthenos* (virgin). The birth initiates the Messianic age of salvation to which the whole OT looks forward.... Jesus realizes the presence of God among his people in an entirely new way..."[13].

Taking elements suggested by McKenzie, I should explain Matthew's *fulfill* by situating it in the context of my whole theory of symbolizing and symbol, applied to Divine-human symbolizing and symbols[14].

---

[9] *Op. cit.*, 8, p. 64 A.
[10] *Ibid.*, 10, p. 64 B.
[11] *Ibid.*
[12] *Ibid.*, 11, p. 65 A.
[13] *Ibid.*, 19, p. 67 A. Behind McKenzie's interpretation of the "fulfillment" texts in Mt. lies the insight of earlier exegetes who recognized the meaning of *fulfill* regarding Jesus' fulfilling the Law. See, for example, Denis Buzy, S.C.J., *Évangile selon saint Matthieu* in *La Sainte Bible [Pirot-Clamer]* (Paris: Letouzey et Ané, 1950) on Mt 5.17: pp. 60-61.
[14] I can refer here only massively to the whole thought elaborated in *Man*

Every symbol is an image of a reality, inadequately representing the total world, objective and subjective, of the symbolizer, and evoking in the perceiver a meaning (cognitive, emotive, volitional, and motor) which is unique as it is set in the whole of his or her total world, subjective and objective. Every element of a complex symbol has its meaning as it is set in the whole: only thus does it contribute to imaging and representing the reality conceived and intended by the symbolizer.

The Bible is one great complex written linguistic symbol, terminating the operation of God and many human writers. God is the principal Symbolizer. The human writers are taken up—with the whole of their human gifts and the whole of their symbolizing effort—to contribute to the elaboration of a Symbol whose total meaning far exceeds their grasp, their meaning and their intention. The total meaning is God's, and we can approach it, but never fully grasp it, only as we transcend the "literal meaning" of the human authors, situating their meaning in the vast, developing total Symbol, and the Reality which it images.

The imaged Reality is God, gradually revealed as Father, Son, and Holy Spirit; his eternal plan for man's fulness of life in Them; and the total process of his revelation and realization of that plan. The process is not in God, but in man, in the Incarnate Word who shares the human condition, and the Church in which the process continues to fulfillment at the end of time. Revelation and basic realization culminate in Jesus Christ: in him God makes his full revelation of himself and of his plan for us; and in him God accomplishes our salvation: in him and through him he offers us, and realizes in us to the extent to which by his grace we respond, the fulness of life which is our potential.

The whole Bible, therefore, has its meaning as it gradually, remotely and most obscurely at first, embodies the revelation of Jesus. It is in the light of the full reality of Jesus, and the fulness of his revelation, that we must interpret the whole. Beyond God's revelation and realization in Jesus, culminating in the Paschal mystery, the process of understanding goes on in the Church, illumined by the Holy Spirit, enlivened by the Spirit, and showing forth in its own life something more of the full meaning of the revealed Reality. In Jesus, then, God's reign is established. In him the Law, revealed gradually in the Old Testament as God

the Symbolizer and *Basics.* I simply recall here elements to which I have referred often and which are necessary here to suggest the intelligible structure within which I situate our present problem.

acted within the human frame, "doing what he could" humanly speaking with a people whose religious sense could develop only slowly—in Jesus the Law comes to its perfection. He is the Law-giver, the new Moses. He brings the Law to a depth and perfection which were beyond the understanding of the religious leaders of the Jews.

The whole of the Old Testament, the "Scriptures", "the Law and the Prophets", projects readings taken by many human authors upon a developing Reality, a transcendent Reality. Individual Old Testament texts had a meaning grasped and intended by their human authors. It was a meaninig, however, which by the very law of the Divine Symbolizer's plan, was bound to make sense ultimately only as it was transformed in the light of further revelation and realization.

Jesus in his full reality, in his words and actions by which he himself could express that reality only imperfectly, utterly transcended all prior human conception, even that of the men who had received earlier revelation and had been inspired to record it.

Fulfillment of Old Testament texts, as recorded in Matthew, often seems to be a complete reversal of all Jewish expectations. One might call *Matthew* "The Great Reversal". Yet that would express only part of what is involved in this Gospel. More properly one might call it the Gospel of transcendent fulfillment. Reversal is only one dimension of this paradoxical fulfillment. I suggest that we see here an analogy with what has been called in classic theology the "triple way" of speaking of God. It involves affirmation, denial, and eminence or transcendence: affirmation of a perfection understood humanly, denial of the imperfections inherent in all human realization of the perfection, and re-affirmation of the perfection thus purified, though in a manner which surpasses all human understanding. It is thus that Jesus fulfills prophecy, and fulfills the Law and the whole of the Scripture. Titles applied to him, affirmed of him, must undergo a process of purification. We witness that process as we read the Gospel; and we come at the end to affirm the same titles in a sense which transcends all prior understanding.

Matthew's understanding of the Old Testament, therefore, can be regarded as a continual reading of the deeper, richer sense of individual Old Testament texts, and indeed of the whole of the Scripture, the whole of the law and the prophets. His Gospel is written from within a life of faith in his early Christian community. He has a Christian understanding of the deeper meaning of the Old Testament.   Moreover he is a theologian who marshals the elements of traditions and written sources in such a way as to bring out strikingly the transcendent reality, the utter newness of Jesus, and of life in Jesus according to the Law, the way of life which he proposed.   *Matthew* is a profound, fascinating Gospel.

FULFILLMENT IN JESUS

(1) *Matthew's prologue-overture* (1-2).   As in the case of John's prologue and what I have called Luke's prologue, so here in the genealogy and infancy narrative according to Matthew we have what could be called a theological prologue or overture to the whole of his Gospel.   He sounds themes here which will be muted for some time, and which will take on their full meaning only as Matthew deploys his sources to effect a gradual reversal and purification.

Significantly the Gospel opens with the announcement of the genealogy of Jesus Christ, the son of David, the son of Abraham. Jesus is rooted in the family of David, who is the son of Abraham. Two things strike me as meaningful here: continuity with Abraham, and the title "son of David".   As in the whole of the New Testament, so here we find the beginning of an account of the fulfillment of God's promise to Abraham.   The theme is not prominent in Matthew, but the link with Abraham is clear.   The Jews, confronted later by John the Baptist and by Jesus, pride themselves on being sons of Abraham (Mt 3.12; cf. Lk 3.7-9; 19.9; Jn 8.31-40).   Jesus will speak of the reward of the believers in terms of sitting at table with Abraham, Isaac, and Jacob in the kingdom of heaven (Mt 8.11; cf. Lk 13.28; 16.19-31).   The God of whom Jesus will speak is the God of Abraham, and the God of Isaac, and the God of Jacob (Mt 22.32; cf. Mk 12.26-27).

The first answer to the question "Who is he?" is this: he is the son of David.   The title will play a considerable role in the course of the Gospel, and yet it is not without paradox from the outset.   Jesus is the son of David, and yet he is not from David by natural generation.   He is David's son obliquely, so to speak: *Joseph* is descended from David; he is the son of David (1.20); and Joseph is the husband of Mary, of whom Jesus was born. And the wondrous manner of his birth is Matthew's first concern.

The child in Mary's womb was conceived of the Holy Spirit, and she conceived as a virgin, fulfilling the prophecy of Is 7.14 in a manner which transcends the literal sense of Isaiah's text. His name will be Jesus ("Savior"), for he will *save* his people *from their sins*. Conceived of the Holy Spirit, born of a virgin, he will be called Emmanuel: "God with us" (1.20-23).

Jesus is called the Christ, the "Anointed". From the outset his name is simply Jesus Christ (1.1), yet *Christ* is a title whose sense will be clarified only in the long process of correction-purification in the Gospel account. Here in the prologue the name-title is mentioned without suggestion of the problems which will be involved in determining in what sense Jesus is God's Anointed, the Christ, the Messiah. When the wise men from the from the East came seeking the *King* of the Jews, Herod inquires where the *Christ* was to be born, and the answer given in terms of Micah's prophecy indicates both the place of his origin and his function: he will be a ruler who will govern God's people Israel (2.1-6). The homage paid by the wise men to the infant Jesus is that given to king (2.11-12).

Finally Matthew points out the significance of the flight into Egypt: "...to fulfill what the Lord had spoken by the prophet, 'Out of Egypt have I called my son'" (2.15): in some unique sense Jesus is the Son of God.

Who, then, is Jesus? The answers given or suggested by Matthew's prologue are these: Son of David, Christ (Anointed-Messiah), Jesus-Savior, God with us, King, and in some special way Son of God. Except for the paradox in his being called Son of David, these titles are mentioned here without apparent problem. In terms of the analogy which I have suggested with regard to transcendent fulfillment, in the prologue we seem to be in the first phase of the so-called "triple way": straightforward affirmation. The second stage, denial, will involve most of the Gospel, in which Jesus will gradually correct the meanings of these titles as they may be eventually applied to him: he will have to reverse all prevailing Judaic notions, and all normal human expectations, before the titles will be applicable to him in a transcendent sense.

In the preceding paragraph I wrote that in the prologue we seem to be in the first stage of simple affirmation, not yet tormented by the problematics of the whole body of the Gospel. Yet the matter is not so simple. We have here Matthew's retrojection of his own faith, and that of his community, long after the resurrection. What he announces here in the titles almost casually given to Jesus really is the result of having lived through the whole process of affirmation-denial-transcendence. He is giving us a deceptively simple theological preview of answers to the question "Who is he?": answers whose sense for us will be established only as we make our way through the tormented dialectic in which alone Jesus himself, by word and action, will make clear who he really is.

One last note seems significant. Jesus is named Savior because he will save his people from their sins (1.21). From the outset, therefore, Matthew suggests the kind of savior he is, and he may be anticipating some of the burden of the correction which Jesus had to make before the title Messiah (Anointed King Savior of his people, with all of the implications of the varying popular judaic notions of a nationalist king-deliverer) could be applied to him.

(2) *The dialectic of titles.* I do not intend to sketch a twofold account of Matthew's presentation of fulfillment in Jesus: one in terms of the interplay of titles; the other in terms of a developing revelation through the course of the Gospel. Yet it seems important to trace the trajectory of the titles, for much of the revelation of who Jesus is and in what sense he fulfills the promise comes by way of the tensions between titles, and of the mutual transformation of meaning which is effected by their interplay. They are a cluster of symbols which are somehow complementary, and which in their manifold interplay gradually contribute together to. the answer to the question "Who is he?"

(a) Son of David. After its appearance in the opening verse of the Gospel, this is used by the blind men calling for mercy (9.27; 20.30, 31), by the people marveling at his works (12.23), by the Canaanite women pleading with persevering faith (15.22), by the crowds at Jesus' entrance into Jerusalem (21.9) and the children hailing him in the temple (21.15). Only in the latter two instances does Jesus seem to encourage their use of the title, in circumstances in which he is clearly symbolizing the kind of davidic King-Messiah he is. In all cases the title is surely messianic in the understanding of those who use it. In the earlier instances Jesus responds to pleas for mercy without indicating any acknowledgment of the title. He himself sharpens the messianic sense of the title when he questions the Pharisees (22.41-45), but makes no application of the title to himself.

(b) Christ, Messiah, Anointed [15]. Though the title *Christ*, with the special sense of *Messiah* appears relatively rarely in

---

[15] For brief accounts of the development of the concept of Messiah in the

Matthew, and only a few times in truly significant instances, still in a sense the tension in the interplay of other titles, and much of Matthew's account of Jesus' actions and words, is somehow concerned with correction of popular notions of the Messiah, and with the establishment of the true sense in which Jesus could be affirmed to be the Messiah: a uniquely Christian sense, reversing and transcending notions prevailing among the people, including the disciples, until the process of correction and transcendence will have been completed. I omit texts in which *Christ* is simply part of the name *Jesus Christ*, reflecting later Christian usage; Herod's question about the place of the birth of the Christ (2.4); Jesus' question to the Pharisees (22.42-45); his warnings about false Christs and rumors about Christ (24.5, 23); the soldiers' use of the title in mocking Jesus (26.68); and Pilate's questions to the people (27.17, 22). Both the soldiers' use of the title and Pilate's question about "Jesus who is called Christ" are signs of widespread use of the title in current talk about Jesus.

Mention of the title in the genealogy is significant, but it represents an element of post-resurrection Christian belief retrojected into the prologue. It is part of Matthew's Christology sounded in the overture to the Gospel.

The first significant occurrence of the title in the body of the Gospel is in the account of John's hearing about the deeds of *the Christ,* and his sending disciples to ask whether Jesus was "he who is to come" (11.2-3). "The one to come" is an equivalent of "the Christ" in the context. The question is significant. More so is Jesus' implicit affirmative answer in terms of the wonders which show who he is (11.4-6). Even here, however, Jesus is beginning to correct any wrong notions about the kind of Messiah he is. His are works of healing and teaching the good news, not what people would expect of some sort of king-savior who would restore the kingdom and thus institute the reign of God. And his closing words reinforce the answer: "blessed is he who takes no offense at me": that is: who is not scandalized at *such* a Messiah.

The account of Peter's profession of faith (16.13-23) is one of the richest in the Gospel. In it we find an intimate link

---

Old Testament and in post-biblical judaism, and for the transformation of the concept in the New Testament, see JOHN L. McKENZIE, "Aspects of Old Testament Thought," JBC, II, 77:152-163, pp. 762-764; and DAVID M. STANLEY, S.J., "Aspects of New Testament Thought," JBC, II, 78:8-10, pp. 770-771.

between Matthew's Christology and his ecclesiology. With regard to the former, which is our present concern, we find what is perhaps the most interesting interplay of three titles. With a notable change of Mark's account, Matthew frames Jesus' question, "Who do men say that the *Son of Man* is?" The disciples' report of varying opinions is itself noteworthy: men identified Jesus with John the Baptist or one of the earlier prophets who had suffered or had been martyred. To Jesus' second question, "But who do you say that I am?" Peter alone replies: "You are the Christ, the Son of the living God" (16.16). Jesus exclaims, "Blessed are you, Simon Bar-Jona! For flesh and blood has not revealed this to you, but my Father who is in heaven. And I tell you that you are Peter, and on this rock I will build my church.... Then he strictly charged the disciples to tell no one that he was the Christ" (16.17-18, 20).

For the moment it is sufficient to note that in Matthew's account three titles are linked: Son of Man, the Christ and the Son of the living God. As we shall see in the course of our account of the titles, these play prominent roles in the dialectic, the mutual interplay, the gradual correction and modification and mutual transformation. By word and action Jesus shows how these titles are to be understood of him. At the end of the process as it is reported in Matthew's account, we have a Christology which is not elaborated in a sharply conceptual theology, but which is held in the complementarity and tension of several intuitive symbols.

The account is clearly theological, clearly a post-resurrection witness to Christian belief. Situation of the original experience is beyond retrieval. That is not lamentable. What we have here is not the report of scientifically empirical historical investigation. It is a witness from within the life of faith in an early Christian community to aspects of the full reality of Jesus which must lie for ever beyond the range of such history.

As it figures in Matthew's account, Peter's profession of faith is held well within the process of the gradual revelation of Jesus. Peter is blessed: he has received a revelation from the Father. He is further blessed by Jesus himself: by the significant change of his name from Simon to Peter, the Rock, and by the promise of his unique role in Jesus' plan for his church. This is the only account which explains the change of name. Though he is blessed by a revelation, he has not yet fully understood. Very shortly he is sharply rebuked: when Jesus makes his first prediction of his suffering, death, and resurrection, Peter simply does not understand, and his protest provokes Jesus' rebuke (16.21-23).

Later, in the context of Jesus' final confrontation with the Jewish leaders, warning the crowds and his disciples against the vanity and hypocrisy of the Pharisees, he tells them how they must act: 'You are not to be called rabbi, for you have one teacher, and you are all brethren. And call no man your father on earth, for you have one Father, who is in heaven. Neither be called masters, for you have one master, *the Christ....*" (23.8-10). There is no doubt whom he means by "the Christ", as there is no doubt about who alone is their teacher. What is surprising is this: Jesus' implicit but open acknowledgment of the title *Christ* is set here in words addressed not only to his disciples, but to the crowds. Seemingly he senses that the process of correction has made clear the meaning of the title as it is applied to him.

Finally, in the "trial" before Caiaphas and the Sanhedrin, the high priest questions Jesus under oath: " 'I adjure you by the living God, tell us if you are the Christ, the Son of God.' Jesus said to him, 'You have said so. But I tell you, hereafter you will see the Son of man seated at the right hand of Power, and coming on the clouds of heaven'" (26.63-64). And Jesus was condemned of blasphemy. Passing over the critical problems of what the titles meant to the high priest and the Sanhedrin, and by what process Jesus was condemned of blasphemy [16], Jesus here affirms in the most solemn circumstances that he, the Son of man, is the Christ, the Son of God [17]. What Jesus adds about the Son of man is to be understood as a combination of allusions to two messianic texts, Ps 110.1 and Dn 7.13. The whole of his response again links three titles whose meanings are mutually conditioned. We can respond in part to the question "Who is he" by holding the three in complementarity, in the dialectical tension of three powerful intuitive symbols.

(c) Emmanuel (1.22). This title occurs only here in the New Testament. It is linked implicitly with Jesus' words in 18.2 and 28.20. More subtly it sounds a theological theme which

---

[16] On the classic critical problems regarding Jesus' trial, see McKenzie's brief account and indication of the literature, *op. cit.*, 189-190, p. 110. As Matthew is not concerned with answering modern critical questions concerning Jesus' very words, so neither is he concerned with a scientifically historical account of the trial, the precise course of the trial and the sense which the titles could have had for his judges, and how his claim in their understanding constituted blasphemy. Matthew is using the titles here with their full Christian meaning, and this is part of his whole theological account of who Jesus is and why he was put to death.

[17] "You have said so" is the equivalent of "I am."

interprets, in the whole account of Jesus' words and actions, the unique manner in which God is present among his people *in him*[18].

(d) King (2.2; cf. *ruler*, 2.6). Used first by the wise men, this title reappears only toward the end of the Gospel. Explicit in the fulfillment text, it is taken now in the sense of the *humble* king of Zechariah's prophecy (Mt 21.5: Zech 9.9). It is implicit in the title *son of David* by which Jesus is hailed by the crowds at his entrance into Jerusalem, and by the children in the temple (21.9, 15). Jesus accepts the title, for by now he has made clear in what sense it can be applied to him. He uses it of himself in a subtle shift from *Son of man* to *King* in his description of the judgment (25.34, 40). He accepts it in response to Pilate (27.11). There is a deep irony in its use in mockery by the soldiers and by the chief priests, scribes, and elders (27.29, 42) and in the sign over his head on the cross, indicating the claim for which he is dying (27.37): the process of correction has been completed, and in a complete reversal of all judaic conceptions—and the natural human ideas of the soldiers—now he is truly King, saving his people in his supreme act[19]. There is no need here for the words added in John's account (Jn 18.33-37): in *Matthew* the great reversal, and the sense of transcendent fulfillment, has been made clear.

(e) Servant. This title is suggested by two brief allusions (3.17; 8.16-17) and especially by the long fulfillment text (12.17-21: Is 42.1-4). I suggest that the bearing of these allusions is far greater than the fragments of texts to which they refer. The figure of the Servant, as it is elaborated gradually in the Servant Songs, is a single great intuitive symbol. Any allusion to him evokes the full power of the whole figure, one of the richest in the Old Testament. All that is said of the Servant somehow bears upon the transcendent fulfillment of the type in Jesus: not by way of a pedantic allegorism applying every detail to a detail of the Reality of Jesus, but by the total evocative power of the full intuitive symbol. There is a vaguely sensed, deep analogy lying beneath any possible explicit conceptual symbolization: a vaguely sensed isomorphism of type and antitype[20].

---

[18] Matthew deepens and enriches the meaning of the name in Is 7.14. There the child is so named because he is a symbol of God's presence among his people. Here, as in the shift from the Hebrew Isaiah's "young woman" to the "virgin" of the Septuagint translation, there is a deepening of the sense of the original. In the strong sense, *in Jesus* God is with his people.

[19] See McKenzie, *op. cit.*, 197, p. 112 A.

[20] On the sense of *isomorphism*, see *Man the Symbolizer*, pp. 172, 192-193, 243-247.

(f) Son of God. This is one of the two principal titles in *Matthew*[21]. After the vague allusion in the fulfillment text, 2.15, we come to the solemn words of the Father at Jesus' baptism: "This is my beloved Son, with whom I am well pleased" (3.17). Three aspects of the words seem significant: the affirmation of Jesus' sonship in some transcendent sense, the love relationship, and the allusion to the Servant in the last clause (Is 42.1). God's words here fix one of the poles of Matthew's Christology: Son of God in some unique sense. The other is *man*: implicit in both *Son of David* and *Son of man*. In a sense the whole Gospel elaborates the unique sense in which Jesus is both. I shall consider this in dealing the title *Son of man*.

The allusion to the Servant suggests from the outset the sense in which Jesus is both Son of God and Son of David or the Christ. The importance of the allusion can be sensed only if the reader goes beyond the fragmentary symbolic element expressed in these few words to the whole figure of the Suffering Servant. Unique in his role is the expiatory value of his vicarious suffering[22].

Six minor texts contain the title in a variety of ways. In the temptations, the devil seems not so much to know that Jesus is Son of God, as to be probing: "If you are the Son of God..." (4.3, 6). At Gadara the two demoniacs seem to know that he is the Son of God (8.29). On Golgotha the title is used in mockery (27.40, 43) and then seriously by the awe-struck soldiers (27.54).

Four texts, besides the Father's words at the baptism, are of major importance. After Jesus had rescued the sinking Peter and the wind had ceased, the disciples in the boat "...worshiped him, saying, 'Truly you are the Son of God'" (14.33): in a situation in which according to Mark they "...were utterly astounded, for they did not understand about the loaves...." (Mk 6.51-52), Matthew attributes to them a full profession of faith[23]. The

---

[21] Jack Dean Kingsbury, in his *Matthew: Structure, Christology, Kingdom* (Philadelphia: Fortress, 1975) maintains that *Son of God* is the central title in Matthew's Christology. It was in part to contest that thesis, and to affirm the equal importance of the title *Son of Man* that Meier wrote the work which I have been citing (cf. p. 1 of that work). Meier, I believe, restores the balance.

[22] In the dialectic of titles, the tension of the interplay in which the sense in which all may be applied to Jesus, it is important, then, to consider the suggestive power of the Servant as he is portrayed in the four Servant Songs. Commentators differ on the portions of Second Isaiah which constitute these songs. JB indicates them thus: 42.1-9; 49.1-6; 50.4-11; 52.13–53.12.

[23] This is one of Matthew's characteristic changes of Mark's version: he attributes considerable understanding and some degree of faith to the disciples.

second text, Peter's profession of faith (16.16) we have already considered; so too the fourth: the high priest's solemn question and Jesus' answer (26.63). The remaining text is Matthew's account of the transfiguration: the Father's words are a repetition of those at the baptism, with the addition, "... listen to him" (17.5).

(g) Son of man. This title is unique in many ways. First, it is used in the Gospel only by Jesus, speaking of himself. In only one text of the New Testament is it used by another: Stephen tells of his vision of the Son of man standing in glory at the right hand of God (Acts 7.56 with allusion the text of Dn 7.13-14). Second, though it has a transcendent sense in Dn 7.13-14, of itself it means simply *man*, or *individual man*. It is, then, utterly simple itself. From this utterly insignificant word Jesus fashions a complex symbol by which he expresses much of his own mystery. Though *man* or *the man* would be the normal translation, the rendering *Son of man* alerts us to its unexpected fulness of meaning. Finally, in so far as the mystery of Jesus is revealed by the use of titles, it is this one which plays the most important role. Jesus is the Son of God. He is the man. In the dialectic in which his mystery is gradually revealed, *Son of God* and *Son of man* play the most important parts. What kind of Son of God is he? What kind of man? What kind of Son of David, and what sort of messianic figure is he? All that bears on the mystery of the unique way in which he is man is taken up into the meaning of *Son of man*, and gradually from the dialectic of *Son of God* and *Son of man* we are given the single complex answer to the question: "Who is he?"

Aspects of the meaning of *Son of man* are classified differently by commentators and biblical theologians. I suggest a threefold division, the first of which holds the paradox of two sharply contrasted sets of characteristics: the Son of man in his life on earth; the climax of his suffering, death, and resurrection; and his future coming in glory.

First, then, in his life on earth, the Son of man is both lowly, humble, and powerful, supremely great. (a) He is poor (8.20), rejected (11.19); he came to serve (20.28). Perhaps for this

---

This is consistent with his theology: Jesus is revealed as the Messiah of the Old Testament; the disciples recognize him as such; the Jews should have. Instead, they reject him in unbelief and hostility, and therefore the kingdom of God will be taken away from them and given to a nation producing its fruits (cf. 21.40-43).

reason Jesus contrasts the gravity of a word against the Son of man and speaking against the Holy Spirit (12.32). (b) He has power to forgive sins (9.6); he is lord of the šabbath (12.8), greater than Jonah or Solomon (12.40-42); he is the Sower and the King in the parable (13.37-43); He is the Christ: it is his question which draws forth Peter's profession of faith (16.13-20); finally, in a variant reading, he came to save the lost (18.11).

Second, with increasing detail, Jesus predicts his delivery into the hands of the chief priests and the scribes, his condemnation, suffering, death, and being raised from the dead. Three solemn predictions stand out: 16.21 (in a context in which Jesus has been speaking of the Son of man: 16.13), 17.22-23, and 20.18-19. To these we may add other partial predictions: 12.40; 17.9; 17.12; 26.2, 24, 45. Finally he explains the purpose: he came to give his life as a ransom for many (20.28).

Third, he will come again in power and glory, suddenly at an unexpected moment, to judge and repay every man for what he has done: 10.23; 13.41; 16.27, 28; 19.28 (cf. 25.31-46); 24.27, 30; 26.64.

(h) Finally, the Son. Three times Jesus speaks of himself simply as the Son. The simplicity of the term is disarming and may be deceptive: for it is charged with all of the meaning which gradually is developed in the dialectic of all the titles, and in the rest of the Gospel narrative and discourses in which Jesus reveals how the promise is fulfilled in himself, and how it may be fulfilled in us if we live according to the project of life which he gradually sets forth.

(3) *Gradual revelation in narrative and discourse.* Without attempting to trace a commentary through the major divisions of the Gospel[24], I shall indicate elements of the revelation of fulfillment in Jesus as Matthew sets them forth both in the narrative of Jesus' actions and words and in the major discourses in which he presents much of Jesus' teaching.

(a) The reign of God. At the outset both John (3.2; cf. 3.7-12) and Jesus call for repentance and proclaim that the kingdom of heaven [God] is at hand (4.17). *Kingdom* (βασιλεία) may be either the *reign* or the *realm*. Usually the context suggests the prior meaning. In a great variety of ways Jesus demonstrates

---

[24] The division into five books, each with a narrative section and a discourse, is not without its difficulties, as McKenzie notes, *op. cit.*, 16, p. 66; yet he adopts it.

what he has proclaimed: in *him* God is present and demonstrating his power.

Jesus has power over the devil/Satan, as he shows in his triple rebuff in the temptations (4.1-11) and his exorcisms (8.16-17, 28-34). He has a singular power of drawing men to follow him and become his disciples, leaving all they had, taking up a new way of life utterly unknown (4.18-22; 9.9-13).

He is the law-giver: new and greater Moses, with authority to bring the Law to a new perfection, to fulfill it (5-7, esp. 5.17-20; 7.24-29). We shall consider details of this fulfillment when we consider fulfillment in us: for the Law, the new, perfect Law, is a charter for the way of life in which we come to fulfillment, and the promise is fulfilled in us.

He has power over disease, regarded somehow as the effect of sin, and the range of diseases which he cures symbolizes the range of his power: the leper (8.1-4), the centurion's slave (8.5-13: making clear the centurion's faith in Jesus' power, authority), Peter's mother-in-law (8.14-15), the numerous healings at evening (8.16-17), the blind and dumb (9.27-31, 32-34). His many healings fulfill Isaiah's prophecy concerning the Servant (12.15-21: Is 42.1-4)[25].

He demonstrates his power over nature (8.23-27, in which Matthew gives a characterisitic apocalyptic touch, changing Mark's fierce gust of wind to an earthquake; 14.22-32) and over death, raising to life by a word (9.18-26). He performs the wonder of multiplying loaves and fishes to feed the multitude (14.13-21).

Going beyond all wonder-working, Jesus forgives sins. When his word of forgiveness provokes the charge of blasphemy, he demonstrates by a healing that the Son of man has authority on earth to forgive sins; and the crowds marveled and glorified God, who had given such authority/power to men (9.1-8).

Finally, he can and does delegate power, giving to his twelve disciples "... authority over unclean spirits, to cast them out, and to heal every disease and every infirmity" (10.1).

(b) Repeated confrontation with the religious leaders of the Jews. Jesus pronounces the doom of the cities of Galilee, whose unbelief and rejection set the pattern of almost universal rejection by his people (11.20-24). Taking the challenge of the Pharisees in controversies over the sabbath, Jesus rejects their narrow

---

[25] See also 14.34-36; 15.29-31; 17.14-21; 20.29-34; 21.14.

interpretation, declares that he is lord of the sabbath, and thus provokes the Pharisees' plot to destroy him (12.1-14).

Accused of healing by the power of Beelzebul, Jesus forces the Pharisees to face the consequences of the alternative: that it is by the Spirit of God that he casts out demons, and he goes on pointedly to affirm the deadliness of blasphemy against the Spirit. If they are guilty of this, they are beyond forgiveness, for they reject the only source of forgiveness and of repentance: attributing the work of the Holy Spirit to the devil, they leave no opening for the action of the only Spirit which could heal them (cf. 12.22-32).

To their demand for a sign, Jesus replies with a ringing denunciation of their evil and adulterous generation (12.38-45): they are adulterous in the full sense of the biblical image: unfaithful to the God to whom in their self-righteousness they profess to be models of fidelity.

Though the scandal of the Nazarenes is not another example of confrontation with the religious leaders, it symbolizes the complementary rejection by his people, and in its most acute form it exposes the root of their trouble: they *know* him, they know all about him. Where does he get all this? How can there be anything special about him? (cf. 13.53-58). They are locked in unbelief.

To the Pharisees' and scribes' criticism of Jesus' disciples' neglecting prescribed ritual purification, Jesus replies with a denunciation of their hypocrisy, tells his disciples to let them alone as blind guides, and teaches what it is that really defiles a man (15.1-20): he rejects the authority of the Pharisees. Again he warns against the leaven (the teaching) of the "Pharisees and Sadducees"[26] (16.5-12). Challenged by the chief priests and elders about his authority, he reduces them to silence with a question about John's baptism, and goes on to accuse them of failure to repent and believe (21.23-32). By his parable of the householder and his vineyard, Jesus draws from the chief priests

---

[26] MEIER, *op. cit.*, p. 20, seizes upon Matthew's linking of Pharisees and Sadducees here as one of two instances which he alleges as proof that Matthew was ignorant of the doctrinal differences between them. This is one of his "precise arguments" to prove that Matthew was not a Jew: no Jew could have made such a blunder. As I have said, I find his argument unconvincing. It rests on syntactical evidence. It could be a slip in syntax: Matthew too can nod. It may not even be a slip, and still not be damning evidence, any more than a warning which one is apt to hear these days against "Capitalism and Communism": it does not confuse them, but regards both as wrong, each in its own way.

and the Pharisees an answer which occasions his affirmation of
the punishment which awaits them, and the transfer of the
kingdom of God to another nation. Stung, they tried to arrest
him, but could not for fear of the multitudes, who held him to be
a prophet (21.33-46). When in turn Pharisees and Sadducees
tried to entangle him, they were reduced to silence by his replies
(22.15-40). Then Jesus in his turn confounded them with his
question about the Christ as Son of David, and from then on no
one dared question him further (22.41-46).

Finally Jesus pronounces seven "Woes" on the scribes and
Pharisees, hypocrites. They are as severe as any condemnation in
the whole Bible: far more severe than the prophets' denunciations
of cities and peoples in the Old Testament, for these are hurled at
the scribes and Pharisees face to face. They are the final ringing
denunciation and rejection of their religious leadership, and a
pronouncement of the punishment which they have brought upon
themselves (23.13-36). In one of the few passages in which
Matthew does not play down Jesus' emotion, he records Jesus'
deeply sorrowful lament over Jerusalem: her sins, his frustrated
desire to embrace her fondly, and her punishment (23.37-39: cf.
Lk 13.34-35).

When we reflect on Matthew's account of the crescendo of
Jesus' confrontation with the religious leaders of the Jews, his
absolute rejection of their authority and his condemnation of
them, and the account of his final confrontation in the "trial",
their final rejection and condemnation of him appears inevitable.
As it had to happen according to the Scriptures, so too humanly
speaking it had to happen: this was the inexorable conclusion. I
shall not recount the final events, for we have considered them
above in treating the title *Christ* (pp. 25-26).

(c) Fulfillment in the passion, death, and resurrection. In
Matthew's Gospel the complex event, passion, death, and
resurrection, is presented as eschatological and apocalyptic: the final
fulfillment which completes the great reversal of all Jewish
expectations[27]. One can distinguish three characteristics of
Matthew's presentation of this fulfillment. First, the eschatological
discourse itself (24.1—25.26)[28] functions as a sort of prelude to

---

[27] See Meier's treatment of "The Turning Point of the Ages", *op. cit.*, pp.
179-219. For an indication of the prominence of apocalyptic themes and
eschatology in his interpretation of *Matthew*, see these terms in his topical index,
pp. 265, 266. Though it seems to me that he tends at times to overplay his
thesis, his insights into the Gospel are stimulating.

[28] 24.1-44 corresponds roughly to Mk 13.1-37 (with Mt 10.17-22
matching Mk 13.9-12). Mt 24.45 – 25.46 expands the account beyond Mk.

Matthew's presentation of the passion, death, and resurrection. Second, running through the account there is a generalization of the sense in which Scripture is being fulfilled. Finally, Matthew's account adds many eschatological-apocalyptic touches which contribute to his presentation of the complex event as the turning point of the ages.

According to Meier, Matthew distinguishes the two strands in the eschatological discourse: the destruction of Jerusalem and the signs of the parousia of Jesus. Yet in the manner of prophetic and apocalyptic writers, he colors what for him is past event (since in this interpretation Matthew wrote after the destruction of Jerusalem) with eschatological and apocalyptic touches. The compenetration of the two makes the historical event itself symbolic of the apocalyptic [29]. The distinction of elements would be made as follows: the destruction of Jerusalem (24.15-22); the period before the parousia (24.23-28); the parousia (24.29-31); and perhaps Jesus' appearance after the resurrection as a "proleptic parousia" (Meier), "... an event which anticipates the parousia and moves closer to it" (McKenzie) [30] (24.29-31).

In speaking of his suffering and death at the last supper and at the moment of his betrayal and arrest, Jesus generalizes his references to the coming events as a fulfillment of the Scriptures: "The Son of man goes as it is written of him...." (26.24); "... but how then should the scriptures be fulfilled, that it must be so?" (26.54); "... But all this has taken place, that the scriptures of the prophets might be fulfilled...." (26.56). The implication seems to be that now there is question not of the fulfillment of a particular text by the indication of its deeper meaning, but of the fulfillment of the whole of Scripture, whose deeper meaning is shown in this culmination of Jesus' revelation and realization of God's plan.

---

[29] On this blurring of historical events and eschatology, see McKenzie, *op. cit.*, 164, p. 104. "... The point is that man in history lives under an eschatological judgment, which means a final judgment. In particular events, such as the fall of Jerusalem, the judgment seems to break into history. When it does, it reminds man of his eschatological destiny; and he is warned in terms such as those used in Mt 25 that the judgment is to be awaited with unremitting vigilance. There is a sense in which the eschatological judgment can and must always be conceived as 'near'; for there is no one to whom it is irrelevant." It is my impression, both here and in his treatment of the concept of fulfillment, that Meier—perhaps not consciously—is more indebted to McKenzie than he acknowledges in his few relatively insignificant citations of McKenzie's commentary.

[30] See Meier, *op. cit.*, pp. 167-168; McKenzie, *op. cit.*, 170, p. 105.

Finally, what are the eschatological-apocalyptic touches which deepen the sense of Matthew's account of the death and resurrection?

First, compare Mark and Matthew in their accounts of what followed immediately upon the death of Jesus:

> And the curtain of the temple was torn in two, from top to bottom. And when the centurion, who stood facing him, saw that he thus breathed his last, he said, "Truly this man as the Son of God!" (Mk 15.38-39).

> And behold, the curtain of the temple was torn in two, from top to bottom; and the earth shook, and the rocks were split; the tombs also were opened, and many bodies of the saints who had fallen asleep were raised, and coming out of the tombs after his resurrection they went into the holy city and appeared to many. When the centurion and those who were with him, keeping watch over Jesus, saw the earthquake and what took place, they were filled with awe, and said, "Truly this was the Son of God!" (Mt 27.51-54).

Second, compare Mark and Matthew in their accounts of the opened tomb:

> And looking up, they saw that the stone was rolled back; ... and entering the tomb, they saw a young man sitting on the right side, dressed in a white robe; and they were amazed (Mk 16.4-5).

> And behold, there was a great earthquake; for an angel of the Lord descended from heaven and came and rolled back the stone, and sat upon it. His appearence was like lightning, and his raiment white as snow. And for fear of him the guards trembled and became like dead men. But the angel said to the women, ... (Mt 28.2-5).

Matthew's apocalyptic coloring of both events is evident.

Finally, in Jesus' appearance to the eleven in Galilee, the only apparition registered by Matthew except for that to the two women, "... Jesus came and said to them, 'All authority in heaven and on earth has been given to me. Go therefore and make disciples of all nations, baptizing them in the name of the Father and of the Son and of the Holy Spirit, teaching them to observe all that I have commanded you; and lo, I am with you always, to the close of the age' " (Mt 28.18-20).

Meier brings out the significance of this conclusion of *Matthew* by contrast with that of *Luke*. Luke has a number of appearances to various disciples, through forty days, and then an ascension, "... a sort of parousia written backward...." Matthew has only one appearance to the eleven, and no ascension. Rather, Jesus comes to his church in a sort of "proleptic parousia". Whereas during his life Jesus had power, authority (ἐξουσία), now *all power* is given to him, and with that power he commands them to go and make disciples of *all* nations, baptizing them in the name of the Father and of the Son and of the Holy Spirit (without suggestion of any distinction in dignity and power), and teaching them to observe all that *he* has commanded. And *he* is with them always, to the close of the age [31].

In treating the theme of fulfillment in Jesus, I have not considered an extremely important portion of the whole Gospel: his gradual formation of his church. My reason was simply that I have chosen to deal with this under the theme of fulfillment in us. Obviously this closing revelation and command mark not only the fulfillment of the promise in Jesus (with the exception of the still future coming in glory, which I shall consider under the heading of further promise), but also that of the constitution of his church, the New Israel (though Matthew never writes of it in those words). Both the exaltation of Jesus and the universal mission to the whole of the church to be constituted from all nations, complete Matthew's great reversal, his account of the transcendent fulfillment.

(d) "Fulfill all righteousness." In my treatment of the fulfillment texts (above, pp. 132-137) I indicated two texts which I have not discussed thus far: 3.15 (fulfill all righteousness) and 5.17 (Jesus' fulfilling the law and the prophets). I intend to deal with the latter in the next section, concerning fulfillment in us. The former remains as one important bit of unfinished business regarding Jesus' (and John's) fulfilling all righteousness through the baptism of Jesus. What is the meaning of Jesus' reply to John's attempt to prevent Jesus' submitting to John's baptism: "... Let it be so now; for thus it is fitting for us to fulfill all righteousness..." (3.15)? It seems to me that only when we have

---

[31] For Meier's treatment of the apocalyptic coloring of the death and resurrection, see *op. cit.*, pp. 32-39, 208. For the implications of this complex apocalyptic event in relation to the law, see pp. 229-234. Compare McKenzie's comment on 24.30 (the parousia): " ... The coming of the Son of Man as Mt conceived it could easily be the establishment of the community of the Risen Son of Man as the new Israel after the destruction of the old Israel. This is not identical with the eschatological parousia, but it is an event that anticipates the parousia and moves closer to it" (*op. cit.*, 170, p. 105).

pondered the whole of Matthew's Gospel may we have hope of answering the question in a way which the tenor of that Gospel itself suggests.

To situate what I propose here it seems to me to be helpful to recall briefly what we have considered thus far regarding fulfillment of the promise in Jesus in the Gospel of Matthew. First, Matthew's prologue-overture announced major Christological themes (above, pp. 137-139). Second, the dialectic of titles brought out some of the tension of the developing response to the question who Jesus really is. In a sense one could say that the central question is this: Is he the Messiah, and if so, what sort of Messiah can he be affirmed to be in the light of Christian revelation? Two elements of the reply go beyond any judaic expectation: he is the Son of God in a transcendent sense, revealing in himself the presence and operation of divine power and authority; he is to suffer, to give his life as a ransom for many, to expiate for sin by his suffering. As far as the development of the conception of the Christian Messiah is indicated in the interplay of titles, the principal roles are played by the titles Son of God and Son of Man. Third, Jesus is gradually revealed in narrative and discourse.

Our present question is simple: in what sense did Jesus and John contribute to fulfilling all righteousness in Jesus' baptism? We find a hint within the narrative of the baptism, in the words [of the Father] spoken from heaven: "This is my beloved Son, *with whom I am well pleased"* (3.17: cf. Mk 1.11; Lk 3.22). The allusion in the clause which I have italicized is to the Servant of Yahweh (Is 42.1)[32]. It introduces what I consider the most powerful symbolic element at play in the whole Gospel: the total figure of the Servant. Note well that I am not referring to the power of Matthew's symbolism: he merely quotes fragments or alludes to the Servant Songs. The power is in the symbolism portraying the unique figure of the Servant: Matthew simply serves to bring us back to that Old Testament symbolism, and to

---

[32] With regard to this and other allusions to or quotations of the Old Testament, there is a critical problem concerning the text quoted or alluded to by Matthew (and by the other evangelists). At times quotations correspond to the Massoretic Hebrew text, at times to the Septuagint, at times to one or more other versions. Many scholars suppose that the explanation is not attributable entirely if at all to quotation from memory, but rather to use of some handbook of quotations used in the early Church. See McKenzie, *op. cit.*, 8, p. 64; compare Fitzmyer, *The Gospel According to Luke* (I-IX), p. 486.

suggest subtly that the total figure of the Servant is the type which is fulfilled and transcended in Jesus as antitype.

I shall proceed as follows. First I shall indicate Matthew's allusions to or quotations from the Servant Songs. Second, I shall point out complementary Old Testament figures who are somehow similar to the Servant. Third, I shall point out aspects of Jesus and of his work which complement Matthew's presentation of him as a transcendent Servant. Finally I shall formulate my answer to the question: in what sense does Jesus fulfill all righteousness?

First, Matthew has four allusions to or quotations from the Servant Songs. The first is in the Father's words at the baptism (3.17). There is the most fleeting allusion to the Servant in these words. They suffice, however, to remind us of the Servant; and they suggest the first indication of the sense in which Jesus in his submission to baptism is beginning the fulfillment of all righteousness. In the context the Father's words are a response of pleasure and praise for the abasement to which Jesus has submitted: accepting the humiliation of a baptism of repentance for sin, though he is sinless, and from the outset of his public life suggesting the kind of righteousness which he himself exemplifies and to which he will call his disciples.

Parallel and somewhat expanded are the words at the transfiguration: "This is my beloved Son, with whom I am well pleased; listen to him" (17.5). Consider the context in *Matthew*. In answer to Jesus' question, "But who do you say that I am?" Peter replied, "You are the Christ, the Son of the living God" (16.15-16)[33]. Having ordered his disciples to tell no one that he was the Christ, Jesus began to tell them what he must suffer, to teach them what following him involved, and to tell them of him own future coming in glory. At this point Matthew tells of the transfiguration, which gives them at once a vision of the future glory of Jesus, a further inkling of the kind of Messiah he is (God's Servant), and a command: "Listen to him." The whole event, embracing glorious transfiguration and the words from the cloud, is a powerful complex intuitive symbol whose full meaning cannot be spelled out in flat propositions. Surely part of the meaning is this: the disciples—and we—are to contemplate the glorious Jesus with a sense of his transcendent dignity, and ponder the Father's words which complement the vision. He is the Servant: in him, glorious as he is at this moment and as he

---

[33] Above, p. 141.

will appear in his coming, we are to ponder the meaning of his
being the Servant, and *listen* to him as he continues to tell us
more of his own mystery and of our discipleship. Contemplate
him, and listen to him: he is the exemplar of righteousness; he is
our law-giver and teacher.

After telling briefly of some of Jesus' healings and deliverance
from demons, Matthew introduces one of his formal fulfillment
texts: "This was to fulfill what spoken by the prophet Isaiah, 'He
took our infirmities and bore our diseases'" (8.17: Is 53.4). The
text is from the fourth Servant Song, quoted according to the
sense of the Hebrew text, with a shift in meaning: the Servant has
borne our griefs and carried our sorrows in his vicarious suffering;
Jesus took our infirmities and bore our diseases by healing,
delivering from them[34]. Yet the symbolism of Jesus' healings
and exorcisms suggests the deeper meaning of his own vicarious
suffering in fulfillment of the prophetic role of the Servant. Once
again, the power lies not in Matthew's words but in the full
symbol of the Servant, and in the Christian insight into Jesus as
the transcendent fulfillment of that figure.

Matthew's fourth Servant text is another formal fulfillment
text, after Jesus' healings and his command not to make him
known. "This was to fulfill what was spoken by the prophet
Isaiah:

> 'Behold, my servant whom I have chosen,
>   my beloved with whom my soul is well pleased.
> I will put my Spirit upon him,
>   and he shall proclaim justice to the Gentiles.
> He will not wrangle or cry aloud,
>   nor will anyone hear his voice in the streets;
> he will not break a bruised reed
>   or quench a smoldering wick,
> till he brings justice to victory;
>   and in his name the Gentiles will hope'" (12.17-21: Is
>   42.1-4).

I shall consider details of this text along with other elements of
the Servant Songs in offering my answer to the question
concerning Jesus' fulfilling all righteousness.

Second, besides the references to the Servant, Matthew
alludes to two other Old Testament figures who somehow
resemble the Servant, and in whom the early Church finds types

---

[34] See McKenzie, *op. cit.*, 58, p. 77.

fulfilled in Jesus. When John sent his disciples to ask Jesus whether he was "he who is to come" [the Christ/Messiah], Jesus answered by citing his works: "Go and tell John what you hear and see: *the blind receive their sight* and the lame walk, lepers are cleansed and *the deaf hear*, and the dead are raised up, and *the poor have the good news preached to them.* And blessed is he who takes no offense at me" (11.4-6). I have italicized fragmentary quotations of Isaiah, the first and second from Is 29.18-19; 35.5-6; 42.16-18; the third from Is 61.1 (cf. the more complete quotation of Is 61.1-2 in Lk 4.17-21). Two elements may be distinguished in these citations: the figure in Is 61: anointed by the Lord and given his Spirit; and the promised blessings which Jesus is conferring, and which he cites as signs that he is indeed the one to come, the Messiah. The figure in Is 61 suggests the Servant and his works. The second figure is the Psalmist, the innocent sufferer in Ps 22. Details of his suffering are quoted in Matthew's account of Jesus' crucifixion: 27.35 (Ps 22.18), 39 (Ps 22.7), 43 (Ps 22.18 and also the innocent suffering just man in Wis 2.18-20). Jesus' cry, "Eli, Eli, lama sabachthani?" ("My God, my God, why hast thou forsaken me?": Mt 27.46) is not a cry of utter desolation, but rather a citation of the prophetic psalm which is being fulfilled in him. The latter part of the psalm, expressing confidence in deliverance and praise of the Lord who will deliver him (vv. 19-31), surely is not prophetic of resurrection according to the sense of the psalmist himself. Yet it too, with the deeper meaning which it takes on in the light of Christian revelation, vaguely prefigures Christ's resurrection and glorification.

Both the complementary figures and the blessings promised in the texts of Isaiah have a bearing on Jesus and his response to John. He is like the Servant and the anointed one of Is 61 and the innocent sufferer of Psalm 22; and his works bring blessings which reveal in what sense he is the saving Messiah. Hence he adds in his reply to John's disciples: "And blessed is he who takes no offense at me" (11.6): blessed is he who is not scandalized at my being *this kind* of Messiah.

Third, Matthew presents, in words attributed to Jesus, aspects of Jesus' character and saving action which complement allusions to him as the Servant. Jesus is gentle, lowly, giving solace to the weary (11.28-30). He came not to be served, but to serve, and to give his life as a ransom for many (20.28). He suggests that he will share the lot of the prophets put to death by his people (23.29-27).   He offers his blood as the blood of the covenant, poured out for many for the forgiveness of sins (26.28).

Finally, in the context of *Matthew*, in what sense does Jesus fulfill all righteousness? His statement in 3.17, "... thus it is fitting for us to fulfill all righteousness", is the announcement of a theme, the beginning of a process which, regarded in terms of Jesus' human action, will come to its term only as he offers himself and freely accepts his death. It is only for a moment here at the baptism that John is included, in so far as he participates in this initial act of the public life of Jesus. From here on we must contemplate Jesus and gradually gather the sense in which he is fulfilling all righteousness. The total process involves a twofold fulfillment: in Jesus himself, and in others. In himself he gradually reveals a righteousness foreshadowed in the Old Testament principally in the figure of the Servant, and transcended in Jesus' personal realization of an ideal vaguely suggested by that most beautiful figure of the Old Testament. In others he fulfills all righteousness in so far as his personal example and his law-giving and teaching gradually reveal a way of life, a righteousness which surpasses that of the Scribes and Pharisees. By his personal example he shows what discipleship means. By his bringing the Law to the perfection of which it was only a remote preparation, he proposes the project of the Christian way, the way in which all of his disciples to the end of time must walk, to realize in themselves the fulfillment of the promise. Obviously I am linking here Jesus' fulfilling all righteousness in himself and his bringing the Law to fulfillment or perfection. As I have said, I regard the latter function as pertaining more properly to the theme of fulfillment in us, and I shall treat it in the next major section of this chapter. Here let us concentrate on Jesus.

In all that he is and does Jesus is the fulfillment of the whole of the Scriptures. If we are to look within the Gospel according to Matthew for indications of how he fulfilled all of the Law and the prophets, I should say that the most powerful Old Testament symbolism suggesting the answer is that of the Servant Songs, along with other elements of the prophetic life and vision of an ideal of righteousness. I say "prophetic life", to allow for the influence of the prophets themselves, principally Jeremiah [35], who

---

[35] Quite probably it is the example of Jeremiah which inspired—taking "inspired" in a broad sense which would include human literary inspiration—Psalm 22. Moreover, significantly Jeremiah is one of the suffering prophets with whom some of the people identify Jesus (16.14). Curiously too,

somehow foreshadowed Jesus in his revelation of God and in the
suffering which he bore as a consequence. His suffering was
more than a consequence: it is precisely in his passion and death,
freely and lovingly embraced, that he comes to the full realization
and revelation of the righteousness which he was to fulfill.

As I have maintained, though Matthew's quotations of and
allusions to the Servant songs are few and fragmentary, they
suffice to call to mind the whole series of songs, and the
extraordinary figure of the Servant which they image. This, to
my mind, is the single most powerful intuitive symbolism at work
in the text of Matthew, and the key to the answer to our question.
Our task, then, is to recall the full symbol constituted by the four
songs, to contemplate the Servant, and then to indicate the
transcendent fulfillment of this prophetic figure in Jesus.

There is no substitute here for the full text of the songs. I
shall not quote them in full: I must presuppose, as my continual
multiple citation of the Bible indicates, that you have the Bible at
hand and are disposed to pause to ponder the songs[36]. I shall
thematize what seem to me to be significant elements of the
songs and the figure of the Servant: I do so only in the hope that
this may help to hold some of the aspects which stand out not
only in the Servant, but also in the eventual transcendent
fulfillment in Jesus. Like most—perhaps all—of my eventual
readers, I must depend here on peering through the veils of
translations. No truly poetic symbolism can be translated, and
only appreciative reading of the Hebrew text—to the extent to
which that is accessible in the present state of the text—could
yield a reasonably grasp of the meaning. I shall indicate what
seem to me to be first characteristics of the Servant, and then
aspects of his mission.

The Servant is *righteous* (53.11), called in righteousness
(42.6). He has God's Spirit (42.1). God delights in him (42.1)
and honors him (49.5). Outstanding among his qualities are his
gentleness and tender considerateness (42.2-3), his strength
(49.2; 50.7), his perseverance (42.4). Taught by God (50.4), he is
docile (50.5) and trusting (50.7-9). Truly it is in the Servant

---

the fulfillment text in 27.9 is attributed to Jeremiah, though in fact it is from
Zechariah. For a brief account of the critical problems concerning the text, and
the element of association with Jeremiah, see McKenzie, *op. cit.*, 193, p. 111.

[36] Once again, for convenience, the songs as indicated by the editors of JB
are Is 42.1-9; 49.1-6; 50,4-11; 52.13-53.12. Exegetes and
commentators differ in this regard as in most, recognizing more or fewer verses
as pertaining to the individual songs.

himself and his works that God is declaring new things, telling us of them before they spring forth (cf. 42.9).

What is his mission? He will bring forth justice to the nations (42.1), establish justice in the earth (42.4)[37]. He will be a covenant to the people (42.6; 49.8; [49.6 LXX]), a light to the nations (42.6; 49.6). He is to open the eyes that are blind, to bring out the prisoners from the dungeon, from the prison those who sit in darkness (42.7). He will bring Israel back to the Lord, raise up the tribes of Jacob, restore the preserved of Israel (49.5-6). As light to the nations he will bring the Lord's salvation to the end of earth (49.6).

He will suffer. He will sense that he has labored in vain (49.4). Despised, abhorred (49.7), he gives his back to the smiters, his cheeks to whose who pull out the beard, and does not hide his face from shame and spitting (50.6). In his suffering his appearance was marred beyond human semblance, and his form beyond that of the sons of men (52.14). He "... had no form or comeliness that we should look at him, and no beauty that we should desire him. He was despised and rejected by men; a man of sorrows, and acquainted with grief; and as one from whom men hide their faces he was despised, and we esteemed him not...." (53.2-3). Yet men will recognize that he has suffered for them: "Surely he has borne our griefs and carried our sorrows; yet we esteemed him stricken, smitten by God, and afflicted. But he was wounded for our transgression, he was bruised for our iniquities; and upon him was the chastisement that made us whole, and with his stripes we are healed. All we like sheep have gone astray; we have turned every one to his own way; and the LORD has laid on him the iniquity of us all. He was oppressed, and he was afflicted, yet he opened not his mouth; like a lamb that is led to the slaughter, and like a sheep that before its shearers is dumb, so he opened not his mouth.... And they made his grave with the wicked and with a rich man in his death, although he had done no violence, and there was no deceit in his

---

[37] Both in the Hebrew Old Testament and in Greek versions, and in the New Testament as well, there is a complicated and developing interplay of the notions of judgment, justice, and righteousness. For a survey of the meanings, see JOHN L. McKENZIE, *Dictionary of the Bible* (Milwaukee: Bruce, c. 1965): *judgment*, pp. 465-466; and *righteous, righteousness*, pp. 739-743. In Matthew's translation of Is 42.1,4, the word is κρίσις, which basically means *judgment, righteous judgment*, but comes to mean also *righteousness*, and is recognized as having this meaning in Is 42.1,4 and Mt 12.18,20. See BAG, κρίσις. For further indications of the interplay of judgment, justice, and righteousness see BAG on δίκαιος and δικαιοσύνη.

mouth.... he bore the sin of many, and made intercession for the
transgressors'' (53.4-7, 9, 12).

God will exalt and reward him. Even while he senses
frustration, he knows that his right is with the Lord, his
recompense with his God (49.4). He knows his mission to restore
Israel and bring salvation to the end of the earth (cf. 49.5-6). He
is assured by the Lord, even as he is despised and abhorred, that
eventually "Kings shall see and arise; princes, and they shall
prostrate themselves; because of the LORD, who is faithful, the
Holy One of Israel, who has chosen you" (49.7). The Lord will
answer him, help him in the day of salvation, give him as a
covenant to the people, make him the instrument of his salvation
(cf. 49.8-11). He shall prosper: "... he shall see the fruit of the
travail of his soul and be satisfied; by his knowledge shall the
righteous one, my servant, make many to be accounted
righteous.... I will divide with him a portion with the great...."
(53.11-12).

How, then, does Jesus fulfill all righteousness? The principal
answer, in my judgment, is this: both in his own personal
righteousness and in his teaching and bringing the Law to its
perfection, he realizes and reveals a righteousness which is utterly
new, a transcendent fulfillment of the character and mission of the
Servant. The Servant, in the Old Testament, is a prophetic figure
which surpasses all other Old Testament understanding and
realization of righteousness. He is portrayed in Songs which are
beautiful, powerful intuitive symbols. Matthew's fleeting
quotations and allusions suffice to evoke the whole complex
symbol, and to suggest it as a key to the answer to our question.
There is no *logic* of such symbols. There is a deep, vaguely
sensed isomorphism of the imaged figure of the Servant and
Jesus, the transcendent fulfillment which goes far beyond what
the prophet understood, and which reveals the deeper, richer
meaning of the Songs. In my judgment, Matthew illustrates a
Christian reading of the Songs, and the symbolism of the Servant
is a powerful catalyst in Matthew's development of the answer to
the question who and what Jesus really is. Beyond Matthew's
own grasp and symbolizing, the Church, pondering the full New
Testament revelation which illumines the whole Bible, senses the
deeper meaning of Matthew. When we celebrate the liturgy of
Holy Week, from Palm Sunday through Good Friday, we read or
hear all of the Servant Songs, portions of Psalm 22 (21), and a bit
of Is 61, and as we worship we *know* that the Church is reading
the deeper meaning of these texts.

Fulfillment of the promise in Jesus, therefore, is set forth by Matthew in the interplay of three principal elements of his Gospel: the dialetic of titles, the gradual revelation in narrative and teaching, and the subtle but powerful transcendent fulfillment of the prophetic figure of the Servant.

FULFILLMENT IN US

At the outset of chapter IV (p. 121), I made some distinctions: first between fulfillment in Jesus and fulfillment in us; then, regarding the latter, between project (proposed in the Gospels) and realization (in part in the Gospels, and further in post-Pentecostal Christian experience). What we shall consider now in the Gospel according to Matthew pertains almost entirely to the project of fulfillment. Matthew traces the gradual revelation of the Christian way, the deeper, richer righteousness, in which we are to come to fulfillment. The Gospel narrative surely records some beginnings of realization of that richer life. Yet in a sense one could say that there is only one event which marks a true fulfillment, and it comes at the very end of the Gospel, after the Resurrection, after the great "eschatological" event, the "turning of the ages". In Matthew 28.18-20 the Risen Jesus *does* what he promised to do and began to do during the course of his public life: with *all* authority he commissions his apostles. Within the frame of Matthew's theology, Jesus establishes his Church.

For the rest, we have Matthew's witness to a fulfillment in us which is now fully revealed, but not yet realized. Still his account is written from within life in a post-Resurrection Christian community. As his account of fulfillment in Jesus is given from within a life of faith in community, in terms of an early Christology, so too his account of the project of fulfillment in us is written from within early Christian experience of a degree of that fulfillment. Consistently with my concern here to hold to Matthew's thought, I have written above of a "post-Resurrection" Christian community, not of "post-Pentecostal Christian experience". I used the latter expression when I drew the distinction regarding New Testament witness as a whole. The simple fact is that Matthew does not refer to Pentecost, and is amazingly sparing in his mention of the role of the Holy Spirit in our fulfillment. We consider Matthew's witness: one of the many complementary witnesses given in the whole of the New Testament, and held in unity in the faith of the Christian community through the centuries.

First, in the prologue two names and a title bear on our theme. The child conceived of the Holy Spirit and born of Mary is to be called *Jesus*: for he will *save* his people from their *sins* (1.21). His very name refers to what he will accomplish in us; he will save, deliver his people: not from their enemies and oppressors, but from their sins. Further, he shall be called *Emmanuel*, "God with us" (1.23). This name too is important not only for its answer to the question "Who is he?", but for the difference it makes to us: in him *God is with us*. Finally, the wise men ask about the *king* of the Jews (2.2). Again the significance of the title is for both Jesus and us: correlative of *king* is *kingdom*, both reign and realm. The gradual revelation of the nature of his reign and realm through the Gospel bears directly on fulfillment in us.

Matthew opens the body of the Gospel with John's proclamation: "Repent, for the kingdom of heaven is at hand" (3.2). After his baptism, temptation, and withdrawal into Galilee, Jesus begins his preaching with exactly the same words (4.17). Though the words are the same, the profound difference of their meaning is borne out only as the Gospel continues. John's call is in the line of the prophets: a last call for preparation for the kingdom of heaven [God], which is near. What he demands is *repentance*: sorrow for sin, confession of sins (cf. 3.6) together with the symbolic baptism of repentance, conversion (change of mind and way of life), fruit (action) which befits repentance (3.8-10). We have no further indication from Matthew of John's moral demands[38]. John himself humbly contrasts both himself and his baptism with Jesus and his baptism with the Holy Spirit (3.11-14).

Jesus' words are the same: he calls for the same action, and proposes the same motive. The rest of the Gospel can be regarded as a gradual revelation of the meaning of both. The kingdom/reign/realm is unique. So too is the new way of life, the righteousness to which Jesus calls. Both are a reversal of all Jewish expectations. There are two lines of development. One

---

[38] Luke's further account of John's moral preaching is unique not only in the details of moral obligation, but in its being directed not only to the multitudes of Jews, but to the tax collectors and to the soldiers. From the outset Luke's concern with the universal scope of the Gospel is apparent (Lk 3.10-14).

elaborates the reign and the realm: God present and reigning in Jesus, and the new kingdom or realm of God which is being established. It involves the call to follow Jesus, and the gradual formation of a structured community, in which some disciples are called to special roles, are given special instructions, and finally are empowered and commissioned to carry on Jesus' work among all nations. The other reveals a new way of life for all who are called and receive the word: a righteousness richer and deeper than that of the Law, greater than that of the Scribes and Pharisees, necessary for entrance into the kingdom. Yet the two lines are intertwined. The Apostles are not the Church: they have special power and roles within the Church to which all are called. The new righteousness is for all: it is the great leveller, for only by becoming like little children can anyone enter the kingdom of heaven (cf. 18.1-4).

In my account of the project of fulfillment according to Matthew, I shall trace the two lines separately: (1) the formation of what will be called Jesus' Church; (2) the new righteousness.

(1) *The formation of the Church.* Before he gives us any inkling of the content of Jesus' first preaching, beyond the call to repentance, Matthew tells of the special call of the first two pairs of his eventual apostles. It is a peremptory call: "Follow me, and I will make you fishers of men" (4.19). Simon and Andrew leave their nets and follow him. Shortly after James and John leave their boat and their father, and follow him (4.21-22). From the outset, these men, who are to play special roles in his Church, make a radical break with their past, and follow Jesus. Later two others, ready to follow him, are faced with a hard decision by two of the hard sayings of Jesus: to one he says, "Foxes have holes, and birds of the air have nests; but the Son of man has nowhere to lay his head" (8.20). Implicitly he tells him: "This is what following me means. Are you ready?" To another who wishes to go first and bury his father, Jesus says, "Follow me, and leave the dead to bury their own dead" (8.22). It makes no sense to deny that these are hard sayings, or to try to soften or sweeten them with explanations. We can balance them with Jesus' clear teaching on our duty to our parents; but Matthew leaves us with the stark paradox, unresolved in the Gospel itself. Jesus makes severe demands of those who would be his close disciples, and challenges their decisiveness. We have no word of their response, but that very silence may suggest that they turned back: this was too much to ask of any man or woman.

Later Jesus calls his twelve disciples and gives them authority over unclean spirits, to cast them out, and to heal every disease and every infirmity. Now they are called the twelve apostles, and Matthew gives their names (10.1-4). Jesus sends them out only to the lost sheep of the house of Israel: explicitly excluding Gentiles and Samaritans. The message of the Kingdom is to be brought first to Israelites. With rare exceptions, which we shall note, this is the rule up to the point where Jesus has been rejected by his people, and he himself has repudiated the religious leaders of the Jews. Before sending them out, Jesus instructs them in his mission discourse (10.5–11.1). They are to travel in poverty, give freely what they have freely received, be at once wise and innocent. When they are delivered up to councils, flogged in synagogues, and dragged before governors and kings to bear testimony before them and the Gentiles, they are not to be anxious how they are to speak, or what they are to say: "... for what you are to say will be given to you in that hour; for it is not you who speak, but the Spirit of your Father speaking through you...." (10.20). They will suffer from division, hatred, and persecution: hated by all for his name's sake. He who perseveres to the end will be saved. They are to proclaim fearlessly, trusting in the Father. "... So every one who acknowledges me before men, I also will acknowledge before my Father who is in heaven; but whoever denies me before men, I also will deny before my Father who is in heaven" (10.32-33).

I have said that our two themes, formation of the Church (especially of its leaders) and the Christian way, are intertwined. Some of the elements of the missionary discourse apply to all Christians: suffering division and persecution and persevering to the end, fearless witness, and trust in the Father. One passage of the discourse with some of the hardest sayings in Jesus' teaching is for all:

> Do not think that I have come to bring peace on earth; I have not come to bring peace, but a sword. For I have come to set a man against his father, and a daughter against her mother, and a daughter-in-law against her mother-in-law; and a man's foes will be those of his own household. He who loves father or mother more than me is not worthy of me; and he who loves son or daughter more than me is not worthy of me; and he who does not take his cross and follow me is not worthy of me. He who finds his life will lose it, and he who loses his life for my sake will find it" (10.34-39).

What is involved here is not simply the renunciation demanded of those who would follow Jesus in a special way as his intimate disciples, his apostles: they are called in a unique way to leave all things and follow him, and in the life of the Church this will be recognized as a special vocation within the kingdom, within the Church. The demands here are made of all. For all who receive the word of the kingdom, following Christ means making these decisions where it is necessary: where father or mother or any other relative, or comfort and pleasure, or anything else would stand in the way of believing and following Jesus. We shall see more of the context of such demands as we trace lines of the project of Christian life, and of the new righteousness.

At the end of the missionary discourse two complementary aspects of life in the Church are linked: "He who receives you receives me, and he who receives me receives him who sent me. He who receives a prophet because he is a prophet shall receive a prophet's reward, and he who receives a righteous man because, he is a righteous man shall receive a righteous man's reward. And whoever gives to one of these little ones even a cup of cold water because he is a disciple, truly, I say to you, he shall not lose his reward" (10.40-42). The general principle is explicit in the first sentence, and it is applied to the case of the twelve disciples: we are to receive them because in them we see both Jesus and the Father. Implicitly the same principle is extended to seeing Christ in all: in the prophet, in the righteous man, and in the little one who is a disciple. This is part of the mystery of life in the Church: we see Christ in all, and respond to them accordingly.

Returning to the special call given to some, Jesus promises the rewards for response to this call. At the moment the disciples are astonished at Jesus' hard saying concerning the difficulty of a rich man's entering the kingdom of God. After Jesus answers their more general question (19.25-26), Peter asked: " 'Lo, we have left everything and followed you. What then shall we have?' Jesus said to them, 'Truly, I say to you, in the new world, when the Son of man shall sit on his glorious throne, you who have followed me will also sit on twelve thrones, judging the twelve tribes of Israel. And every one who has left houses or brothers or sisters or father or mother or children or lands, for my name's sake, will receive a hundredfold, and inherit eternal life. But many that are first will be last, and the last first' " (19-27-30) [39].

---

[39] Matthew's abbreviation of Mark here is interesting. He omits the explicit

Two more elements call for attention. One is the gradual opening of the Gospel to the Gentiles. It is suggested in Jesus' response to the centurion's faith:

> When Jesus heard him, he marveled, and said to those who followed him, "Truly, I say to you, not even in Israel have I found such faith. I tell you, many will come from east and west and sit at table with Abraham, Isaac, and Jacob in the kingdom of heaven, while the sons of the kingdom will be thrown out into the outer darkness; there men will weep and gnash their teeth." And to the centurion Jesus said, "Go; be it done for you as you have believed...." (8.10-13).

After severely testing the faith of the Canaanite woman, Jesus answered her reply, at once humble and beautiful and persevering: "Oh woman, great is your faith! Be it done for you as you desire" (15.28). In the context, in which Jesus has insisted on limits of his mission to the house of Israel, this is another striking opening upon the Gentile world. Later, when his people have rejected him, and Jesus has repudiated their religious leaders, Jesus declares: "...this gospel of the kingdom will be preached throughout the whole world, as a testimony to all nations...." (24.14). Finally, establishing his Church, Jesus sends his disciples to go and make disciples of *all nations* (28.19).

The second remaining significant element is Jesus' gradual conferring of authority on his apostles. The commissioning in chapter 10 mentions explicitly only authority over unclean spirits and to heal (10.1). Yet in the mission discourse in which Jesus instructs them it is apparent that they have teaching authority (cf. 10.14, 27, 40). After Peter's profession of faith, Jesus tells him of the role which will be his in the Church: on this rock he *will* build his Church; he *will* give Peter the keys of the kingdom of heaven (symbols of authority), and then whatever he will bind on earth shall be bound in heaven, and whatever he looses on earth shall be loosed in heaven (16.18-19). This is a promise of authority, given to Peter alone. Later, in a context which is extremely obscure, Jesus gives power to all of his apostles: "Truly, I say you, whatever you bind on earth shall be bound in heaven, and whatever you loose on earth shall be loosed in

---

contrast between rewards "now in this time" and "in the age to come eternal life"; the details of the rewards corresponding to what has been given up; and the salutary sting: "with persecutions". See Mk 10.28-31. Still the contrast between the hundredfold [or manifold in other readings] and eternal life is sufficiently clear even in Matthew.

heaven" (18.18)[40]. Finally the Risen Jesus, with all authority, commissions his Apostles to teach and baptize (28.18-20).

Unquestionably Matthew's witness to the formation of the Church is fragmentary, and no one could dream of developing an ecclesiology on this narrow base. Yet his witness is one of several complementary New Testament witnessess, and it is precious.

(2) *The new righteousness.* Important as are Matthew's indications of Jesus' formation of his Church, I should say that his extensive presentation of Jesus' call to a new way of life, a new righteousness, is even more important: for this is to be the life which characterizes his Church and all who live in it, and which they are to witness to the world. Here too Matthew's Gospel could be rightly called the great reversal: Jesus calls to a way of life, and offers a fulness of life and blessedness which reverse much of Jewish expectation, upset old scales of values, and repudiate the traditions and the practices of Jewish religious leaders.

In what order can I present this project for fulfillment? One could attempt some sort of theological reconstruction of the contents of Jesus' teaching as presented by Matthew; yet it would be arbitrary, and in any case would lose the power of Matthew's own presentation. On the contrary, to proceed simply by way of commentary, taking the teaching bit by bit in the order in which it

---

[40] The passage is unparalleled, and seems to be made up of elements from diverse sources. 18.15-17, addressed to the second person singular, sets rules for stages of fraternal correction, culminating in action by the church (here reasonably the local church: not the universal Church of 16.18-19). 18.19-20 regards another aspect of life in the Church: the efficacy of prayer of two or three gathered in Jesus' name: he is in the midst of them. 18.18 obviously is linked with the authoritative act of the church mentioned in the preceding verse. What remains obscure is who have the authority of binding and loosing here? There is a shift from second person singular to plural. I judge that the apostles (and eventually their successors in position of authority in the local churches) have this power. When the church acts (in the case of the "excommunication" of v. 17), the power resides not in the whole assembly indiscriminately: the "church" has the authority, but it is an authority residing in and exercised by those who have been given special power in the church. I see no grounds for the contrary view, expressed, for example, by McKenzie, *op. cit.*, 128, p. 95. Interesting as parallels are, the local Christian church is not a Qumran community. It is true that acts of the Church are always acts of the whole Church, yet its acts are acts of its officers, for in judicial action as in legislation, authoritative teaching, and public worship, the Church acts through its qualified members. Here, as elsewhere, I am not interested in alleging the opinions of exegetes. For brief indications that the view which I have presented has support among exegetes, see the notes of the editors of RSV and JB on 18.18.

occurs in the Gospel, would contribute little to understanding the prominence of major themes. I have decided to preserve as well as possible an order which introduces major themes as Matthew himself does, and to cite along with them resonances and variations which follow later in the Gospel.

(a) Christian blessedness. Matthew had his reasons for composing the Sermon on the Mount and placing it prominently at the beginning of the Gospel (ch. 5-7). He must have sensed too that in beginning with the beatitudes (5.3-12) he was employing what could be called a strategy of maximum shock. I shall not attempt here to reflect at length on the beatitudes, partly for reasons of the limitations of what can be only a sketch of Matthew's principal themes, partly because I hope to return to them in the second volume of this work.

It is difficult now for a Christian to read the beatitudes and sense how they must have shocked the Jews who heard them for the first time, and how they must sound like utter nonsense to any man or woman with a normal merely human sense of what makes for happiness or blessedness. We read them from within a Christian experience, having been drawn by the beauty of Jesus' own example, and being moved by the Spirit who animates the word of the Gospel received in faith. Yet, humanly speaking, and also in the light of Jewish sense of values and Jewish hopes, the beatitudes are unintelligible.

In what sense are the poor in spirit blessed, and in what sense do they possess the kingdom of God? In what sense shall the meek inherit the earth? When and how shall the mourners be comforted, those who hunger and thirst after righteousness be satisfied, the merciful obtain mercy, the pure in heart see God, and the persecuted possess the kingdom of heaven and feel blessed? These questions can be answered only in terms of two radical reversals of convictions. The first involves a revision of very notion of the blessedness which is promised within the limits of this life. The second involves firm hope in the blessedness of eternal life, and the mysterious blessedness which here and now can fill the man or woman who lives in that hope and knows that this life with all of its trials makes sense.

I shall say no more here than this. Matthew could hardly have chosen a more spectacular way of proclaiming, and calling attention to his further presentation of, this aspect of the Christian revolution. His account of fulfillment in Jesus reversed all previous messianic notions. His account of Christian blessedness, and his further account of the new righteousness, reverse all previous sense of values and of true human happiness, even as it was understood with the wisdom of the Law.

Variations on the themes of the beatitudes appear through the Gospel. To follow Jesus without reservation (and so to come to the fulness of the life which he offers) one must embrace poverty (8.20) and renounce action which normally would be judged good (8.21-22); one must sacrifice family relationship where that would stand in the way (10.34-37), take the cross, and lose life to find it (10.38-39). Jesus thanks his Father for having hidden [the truth about the kingdom] from the wise and understanding and revealed it to babes (11.25). He invites all who are weary and burdened to come to him, and he will give them rest. "...Take my yoke upon you, and learn from me; for I am gentle and lowly in heart, and you will find rest for your souls. For my yoke is easy, and my burden is light" (11.28-30). He reverses the order of servant and served: "...You know that the rulers of the Gentiles lord it over them, and their great men exercise authority over them. It shall not be so among you; but whoever would be great among you must be your slave; even as the Son of man came not to be served but to serve...." (21.25-28). His followers are not to covet places of honor, respectful greetings, and titles of honor: "...He who is greatest among you shall be your servant; whoever exalts himself will be humbled, and whoever humbles himself will be exalted" (23.11-12: cf. vv. 2-10).

(b) Bringing the Law to its perfection. As I have suggested, Matthew may have intended to shock hearers and readers of the Gospel by beginning his "Sermon on the Mount" with the beatitudes. Having brought us up short with the paradoxical presentation of Christian blessedness, he moves to Jesus' reassurance concerning his intention:

> Think not that I have come to abolish the law and the prophets [the whole of the Scriptures for the Jews]; I have come not to abolish them but to fulfill them. For truly, I say to you, till heaven and earth pass away, not an iota, not a dot, will pass from the law until all is accomplished.... (5.17-18).

Two questions rise here: the sense of "fulfill", and the sense in which not a bit of the law will pass *until all is accomplished.*

I have dealt with the notion of *fulfill* in Matthew (above, pp. 132-137), and with the sense in which Jesus fulfilled all righteousness (pp. 152-161). The two notions, *fulfill all righteousness* and *fulfill the law and the prophets,* are intimately connected. Their meaning in Matthew is to be gathered similarly from the whole tenor of the Gospel. With regard to Jesus' fulfilling the law, we must look directly to those elements of his teaching which regard interpretation or modification of the Law; but we must consider too his gradual revelation of the true righteousness to which he calls all of his disciples, and without which they—we—cannot enter the kingdom of heaven. I shall deal with these two complementary aspects of the Gospel in this sub-section and the next.

First, then, recalling what we have established concerning the meaning of *fulfill*, we must note how Jesus goes about his task by interpreting or modifying prevailing understanding of the Law. He does so most strikingly in a series of six contrasts, all formulated in the same way: "You have heard that it was said.... But I say to you...." (5.21-48). The words with which he concludes the sixth case could be understood of the teaching regarding all six: "... You, therefore, must be perfect, as your heavenly Father is perfect" (5.48).

In general Jesus brings the Law to its perfection by a radical re-interpretation which makes much greater demands. Where the Law forbids a sin, Jesus cuts to the vice which is the root of the sin. Moreover, in such instances and in those in which a good action is commanded, he reveals the full virtue by which we are to avoid sin and come to a fulness of perfection, righteousness.

The Law forbade killing. Jesus warns of the anger which is the vice, and demands reconciliation (5.21-26). The Law forbade adultery. Jesus forbids the lustful look, and calls for radical sacrifice of what could lead us to sin: pluck out the eye and throw it away, cut off the hand and throw it away (5.27-30). The Law prescribed the procedure for divorce. Jesus forbids all divorce (5.31-32; cf. 19.3-9, esp. v. 9)[41]. The Law forbade swearing falsely. Jesus forbids a variety of evasive forms of oath, which could have been regarded as ways of avoiding perjury by avoiding the Divine name; and he calls for simple, straightforward "Yes" or "No", without need of oath. Again, he is cutting to the

---

[41] This is not the place to go into the classic controversy over the interpretation of the apparent exception: "except on the ground of unchastity" (5.32), "except for unchastity" (19.9). Among the many interpretations offered I judge that of J. BONSIRVEN, S.J. most satisfying: *Le divorce dans le Nouveau Testament* (Paris, 1948) and "Excepta fornicationis causa," *Rech. sc. rel.* 35 (1948) pp. 442-464. His solution was judged to be clear, perhaps definitive by P. BENOIT, O.P., *Revue Biblique* 58 (1951) pp. 116-118; and definitive by C. SPICQ, RSPhTh 34 (1950) pp. 47-48.

vice at the root of any perjury or evasiveness and demanding a basic honesty which makes swearing unnecessary (5.33-37)[42]. The Law set down norms of retaliation: "An eye for an eye and a tooth for a tooth" (cf. Ex 21.24; Dt 19.21). Revenge was a right, and avenging murder or injustice to one's relative was a duty: the law set limits of proportionate vengeance. Jesus reverses the whole basic principle and commands a basic law of non-resistance and yielding, which he illustrates with three examples. Taken as it should be, without dilution, Jesus' principle is one of the most radical reversals of the Law (5.38-42)[43]. It was said, "You shall love your neighbor and hate your enemy." The love of neighbor commanded in Lev 19.18 seems to have referred to one's fellow-Israelite; but in Lev 19.33-34 it was extended to the stranger sojourning among Israelites. Hatred of enemy is not commanded in the Old Testament, nor is there evidence of it as an explicit rabbinical teaching. It is enough to read many of the Psalms, however, to know that it was part of Israelite mentality. Jesus' command of love of one's enemies must have seemed the sharpest reversal of prevailing moral standards (cf. 5.43-48). The universality of our love of our fellow men, and its supreme importance in Jesus' teaching, is brought out finally in Matthew's unparalleled account of the judgment which will take place at the coming of the Son of Man in his glory. Eternal punishment or eternal life will depend on one criterion: the way we shall have treated our fellow man. As we shall have treated him, so we shall have treated Jesus in him (25.31-46).

The second question is more difficult: in what sense does Jesus teach that not a bit of the law will pass *until all is accomplished*. I think that there are two answers which are complementary. The first is more obvious: the Law *as brought to perfection by Jesus* will never pass: it will last to the end of time, when all is accomplished in the true eschatological coming of the Son of Man. The second is obscure, but highly suggestive, and it fits some other elements of Jesus' teaching. *All is accomplished* when the whole of the Law and the prophets—the whole of the Scripture—is fulfilled in the passion, death, and resurrection of Jesus. In Matthew's account, as we have seen, this complex event is portrayed in apocalyptic colors. It is the "turning of the ages", the great eschatological-apocalyptic event

---

[42] Compare McKenzie, *op. cit.*, 39, p. 72.
[43] See McKenzie, *ibid.*, 40, pp. 72-73.

which marks the end of the Temple cult (in the rending of the veil), and the end of the Law on which it was grounded. It comes when in his final confrontation with his people and their religious leaders Jesus has repudiated their authority. His coming after his resurrection is an anticipation of his final coming. Even now he comes with *all* authority. Henceforth the Apostles are to teach disciples of all nations to observe all that *Jesus has commanded* (28.18-20). Thus the symbolism of the transfiguration takes on a deeper meaning: at the outset Jesus appeared with Moses and Elijah, who symbolize the Law and the prophets. The Father declares: "This is my beloved Son, with whom I am well pleased; *listen to him*" (17.5). When at the end the disciples looked up, they saw no one but Jesus only. Moses and Elijah—Law and prophets—have disappeared. Jesus alone is there: "listen to him!" The whole of the Scripture, Law and prophets, were prophetic of Jesus. In him they are fulfilled in their entirety. He is the embodiment of the Law, the will of the Father. Hence it is that during his public life he could instruct his disciples to obey the teaching of the Scribes and Pharisees: "The scribes and Pharisees sit on Moses' seat; so practice and observe whatever they tell you, but not what they do; for they preach, but do not practice" (23.2-3). *For the present* their teaching authority remains: when all is accomplished in Jesus, that authority will have come to its end [44].

One other element of the Gospel fits this second inter-pretation, namely that *all is accomplished* in the death and resurrection of Jesus. It is the puzzling statement in Jesus' eschatological discourse, concerning the coming of the Son of Man in his glory: "...Truly, I say to you, this generation will not pass away till all these things take place...." (24.34) [45].

---

[44] The matter is by no means simple, for Jesus has already modified the Law and rejected the traditions of the leaders: see, for example, 5.17-43; 12.1-14; 15.1-20; 19.1-12. For the basic problem, see McKenzie, *op. cit.*, on 5.17-48: 34, pp. 70-71. There are apparent inconsistencies in the New Testament regarding the relation of the Law to the Gospel. Rather than inconsistencies, they could be taken as signs of the tension and the difficulty in the development of Christian understanding of this difficult matter. If, as seems probable, Matthew is writing from within a Christian community which has problems similar to those faced by Paul regarding Jewish and Gentile Christians and their relationship to the Law, it is not surprising that no perfectly harmonious explanation of all elements in Matthew can be worked out.

[45] On the whole matter of *accomplishment* in the death and resurrection of Jesus, see Meier, *op. cit.*, pp. 189-191; 224-234; 262-264.

(c) True and false righteousness. In what follows I do not seek to establish the only order which could be found in the many sayings of Jesus which Matthew reports in both his narrative portions and his discourses. I suggest some plausible grouping of elements of Jesus' teaching which somehow concern true and false righteousness, and which complement what we have considered concerning his direct re-interpretation of the Law.

[1] Christian witness. I gather here several elements which seem to me to be intimately related. First, Jesus' disciples are the salt of the earth, the light of the world: they must witness by their good works, and bring men to give glory to God (5.13-16). Theirs must be a righteousness greater than that of the Scribes and Pharisees: otherwise they will never enter the kingdom of heaven, much less give witness by the genuine good works of which Jesus has spoken (5.19-20).

In part Jesus makes his meaning clear by repeated warnings against hypocrisy. Surely they must practice good works: this he has insisted on (5.14-16). But they must avoid all hypocritical intention: "Beware of practicing your piety before men *in order to be seen by them*; for then you will have no reward from your Father who is in heaven" (6.1). And Jesus instructs them on how they are to give alms, pray, and fast (6.2-18). Most of all he denounces the hypocrisy of the Pharisees and scribes. He accuses them of insisting on their own traditions and neglecting the commandment of God, and teaches the importance of interior cleanness as contrasted with the exterior cleanness on which they insisted: "... what comes out out of the mouth proceeds from the heart, and this defiles a man. For out of the heart come evil thoughts, murder, adultery, fornication, theft, false witness, slander. These are what defile a man; but to eat with unwashed hands does not defile a man" (15.18-20; cf. vv. 1-17). Here, as in bringing the Law to perfection, Jesus is cutting to the sources of sin. Finally, he makes his scathing denunciation of the hypocrisy of the scribes and Pharisees in the series of woes (23.13-36).

Linked with Jesus' teaching on genuine witness is his insistence on not just hearing his words, nor just calling on his name, but on *doing* what he says (7.15-27; cf. 12.33-37).

.   [2] Decisive response and singleness of purpose. Under this double heading I should gather a number of related elements of Jesus' teaching. Strangely Matthew does not report much explicitly on the need of faith in Jesus; yet in various ways, explicitly or implicitly, it is obviously the beginning of response to him. He praises the faith of the centurion, and contrasts it with lack of faith in Israel (8.5, 13). He rewards the persevering faith of the Canaanite woman (15.21-28). Faith is implicit in receiving or listening to Jesus' words or those of his disciples speaking for him (10.14-15), and in acknowledging him (10.32.33). Besides the faith necessary for salvation, he teaches of that which is necessary for wonder-working (17.19-20; 21.21-22).

Jesus demands a sense of priority which prizes the kingdom of heaven above all other good things, and a singleness of purpose, expressed in terms of the soundness of the eye which lights the whole body (cf. 6.19-34). We must enter by the narrow gate and follow the hard way which leads to life (7.13-14). We have already considered the decisive renunciation demanded for full following of Jesus (8.19-22), the necessity of taking up the cross and following him, and of losing one's life for his sake in order to find life (16.24-26); and the resolute rejection of what would cause us to sin (18.7-9). By the parables of the hidden treasure and of the pearl of great value Jesus again teaches that the kingdom is to be prized above all else (13.44-46).

[3] Forgiveness of those who have offended us. This is one of the most radical reversals of Israelite practice. I know of a single example of it in the Old Testament: Sir 27.30 – 28.7. Jesus' teaching is emphatic. First, in teaching us how to pray, he includes the petition: "And forgive us our debts, *as we also have forgiven our debtors*; ..." (6.12). I have italicized the clause which should suffice to make us pause and examine our conscience. But Jesus is not content with this. In Matthew's version, this is the only petition of the Lord's prayer to which Jesus adds a forceful commentary: "For if you forgive men their trespasses, your heavenly Father also will forgive you; but if you do not forgive men their trespasses, neither will your heavenly Father forgive your trespasses" (6.14-15) [46].

[4] Avoidance of judging. Jesus' teaching on this is one of the "detached sayings" of chapter 7, many of which we have considered. It is closely related to forgiveness, and equally important: "Judge not, that you be not judged. For with the judgment you pronounce you will be judged, and the measure you give will be the measure you get...." (7.1-2).

---

[46] Compare the variant reading of Mk 11.25-[26].

[5] Perseverance in prayer: we are to ask, trusting in the goodness of our Father in heaven (7.7-11).

[6] Various other aspects of life in the kingdom. I note here some further elements of Jesus' teaching in parables and other sayings. First, the parable of the sower and the seed stresses the importance of the disposition of the recipient of the word (13.18-23). The parable of the good seed and the weeds, and that of the net (13.24-30, 36-43; 47-50) suggest a healthy realism concerning life to the end of time: righteous and sinners will share the world, and will be separated only at the judgment. The kingdom will grow (cf. 13.31-33): though the parables seem to regard the kingdom as the "realm", it seems reasonable to find implicit a sense of process, of growth, in the life of a person in the kingdom. Though judgment is forbidden, fraternal correction is enjoined (18.15-17). Prayer in union even with one or two gathered in Jesus' name is effective, and he is with us when we pray thus (18.19-20). One of the mysteries of the call to the kingdom is that of celibacy freely chosen for the sake of the kingdom: for a greater dedication to the supreme value of the kingdom (19.10-12). Finally, we all live in expectation of the coming of the Son of Man, with no inkling of when it will be: we must be vigilant (24.32 – 25.13).

(d) God's free gift. Finally, I should point out the importance of the parable of the householder and the workers in his vineyard (20.1-16). It makes no sense in terms of labor relations or social justice. It teaches the transcendent truth that God is the Creator and Lord, and that he gives his gifts freely, out of a goodness and love which is beyond criticism. In Matthew's Gospel it teaches a truth which is brought out differently, for example, by Paul and John. We are not saved, we do not come to life in the kingdom, thanks to our own works done with a sense of self-righteousness. Jesus calls from the outset for repentance, and he mingles with sinners. The kingdom is given mysteriously to those who have a deep sense of their need, those who are open to the wonder of the gift. The self-righteous are closed in their complacency.

FURTHER PROMISE

By "further promise" I refer to promise to be fulfilled in the consummation, as distinct from fulfillment in Jesus in his death and resurrection, and fulfillment in us in the course of the life of the Church up to the Coming of the Son of Man in glory. Little is to be said.

With regard to Jesus, the essential further promise regards his coming in glory and his judgment, which we have already noted.

With regard to us, there is the judgment in so far as it regards not Jesus' action but its decisive effect for us: reward or punishment (cf. 7.21-23; 13.30, 47-50; 25.31-46). A number of elements pertain to the reward. There is, first, what I have indicated as the eschatological aspect of the beatitudes: besides the mystery of a paradoxical blessedness in this world, there is the blessing in eternal life. For the most part this is implicit; regarding the last beatitude it is explicit (5.12). For all who have lived according to Jesus' word, there is the symbolism of the treasure in heaven (6.9) and of the messianic banquet (8.11-12; 26.29). For those who will have left all to follow him there will be a special reward (19.28-29).

CONCLUDING REFLECTIONS

I should say that two qualities characterize Matthew's profoundly theological Gospel: the power with which he has witnessed to the Christian revolution, the Great Reversal; and what I can only call the starkness of his Gospel. They need not go together: there can be an equally powerful witness which is not stark, but more richly human and also more profoundly theological. Perhaps we can say that for Matthew this was the only way. He is unique, and his witness is unique. It is one witness among many, one theological elaboration which calls for complements. We can thank God both for Matthew's great contribution and for the many complements which we have in the works of other New Testament writers: Mark's freshness, vividness, narrative detail, and portrayal of Jesus' emotion; Luke's gentleness; John's greater theological depth and intimate revelation of Christian experience; Paul's sharing of his own life in Christ and in the Spirit, his different way of bringing out the relation of Gospel to Law, and his profound sense of the Law of the Spirit and of freedom. In the life of the Church we hold all in unity and complementarity. From many points of view, from within many unique personal worlds, we take readings on the one great Reality, which evokes in every one of us a unique personal response.

One more observation seems salutary. Matthew is not a moral theologian. In his Gospel Jesus cuts to the roots of sin, and seeks to plant the seed of true righteousness. We have here no carefully drawn distinctions of degrees of obligation and counsel on the one hand, and degrees of sin and imperfection on the other. We have a ringing proclamation of the Christian revolution, the new righteousness, and a call to a fulness of life. In God's good time in the life of the Church others would come to make other contributions: different, surely not greater, than Matthew's.

CHAPTER VI

JOHN

FULFILLMENT IN JESUS

(1) *Continuity with Abraham, Moses, and the prophets.*
Jesus himself makes the massive affirmation in this regard: "You
search the scriptures, because you think that in them you have
eternal life; and it is they that bear witness to me" (5.39); and
again, "If you believed Moses, you would believe me, for he
wrote of me. But if you do not believe his writings, how will you
believe my words?" (5.46-47). To the Jews who prided
themselves on being sons of Abraham (8.33-53) Jesus affirmed:
"Your father Abraham rejoiced that he was to see my day; he saw
it and was glad" (8.56). When they challenged him, asking how
he, not yet fifty years old, had seen Abraham, Jesus said: "Truly,
truly, I say to you, before Abraham was, I am" (8.58)[1]. John
contrasts Moses' role and contribution with Jesus'; "...the law
was given through Moses; grace and truth came through Jesus
Christ" (1.17)[2]. The prophets wrote of Jesus: 1.45; cf. 1.23;
6.45; 12.38-41. In his account of the crucifixion, John has three
allusions to fulfillment of texts of Psalms: 18.24: Ps 22.18; 18.28:
Ps 22.15; 18.29: Ps 69.21.

(2) *Who is he? Titles.* We may follow the common
distinction between titles used by others and those used or
implicitly accepted by Jesus.

John's most characteristic title is the *Word* (1.1, 14; 1 Jn 1.1;
cf. Ap 19.13). Unique in the Bible in the sense in which John uses

---

[1] For the significance of "I am" see above, pp. 96-102. In my citations
of John, mere chapter and verse refer to the Gospel; for the First Letter I prefix
"1 Jn".

[2] John's statement here is pregnant. "Grace" here seems to stand for
God's loving-kindness or redeeming love; "truth", his faithfulness to his
promises. These are the two great, constant covenant virtues of God in the Old
Testament. "Moses" surely wrote of them. Jesus, the full realization and
revelation of God's love, embodies them.

it, it is related to Old Testament, Jewish, and early Christian conceptions, but transcends them all: Jesus is the Word spoken by God, the full revelation of God, the dynamic, creative Word, one with the Father and yet distinct from him[3]. Moreover, John in his prologue writes of the *life* which was in him, and affirms that he is the *light* (1.4; 1.5, 7-9). In John's Gospel Jesus takes up both *life* and *light* as metaphors which express his attributes.

John the Baptist call Jesus the *Lamb of God* (1.29, 36), and the title probably includes and goes beyond elements of the conquering lamb of Ap 7.17; 17.14, the Suffering Servant, and the paschal lamb[4]. Titles used by others in the Gospel are *Messiah* or *Christ* (1.41; 4.25, 29; 11.27), and the title appears in accounts of speculation or questioning by the people (7.26-31, 40-42; 9.22). Jesus is called the *Son of God* in some transcendent sense (1.34, 49; 11.27). For Nathaniel and the crowds at his entrance into Jerusalem he is *King of Israel* (1.49; 12.13), and in the interplay involving the soldiers, Pilate, and the Jews, the titles *King of the Jews* and *King* figure (19.3, 12, 14, 15, 19, 21).

Once, reflecting Jesus' own use, the people call him the *Son of Man*, seemingly with the meaning of Messiah (12.34). He is called a *prophet* (4.19; 9.17) or *the Prophet* (6.14; 7.40), and the *Savior of the world* (4.42; cf. 1 Jn 4.14). For Peter Jesus is the *Holy One of God* (6.69; or *Son of God* in some variant readings). Finally, Thomas, in full belief, exclaims: "My *Lord* and my *God*" (20.23).

Jesus himself uses most of all the simple title *the Son,* with variations: *the only Son of God* (3.16-18)[5], and *the Son of God*, in a transcendent sense (11.4). Except for the instance in which people reflect his usage, Jesus is the only one to speak of himself as the *Son of man*, with the suggestion of transcendent dignity and power (1.51; 3.13, 14; 5.27; 6.27; 6.27, 53, 62; 8.28; 9.35; 13.31). Even where he refers to his being lifted up, the expression in Johannine thought means the whole process of Jesus' glorification: suffering, death, resurrection, and return to the Father.

---

[3] See *The Mystery*, pp. 148-149, and sources indicated there.

[4] See R. E. BROWN, S.S., *The Gospel according to John.* Anchor Bible, 29 (N.Y.: Doubleday, 1966) pp. 58-63.

[5] John may not attribute these words to Jesus: see BROWN, *op. cit.,* 135-137, 149.

Four times Jesus says of himself absolutely: *"I am"* (8.24, 28, 58; 13.19), with highly probable reference to the divine name in Exodus 3.14 [6].

Though he does not use the titles *Christ (Messiah)* or *King*, at times he implicitly accepts them as used by others (4.25-26; 7.27; 10.24; 18.33, 36-37).

Finally Jesus uses metaphors which express his attributes or his relationship to men: *life* (11.25; 14.6), *light* (8.12; 9.5; 12.35-36, 46), *door* (10.7), *good shepherd* (10.11), *resurrection* (11.25), *Teacher* (13.13), *Lord* (13.13), the *way*, the *truth*, and the *life* (14.6), and the *true vine* (15.1, 4-5).

(3) *Who is he? His unique being and functions.* First, he is intimately united with the Father:

> ... In the beginning Jesus was [*is*] with the Father, in the bosom of the Father (1.18), and before the world was made he had glory with the Father (17.5). He came from the Father and goes to the Father (13.3; 16.28). He has seen and heard God (1.18; 3.32; 5.30; 6.46; 8.26-28, 38).
>
> He and the Father are one (10.30; 17.11): he is in the Father and the Father is in him (10.38; 14.10-11, 20; 17.21-23); the Father is with the Son (8.29; 16.32). The Father has given all things into the Son's hands (3.35; 16.15; 17.6-10): judgment (5.22), life (5.26), his works (5.36); the men who are to believe in him (6.37, 39), and power over all flesh, to give eternal life (17.2). Consequently, Jesus' words are God's words (3.34; 14.24) and so for his judgment (8.16), his works (5.17-21; 10.37-38), and his witness to himself (8.18). Jesus does nothing on his own authority, but seeks the will of the Father (5.30; 7.16-18; 8.42). The glory of the Son is also the glory of the Father (13.31-32). Finally, Father and Son send the Spirit (14.16; 15.26; 16.7).
>
> Not only is there an intimate union of Father and Son, but also on the part of men there is an identity of relatioship to Father and to Son. To know Jesus is to know the Father (8.19; 14.7). To believe in Jesus is to believe in him who sent him (12.44). Seeing Jesus is seeing the one who sent him (12.45; 14.7, 9). Receiving Jesus is receiving the one who sent him (13.20). To hate Jesus is to hate the Father (15.23-25); to dishonor Jesus is to dishonor the Father (5.23). "And this is eternal life, that they know thee the only true God, and Jesus Christ whom thou hast sent" (17.3) [7].

---

[6] For the meaning of the expression in these texts and others, see above, pp. 96-102.

[7] *The Mystery*, pp. 149-150.

What are his qualities? He is truly man: for the Word became flesh and dwelt among us (1.14). He is God (1.1; cf. 20.28). As God and man, Jesus is utterly unique: he is

> ... full of grace and truth (1.14); he is superior to John (1.15, 27, 30) and to Moses (1.17); he is teacher and Lord (13.13). He is from God (9.30; 13.3; 16.28), from above, from heaven (3.31; 8.23). He has the fulness of the Spirit (3.34). He has life in himself and is the source of life for others (5.26; 6.68; 1 Jn 5.11; 6.35-36, 41, 47, 51). Though he was not known to have studied, he has extraordinary knowledge of men and of what is to befall him (2.25; 6.64; 7.15-16; 18.4). He is the light of the world (1.4-9; 8.12; 9.5; 12.46). His judgment is true (8.16) and he tells the truth (8.45). He has the power to lay down his life and to take it up again (10.17-18).
>
> Jesus loves the Father (14.31), and seeking the glory of his Father (7.18; 8.50) he does the Father's will (4.32, 34; 5.30; 6.38-40; 8.28-29, 42; 12.49-50; 17.4). He loves his own (13.1, 34; 15.9, 12, 13; 1 Jn 3.16). He is not a sinner (9.16; 1 Jn 3.5). He is the revelation of his Father (12.45; 14.7, 9) [8].

(4) *His work.* Jesus' work is to do the work of God: "My food is to do the will of him who sent me, and to accomplish his work" (4.34). What is the *work* of God? "This is the work of God, that you believe in him whom he has sent" (6.29). At the end of his life he could pray: "I have glorified thee on earth, having accomplished the work which thou gavest me to do; ...." (17.4). The Father has given Jesus a command (10.17-18; 12.50; 14.31), a work to be done (17.4), a cup to be drunk (18.11). In the accomplishment of the work, the Father himself is working (5.17, 19; 14.10-11) [9].

For Jesus, the work means laying down his life for his sheep (10.11-18), offering his flesh for the life of the world (6.51), dying for the nation and for the scattered children of God (11.51-52). In this he shows supreme love (15.13). For the sake of those who have been given to him, he consecrates himself (17.19). Dying, he bears much fruit (12.24); lifted up from the earth, he will draw all men to himself (12.32-33). His blood cleanses us from all sin (1 Jn 1.7), expiates for our sins and those of the whole world (1 Jn 2.2; 4.10), takes away sins (1.29; 1 Jn 3.5) and destroys the works of the devil (1 Jn 3.8).

---

[8] *The Mystery*, p. 149.

[9] For an ample treatment of the roles of Father, Son, and Spirit in the accomplishment of the work, see *The Mystery*, pp. 151-158.

(5) *His glory and glorification.* In John's Gospel we find the account of a gradual showing forth of Jesus' glory during his public life, and the unique glory and glorification which are reserved for the *hour*, carefully set off from the rest of his life [10].

In both the gradual glorification of Jesus and the consummation in the *hour* (cf. 12.23, 28; 17.1) the glorification of Jesus and of the Father are one. In the raising of Lazarus from the dead this is clear: informed of Lazarus' illness, Jesus replied, "This illness is not unto death; it is for the glory of God, so that the Son of God may be glorified by means of it" (11.4). In his supreme glorification in the *hour* both Jesus and the Father act, and both are glorified.

Jesus obeys his Father's command, which is twofold: to lay down his life, and to take it up again: "... For this reason the Father loves me, because I lay down my life, that I may take it again. No one takes it from me, but I lay it down of my own accord. I have power to lay it down, and I have power to take it again; this charge [command] I have received from my Father" (10.17-18). There is no command simply to die. Moreover, in Johannine thought, Jesus is not *raised* from the dead, but *rises*, takes up his life again. This is consistent with the theology of the Incarnate Word proclaimed from the beginning of the Gospel. Because Jesus is God and man, he can lay down his life and he can take it up again.

According to his Father's command, Jesus *goes*, and he *will come* (14.28). In the context of the Gospel, Jesus' *going* means both his death and his return to the Father; his *coming* means both his coming after his glorification and his final coming in the parousia.

Again, in Johannine thought, Jesus' triple statement that he must be *lifted up* (3.13-14; 8.28; 12.32-33) corresponds to the triple prediction of his passion, death, and resurrection in the Synoptic Gospels. Being *lifted up* involves the total process of dying, rising, returning to the Father.

What, then, is the Johannine conception of glory and glorification?

> By works-signs Jesus manifests the divine glory, his own as well as that of the Father. He reveals the Father, makes his name known, gives his words and his commandments to men. He glorifies the Father by manifesting him and making him known.

---

[10] Again, for a fairly ample treatment of glory in John's Gospel, see *The Mystery*, pp. 158-170.

Glory is not merely manifestation, but the divine presence, power, and love manifested, shown to be present and operative. Glorification is not merely manifesting the divine excellence: it is a manifestation which terminates in knowledge, belief, acknowledgment, love expressed in keeping God's commandments, and oneness with Father, Son, and Spirit and with others who have fellowship in eternal life. A manifestation which did not come to this term would be meaningless.

What, then, is glory and glorification? Going beyond John, yet consistently with the dynamic pattern of his thought, we may say this: Glory is not merely divine excellence (light, life, love, spirit...) in itself, but that divine excellence as knowable and known, believed, loved. It is the mystery of a oneness by knowledge and love, beginning with the oneness of Father and Son (and Spirit) and terminating in the oneness of Father, Son, and Spirit in the men in whom they dwell, who by their own union of love show forth the divine union. At the root, in the glory of Father and Son, there is no question obviously of a sensible brilliance and the knowledge which it mediates. It is the divine life of mutual knowledge and love. This divine life is shown forth to bring men to eternal life: to a knowledge and love of Father, Son, and Spirit, to oneness with them and with all who share the same life, and who on the last day will be raised to life again and brought to be with Jesus in his glory in the presence of the Father [11].

FULFILLMENT IN US

John's thought moves in a spiralling fashion. He returns often to the same themes, but every time, in the gentle movement of his thought, he adds another touch. One cannot find in the Gospel and the First Letter the structure of a theology elaborated by John himself. Yet there are hints of priorities and of a certain underlying intelligible order. Without illusion of working out the only possible account of such an order, I shall set forth the elements of John's thought in an order which seems to me to be reasonable.

One could begin, of course, with one or other of the major themes which recur often and are most conspicuous, such as faith and eternal life. Yet careful reading and reflection may suggest factors which, though less often mentioned, are prior. These seem to me to be the easiest to fix in an order which may seem acceptable to most who will have pondered the matter. I shall

---

[11] *The Mystery*, pp. 169, 170.

begin with the roles of Father, Son, and Spirit, and then follow with the effects which together constitute fulfillment of the promise in us.

I wish to note two things regarding this treatment of the roles of Father, Jesus, and the Spirit, both in this consideration of John and in the following chapter on Paul. First, there is an inevitable partial repetition of treatment of texts: some regard both fulfillment in Jesus and fulfillment in us. It is necessary to mention them here in so far as they regard not Jesus, but us. Second, and more important, it would not be sufficient to consider only the "effects" in us, as if these were somehow just "objective" modifications of our mode of being. We must consider these effects in relation to the roles of Father, Jesus, and the Spirit, because we *are* in a transcendent way both as a result of their actions, and in transcendent interpersonal relations with Them, relations which correspond to their roles in our salvation and transformation. Consequently this reflection is an essential part of the total reflection on the dialectic of promise and fulfillment. That dialectic, as we are aware of it, conditions all of our experience of God. Our experience of God, Father, Jesus, and Holy Spirit, is realized as we are conscious of being affected by them and of responding to them. We grasp the manner of their action, and of our response, and we come more and more to sense the shape of our experience of Them, not by just an introvertive "reading" and "discernment" of our "feelings", but by a reflection which is illumined continually by revelation and faith. Taking the biblical account of God's revelation, we believe what They have told us of their roles in our lives, and of our potential response. Believing what They tell is, breaking through the barriers of the unseen and unfelt, we respond to Them, come to fulfillment, and sense the shape of our total experience.

(1) *The roles of Father, Son, and Spirit.*

(a) The Father, God. God is *love* (1 Jn 4.8), and all of his action regarding both Jesus and us springs from love. He loves the Son (3.35; 5.20; 10.17; 15.9; 17.23). He loves us: "... God so loved the world that he gave his only Son, that whoever believes in him should not perish, but have eternal life" (3.16). "In this is the love, not that we loved God, but that he loved us and sent his Son to be the expiation for our sins. Beloved, if God so loved us, we also ought to love one another" (1 Jn 4.10-11; cf. also 14.21, 23; 16.27; 17.23; 1 Jn 3.1; 4.8-19). He gives us to the Son (3.35; 6.37, 39; 10.26-29; 17.6-9). He draws us to the Son (6.44), permits us to come to the Son (6.65). He commands

the Son what to say and what to speak (12.48-50), and
consequently it is he who is speaking to us through the Son. He
begets us (1.12-13; 1 Jn 4.7; 5.1, 4), teaches us (6.45), sanctifies
us (17.17), keeps us (10.29; 17.15), abides in us (14.23; 1 Jn 3.24;
4.4, 12-16) and gives us the Spirit (14.16-17, 26; 15.26).

   (b) Jesus, the Son. "... from his fulness we have all received,
grace upon grace ... grace and truth came through Jesus
Christ ... " (1.16-17). He loves us (13.1, 34; 15.9, 12-15; 1 Jn
3.16).

> He laid down his life for his sheep (10.11-18), offering his
> flesh for the life of the world (6.51), dying for the nation, "... and
> not for the nation only, but to gather into one the children of God
> who are scattered abroad" (11.51-52). "Greater love has no
> man than this, that a man lay down his life for his friends"
> (15.13). For the sake of those who have been given to him and
> who have believed in him, he consecrates himself (17.19). Dying,
> he bears much fruit (12.24); liften up from the earth, he will draw
> all men to himself (12.32-33). His blood cleanses us from all sin
> (1 Jn 1.7). An expiation for our sins and those of the whole world
> (1 Jn 2.2; 4.10), he takes away sins (1.29; 1 Jn 3.5) and destroys
> the works of the devil (1 Jn 3.8).
> He is the light (1.4-5, 7-9; 8.12; 9.5; 12.46) and the
> source of life.... To those who receive him, who believe in him, he
> gives the power to become the children of God (1.12). He gives
> life (5.21-29), gives the food of eternal life (6.27): he *is* the bread
> of life (6.35, 51-58). Those who believe in him *have* eternal life
> (3.15, 16, 36; 6.40, 47; 8.51; 10.10, 27-29; 11.25-27; 14.19;
> 20.31).
> He who believes in Jesus, who loves him and keeps his
> commandments, who eats his flesh and drinks his blood, abides in
> Jesus, and Jesus abides in him (6.56; 14.20, 23; 15.4, 5; 1 Jn 1.3;
> 2.5, 6; 3.24) [12].

Jesus gives the Spirit (1.33; 4.10-14, 20-24; 7.37-39; 15.26;
16.7; 20.22-23). He keeps those given to him (6.37-39).
Those who do what he commands are his friends: not servants,
but friends, for all that he has heard from the Father he has made
known to them (15.13-15).

   Implicit in some aspects of the preceding account of Jesus'
role, his function as revealer must be noted explicitly. He came,
sent by the Father, and he accomplished his work, that we might
have eternal life. He gave us the power to become children of

---

[12] *The Mystery*, p. 153.

God.   But how do we come to this life, how can we become
children of God, how can we be aware of the very possibility of
that fulness of life which he came to give?   He must first of all
tell us about God (cf. 1.18) and about the eternal life which God
offers us.   He has the *words* of eternal life (cf. 6.68), the words
which tell us who he is and what is the meaning of his life and
work. He is the light which illumines us interiorly; we are drawn
to him by the Father; the Father and he give us the Spirit to
teach us, to illumine us interiorly: all of these factors bear on
God's action within us.   But the words which he speaks are the
principal bearers of his revelation.   That revelation opens to us
the way to a new fulness of life.   To it we must respond in faith:
we must believe him, believe in him, believe what he tells us,
trust him and commit ourselves to him.   Jesus' words of
revelation, then, ground our personal relation to him, the
revealer.

(c) The Spirit.   To see the kingdom of God, enter the
kingdom of God, one must be begotten anew from above,
begotten of water and the Spirit.   What is begotten of the flesh is
flesh; what is begotten of the Spirit is spirit (3.3, 5-8). Referring
to what he has said about the bread from heaven, and the
necessity of belief in him, Jesus affirms: "It is the Spirit that gives
life, the flesh is of no avail; the words which I have spoken to you
are spirit and life...." (6.63): "flesh" (mere human manners of
understanding) will not enable men to penetrate the meaning of
Jesus' life-giving words; the Spirit (which he has, and which he
will give) gives understanding and life.

> "If you love me, you will keep my commandments.   And I will
> pray the Father, and he will give you another Counselor, to be
> with you for ever, even the Spirit of truth, whom the world cannot
> receive, because it neither sees him nor knows him; you know
> him, for he dwells with you, and will be in you.... These things I
> have spoken to you, while I am still with you.   But the Counselor,
> the Holy Spirit, whom the Father will send in my name, he will
> teach you all things, and bring to your remembrance all that I have
> said to you...." (14.15-17, 25-26).

The Spirit will bear witness to Jesus, and we too (implicitly by the
light, and in the power, of the Spirit) shall bear witness (cf.
15.26-27; 1 Jn 5.6-8).

> "... it is to your advantage that I go away, for if I do not go away,
> the Counselor will not come to you; but if I go, I will send him to
> you.   And when he comes, he will convince the world of sin and of

righteousness and of judgment.... I have yet many things to say to you, but you cannot bear them now. When the Spirit of truth comes, he will guide you into all the truth; for he will not speak on his own authority, but whatever he hears he will speak, and he will declare to you the things that are to come. He will glorify me, for he will take what is mine and declare it to you. All that the Father has is mine; therefore I said that he will take what is mine and declare it to you" (16.7-8, 12-15).

In the "Johannine Pentecost" Jesus gives the Holy Spirit to the Apostles, implicitly to enable them to fulfill the mission which he has given them, explicitly empowering them to forgive or retain sins (20.21-23).

In Volume II of this work we shall have to consider John's many norms for discernment of our experience of God. Here it may suffice to indicate the role of the Spirit which God has given us (cf. 1 Jn 3.24; 4.12-13).

(2) *The effect in us: abundant life.* "...I came that they may have life, and have it abundantly" (10.10: RSV; or, with JB: "...and have it to the full"). Writing now of fulfillment in us according to John, I choose deliberately to bring all aspects under a single effect: full life. I shall enumerate many aspects or factors, but it seems to me that all bear upon one great complex reality, and that the term which expresses that reality most satisfactorily is *abundant life,* or *full life.* Having completed my account of the elements, I shall reflect on the nature of John's symbolism and on the reality which it images.

(a) "... [The] Father has life in himself, ..." (5.26).

(b) "... [As] the Father has life in himself, so he has granted the Son also to have life in himself, ..." (5.26). As some editors punctuate verses three and four of the prologue, and some commentators correspondingly interpret it, "In him was life, and the life was the light of men" (1.4)[13]. Jesus affirms: "...because I live, you will live also" (14.19). Without explicit mention of the word *life,* Jesus' symbol of the vine and the branches expresses our participation of his life. Finally, John writes of the word of life: "—the life was made manifest, and we saw it, and testify to it, and proclaim to you the eternal life which was with the Father and was made manifest to us—" (1 Jn 1.2).

(c) "In this is the love, not that we loved God but that he loved us and sent his Son to be the expiation for our sins" (1 Jn

---

[13] See above, pp. 92, 95.

4.10); "... he is the expiation for our sins, and not for ours only but also for the sins of the whole world" (1 Jn 2.2). Jesus is the Lamb of God, who takes away the sin of the world (1.29; cf. 1 Jn 3.5). "If we confess our sins, he is faithful and just, and will forgive our sins and cleanse us from all unrighteousness" (1 Jn 1.9; cf. 2.2).

(d) We, in turn, must *come* to Jesus, drawn by the Father (5.40; 6.35, 44-45), *hear* him, for he comes from above and bears witness to what he has seen and heard (3.31-32; 5.24), *receive* him (1.12; 3.33; 5.42-43), and *believe*: believing in him, with all of the nuances of the nature of the act, is at once the condition of coming to full life (e.g. 1.12; 3.16; 6.40; 11.25-26) and an abiding dimension of the fulness of life (3.36; 6.47). I shall not multiply citations of texts, nor attempt to consider all of the nuances suggested by the extremely varied syntax of the verb *believe*[14]. Human faith in itself is an act and an attitude which involve many factors and interpersonal relations. All the more complicated is faith in God, and in Jesus the God-man. Believing, trusting, and entrusting of self are of supreme importance, and their full significance can be suggested only as they are considered as elements of that fulness of life which we are attempting to sketch.

(e) Both Father and Son *give* life (5.21; 10.10; 11.25; 14.6, 19; 17.2; 1 Jn 4.9; 5.11-12). *Begotten/born* of God (1.12-13; 1 Jn 3.9; 4.7; 5.1, 4, 18), *anew from above*[15] (3.3), *of water and spirit*[16] (3.5-8), we are *children of God* (1.12; 1 Jo 3.1-2). We are *of God* [or: *from God*] (1 Jn 4.2, 4, 6; 5.19). Since we are

---

[14] Anyone interested in finding all of the texts regarding elements of our response can do so by consulting a concordance to the Greek New Testament for the words ἔρχομαι (come), ἀκούω (hear), λαμβάνω (receive), and above all πιστεύω (believe). For the basic senses of *believe* (believe/be convinced of something; trust; entrust) and for the bewildering variety of the syntax of the verb, used absolutely or governing cases, or with prepositions and a variety of cases, see BAG, πιστεύω.

[15] The Greek ἄνωθεν, as it occurs in 3.3, seems to be used deliberately by John with the double sense *anew* and *from above*: cf. BAG.

[16] The Greek text is simply "water and spirit" in 3.5. Both RSV and JB translate "the Spirit", and their interpretation seems justified by the immediate context, regarding what is begotten/born of *the Spirit*, as contrasted with the flesh, and the spirit's [or "the wind's"] blowing where it wills. I should say, however, that the interpretation of "the Spirit" is grounded not so much on the text and immediate context as on the whole of the Gospel, in which Jesus promises another Counselor, the Spirit of truth, the Holy Spirit (14.16-17, 26; 15.26; 16.7-15).

begotten of God, God's *seed* remains in us[17]. We *have* the *Father* (1 Jn 2.23), the *Son* (1 Jn 5.12); God has given us of his own *Spirit* (1 Jn 4.13). Father (1 Jn 4.12, 13, 15-16), Son (6.56; 15.4-5), and Spirit (14.17; cf. 14.16) *abide* in us[18]. We abide in the Father (1 Jn 2.24; 4.13, 15-16), in the Son (6.56; 15.4, 5, 7; 1 Jn 2.6; 2.24, 28). We *are* in the Son (1 Jn 2.5; 5.20).

The life which we are given is *eternal, everlasting* (3.15-16, 36 and *passim*): this is John's most common expression. At times when he writes of it simply as *life*, he plays on the contrast between eternal, everlasting life and natural, human, mortal life, or life in this world. Moreover he plays on the corresponding contrast between two kinds of death. The interplay of these two sets of contrasts, and of corresponding characteristics of the lives and deaths, are the source of some of the striking paradoxes in John. The contrasts figure most prominently in relation to believing and not believing in the Son, and in relation to eating or not eating his flesh, drinking or not drinking his blood.

He who believes in the Son *has* eternal life (3.15, 16; 6.47); he will not perish (3.16; cf. 6.50-51; 8.50.51), will not be condemned (3.17-18), has passed from death to life (5.24; cf. 1 Jn 3.14). The paradoxes appear in these texts: "For this is the will of my Father, that every one who sees the Son and believes in him should *have* eternal life; *and* I *will raise him up* at the last day" (6.40; cf. 6.44, 47). "I am the resurrection and the life; he who believes in me, *though he die*, yet shall he *live*, and whoever lives and believes in me *shall never die*" (11.25-26). "He who believes in him [the Son] is not condemned; he who does not believe is condemned already, because he has not believed in the name of the only Son of God. And this is the judgment, that the light has come into the world, and men loved darkness rather than light, because their deeds were evil...." (3.18).

"Truly, truly, I say to you, unless you eat the flesh of the Son of man and drink his blood, you *have no life in you*; he who eats

---

[17] 1 Jn 3.9: σπέρμα. There is no agreement on how *seed* here is to be understood. Among the opinions are these: *nature* (RSV and others); the word of God; the beginning or germ of a new life, planted in us by the Spirit of God; word or spirit; grace that makes us holy; Christ; the Spirit. JB simply translates it as *seed*, perhaps the best solution of all, leaving the word with all of the suggestive power indicated by the range of interpretations. See BAG on σπέρμα and JB, note "f" on 1 Jn 3.9.

[18] μένω means *abide, dwell, stay, live, continue*, etc. See BAG.

my flesh and drinks my blood *has eternal life, and* I *will* raise him up at the last day.... he who eats me *will live* because of me.... he who eats this bread *will live* for ever" (6.53-54, 57, 58).

Finally, there is Jesus' paradoxical teaching: "...The hour has come for the Son of man to be glorified. Truly, truly, I say to you, unless a grain of wheat falls into the earth and dies, it remains alone; but if it dies, it bears much fruit. He who *loves* his *life* loses it, and he who hates his life in this world will keep it for eternal life. If any one serves me, he must follow me; and where I am, there shall my servant be also; if any one serves me, the Father will honor him" (12.23-26)[19].

What are we to make of these texts concerning life and death? There are two kinds, or levels, of life: our natural human life in this world, which terminates in death; and the "full" life which is portrayed in John. There are two kinds of death: that which is the end of natural life; and that which is a state which can endure during this natural life and, implicitly, eternally after the end of life in this world. One can be alive in this world, and yet dead: to pass from death to life he or she must believe in the Son (5.25; cf. 1 Jn 3.14). One who does not believe remains in his death of sin, is already condemned, judged (3.18, 19). One who dies in his sins (8.21, 24) comes to that death which is the end of natural life, and passes into what is called judgment, and what is implicitly eternal death. Hence there is a twofold resurrection: "Truly, truly I say to you, the hour is coming, and now is, when the dead will hear the voice of the Son of God; and those who hear will live. For as the Father has life in himself, so he has granted the Son also to have life in himself, and has given him authority to execute judgment, because he is the Son of man. Do not marvel at this; for the hour is coming when all who are in the tombs will hear his voice and come forth, those who have done good, to the resurrection of life, and those who have done evil, to the resurrection of judgment" (5.25-29).

One who believes in the Son will come to the end of his natural life, but he has eternal life and will never perish. He may be killed for hatred of Christ (cf. 16.2), he may lose his life, not clinging to it at the cost of eternal life, "hating" his life in this world in the sense that he does not prefer it to eternal life, and is willing to sacrifice it for the sake of eternal life. He will not *perish*, he will *live*: he *has* eternal life, *and* he *will be raised* to

---

[19] Compare the Synoptics: Mk 8.35; Mt 16.25 and 10.39; Lk 9.23-24 and 17.35.

life at the last day. The full life, then, has two stages: now, and from the resurrection at the last day. Natural life will pass, come to its end in death. The "death" of sin also has two stages: now during life in this world, for the one who refuses to believe: he or she is already "judged", condemned; and from the resurrection of "judgment": implicitly eternal death. Those, then, who "die in their sins" (cf. 8.21, 24) will die a double death: the end of life in this world, the continuing death of judgment at the resurrection and after.

(f) John's complementary symbolisms of *hunger and thirst, food and drink,* contribute to suggesting the uniqueness of the great transcendent reality: new life from above, from God, eternal life. Our food is the Son, the bread from heaven; his flesh; and (as he did) doing the will of our Father (4.32-33). Our drink is implicitly the Spirit (4.14) and Jesus' blood. Only within the mystery of believing him and believing in him can we eat this food and drink this drink. If we do, we shall never hunger and never thirst (4.14; 6.35). The bodily symbolisms of hunger and thirst, food and drink, in the context of this message represent an appetite for Father and Son and for life in them, an appetite which is fully satisfied in the life which never fails.

(g) Our life is one of *love*. The life which is symbolized is not merely bodily, but *fully human*, personal and interpersonal. The interpersonal world in which we live is transcendent both in our relations with Father, Son, and Spirit and in our relations with one another. We love the Father (1 Jn 4.19-20; 5.1-4) and the Son (8.42; 14.15, 21, 23). Yet the mystery and the great reality is not merely of our individual personal love of them. Jesus gradually reveals that our life and love are realized only in fellowship, as we are together in them, love one another, and are truly one. From the outset Jesus drew disciples who together followed him (cf. 1.35, 39-51) and together were formed by him. There is to be one flock and one shepherd (10.16; cf. 11.52). Within the community of his disciples there are some whom Jesus loves especially: John (13.23; 20.2; 21.20), and Mary, Martha, and Lazarus (11.3, 5, 11, 35-36). He calls his disciples not servants, but friends: "You are my friends if you do what I command you. No longer do I call you servants, for the servant does not know what his master is doing; but I have called you friends, for all that I have heard from my Father I have made known to you" (15.15). His new commandment is that we love one another as he has loved us (13.34; 15.12, 17; 1 Jn 4.7-12, 20-21). We must "...not love in word or speech but in deed and in truth" (1 Jn 3.18). In our love we must be one, as the Father and the Son are one (17.11, 20-23).

The command is unequivocal in the Gospel, and it goes far beyond that love of enemies which is Jesus' deepening of the law of love according to Matthew and Luke (Mt 5.43-48; Lk 6.27-28, 32-36). John's theological insight into the command, as he develops it in the letter, is profound. Our love of one another is the sure test of our love of God, of our being born of God and knowing God. We have never seen God. How do we know that we love him? If we cannot recognize God's goodness in one another, in its most perfect manifestation among us, how do we love him? If we hate our brother, whom we see, we are liars if we say that we love the God whom we have not seen. God is love. We have an experiential knowledge of him when we love: knowing what it is to love, we have some sense of what God really is: he has given us something of his own Spirit, which is a Spirit of love.

I have said that this love of one another, within the community of believers, goes beyond the love of enemies. Why? The love of our enemy cannot be the ideal, the supreme degree of love. If indeed we love our enemy who seeks to injure us, we desire that he or she be healed of that hatred which is a disease and deformity, that he or she come to acknowledge and return our love, that we may live together in that mutual knowledge and love which alone can be the perfection of love. The new commandment, of mutual love within the community of believers, calls for perfect love, the ideal of love [20].

I make one more personal reflection regarding the deep sense of Jesus' prayer: that we may be one, so that the world may believe that the Father has sent him. Why should our oneness in love lead the world to believe that the Father has sent Jesus? I suggest a possible answer. For any one who knows of the promise, of how men and women are to live together in the age of the promised blessings, our love should be such as to convince them that the promise has been fulfilled, that the Savior has been sent and the blessings realized at least in part. For mutual Christian love in fellowship is a mystery. Its beauty and the fulness of life to which it witnesses surpass any purely human love.

---

[20] In this paragraph, obviously, I am presenting not John's theological reflection, but my own. I have treated the matter more fully in *The Mystery*, "Love in Fellowship", pp. 269-284. I have developed it further in *Basics*, "The Dialectic of Charisms", pp. 198-212, esp. pp. 209-211.

(h) We must *keep the commandments.* The Father's commandment *is* eternal life (12.50). As for Jesus himself, his food is to do the will of him who sent him, to accomplish his work (4.34); he has kept his Father's commandments and abides in his love (15.10). We must continue in his word, to be truly his disciples (8.31); keep his word, that we may never see death (8.51; cf. 12.47-50). "If a man loves me, he will keep my word, and my Father will love him, and we will come to him and make our home with him. He who does not love me does not keep my words; and the word which you hear is not mine but the Father's who sent me" (14.23-24). "My sheep hear my voice, and I know them, and they follow me; and I will give them eternal life, and they shall never perish, ..." (10.27-28). "If you love me, you will keep my commandments" (14.15; cf. 14.21; 15.10, 14; 1 Jn 2.3-6; 3.21-24; 5.2-3). His new commandment is that we love one another (13.34; 15.12, 17; 1 Jn 2.3-6, 7-11; 3.11-24; 4.7-21).

(i) We have the *light, know* the truth and are free, have what may be called an *experiential or connatural knowledge* of God and of aspects of our being in him, and are able to test and *discern* the Spirit of God and the quality of our lives.

The Word is the light of men, the true light that enlightens every man (1.4, 9). "I am the light of the world; he who follows me will not walk in darkness, but will have the light of life" (8.12; cf. 9.5). Judgment depends on one's attitude to the light: "And this is the judgment, that the light has come into the world, and men loved darkness rather than light, because their deeds were evil. For every one who does evil hates the light, and does not come to the light, lest his deeds should be exposed. But he who does what is true comes to the light, that it may be clearly seen that his deeds have been wrought in God" (3.19-21). What is affirmed first of the disciples during Jesus' life on earth is true of all who believe: "The light is with you for a little longer. Walk while you have the light, lest the darkness overtake you: he who walks in the darkness does not know where he goes. While you have the light, believe in the light, that you may become sons of light" (12.35-36). "I have come as light into the world, that whoever believes in me may not remain in darkness" (12.46).

"... God is light and in him is no darkness at all. If we say we have fellowship with him while we walk in darkness, we lie and do not live according to the truth; but if we walk in the light, as he is in the light, we have fellowship with one another, and the blood of Jesus his Son cleanses us from all sin" (1 Jn 1.5-7). "... I am

writing you no new commandment, ... Yet I am writing you a new
commandment, which is true in him and in you, because the darkness is passing away and the true light is already shining. He who
says he is in the light and hates his brother is in the darkness still.
He who loves his brother abides in the light, and in it there is no
cause for stumbling. But he who hates his brother is in darkness
and walks in the darkness, and does not know where he is going,
because the darkness has blinded his eyes" (1 Jn 2.7-11).

"Jesus then said to the Jews who had believed in him, 'If you
continue in my word, you are truly my disciples, and you will
know the truth, and the truth will make you free.... if the Son
makes you free, you will be free indeed" (8.31-32, 36): free
from slavery to sin (cf. 8.33-35). "... [This] is eternal life, that
they *know* thee the only true God, and Jesus Christ whom thou
hast sent. I glorified thee on earth, having accomplished the
work which thou gavest me to do; .... I have manifested thy name
to the men whom thou gavest me out of the world; .... Now they
know that everything that thou has given me is from thee; for I
have given them the words which thou gavest me, and they have
received them and know in truth that I came from thee; and they
have believed that thou didst send me.... O righteous Father, the
world has not known thee, but I have known thee; and these
know that thou hast sent me. I made known to them thy name,
and I will make it known, that the love with which thou hast
loved me may be in them, and I in them" (17.3-4, 6-8,
25-26). We "... *know* him who is from the beginning" (1 Jn
2.13-14): probably to be understood in the sense of knowing
Jesus Christ. We "...know the Father" (1 Jn 2.13). "...you
have been anointed by the Holy One [most probably the Holy
Spirit], and you all *know*. I write to you, not because you do not
know the truth, but because you know it, and know that no lie is
of the truth. Who is the liar but he who denies that Jesus is the
Christ? This is the antichrist, he who denies the Father and the
Son. No one who denies the Son has the Father. He who
confesses the Son has the Father also. Let what you heard from
the beginning abide in you. If what you heard from the
beginning abides in you, then you will abide in the Son and in the
Father. And this is what he has promised us, eternal life. I write
this to you about those who would deceive you; but the *anointing*
which you received from him abides in you, and you have no need
that any one should teach you; as his anointing teaches you about
everthing, and is true, and is no lie, just as it has taught you,
abide in him" (1 Jn 2.20-27).

Finally, we have a certain experiential or "connatural" knowledge of God and of aspects of our being in him; and we are able to test spirits to know whether they are of God, and to discern aspects of our being in God.

In his confrontation with the leaders of the Jews, Jesus affirms the basic truth which is involved here: "... My teaching is not mine, but his who sent me; *if any man's will is to do his will, he shall know whether the teaching is from God or whether I am speaking on my own authority.* He who speaks on his own authority seeks his own glory; but he who seeks the glory of him who sent him is true, and in him there is no falsehood" (7.16-18). I have italicized the words which formulate the basic principle. What follows may be regarded as a sort of confirmatory criterion. The basic principle is this: any one who is determined to do God's will is able to recognize God's teaching. Why is this so? The man or woman who does God's will is living in God, has a sense of the "shape" of the experience of living in God and doing his will, and can recognize what is in harmony with what he or she believes concerning God. Such a man or woman has a sort of connatural knowledge of God which is a criterion of God's teaching and God's truth. Living in God, doing his will, we experience God, we have a vague, massive knowledge of the shape of the experience, and a vague, massive knowledge of the God whom we experience. Such experiential knowledge is a touchstone, a criterion of what is in harmony with what we hold by faith. In other words, what is involved here is a sense of the *analogy of faith*: a sense of the harmony, proportion, and intelligible structure of the whole of revealed truth[21]. It is a reliable guide in the life of the individual believer living within a community of believers. All the more surely it functions in the Church as a whole. As Jesus indicates here according to John, it functioned in the life of the Jews, as a criterion of God's continuing revelation.

Those who do not have the love of God within them will not recognize his voice, receive his testimony, receive Jesus who is sent by him, and believe: "... The Father who sent me has himself borne witness to me. His voice you have never heard; and you do not have his word abiding in you, for you do not believe him whom he has sent. You search the scriptures, because you think that in them you have eternal life; and it is they that bear witness to me; yet you refuse to come to me that you may have life.... I

---

[21] On the analogy of faith, see *Basics*, pp. 142-148.

know that you have not the love of God within you" (5.37-42).
Again, "...If God were your Father, you would love me, for I
proceeded and came forth from God; I came not of my own
accord, but he sent me. Why do you not understand what I say?
It is because you cannot bear to hear my word. You are of your
father, the devil, and your will is to do your father's desires. He
was a murderer from the beginning, and has nothing to do with
the truth, because there is no truth in him. When he lies, he
speaks according to his own nature, for he is a liar and the father
of lies. But because I tell the truth, you do not believe me.... He
who is of God hears the words of God; the reason why you do not
hear them is that you are not of God" (8.42-47).

In a similar manner Jesus indicates two attitudes toward the
promised Spirit: "If you love me, you will keep my
commandments. And I will pray the Father, and he will give you
another Counselor, to be with you for ever, even the Spirit of
truth, whom the world cannot receive, because it neither sees him
nor knows him; you [who love me and keep my commandments]
know him, for he dwells with you and will be in you"
(14.15-17).

This interior principle of recognition of God's word can be
called a sort of transcendent connatural knowledge. It is not
connatural if we regard what is according to our merely human
way of being. It is connatural in a transcendent sense, in so far as
we have been begotten and born again from above, of God, of the
Spirit. We are *of* God, children of God, with God's seed within
us, loving God and living according to his will. Living in this
higher life, we can recognize and believe in God's word, recognize
and believe in Jesus and in the Father who sent him.

Similarly, according to John's teaching in the letter, we have
been anointed by the Holy One, and the anointing abides in us.
Hence we *know* the truth:

> But you have been anointed by the Holy One, and you all know. I
> write to you, not because you do not know the truth, but because
> you know it, and know that no lie is of the truth. Who is the liar
> but he who denies that Jesus is the Christ? This is the antichrist,
> he who denies the Father and the Son. No one who denies the
> Son has the Father. He who confesses the Son has the Father
> also. Let what you heard from the beginning abide in you. If
> what you heard from the beginning abides in you, then you will
> abide in the Son and in the Father. And this is what he has
> promised us, eternal life.... the anointing which you received from
> him abides in you, and you have no need that any one should

teach you; as his anointing teaches you about everything, and is true, and is no lie, just as it has taught you, abide in him (1 Jn 2.20-27).

One of the most fascinating elements in John's witness to Christian experience is that which bears on the knowledge which he and his fellow-believers have of aspects of the mystery of the new life which they have received. The texts can be divided into three classes: (1) John's absolute statements about his fellow-believers, his "little children" (τεκνία: 1 Jn 2.1, 18, 29; 3.7 in a variant text and 3.18; 4.4; 5.21) or simply "children" (παιδία: 2.14, 18; 3.7 var.); (2) his absolute statements about what they know; (3) his complicated series of criteria of their knowledge of aspects of their own life and of the larger mystery.

First, then, John makes a series of statements about the interior life of his fellow-believers: "...your sins are forgiven for his sake" (1 Jn 2.12); "...you have overcome the evil one" (2.13, 14; 4.4); "...you are strong, and the word of God abides in you, ..." (2.14); "...you are of God, ..." (4.4); "...we are in him who is true, in his Son Jesus Christ ..." (5.20).

Second, John states absolutely what they *know*: him who is from the beginning (2.13, 14); the Father (2.13); "...you all know" (2.20); the truth (2.21); that no lie is of the truth (2.21); everything (2.27); that we are of God, and the whole world is in the power of the evil one (5.19); that the Son of God has come and has given us understanding, to know him who is true (5.20).

Third, John gives bewildering sets of criteria and of truths which we know according to those criteria, some positive, some negative. To introduce some order into these sets, I shall list in two columns the criteria and the truths known. I reduce both to brief expressions of the substance. I group criteria, giving variations of what I regard as basically the same criterion: these are numbered in the left column. In the right column I list the truths known, often several quite distinct truths concerning aspects of the believers' lives or of the mystery more generally. From the outset I make clear that I have no illusion of working out a neat set of "rules for the discernment of spirits". Rather I regard them as significant indications of John's symbolism and of the reality which it images, and I shall reflect on them in the closing section of this chapter.

Criteria	*Truths*
(1) believe	abide in Son and Father (2.24)
let what you heard from	overcome the world (5.4-5)
the beginning abide in you	have testimony of God in
confess the Son	ourselves (5.10)
confess that Jesus Christ	have eternal life (5.13)
has come in the flesh	have confidence of receiving
	what we ask (5.14-15)
	have [Son] and Father (2.23)
	be spirit of God (4.2)
(2) deny Jesus is the Christ	be the antichist (2.22)
not confess Jesus	not have the Father (2.23)
	not be of God (4.3)
	make God a liar (5.10)
(3) keep the commandments	be sure that we know him
walk as he walked	(2.3)
walk in the light	love for God is perfected (2.5)
keep his word	be in him (2.5)
do right	abide for ever (2.17)
be as he is	be born of him (2.29)
[the commandment:	be righteous (3.7)
(a) believe in the name	know that we are of the truth
of the Son Jesus Christ	(3.19)
(b) love one another]	reassure our hearts (3.19)
	have confidence (3.21; 4.17)
	receive what we ask (3.22)
	abide in him (3.24)
	He abides in us (3.24)
	know that we love the children
	of God (5.2)
	love God (5.3)
(4) walk in darkness	have no fellowship with him
sin	(1.6)
disobey his commandments	not live according to truth (1.6)
	be guilty of lawlessness (3.4)
	never have seen or known him
	(3.6)
	be of the devil (3.8, 10)
	not be of God (3.10)
	not know him (2.4)

Criteria	Truths
(5) love our brother love one another abide in love	abide in light (2.10) pass out of death into life (3.14) lay down life for brethren (3.16) be of God (4.7) be born of God (4.7) know God (4.7) God abides in us (4.12) his love is perfected in us (4.12, 17) he has given us of his own Spirit (4.13) we abide in him (4.13) abide in God and God in us (4.16) have confidence (4.17) not fear (4.18)
(6) hate brother not love close heart	be in darkness (2.9, 11) not be of God (3.10) remain in death (3.14) be a murderer (3.15) not have eternal life (3.15) not have God's love in him (3.17) not know God (4.8) not love God (4.20)
(7) be born of God be of God be God's children now	not sin (3.9, 5.18) be listened to by him who is of God (4.6) overcome the world (5.4) keep him (5.18) not be touched by the evil one (5.18)
(8) love God	love brother (4.21)
(9) love parent (God)	love child (5.1)
(10) love the world	not love the Father (2.15-17)
(11) be of the world	be listened to by the world (4.5)

Criteria	*Truths*
(12) not listen to us	not be of God (4.6)
(13) leave us	never have been of us (2.19)
(14) say we have no sin	truth is not in us (1.8) make him a liar (1.10)
(15) confess sins	he will forgive, cleanse (1.9)
(16) abide in Son, Father abide in him	have eternal life (2.24-25) have confidence (2.28) not shrink from him in shame at his coming (2.28) not sin (3.6)
(17) have Son	have life (5.12)
(18) not have Son	not have life (5.12)
(19) not know him	not know us (3.1)

(j) We must *purify ourselves*: "Beloved, we are God's children now; it does not yet appear what we shall be, but we know that when he appears we shall be like him, for we shall see him as he is. And every one who thus hopes in him purifies himself as he is pure" (1 Jn 3.2-3).

(k) We must have *confidence* (1 Jn 3.21; 4.17) and have *no fear* (1 Jn 4.18).

(l) We are *sent* to *witness*, guarded by the Father, and (implicitly) empowered. Mission and role of witness are far more explicit in the case of John, the forerunner, than in the case of the apostles and those who would believe after them. John's mission and role are clear: (1.6-7, 15, 19-23, 29-34; 3.25-30; 5.33-36). Jesus' explicit call is clear especially in accounts of Peter (1.43; 21.19, 22). So too is his sending into the world those whom the Father has given to him (17.9, 18). Jesus chose his apostles out of the world (15.19) and they are to witness to Jesus (15.26-27). As he prays that the Father may keep, guard them, it is clear that he has in mind not only his apostles, but also "...those who believe in me through their word..." (17.18).

Implicitly too their mission is to witness by their very lives, especially by their unity in love, that the Father has sent the Son (17.20-23). He chose us, and appointed us to go and bear fruit which will abide (17.16). To the Apostles [and implicitly to their successors] Jesus gives the Spirit in a special manner, with the power of forgiving or retaining sins (20.22-23). To Peter [and implicitly to his successors] he gives the command and the power: "Feed my lambs.... Tend my sheep.... Feed my sheep" (21.15-17). The evidence admittedly is sketchy, but it is recognizable as a remote base for the manner in which the Church has understood the mystery of our continuing sending, to witness. John's letter gives further suggestion of the role and importance of *confessing* Jesus, of testifying (1 Jn 4.14-15; 2.23; 4.2-3).

(m) We have *overcome the evil one* (1 Jn 2.12-14; 5.4-5).

(n) As the apostles could expect the world's *hatred* and *persecution,* so too can his other followers (15.18-25; 16.1-4, 20-22).

(o) So too can we expect *sorrow, joy,* and *peace* (14.27; 16.20-24, 33; 20.19, 21, 26).

(p) Though a share in Jesus' glory pertains to the further promise, rather than to present fulfillment (cf. 17.24), still in a sense Jesus can speak of having given glory to those who have believed in him (17.22)[22].

FURTHER PROMISE

With regard to Jesus, we consider here what could be termed aspects of the consummation of the process of his glorification and of his action on our behalf. They are indicated both in his promises and his prayer to the Father. (a) Jesus goes to the Father (13.3, 31-36); he is no more in the world (17.11). His glorification is a process beginning on earth. In his "signs", beginning at Cana, Jesus manifested his glory (2.11). Lazarus' death is "... for the glory of God, so that the Son of God may be glorified by means of it" (11.4). The Father seeks Jesus' glory

---

[22] One cannot find in John, as far as I know, any clear indication of the sense in which Jesus has given glory to those who believe in him. Elsewhere I have gathered the elements of the Johannine conception of glory and glorification: see *The Mystery*, pp. 169-170. One may find inklings of the meaning of the glory given to believers in my effort to go beyond John's explicit thought. See the text quoted above, pp. 182-183.

(8.50, 54). In a very special sense Jesus will be glorified in his "hour" (cf. 7.39; 12.16, 23, 28; 13.3, 31,36; 17.1-5). In that hour he departs out of this world and goes to the Father (13.1, 3, 31-36). This is part of the whole of his being "lifted up", which includes his dying on the cross, rising, and ascending to the Father. Thus in John Jesus' triple statement of his having to be lifted up corresponds to the triple prediction of his passion, death, and resurrection in the Synoptics (3.13-14; 8.28; 12.32-33). The consummation comes in that glorification in the Father's presence, with the glory which the Son had with him before the world was made (17.5, 24)[23]. (b) Jesus goes to prepare a place for us (14.2). (c) He will come again and take us to himself, so that where he is we may also be (14.3, 28). (d) He will raise us on the last day (cf. 6.40, 44, 54). There will be a resurrection for all, but it will be twofold: resurrection of life for those who have done good, and resurrection of judgment for those who have done evil (5.28-29). Concerning judgment, there is a dialectic in the texts. On the one hand, the Father judges no one, but has given all judgment to the Son (5.22; cf. vv. 27-29, 30); yet Jesus and the Father judge (8.16, 26); the Father judges (8.50). On the other hand, Jesus does not judge: "For God sent the Son into the world, not to condemn the world, but that the world might be saved through him. He who believes in him is not condemned; he who does not believe is condemned already, because he has not believed in the name of the only Son of God. And this is the judgment, that the light has come into the world, and men loved darkness rather than light, because their deeds were evil...." (3.17-19; cf. 8.15; 12.47-48).

Concerning men, further promise or threat regards judgment (12.46-48); resurrection (5.26-29; 6.39-40, 44, 54; 11.25); the place prepared for us (14.2-3); being with Jesus to behold his glory given to him before the foundation of the world (17.24). Finally, there is a mysterious, fascinating text in 1 Jn: "Beloved, we are God's children now; it does not yet appear what we shall be, but we know that when he appears we shall be like him, for we shall see him as he is" (1 Jn 3.2). To me the mystery and the fascination lie in the link between seeing him as he is and being like him. It seems insufficient to understand it in the sense that the perfection of vision in itself, as contrasted with our veiled knowledge by faith in this life, will make us like him. I take *him* as designating God, not Jesus. I suggest an interpretation which

---

[23] For a more ample treatment of *glory* in John, see *The Mystery*, pp. 158-170.

seems far more satisfying, and fully consistent with Johannine thought. We shall be like him, not simply by virtue of seeing him as he is, but because of the *love* which will be the consequence of such vision. Knowing God by faith in this life, we should love him, but because of the imperfection of a knowledge which does not reach him as our full, compelling Good, we can fall away from love, or love only imperfectly. When we see him as he is, and as our supreme Good, drawing us so powerfully that we cannot but respond in fulness of love, we shall reach the fulness of our potential life in that love. And loving him fully, with the full power of our being, we shall be like him, for he is love.

REFLECTIONS

I propose here a number of reflections on John's thought, beginning with some particular features, and moving towards a more general characterization which hopefully will make the particular features intelligible.

(1) I note first one element which is almost completely lacking in John: what might be termed a moral code of Christian life, such as can be gathered, for example, from *Matthew* or from Paul's letters. Throughout John's presentation of Jesus' message and John's own witness to Christian experience faith and love are foremost, and all seems to be summed up in them. Keeping the commandments itself is somehow reduced to them, for "... this is his commandment, that we should believe in the name of his Son Jesus Christ and love one another, just as he has commanded us" (1 Jn 3.23). John's thought is lofty, intuitive, contemplative, inspirational, calling for a fulness of life which consists in knowing-believing and loving. Obviously John makes a precious contribution to the rest of the New Testament, but his thought complements others': it would not suffice in itself to give us a knowledge of the fulness of Christian life.

(2) It is extremely important to reflect on the sense of *know* in John. He uses two verbs especially: οἶδα, γινώσκω. Both are used of (a) what can be called simple natural, human knowledge (and even of sheeps' "knowing"); (b) the range of knowledges which men and women have or could have on the basis of revelation and faith; (c) Jesus' knowledge, which obviously raises special problems. I shall not cite all of the texts: I merely refer to any standard concordance of the Greek New Testament. John uses the verbs with roughly the same frequency in all three senses

in the Gospel.   In the letter, with two exceptions [24], he uses it only
of (b).   As for the objects of the verbs expressing human
knowledge by revelation and faith (b), they fall into three general
classes: (i) Jesus, or a truth about Jesus, or God; (ii) some other
aspects of revealed truth; (iii) what we can discern about ourselves
or others.

    Given the range of uses and objects in John's works, one
cannot determine the meaning of *know* solely on the basis of
profane Greek usage.   Much less can one elaborate any "theory"
of "Johannine knowledge".   In the cases in which merely human
knowledge is concerned, what is involved is some sort of common
sense knowledge of men of the period and culture, or some
knowledge of "fact".   In the far more important class of texts in
which John is concerned with the range of our knowledge by
revelation and faith (in varying degrees), all of the knowledge is
grounded on a transcendent factor, and it is unique even in its
cognitive dimension.   Moreover, all such knowledge involves
other dimensions besides the merely cognitive.   It presupposes
what Jesus *tells* us, reveals to us.   It is possible only for those
who are drawn by the Father, come to Jesus, and *believe*: making
the leap of faith, trust, and commitment of self to Jesus and to the
Father.   It opens upon a wholly new world, beyond the range of
all merely human knowledge.   It is enmeshed in a total religious
act and way of life, in a blend of factors which defies all
satisfactory analysis and explanatory account in any sort of
"*philosophy* of religion".   Some account could be given in a
Christian *theology* of religious experience.   No such theology
could be attributed to John himself, and no rigorous account of
Johannine usage of verbs for *know* can be elaborated.

    One further reflection on the role of knowledge in Christian
experience seems imperative.   On the one hand, we must
acknowedge that *knowing* is part of a total Christian experience of
Jesus, of the Father, and of the full mystery of ourselves and
others: it is not merely cognitive.   On the other hand, we must
not neglect the importance of the cognitive element in the total
experience.   As intellect permeates and penetrates all conscious
human operation, since consciousness itself is part of the mystery
of knowledge [25], so intellect enlightened by revelation and faith
permeates and penetrates all Christian experience.   Without the
cognitive factor of a knowledge reached only by revelation and

----

[24] Cf. 1 Jn 2.11, which may refer to merely human knowledge, from which
John's image is drawn; and 1 Jn 3.20 on God's knowledge.
[25] See MS, pp. 113-123.

faith, a transcendent divine-human knowledge, there would be no Christian experience. For Christian experience, like all human experience, is conscious; and all conscious experience is part of the mystery of knowledge. The knowledge in this case is not merely human, but transcendent. None the less it is knowledge. Without the transcendent cognitive factor of uniquely Christian knowledge, we could have no knowledge of Christian experience, no awareness of experiencing God, no vague sense of the shape of that experience. All talk of experiencing God, and of the God whom we experience would be meaningless. Much less would there be any drive for further understanding within a life of faith [26].

(3) John's *light* symbolism calls for similar reflections. The Word is light (1.4, 5, 7-9). Jesus, the Son, the Incarnate Word is light (8.12; 9.5; 12.35-36, 46). God is light (1 Jn 1.5). Such expressions suggest statements about their "nature". Yet their action upon us has a cognitive dimension: the true light enlightens every man (1.9). The total symbolism suggests a blend of all of the elements which comprise our total response: we must receive the light (1.12), believe in his name (1.12), follow him to have the light of life (8.12), work while we have the light (9.4-5), walk in the light and believe in the light, that we may become sons of the light (12.35-36) not walk in the darkness nor remain in the darkness (12.35, 46; cf. 1 Jn 1.6-7). To be enlightened and walk in the light transcend all merely human knowledge and life.

(4) Sharp contrasts and at times unresolved tensions make John's thought stark and jagged. In a sense one could say that John's thought is portrayed entirely in black and white. Some of the contrasts are these: light and darkness, believers and the "world", love and hate. In the criteria and truths which I arranged in sets (pp. 235-237 above) one can recognize variations upon sets of such contrasts. For John, "we" are of God; "they", unbelieving and already judged, walking in darkness, sinning, are of the devil; they never were of God; those who left "us" never were of us. One of John's stark contrasts involves an unresolved tension in his own thought: it concerns sin. In one of the most severe passages in John he makes these extreme statements about one who sins: he is guilty of lawlessness; he does not abide in God; he has neither seen him nor known him; he is of the devil: "No one born of God commits sin; for God's seed [or "nature": RSV] abides in him, and he

---

[26] See above, pp. 8-9, 13-14, 22-26, and the portions of *Basics* cited there: on revelation, pp. 71-93, and on faith, pp. 137-142.

cannot sin because he is born of God. By this it may be seen who
are the children of God, and who are the children of the devil:
whoever does not do right is not of God, nor he who does not
love his brother" (1 Jn 3.9-10; cf. vv. 4-8). Between this text
and another there is a tension which John himself does not seem
to recognize, and certainly does not resolve: "My little children, I
am writing this to you so that you may not sin; but if any one
does sin, we have an advocate with the Father, Jesus Christ the
righteous; and he is the expiation for our sins, and not for ours
only but also for the sins of the whole world" (1 Jn 2.1-2).
Contrast the implications of this latter text with the details of
John's denunciation in 1 Jn 3.4-10. There is an absolute
opposition between them. It is vain to introduce the sort of
distinctions which theologians make later. John himself makes
no such conciliatory distinctions. If we are to assess John's
thought honestly, we must take it as it stands, not as it could be
re-touched with the distinctions of a later, more conceptual type
of symbolism. Just as his severe statements about sin and sinner
exclude all reconciliation, so too does his denunciation of those
who left his community: they never were of "us"; implicitly they
never were of God, but were and are of the devil; that they should
be converted and reconciled seems unthinkable for John.

(5) If I read John right, one great symbolism dominates his
thought: imaging the full reality of life (and death), playing upon
all aspects of one great analogy. His symbolism is total,
embracing all factors: hunger and thirst, food and drink, life and
death, the full range of life from its bodily aspects to the fully
human life, personal and interpersonal, all taken up into a fulness
of a life which is divine-human. To eat the bread of life, the
bread from heaven, is to believe, to yield and respond to God's
drawing, to come recognize, acknowledge Jesus and the One who
sent him, to have life, to abide in Them and have Them abide in
us, to be one in the fellowship of believers. All aspects of our
fulfillment are elements of one transcendent divine-human
reality, of one process in which the Life which is in the Word
eternally comes into the world in a new manner as the Word
becomes flesh, expiates for our sin, gives life to those whom the
Father has given to him and drawn to him, life which is eternal
and continues into eternity, life which is fellowship now with
Them and with our fellow sharers, and which will be
consummated when we are raised, to be with Jesus in the glory
which he had with the Father before the world was made. John's
symbolism is manifold, but it bears on this one great Reality.

(6) I have characterized John's thought as spiralling. One could say that it is a dialectic: not a dialectic of a highly conceptual symbolism which sharpens concepts and draws clear distinction as it moves, but the dialectic of a highly intuitive symbolism. In such a symbolism there is no "logic". One can fix no one intelligible order and linear conceptual development. Rather, as in a single great intuitive symbol, every symbolic element is related to all others. Any one element is somehow symbolic, representative of the whole. Any one is a touchstone, a criterion of the reality of the whole. Consequently, in the sets of criteria and truths which I have proposed above, one does not have a neat, manageable set of "rules for the discernment of spirits". John proposes a bewildering multiplicity of criteria and truths which often are reversible, reciprocal. All of them, positive and negative, bear upon one great reality, the transcendent life and death which together are the mystery.

It is in the highly intuitive character of John's symbolism that one may find the explanation of his stark contrasts, his black-and white total image, his unresolved tensions, his great paradoxes. There is a dialectic, but it is intuitive, without sharp conceptualization and fine distinctions. He has a richness which leaves such further tasks of conceptualization and distinction to others. What he has elaborated is precious. It is highly personal and distinctive. It should be recognized and esteemed as such.

(7) It may be presumptuous to "evaluate" John's thought, but it is reasonable, I believe, to indicate its unique value and its relation to the rest of the New Testament and the Bible.

I should say that John merits his characterization as "the theologian". Obviously there is no question here of a highly conceptual theology, yet in John we have a "word" about God, and the mystery of Jesus, and the mystery of our fulfillment, which in many respects is unparalleled for depth, beauty, and evocative power as a call to a full response of faith, love, and full life of interpersonal union with Them and with all who are of Them, abide in Them, and have Them abiding in themselves in eternal life.

I have marked the starkness of John's thought. In his own way John is as stark as Matthew. Yet the thrust of his black-and-white opposition is different from that of the contrasts in Matthew and Paul between Jewish and Gentile Christians, or judaizers and Christians. John's opposition is between faith and love and full life on the one hand, and darkness, unbelief, sin, and the world on the other. John surely

portrays Jesus' condemnation of the blindness of the "Jews", yet
their sin is part of the whole surd of the darkness opposed to the
light.   He portrays their absolute rejection of Jesus, not the
reversal of all Judaic expectations which is involved in Matthew's
and Paul's reaction to the challenge of judaizing within the
Church.   In his own way John challenges his readers as forcefully
as do Matthew and Paul.

What is John's relation to the rest of the New Testament, and
what is his unique role?   I have attempted to formulate what I
think his unique qualities are.   As for his relation to the other
New Testament writers, clearly his role is complementary.   Rich
as his thought is, it is only part of the total riches of the New
Testament, and of the Bible as a whole.   Obviously John's work
could never suffice alone as a presentation of the message.   It is
inconceivable that anyone regard it as sufficient, or that anyone
could have had an exclusively Johannine Christian experience, in
the sense of an experience mediated solely by *John* and *1 John*.
That could not have been the experience of John himself or of any
of his community of believers.   The Gospel and Letter of John are
particular works, particular symbolic elements.   They cannot be
conceived of as portraying the full reality experienced by John or
by any of his community.   Their experience must have been
mediated by all that John and his community held of the full
Christian message.   John's Gospel and Letter were written from a
unique perspective, with unique motivation conditioned by the
circumstances of the author and his community.

Consequently the *meaning* of John's Gospel and Letter can
be reached only as they are held in the whole, of which they are
symbolic elements: the whole of the New Testament, and of the
Bible.   In John's case, as in that of any other human author of a
portion of the Bible, the ultimate meaning, the full meaning, of
what he wrote is God's meaning.   We grasp more and more of
that meaning as we grasp more and more of the intelligible
relationships of portions of the whole Bible, and as, under the
continuing illumination of the Spirit in the life of the individual
believer and of the Church, we come to a deeper penetration, a
richer insight and understanding.   That process will continue till
the end of time.

Christian reading of John, therefore, like that of any other
part of the Bible, plays an important role in the total dialectic,
personal and interpersonal, which characterizes full Christian
experience.   Within that total dialectic, the dialectic of knowledge
and understanding is a part: what we understand from one part

of the Bible helps us to understand another, for they all bear on one Reality. Our knowledge and understanding themselves function in a dialectical process involving faith, love, and fidelity, and a deepening awareness of the shape of our experience which in turn impels us to seek to understand more fully. Moreover, our knowledge itself is mediated only in part—if principally—by prayerful Christian reading of the Bible. Worship, especially in the Eucharist, a developing sense of the presence of Father, Jesus, and the Spirit within us, and a deepening sense of their presence in one another, play their role in the total process[27].

---

[27] What I have affirmed summarily in these paragraphs may be found developed in *Basics*. I have not made explicit citations, but readers of that work will recognize the elements. Others who may desire to find them may do so by consulting the index of *Basics*, especially under the words *Bible*, *dialectic*, *growth* in knowledge and love of God.

CHAPTER VII

PAUL

THE MYSTERY: GOD'S MASTER PLAN

In presenting Paul's conception of fulfillment and further promise, I have chosen not to begin directly with details of fulfillment in Jesus and then go on as I have in preceding chapters. To do so would involve shredding some great Pauline texts which provide precious contributions to a synthesis holding God's eternal plan and its gradual revelation and realization. Eventually, of course, I shall have to shred the texts, to gather elements bearing on our three themes: fulfillment in Jesus, fulfillment in us, and further promise. It seems to be far better here to present the elements of a synthesis which may occasion deeper insight and understanding of the Christian mystery, and stimulate continuing growth in a genuine Christian wisdom.

I am not proposing a Pauline synthesis. The elements are Paul's. The thematizing, elaboration of an intelligible order, and presentation of a synthesis are mine. I presuppose the exegesis of seven texts in which Paul uses the word mystery (μυστήριον)[1], and two great passages which could be called Pauline prologues, in the sense in which I have used the word prologue[2]: Eph 1.3-14, in which the word *mystery* occurs; and Col 1.12-23, closely related to explicit use of the word. I have quoted and treated Eph 1.3-14 at length in chapter III, pp. 105-108. Though I regard Col 1.12-23 as a complementary prologue, equal in importance, I shall not quote it here, nor any other of the texts in which the word *mystery* occurs. Here, as elsewhere especially in this volume, I can only hope that my reader will have the Bible at hand, and will take my indications as a helpful guide to reading and reflection upon the texts which I cite. I am

---

[1] 1 Cor 2.7-10; Rom 16.25-26; Col 1.26-27; 2.3; 4.3; Eph 1.9-10; 3.3-12.

[2] See my Introduction, pp. 17-22, and chapter III, pp. 89-120.

drawing the Pauline elements from the texts which refer explicitly
to the mystery. The two "prologues" are rich developments of
the theme.

(1) There is question of the secret (ἐν μυστηρίῳ), hidden
wisdom of God (1 Cor 2.7), his eternal purpose (Eph 3.11), which
he decreed before the ages for our glorification (1 Cor 2.7),
concerning what he has prepared for those who love him (1 Cor
2.9-10).

(2) It is the mystery of his will, according to the purpose
which he set forth in Christ, as a plan for the fulness of time, to
unite all things in him, things in heaven and things on earth (Eph
1.9-10). The mystery is Christ (Col 4.3; cf. 2.2), Christ in
whom all the treasures of wisdom and knowledge are hidden (Col
2.3), Christ in you (Col 1.27); the mystery of how the Gentiles are
fellow heirs, members of the same body, and partakers of the
promise in Christ Jesus through the gospel (Eph 3.6).

(3) The divine plan was kept secret for long ages (Rom 16.25;
cf. Col 1.26; Eph 3.5, 9). None of the rulers of this age
understood it (1 Cor 2.8).

(4) Now it is disclosed and through the prophetic writings is
made known to all nations, to bring about the obedience of faith
(Rom 16.26). God has revealed it to us through the Spirit (1 Cor
2.10). The mystery is now made manifest to his saints (Col 1.26),
to his holy apostles and prophets (Eph 3.5), and to Paul (Eph 3.3).

(5) Through the Church the manifold wisdom of God is to be
made known to the principalities and powers in the heavenly
places (Eph 3.10).

(6) Paul imparts this in words taught not by human wisdom,
but by the Spirit, interpreting spiritual truths to those who
possess the Spirit. The unspiritual man does not receive the gifts
of the Spirit of God, for they are folly to him, and he is not able to
understand them because they are spiritually discerned (1 Cor
2.13-14).

(7) God has realized his eternal purpose in Christ Jesus our
Lord (Eph 3.11). The mystery, Christ in us, is the hope of glory
(Col. 1.27). In Christ we have boldness and confidence of access
through our faith in him (Eph 3.12).

In Pauline usage, *mystery* means hidden, as opposed to
revealed or manifested. The divine plan, the mystery, was
hidden, kept secret for long ages. Even now that it has been
revealed and realized in Christ, it is a mystery, because it has been
revealed only by the Spirit, and it is communicated only in words
taught by the Spirit to those who possess the Spirit: to the

unspiritual it remains hidden. Hence in general *mystery* indicates
directly a relationship to human knowledge.

FULFILLMENT IN JESUS

In this section I shall propose a synthesis of elements of
Paul's teaching regarding fulfillment in Jesus. In doing so I shall
attempt to be faithful to Paul, attributing to Jesus, the Son, what
Paul affirms of him: I shall use Pauline terminology. I make
certain divisions in elaborating a synthesis which is not explicitly
Pauline, but which I consider to be grounded in implicit
distinctions of aspects of the mystery of Christ. In doing so I
deliberately avoid foisting upon Paul a terminology which was
developed only later in the history of dogma and of a conceptual
theology, such as the distinction between time and eternity. Even
more I attempt to avoid any pseudo-conceptualizations which fit
neither Pauline thought nor conceptual theology. In particular I
avoid referring to the "pre-existent Son": it makes no sense to
use the word "pre-existent" as a surrogate for a not-yet
developed concept of eternal. "*Pre*-existent" involves a
temporal relationship. My father was pre-existent to me for a
time. I was pre-existent to my younger brother for a time. I
exist in this earthly life after both of them, for they have died. All
relationships of before and after make sense only within the
frame of time. At the moment of creation of a bodily universe,
bodily existence, extension, movement, and time "begin". We
cannot speak of any existence as being *prior* to creation in any
proper sense. We can speak intelligibly of existence which is not
within the frame of time, not within history. History as process
extends from creation to the "end" of time.

I acknowledge that in some texts Paul himself, regarding
what theologians would call God's eternal action, writes in a
human way which has temporal coloring. For example, God
"... *fore*knew ... *pre*destined..." (Rom 8.29); and he "... *chose* us
him *before* the foundation of the world ... [and] *destined*
[*pre*destined according to the Greek] us..." (Eph 1.4-5; cf. v.
11). Still, in his principal affirmations about the Son "in the form
of God" (Phil 2.6), Paul very aptly uses the present tense or
present participle of *to be* or an equivalent[3]. I am not suggesting
that in doing so Paul had any awareness like that which John

---

[3] Thus ὑπάρχων in Phil 2.6.

seems to have had in reporting Jesus' "*I am*", especially in that affirmation which shatters all normal human usage: "...before Abraham *was*, I *am*" (Jn 8.58). The fact remains that Paul does use the present tense, as I shall point out in the relevant texts, and that in doing so he uses human language which needs the slightest critical nuancing in the later development of conceptual theological affirmations concerning God in his eternal being. In short, there are Pauline texts in which he gives a human temporal coloring to speech about God in his eternal being and action. I am not attempting to deliver Paul from his own limitations. I am determined to avoid any further "temporalizing" of the eternal which would be involved in such an expression as "the pre-existent Son".

Admittedly it is difficult to remain faithful to Pauline terminology in the elaboration of a synthesis which itself is not explicitly Pauline. No doubt various acceptable solutions are possible. For my part these are the principles which govern my procedure. (1) All of Paul's affirmations concerning Jesus are made concerning *one subject*, variously designated as Jesus Christ, the Son, the Lord, etc. (2) Yet there is an implicit distinction to be made between affirmations which regard different spects of his existence. I say *aspects* in the attempt to find a sort of neutral, non-conceptually-theological term. It is not a Pauline word, and I do not use it in designating the headings of my divisions. What do I mean by *aspects*? Simply different considerations of the ways in which Jesus is *as* God, *as* incarnate, *as* man, *as* he was during his earthly existence, *as* he is from the moment of his resurrection, *as* he will be and will act at the last day.

I distinguish four aspects: (a) as he is in the form of God, not within the frame of time; (b) as he was in time during his earthly existence; (c) as he is in glory from the moment of his resurrection: transcending the conditions of earthly existence, yet acting now and until the end of time; (d) as he will be at the last day, at the end of time.

(3) My third principle is this: there is a significant difference between the first aspect and the other three as they figure in Paul's thought. What is affirmed of Jesus in the form of God is true of him absolutely, independently of the frame of time, and permeating all other aspects of his existence. Properly all fulfillment, in the sense of something occurring in Jesus or happening to him, pertains to aspects two, three, and four, which can be regarded analogously as *phases* of his existence from the

moment in which he takes the form of a servant. Only in these phases of his existence can anything *occur* in fulfillment of the promises. Yet the first aspect is relevant, indeed of maximum importance in the full conception of fulfillment in Jesus. For he who fulfills all promises, and in whom all the promises are fulfilled, *is* all that is affirmed of him in the form of God. It is this supreme truth about him which transcends all Jewish expectations and poses the utterly new mystery of the relationships of Father, Son, and Spirit. This is the greatest mystery of our faith, and it will call for the supreme effort of theologians through the centuries in the development of a theology of the Trinity.

Finally, though I distinguish here four aspects, I treat only the first three in this section, which regards fulfillment already accomplished. The fourth regards fulfillment of further promises concerning what will happen at the last day. These promises are either new promises made in the New Testament, or formulations of aspects of the deeper meaning of Old Testament promises, now understood in the light of new revelation and illumination by the Holy Spirit.

Before proposing elements of Paul's thought which regard successively the first three aspects, I wish to point out three texts which affirm massively the relation of the Son, Jesus Christ, to all of the promises of the Scripture. (1) "For the Son of God, Jesus Christ, ... was not Yes and No; but in him it is always Yes. For all the promises of God find their Yes in him..." (2 Cor 1.19-20). Paul's gospel is "... the gospel of God which he promised beforehand through his prophets in the holy scriptures, the gospel concerning his Son, ... Jesus Christ our Lord...." (Rom 1.1-4). (3) "... Christ is the end of the law, that every one who has faith may be justified" (Rom 10.4; cf. Gal 3.19-29).

(1) *In the form of God.* I take this phrase from the great text in *Philippians*: "Yours is to be the same mind which Christ Jesus shewed. His nature is, from the first, divine, and yet he did not see, in the rank of Godhead, a prize to be coveted, he dispossessed himself, and took the nature of a slave, fashioned in the likeness of men, and presenting himself to us in human form; ...." (2.5-7: Knox). Having pondered several translations[4], I offer this as least unsatisfactory. I should render Paul in some such fashion as this: "In this [in Paul's preceding counsels] think as does Christ Jesus, who, *being* divine, did not consider equality

---

[4] RSV, JB, NEB, Goodspeed, Spencer.

with God a thing to be clung to, but emptied himself, taking the nature of a slave...." I say "being divine", since Paul has simply a present participle, equivalent of *being*. A literal translation of the Greek, from which I draw the title of this section, is this: "... *being in the form of God,...*" I am concerned with not injecting more "temporalizing" elements into the thought than Paul's own wording indicates: obviously there are some, in the past tenses of *consider* and *empty*. Christ Jesus *is* divine. He *did* not, or rather he *does* not, and indeed *cannot* empty himself of his being divine, being equal to God. He does not cling to the external glory and the regard and treatment which befit him. From the moment in which he strips himself of external glory in taking the form of a slave, the likeness of man, *he is* both divine and human.

A brief, rather cryptic verse of 2 Cor seems to express less explicitly the teaching formulated in Phil 2.5-8: "For you know the grace [or favor] of our Lord Jesus Christ, that though he was rich, yet for your sake he became poor, so that by his poverty you might become rich" (2 Cor 8.9)[5].

Jesus is the *Son of God* (Gal 2.20; 2 Cor 1.19; Eph 4.13); *his* [the Father's] *Son* (1 Th 1.10; Gal 1.16; 4.4, 6; 1 Cor 1.9; Rom 1.3, 9; 5.10; 8.3, 29, 32 [his own Son]; Col 1.13 [the Son of his love]). What is the meaning of *Son of God* and the variations in these texts? It is not the same in all. In some of the texts Paul seems to be using the term as referring to Jesus as divinely elected for a God-given task[6]. Such texts would involve affirmations about Jesus in the second, third, and fourth (1 Th 1.10) aspects of his existence. Others, however, most probably must be understood as absolute, concerning the Son in his unique relation to the Father, in the first aspect of his existence: as he is in the form of God, independently of any reference to the frame of time. I should understand Rom 1.3 in this sense: "... the gospel concerning his Son, who was descended from David according to the flesh, and designated Son of God in power [or: set up as the Son of God with power: Fitzmyer] according to the Spirit of holiness by his resurrection from the dead, Jesus Christ our Lord...." (Rom 1.3-4). There are two contrasts in this text.

---

[5] Which of the two letters was written first is disputed: see JOSEPH A. FITZMYER, S.J., "The Letter to the Philippians," JBC, II, 50:5-6, p. 248. For a brief indication of the doctrinal relation to Phil 2.5-11, see JOHN J. O'ROURKE, "The Second Letter to the Corinthians," JBC, II, 52:28, p. 284.

[6] See FITZMYER, "Pauline Theology", JBC, II, 79:54-55, p. 811.

One is that noted by Fitzmyer [7]: between Jesus as descended from David and as set up as the Son of God with power by his resurrection [or, temporally, from the moment of his resurrection]. The other is implicit, but important: between the Son (implicitly in an absolute sense) and the Son as descended from David (and subsequently designated or set up as Son of God with power). This important implicit contrast is drawn more sharply in two other texts: "But when the time had fully come, God sent forth his Son, born of a woman, born under the law, to redeem those who were under the law, so that we might receive adoption as sons. And because you are sons, God has sent the Spirit of his Son into our hearts, crying, 'Abba! Father!' So through God you are no longer a slave but a son, and if a son then an heir" (Gal 4.4-7). "For God has done what the law, weakened by the flesh, could not do: sending his own Son in the likeness of sinful flesh and for sin [or: and as a sin offering], he condemned sin in the flesh, in order that the just requirement of the law might be fulfilled in us, who walk not according to the flesh but according to the Spirit" (Rom 8.3-4).

Each text sets forth two contrasts, and in both texts the first contrast is between what I have called the first aspect of Jesus' existence and the others. He *is* the Son, the Father's own Son, absolutely, without reference to the frame of time. *When* the fulness of time had come, within human history and the process of salvation history, God sent forth his Son, born of a woman, born under the law. *When* the law had been shown to be unable to assure fulfillment of its just requirement, *then* God sent his own Son in the likeness of sinful flesh. The purpose of the sending in the two texts is formulated similarly in part: to redeem those who were under the law, to condemn sin in the flesh. In part the texts differ, and in each a second contrast is drawn. In *Galatians*, the purpose is that we might receive adoption as sons, and the contrast is between two sonships: that of his Son, whose Spirit [also elsewhere in Paul the Spirit of God, the Father] is sent into our hearts; and our adoptive sonship. In *Romans*, the purpose is fulfillment of the just requirement of the law in us, and the contrast is between walking according to the flesh and walking according to the Spirit. In each case, or from each point of view, it is only a divine principle which can accomplish the purpose. Jesus *is* the Son, the Father's own Son. Only *he,* now born of a woman, born under the law, in the likeness of sinful flesh, can

---

[7] "The Letter to the Romans," JBC, II, 53:15-16, p. 294.

redeem us, condemn sin in the flesh, give us adoptive sonship, give us his Spirit to move us to call upon God as our Father, and to enable us to fulfill the just requirement of the law by walking according to the Spirit: the Spirit of God, the Spirit of Christ (Rom 8.9). Later in *Romans* (8.14-17) Paul returns to the theme of our sonship, and of the Spirit of God bearing witness within our spirit that we are children of God and heirs.

Any lingering doubt, any suggestion that the *sending* is merely a divine commissioning of a mere man, called "son of God" because of his mission and his devotion to accomplishing it, is banished by these two texts. If they were not enough, however, then the complementary teaching of Phil 2.6 should settle the question. Jesus, the Son who is sent, according to *Galatians* and *Romans*, *is* divine [in the form of God, or of divine nature], *equal to God*, according to the ancient hymn incorporated into *Philippians*[8].

Col 1.15-20 is generally considered an ancient hymn celebrating Christ's pre-eminence and his role in the universe. "He [Christ Jesus, the Son] is the image of the invisible God, the first-born of all creation; for in him all things were created, in heaven and on earth, visible and invisible, whether thrones or dominions or principalities or authorities—all things were created through him and for him. He is before all things, and in him all things hold together (vv. 15-17). He is the head of the body, the church; he is the beginning, the first-born from the dead, that in everything he might be pre-eminent. For in him all the fulness of God was pleased to dwell, and through him to reconcile to himself all things, whether on earth or in heaven, making peace by the blood of his cross (vv. 18-20)."

In what sense is Christ the *image* of the invisible God? Exegetes differ as to whether Paul means the "pre-existent" Christ or the "incarnate" Christ[9]. Preferring the terminology which I have proposed, I should say that in vv. 15-17 Paul is writing of Christ in the first aspect of his existence. Absolutely, without reference to time, he *is* the image of God. Yet this is true of him also in the other three aspects of his existence. What is affirmed of him in vv. 15-17 can be understood, I think, only of

---

[8] On the bearing of Gal 4.4-7, Rom 8.3-4, and Phil 2.6-11 on Jesus' sonship, see FITZMYER in the places cited, JBC, II, 53:81-82, pp. 314-315; 79:53-55, pp. 810-811.

[9] For a brief introduction to the views and discussion of the text, see JOSEPH A. GRASSI, M.M., "The Letter to the Colossians," JBC, II, 55:12-17, pp. 336-337.

Christ as he is in the form of God. What is affirmed in vv.
18-20 can be true only consequently to his taking the form of a
servant, being in the likeness of man. In the first aspect of his
existence, and in the three successive phases of his existence which
begin with his taking human nature, *he* is the image of God
analogously: as divine, he is the perfect image, the perfect symbol,
of God; as man, in his earthly existence, as the glorified risen
Lord, and at the last day, he is the inadequate image, symbol, of
God; for in all of these phases it is in his human reality that he
images God. That reality, even in his glory, is the supreme but
necessarily inadequate image or symbol of God [10].

Taking *image* as applying to Christ as he is in the form of
God, as he is divine, we must recognize the other affirmations in
the first part of the hymn, Col 1.15-17, as bearing on the first
aspect of Jesus' existence: he is "the *first-born of all creation*":
not that he himself is created, the first of all that is created, but
that he is "prior" to all creation, pre-eminent over all creation.
He is *before all things*. *In him, through him,* and *for him* all
things were created: he *is* the *creator*. *In* and *through* cannot be
understood as suggesting any role unequal to that of God, the
Father. Rather they are inadequate human efforts to suggest the
unique relation of Son to Father in all, equal as he is to God, the
Father.

He is the *Lord*. After the first part of the great hymn in
Philippians, in which Jesus is the subject, the second part details
the actions of God in response. Jesus, being divine, did not cling
to being manifest as equal to God, but emptied himself, took the
form of a servant, was born in the likeness of men, and humbled
himself, obedient even to undergoing death on a cross (Phil
2.6-8). In response, "Therefore God has highly exalted him
and bestowed on him the name which is above every name, that
at the name of Jesus every knee should bow, in heaven and on
earth and under the earth, and every tongue confess that Jesus
Christ is Lord, to the glory of God the Father" (Phil 2.9-11).
Regarding my fourfold division of affirmations concerning aspects
of Jesus' existence, one might be inclined to take this series of
affirmations, and the title *Lord*, as pertaining to the third aspect,
that of the risen Jesus. Yet the divine irony and paradox, and the
mystery, are more profound. The hymn comes full cycle.
Having begun with Jesus who *is* divine, the hymn as taken over
by Paul returns to the bestowal of the name which is above all

---

[10] See *Basics*, pp. 53-64; and MS, pp. 329-337.

names, the divine name, *Lord* (κύριος). The bestowal is part of the glorification of Jesus. Yet it is not a bestowal of a title which now for the first time is his. Through all of the process of emptying, humiliation, and death, Jesus *is* divine, though he is not manifest as such. Now he is shown forth as what he *is* absolutely, without reference to time and to the process of salvation history. He *is* the *Lord*. The *name* is *Lord*: every knee should bow at the name of *Jesus* precisely because now it is fully revealed that Jesus Christ *is Lord*, to the glory of God the Father. Paul does not give later dogmatic affirmations of the Trinity and of the Incarnate Word. In his own way he parallels John, for whom "I am" is the divine name, and the glory of the Son is the glory of the Father. *Lord*, therefore, is not a title which is Jesus' only from the moment of his glorification. "Jesus Christ is Lord" is an affirmation which is true of him as he is in the form of God. Like all such affirmations it is true of him always, permeating all other affirmations regarding other aspects of his existence. All affirmations concerning Jesus are made concerning *one subject*. Always, in and through all aspects of his existence, despite all appearances, what is true of him as divine is true of him absolutely.

So "... for us there is one God, the Father, from whom are all things and for whom we exist, and one Lord, Jesus Christ, through whom are all things and through whom we exist" (1 Cor 8.6). "Now there are varieties of gifts, but the same Spirit; and there are varieties of service, but the same Lord; and there are varieties of working, but it is the same God who inspires them all in every one" (1 Cor 12.4-6).

Finally, without multiplying citations of texts, and without attributing to Paul an explicit trinitarian dogma or theology, I should say that in many ways Paul indicated roles of God (the Father), Jesus (the Lord Jesus Christ, and other variants), and the Spirit (of God, of Christ, the Holy Spirit) which are at once diverse and equally divine. Only a later explicit trinitarian dogma and theology can do full justice to the implications of Paul's usage. In this sense one can say that Paul contributes to New Testament foundations of trinitarian dogma. The role of Jesus as he figures in Paul's greetings, attributions of saving and sanctifying actions, prayers, and absolute statements about Jesus Christ all have a bearing upon what must be regarded as affirmations concerning Jesus as he is in the form of God.

(2) *In the form of a servant, in the likeness of men.* On the Father's part, he sent forth his Son, born of a woman, born under

the law (Gal 4.4). He "... did not spare his son but gave him up for us all...." (Rom 8.32). Jesus emptied himself, took the form of a servant, was born in the likeness of men, humbled himself, became obedient even to death on a cross (Phil 2.6-8). Being rich, for our sake he became poor (2 Cor 8.9). Descended from David according to the flesh (Rom 1.3), he was the offspring of Abraham, heir to the promise (Gal 3.16; cf. 3.29), of the race of the Israelites according to the flesh (Rom 9.5), "... a servant to the circumcised to show God's truthfulness, in order to confirm the promises given to the patriarchs, and in order that the Gentiles might glorify God for his mercy" (Rom 15.8-9).

He loved us and gave himself up for us, "... for our sins to deliver us from the present age, according to the will of our God and Father...." (Gal 1.4; cf. 2.20). Christ "... loved the church and gave himself up for her, that he might sanctify her, having cleansed her by the washing of water with the word, that he might present the church to himself in splendor, without spot or wrinkle or any such thing, that she might be holy and without blemish" (Eph 5.25-27).

Most of Paul's teaching concerning Jesus in the form of a servant regards his death and its consequences for us. He was handed over (to death) for our trespasses (Rom 4.25). Crucified (1 Cor 1.23; 2 Cor 13.4), he died on a cross (Phil 2.8). He died for us (1 Th 5.10), for our sins (1 Cor 15.3; Cor 5.15). He died to sin once for all (Rom 6.10).

The effects of his death are expiation (propitiation) by his blood (Rom 3.25), deliverance and freeing (Gal 1.4; 1 Th 1.10), redemption (Gal 3.13; 4.4-5; Rom 3.24; Col 1.14; Eph 1.7), forgiveness of sins (Col 2.13; Eph 4.32), reconciliation (2 Cor 5.19; Rom 5.10-11; Col 1.20, 22). We are justified by his blood, saved from the wrath of God (Rom 5.9).

(3) *The risen Son of God in power.* God, the Father, raised Jesus from the dead (1 Th 1.10; Gal 1.1; 1 Cor 6.14; 15.12-23; 2 Cor 4.14; Rom 4.25; 6.4, 9; 8.11, 34; 10.9; Col 2.12) for our life (Rom 4.25). "... Christ being raised from the dead will never die again; death no longer has dominion over him" (Rom 6.9). He is the first to rise, the first fruits of those who have fallen asleep (1 Cor 15.20-23). "The death he died he died to sin, once for all, but the life he lives he lives to God" (Rom 6.10).

God has exalted him (Phil 2.9); he has ascended (Eph 4.8-10); he is at the right hand of God (Rom 8.34; Col 3.1; Eph 1.20). Jesus Christ is *Lord* (Phil 2.11; and continually Paul uses the title *Lord*).

The Lord is the Spirit (2 Cor 3.17-18), the likeness of God (2 Cor 4.4). He is the power and wisdom of God (1 Cor 1.23-24, 30: the crucified Christ, but Christ Jesus, whom God made our wisdom, our righteousness and sanctification and redemption). In him "... are hid all the treasures of wisdom and knowledge" (Col 2.3; cf. Eph 3.8). He lives by the power of God (2 Cor 13.4). He is the Lord of glory (1 Cor 2.8; cf. 2 Cor 3.14-18). In him "... all the fulness of God was pleased to dwell" (Col 1.19); "... in him the whole fulness of deity dwells bodily...." (Col 2.9). The substance of what is to come belongs to Christ (Col 2.17). He has the power to subject all things to himself (Phil 3.21). Paul desired to know [to experience] the power of his resurrection (Phil 3.10).

Prefigured as the Rock from which the Israelites drank in the desert (1 Cor 10.4), Jesus Christ is the foundation on which Paul (and all apostles) must build (1 Cor 3.11). He is the cornerstone, in whom the whole structure of the household of God is joined together and grows into a holy temple in the Lord (Eph 2.19-22). He is the head of the body, the church (Col 1.18), the head of all rule and authority (Col 2.10); "... we are to grow up in every way into him who is the head, into Christ, from whom the whole body, joined and knit together by every joint with which it is supplied, when each part is working properly, makes bodily growth and upbuilds itself in love" (Eph 4.15-16). The kingdom is his: having delivered us from the dominion of darkness, the Father has transferred us to the kingdom of his beloved Son (Col 1.13): it is the kingdom of Christ and of God (Eph 5.5).

He intercedes for us (Rom 8.34). In him the Father has blessed us with every spiritual blessing (Eph 1.3-14).

(4) *What God has revealed of himself in this fulfillment.* In the course of Paul's treatment of fulfillment of God's promises in Jesus, he makes several profound reflections on God's self-revelation in the process of this fulfillment. It is important for our purpose in tracing lines of the dialectic of promise and fulfillment to note these Pauline reflections. Our whole purpose is to elaborate the framework of biblical revelation within which we locate ourselves in the process of salvation history, and to bring out important elements in that revelation which mediates our own experience of God. Consequently the reflections which I gather here are important for our reflections on experiencing God, and on the God whom we experience, in Volume II of this work.

(a) Love.   There is a classic text in *Romans* which can seem
paradoxical, and which upon further reflection can occasion a
profound insight into the Mystery:

> While we were yet helpless, at the right time Christ died for the
> ungodly. Why, one will hardly die for a righteous man—though
> perhaps for a good man one will dare even to die. But *God shows
> his love for us* in that while we were yet sinners Christ died for us.
> Since, therefore, we are now justified by his blood, much more
> shall we be saved by him from the wrath of God. For if while we
> were enemies we were reconciled to God by the death of his Son,
> much more, now that we are reconciled, shall we be saved by his
> life. Not only so, but we also rejoice in God through our Lord
> Jesus Christ, through whom we have now received our
> reconciliation (Rom 5.6-11).

I have italicized the apparently paradoxical words. From the
whole movement of Paul's thought here, one would expect him to
affirm that *Christ* shows his love for us, and we might take this as
going beyond Jesus' words reported by John: "Greater love has
no man than this, that a man lay down his life for his friends" (Jn
15.13). But Paul does not say *Christ*, but *God*. Why? I suggest
that Paul's thought here, as often, is elliptical and cryptic. One
can find a profound meaning by expanding the text consistently
with Paul's own thought. Christ, variously in all aspects of his
existence, is the *image* of the invisible God. Christ shows *his* love
for us in the special circumstances in which he died for us. Since,
however, he is the image of God in all that he is and does,
through Christ God reveals his own love for us.

Paul's rather cryptic expression here is complemented by
another great text in which Paul blends the love which God and
Christ Jesus have for us, and the actions by which they prove their
love for us (Rom 8.28-39). Paul asks: "Who shall separate us
from the love of *Christ*?" (35), and he concludes: "... in all these
things we are more than conquerors through him who loved us.
For I am sure that neither death, nor life, nor angels, nor principalities, nor things present, nor things to come, nor powers, nor
height, nor depth, nor anything else in all creation, will be able to
separate us from the love of *God* in Christ Jesus our Lord"
(37-39: RSV) [11].

---

[11] JB very aptly translates the last portion of the text thus: "... nor any
created thing, can ever come between us and the love of God made visible in
Christ Jesus our Lord."

(b) Power.   In his prayer for the Ephesians, Paul prays that they may know "... what is the immeasurable greatness of his power in us who believe, [which they can judge] according to the working of his great might which he accomplished in Christ when he raised him from the dead and made him sit at his right hand in the heavenly places, far above all rule and authority and power and dominion, and above every name that is named, not only in this age but also in that which is to come...." (Eph 1.19-21) [12]. Paul is not speaking of the sort of power which can be observed in the physical universe, nor of that aspect of the power of God which we can clearly perceive in the things that have been made (Rom 1.20).   What is revealed here is a range of God's power in a mysterious higher realm of reality, beyond the reach of all natural human knowledge.   The prime manifestation of this power is God's work in the resurrection and glorification of Christ.   In derived senses, Christ crucified, the cross of Christ, the word of the cross (1 Cor 1.17, 18, 23-24), the gospel of God (Rom 1.16) are the power of God; and our faith rests not in the wisdom of men but in the power of God (1 Cor 2.5).

(c) Wisdom.   Christ is also the wisdom of God (1 Cor 1.24-25;   2.6-7):   a wisdom   contrasted   with   the   human wisdom of the wise, of the world, of this age and the rulers of this age (1 Cor 1.19-25; 2.6-7).   It is not that aspect of God's wisdom which can be known naturally by pondering the order of the universe.   Rather it is a secret and hidden wisdom (1 Cor 2.7), the wisdom of the hidden plan which is now revealed and preached (cf. Eph 3.8-11), Christ, in whom are hid all the treasures of wisdom and knowledge (Col 2.2-3).

(d) Righteousness, mercy, forgiveness.   I link these three "qualities" of God, and I barely touch here upon the deep mystery which they suggest.   They are indicated in Paul's thought partly in those elements which I have selected to show fulfillment of the promises in Jesus.   In part they figure in his conception of fulfillment of the promises in us.   I shall have to return later in this work to gather other biblical witness concerning these aspects of the mystery of the kind of God in whom we believe, the God whom we experience.   There is a further limitation of my treatment of God's "righteousness" here: what Paul says in the

---

[12] The text is difficult to translate, for Paul uses three words, δύναμις (power, might, strength ...), κράτος (power, might), and ἰσχύς (strength, power, might). JB turns it thus: "... how infinitely great is the *power* that he has exercised for us believers. This you can tell from the *strength* of his *power* at work in Christ...."

texts which I shall cite brings out only some aspects of the
"righteousness" of God. I cannot say more than this here, for to
go farther in indicating my limitations would involve undertaking
the more ample reflection which I reserve for later.

For my present purpose it is sufficient to propose two
"capital" texts, fountainheads of Pauline thought:

> For I am not ashamed of the gospel: it is the power of God for
> salvation to every one who has faith, to the Jew first and also to
> the Greek. For in it the *righteousness* of God is revealed through
> faith for faith; as it is written, "He who through faith is righteous
> shall live" (Rom 1.16-17).

> But now the *righteousness* of God has been manifested apart from
> the law, although the law and the prophets bear witness to it, the
> *righteousness* of God through faith in Jesus Christ for all who
> believe. For there is no distinction; since all have sinned and fall
> short of the glory of God, they are justified by his grace as a gift,
> through the redemption which is in Christ Jesus, whom God put
> forward as an expiation by his blood, to be received by faith. This
> was to show God's *righteousness*, because in his divine
> forbearance he had passed over former sins; it was to prove at the
> present time that he himself is *righteous* and that he justifies him
> who has faith in Jesus (Rom 3.21-26).

Obviously both texts anticipate what we shall have to consider
regarding fulfillment in us. Yet they are to be noted here, for in
what God did in Jesus, in fulfillment of his promises, he shows his
righteousness: he himself is *right*, in conformity with what he
should be and do, true to himself, showing what kind of God he
really is. And mysteriously his *rightness* involves mercy,
forbearance, passing over sins, forgivenness: all this is manifested
in his putting Christ Jesus forward as an expiation by his blood,
passing over sins in his forbearance, justifying by his grace as pure
gift.

(e) Glory. Here again I merely touch an aspect of the glory
of God, revealed in his fulfillment of his promises both in Jesus
and in us. I mention it here with regard to Jesus, and shall
return to consider it in our fulfillment. As in the case of all of the
other "qualities" of God which I have mentioned in this brief
section, glory is one of a cluster of concepts which serve in
complementarity to bring out something of the mystery of what
kind of God it is in whom we believe, and whom we experience.

As one can quickly ascertain from any fairly adequate biblical
theology, glory (δόξα) and its Old Testament antecedent have a

wide range of meanings. *Glory* is an intuitive symbol, and its sense in any one passage is not to be held in sharply defined conceptual symbolism. I shall suggest some of the implications of the word as it is used by Paul concerning the glory of God in his work in Jesus.

Three texts, in my judgment, bring out best the sense in which Paul thought of God's glory in relation to the fulfillment wrought in Jesus:

> We were buried therefore with him by baptism into death, so that as Christ was raised from the dead by the *glory* of the Father, we too might walk in newness of life (Rom 6.4).

> In their [the Jews' (of Paul's time)] case the god of this world has blinded the minds of the unbelievers, to keep them from seeing the light of the gospel of the *glory* of Christ, who is the likeness (εἰκών: image) of God. For what we preach is not ourselves, but Jesus Christ as Lord, with ourselves as your servants for Jesus' sake. For it is the God who said, "Let light shine out of darkness," who has shone in our hearts to give the light of the knowledge of the *glory* of God in the face of Christ (2 Cor 4.4-6).

> And my God will supply every need of yours according to his riches in *glory* in Christ Jesus (Phil 4.19).

I believe that it is obvious that Paul's sense of *glory* contrasts notably with dominant Old Testament usage, and also with some senses of the word in other New Testament writings. There is nothing here of the sensibly perceptible brilliance of light especially which in the Old Testament frequently symbolized the presence, power, majesty, and holiness of God. Since Paul gives no account of the public life of Jesus, there is nothing of the perceptible signs or works which in the Gospels symbolized the divine presence, power, and operation, and which were intended to move men and women to believe in Jesus. There is nothing like the account of the transfiguration of Jesus. Nor does Paul himself narrate the experience in which, according to Acts 22.6-11, Jesus appeared to him in a brilliant, blinding light. Paul shifts from the sensibly perceptible intuitive symbol to the reality symbolized: the majesty, sublimity, power of God. He interiorizes the light. Thus Jesus was raised by the power of the Father (Rom 6.4): only by the interior enlightenment of the Spirit do we know the power which is at work. The resurrection itself was not visible, and could not be a sensibly perceptible symbol of the Father's power.

The text from 2 Cor subtly suggests the shift, the interiorization, of which I am speaking. In the context Paul is contrasting the splendor or glory of the Old Covenant (the dispensation of death) and that of the New Covenant (the dispensation of the Spirit). Even the fading splendor of Moses' face was too bright for the Israelites to behold, and Moses veiled his face. "Yes, to this day whenever Moses is read a veil lies over their minds; but when a man turns to the Lord the veil is removed. Now the Lord is the Spirit, and where the Spirit of the Lord is, there is freedom. And we all, with unveiled face, beholding the glory of the Lord, are being changed from one degree of glory to another; for this comes from the Lord who is the Spirit" (2 Cor 3.15-18; cf. vv. 7-14). In Paul's account of the old dispensation, he shifts subtly from the sensibly perceptible light of Moses' face, and the physical veil, to a veil over the minds of the unbelievers. The glory which we behold with unveiled face is no sensibly perceptible splendor. The light of the gospel of the glory of Christ, the light of the knowledge of the glory of God in the face of Christ, is the interior light of God, who has shone in our hearts.

The third text which I have cited, brief as it is, is consistent with the interpretation which I propose. In their article on δόξα, BAG suggest for the phrase "riches in glory" (RSV, which I quoted) this translation: "the wealth of his glory", but they include this text among others for which they indicate that Paul's word *glory* has the broader sense of majesty, sublimity, power, might. In short, Paul's sense of glory is consistent with his sense of the wisdom of God and of the Mystery: in the fulfillment accomplished in Jesus, God's hidden plan, and his wisdom are revealed, not in any external, luminous symbolic brilliance, but by the Spirit; they are grasped only by the spiritual. For the unspiritual they are folly, beyond understanding[13].

FULFILLMENT IN US

Keeping in mind what we have considered both of God's master plan, the Mystery, and the first stage of its fulfillment Jesus, I concentrate here on the further realization of the plan as it comes to relative fulfillment in us *now*: that is, from the glorification of Jesus until the end of time. What remains to be considered of final fulfillment at the last day is reserved for the next section, regarding both Jesus and us.

---

[13] See above, on mystery, pp. 210-212, and wisdom, p. 223.

I acknowledge from the outset that in thematizing elements, or factors, or stages of that fulfillment, any theologian is going beyond Paul. Paul himself describes concrete experience, for example: that of hearing or receiving the word. Reflecting on his portrayal of that experience, we can find several elements or factors in this very beginning of the process of fulfillment: preaching the word (preceded by Paul's own hearing the word), hearing, receiving the Spirit in the very experience of believing, believing as one takes the word for what it is: God's word, not man's, and the whole concrete response. The process of thematizing, then, involves a discernment and differentiation and initial conceptualization which demands a linear consideration of the individual elements. When we have done this with a relative degree of adequacy, we must return and hold all of the elements in our contemplation of the experience itself.

Second, fulfillment is a process, and we must recognize that elements discerned and differentiated at any one stage of the process recur in a dialectic which ends only with life itself. Consequently we must consider faith, love, and Spirit, for example, as they are constants in that dialectic.

Third, the order in which elements of the total process are set forth is the result of one theologian's reflection. I can proceed only along the line of development which seems to me to provide an intelligible account of the process. Other orders could be determined by other theologians, or by me in another effort. Any such linear order and initial conceptualization goes beyond Paul's vivid, highly figurative, intuitive symbolizing. And when we have done our work of conceptualizing and ordering, we must return continually to contemplate the full concrete reality which Paul himself projects only inadequately in his own type of symbols.

Fourth, I regard Paul's thought as the most difficult of all to present in any satisfactory intelligible order, in any effort to elaborate a "theology" which is faithful to the author and yet goes beyond him in the discovery of an order which at best can be said to be implicit in Paul. I should say that Paul is a tormented, haunted thinker. Some serious problems rise to the surface repeatedly, only to sink again in the whirling movement of Paul's thought. Eventually, in some cases, he faces the problems squarely. Such is the case, for instance, with the problems of sin, the Law, and the mystery of Israel. Anyone seeking to work out a Pauline theology may feel constrained, as I have, to introduce Paul's treatment of these problems at a different point from that at which he faces them in *Romans*.

Two features of Pauline thought in particular make it extraordinarily difficult to hold in an intelligible order. One is what I have referred to at the outset of this work as the contrapuntal dialectic of promise and fulfillment, threat and punishment; of faith, love, and fidelity on the one hand, and of sin and diverse patterns of repentance and forgiveness or obdurate rebellion on the other[14]. For the most part in developing this work I have stressed the dialectic of promise and fulfillment. Moreover, admittedly there is a relative stress on promise in the Old Testament and on fulfillment in the New. In dealing with Paul I think that one cannot refuse to face the full complexity of the contrapuntal dialectic, and the consequent heightened difficulty of holding the line of his thought.

The second feature adding to the difficulty is that the letters suggest many different orders. Most prominently, *Romans* is most like a "treatise" which commentators succeed in outlining to their own apparent satisfaction, but which I regard as extremely tormented and in a sense "disorderly". Even if one could be content with an "order" of *Romans,* however, he or she would have to come to terms with different orders and emphases in the other letters.

What is the solution? Perhaps no two theologians would agree completely. Surely I should say that one cannot disregard Paul's own efforts at ordering his thought, and the prominence, for example, of his thesis of justification by faith. One cannot reasonably propose an "absolute" theological intelligible order. The only solution seems to lie in finding the least uneasy accommodation to Pauline thought and Pauline priorities. It would be relatively easy to "reduce" Paul to a commentary on *Romans*—at first sight, at least, it might seem to be easy. I think, after having tried it, that such an attempt is doomed to failure. What I propose is the result of about six or seven efforts to elaborate a plan. Some may observe wryly that I should have tried six or seven more, or given up in the first place. All I can say is that I am driven to the effort, and that I propose my order as simply mine, hoping that it may be of some help to others in the effort to understand Paul.

(1) *Paul's gospel.* Paul's greeting describes his gospel in a way which foreshadows his later formulations of his basic thesis. It is "... the gospel of God, which he promised beforehand through his prophets ... concerning his Son ... Jesus Christ our

---

[14] See above, pp. 50-51.

Lord, through whom we have received grace and apostleship to bring about the obedience of faith for the sake of his name among all the nations, including yourselves who are called to belong to Jesus Christ" (Rom 1.1-6).

(2) *First formulation of the thesis*: "... I am not ashamed of the gospel: it is the power of God for salvation to every one who has faith, to the Jew first and also to the Greek. For in it the righteousness of God is revealed through faith for faith [or: from faith to faith[15]]; as it is written, 'He who through faith is righteous shall live'" (Rom 1.16-17). I reserve reflections on this formulation, which I shall consider together with the second formulation in Rom. 3.21 ff. At that point too I shall indicate significant differences between Paul's thesis announced earlier in Gal 2.16 and the two formulations in *Romans*.

(3) *A prior question: the wrath of God*. Instead of proceeding with a development of this thesis, Paul turns to what seems to have occurred to him as a prior question, concerning the wrath of God, and the apparent contrast between the righteousness and the wrath of God. Reviewing the history of mankind, Gentiles and Jews, Paul affirms that God has revealed his wrath against all. The Gentiles (2.14) or "Greeks" (2.9-10) knew God, but did not honor him as God or give thanks to him (1.18-21). They became futile in their thinking, fools, and God abandoned them, letting them run the full course of their own perversion (cf. 1.21-32). The Jews, relying upon the law and boasting of their relation to God, dishonored God by breaking the law (cf. 2.1 – 3.9). Paul's conclusion is a massive condemnation: "... all men, both Jews and Greeks, are under the power of sin" (3.9). He supports his judgment with a chain of witnesses from Scripture (3.10-18)[16]. The whole world is accountable to God (cf. 3.19)[17].

Paul begins with an apparent contrast between God's righteousness and his wrath. Without explicit treatment of the contrast, he approaches a conciliation of the two in the course of

---

[15] FITZMYER, *ibid.*, 21, p. 295.

[16] Ps 14.1-2; 5.9; 140.3; 10.7; Is 59.7-9; Ps 36.1.

[17] Compare Paul's other treatments of the same theme: "... scripture imprisoned all in sin, that what was promised to faith in Jesus Christ might be given to those who believe" (Gal 3.22); we were helpless: ungodly, sinners, enemies of God (Rom 5.6-10); death reigned because of one man's trespass; one man's trespass led to condemnation for all men; by one man's disobedience many were made sinners; all men sinned (Rom 5.12-19); "... God has imprisoned all [men] in disobedience, that he may have mercy on all" (Rom 11.32).

his reflection upon God's wrath, judgment, and punishment.
God's judgment "... *rightly* (κατὰ ἀλήθειαν: according to truth)
falls upon those who do such things" (2.2). On the day of wrath
"... God's *righteous judgment* (δικαιοκρισία) will be revealed"
(2.5). "... God shows no partiality" (2.11). The faithlessness of
some Jews does not nullify the *faithfulness* of God (cf. 3.3). "But
if our wickedness serves to show the *justice* (δικαιοσύνη) of God,
what shall we say? That God is unjust to inflict wrath on us? (I
speak in a human way.) By no means! For then how could God
judge the world? But if through my falsehood God's
truthfulness abounds to his glory, why am I still being
condemned as a sinner? And why not do evil that good may
come?—as some people slanderously charge us with saying..."
3.5-8)[18]. God's wrath and righteous judgment, are, then, at
least an aspect of God's righteousness or justice or uprightness
(δικαιοσύνη). For our present purpose this suffices to reveal a
dialectic in Paul's thought regarding wrath and righteousness.

    There is one apparent inconsistency in Paul's portrayal of all
human history up to Christ. On the one hand, he pronounces a
massive, universal condemnation: all men, both Jews and Greeks,
are under the power of sin (3.9); the whole world is accountable
to God (3.19). On the other hand, there is the problem of Jews
and Greeks who do good (2.6-10); of the Gentiles who do by
nature what the law requires: it is written on their hearts (cf.
2.13-16); in their own way they are doers of the law, who will
be justified, and who will face a favorable judgment (cf.
2.13-16); and of the many righteous men and women of the
Old Testament. The question does not seem to have occurred to
Paul, and so it would be futile to propose a Pauline answer. There
is an answer, however, which is consistent with Paul's thesis of
justification as pure gift, through faith in Jesus Christ. First, men
and women in Israel were justified and sanctified radically by their
faith in the promises given to Abraham. I say *radically*: they had
to do what the law, when given, prescribed; but they were *right*
with God, righteous, not by virtue of the external performance of
works of the law, nor by any vaunted righteousness of their own,
but by faith in God's promise, his fidelity, his righteousness. Men
and women who did not have the Mosaic law, but who lived

---

    [18] Paul does not bother to refute the sophism: he is concerned here simply
with the opposition of man's falsehood and God's truthfulness (see FITZMYER,
ibid., 34, p. 300). For the sophistic argument itself and Paul's refutation, see
Rom 6.1 ff.

according to their conscience, followed the hidden ways of God for them, lived as they recognized that they should, but did so by the grace of Christ which they shared without ever having heard of it. Radically their righteousness too is not a self-wrought righteousness, but pure gift. That is the core of Paul's teaching (cf. 3.23-24). For Paul, they too will be judged by Christ Jesus (cf. 2.15-16).

Finally, here and elsewhere, as I shall note, there are elements of Paul's statements about the law which seem to be a ferment in his thought, unresolved questions and tensions which must have agitated him, and which eventually called for his explicit consideration of the role of the law, in chapter seven. Here, in 2.1 – 3.20, these are the elements to which I refer: the doers of the law (2.13), the real Jew and real circumcision (2.25-29), the advantage of the Jew in the possession of the "oracles of God" (3.1-2)[19], the question of *some* who were unfaithful [implicitly *only* some] (3.3), and the bare statement "...no human being will be justified in his sight by works of the law, since through the law comes knowledge of sin" (3.20).

(4) *Probing deeper: sin and death.* I have affirmed that Paul was a tormented, haunted thinker, and that one of the "problems" or "mysteries" which haunted him is sin. His treatment of the universality of sin and of the power of sin raises more questions than it answers. He returns to a reflection on the "cause" of sin *Romans* 5.12-21, but only obliquely, so to speak, in his comparison of the influences of Adam and Christ. When I write that sin is a "problem" or a "mystery" which haunted Paul, I am suggesting quite deliberately that I use the words in a somewhat improper sense. And in doing so I am suggesting that as a theologian, not merely a biblical theologian, I am tormented and haunted by further questions which cannot even be formulated within a biblical theology. Eventually, in the final volume of this work, I shall have to give a theologian's account of sin, but that lies beyond my present concern, which is to present a reasonably intelligible account of the development of Paul's thought. He is not a conceptual theologian. His symbolism is highly intuitive. For him sin and death are Sin and Death, great personified forces, as it were actors in the drama which portrays human history. They have a great "power" and a "causal influence" over mankind, contrasted by Paul with the power and

---

[19] The whole of the Old Testament, including the Law: cf. Fitzmyer, *ibid.*, 34, p. 299.

influence of Christ. When Paul faces the "mystery" of sin, as later when he faces the "mystery" of the Law and of Israel, again he raises more questions than he answers. Indeed, he raises questions of two orders: one for the biblical theologian who by the terms of his mandate holds to biblical symbolism as he seeks to work out an explicit synthetic order which is only implicit in the biblical author or authors; another for the conceptual theologian who is driven to formulate questions and answers which are proper to the movement of his kind of thought and symbolism[20].

Paul's deeper probing into sin comes in his comparison of the grace which we have received through Christ and the effects of the sin of one man, Adam, upon all mankind (Rom 5.12-21: the occasion of the comparison is his treatment of the grace in 5.1-11). I take here only the elements which bear directly upon sin[21].

Through one man Sin came into the world, and through Sin Death, and thus Death spread to all men, since all sinned (v. 12). Sin is portrayed as a personified evil power, alienating man from God. Death similarly is a personified force: not physical death alone, but spiritual death, the separation of man from God. Paul clearly affirms the causal influence of one man, Adam, but in the most probable interpretation the last part of the verse (since all sinned), refers also to the personal sins of all. Personal sins, therefore, play some part in the condition of mankind before Christ; yet Paul clearly affirms the primary causal influence of one man, as the rest of the passage makes certain[22].

Before the Law Sin was in the world, but sin is not imputed when there is no law. But Death reigned from Adam to Moses, even over those who had not sinned as Adam had [or: in the likeness of Adam's transgression] (vv. 13-14). Adam's sin was

---

[20] I have developed my concepts of conceptual and intuitive symbolizing and symbols in MS, ch. VII, pp. 183-214; and I have applied them to theology in Basics, ch. VIII, "Symbolizing and Symbols in Theology," and ch. IX, "Theology in the Life of the Church," pp. 240-302. I am fully aware that what I have written in this paragraph is extremely cryptic. I wish simply to register the fact that what I am doing here is a very limited operation, all that I can attempt at this stage of my Telling About God.

[21] For a concise treatment of 5.12-21 see FITZMYER, "Romans", JBC, II, 53:52-60, pp. 306-308. In the long history of interpretation of Rom 5.12-21 and its bearing on the dogma of original sin there have been, and remain, some sharp divergences. I refrain from entering into the matter here, for it would lead us far afield.

[22] "Since" in the last part of the verse translates Paul's obscure, much debated phrase, ἐφ' ᾧ. For a summary and critique of the principal interpretations of the phrase, see FITEZMYER, ibid., 56, p. 307.

a transgression: a sin formally considered as the violation of a precept. Adam had received a precept from God; others before the Law did not[23].

In the continuing contrast of the influences of Adam and Christ, Paul brings out clearly the universal effect of Adam's transgression, or offense: by one offense [or: the offense of one man] many [or: the mass of mankind] died; the judgment from one offense [or: the offense of one man] brought condemnation [to all]; because of one man's offense Death reigned through the one man; one man's offense led to condemnation for all men; through one man's disobedience many ["all"] were made sinners (cf. vv. 15-19)[24].

(5) *Abraham: promise, faith, righteousness.* Paul's treatment of Abraham is highly abstractive: Abraham's faith and righteousness serve as an argument to confirm Paul's thesis of justification not by works of the Law but by faith (Rom 4; Gal 3.6-18, 29; 4.22-31). The only chronological reference is one which serves Paul's purpose: Abraham's experience was prior to both circumcision and the Law. Hence his righteousness could not depend on works of the Law (cf. Rom 4.9-17a; Gal 3.15-18). Paul does not situate Abraham in the history of a universally sinful mankind; he makes no reference to Abraham himself as a sinner; nor does he indicate any factor in Abraham's righteousness besides faith. In introducing Abraham's case here, consequently, I am following an order which situates him somehow in the history of salvation as a whole. Obviously this is not Paul's order.

First, Paul establishes his thesis concerning Abraham's righteousness (Rom 4.2-9; Gal 3.6); and he reflects on the structure of Abraham's experience in believing (Rom 4.17b-22). Second, he considers what was the blessing, the good, which was

---

[23] In verse 14 Paul uses παράβασις for Adam's sin; in the following verses he uses παράπτωμα. The words both mean *transgression*.

[24] " ...The formal effect of Adam's disobedience (Gn 3:6) was to make mankind not only liable to punishment, but actually sinners. So astute a commentator as V. Taylor remarks, 'No one is made a sinner or made righteous' (*Romans*, 41). And yet, this is what Paul says, and he is not speaking of man's personal sinful actions. The vb. *katestathêsan* does not mean, 'were considered' (to be sinners), but 'were made, were caused to be, were constituted' (such). Adam's disobedience placed the mass of mankind in a condition of estrangement from God. The text does not imply that they became sinners merely by imitating Adam's transgression. Rather they were affected by him...." (FITZMYER, *ibid.*, 60, p. 308).

promised. Third, he declares who are the sons and heirs of Abraham, sharers of the inheritance.

As is often the case, Paul's argument concerning Abraham's righteousness is somewhat eliptical, obscure, and not always quite in focus. He contrasts this righteousness with the wages which a man earns by work, which are his due, and about which he could boast before his employer: "I earned this from you." Abraham did nothing of the kind. He simply believed, trusted in the promising God and the promised good; and his belief and trust were "reckoned as righteousness": put to his account as righteousness[25]. Consequently the blessing, the promised good, came to Abraham and his descendants not because of works of the law ["from" works], but simply *from* the righteousness of faith, *from* faith (4.13-16). The element of the argument which I mentioned as being not quite in focus is the text of the Psalm 32.1-2 quoted in Rom 4.7-8. It does indeed give an example of God's reckoning righteousness without works, but it involves God's freely forgiving sin, not reckoning sin. In Abraham's case, as Paul recounts it, there is no suggestion of his being a sinner who is forgiven. Rather God promises, Abraham believes and trusts, and his faith is put down as righteousness. Note here that faith is not an act which itself is meritorious, and in return for which God gives him righteousness and the promise good. No: the contrast is between work and wages as due on the one hand, and pure faith-trust and pure gift on the other hand. By *believing* the promising God, Abraham *is right* before God, and the promised good when given is pure gift.

In a remarkable bit of phenomenology before its time, Paul probes the structure of Abraham's experience. Abraham stood before the God who had promised: a God who gives life to the dead and calls into existence the things that do not exist (4.17), a God who could do what he promised (4.21), [and implicitly a God whom he trusts as faithful, who surely would do what he promised]. He did not consider his own body, as good as dead at the age of about a hundred years, and Sarah's barren womb. In hope he believed against hope, that he should become the father of many nations. No distrust made him waver concerning the promise of God, but he grew strong in his faith as he gave glory to God (cf. 4.17b-22).

---

[25] ἐλογίσθη is a figure taken from accounting: it was accredited to him. The prepositional phrase εἰς δικαιοσύνην functions as a predicate noun (cf. BDF 145; and BAG, εἰς with accusative, 8.

What was the promised blessing? Abraham would become
the father of many nations (Rom 4.18). In him all the nations
would be blessed (Gal 3.8). Abraham and his descendants would
inherit the world (Rom 4.13).

Who are the sons, the descendants of Abraham, heirs to the
the promise? The blessing was pronounced, and Abraham's faith
was reckoned as righteousness, before he was circumcised:
circumcision was a sign or seal of the righteousness of faith, which
he had while he was still uncircumcised. "... The purpose was to
make him the father of all who believe without being circumcised,
to have righteousness reckoned to them, and likewise the father
of the circumcised who are not merely circumcised but also follow
the example of the faith which our father Abraham had before he
was circumcised" (Rom 4.11-12). So too the promise did not
come through the law (Rom 4.13-17a; Gal 3.15-18). All who
share Abraham's faith are his sons (Rom 4.11, 16). We are not
sons of the slave, Hagar, born according to the flesh, but sons the
free woman through the promise, according to the Spirit (cf. Gal
4.22-31).

(6) *The Law*. Given after Abraham, the Mosaic Law has an
important role in the history of salvation. In Paul's account of
man before Christ, the Law is a troublesome factor. He deals
with the role of the Law for the first time in *Galatians*, and
returns in *Romans* to attempt to solve a problem which obviously
is bothering him. His only other explicit mentions of the Law
come in 1 Cor, Eph, and Phil. In 1 Cor, between his two major
considerations of the Law, his attitude seems to be ambivalent.
On the one hand, he cites the Law to support his argument in
9.8-9 and 14.21, 34. On the other, he is careful to affirm that
he himself is not under the law, and he emphasizes the negative
role of the Law: "The sting of death is sin, and the power of sin is
the law" (15.56). What he states about the law in Eph and Phil
is based on the thought developed in Gal and Rom. Christ
abolished in his flesh the law of commandments and ordinances
(cf. Eph 2.15). He contrasts his own attitude to the Law before
and after coming to know Christ (Phil 3.5,6,9).

Though seemingly he thinks that he has dealt with the Law
sufficiently in Gal to ward off the danger of judaizing, there are
repeated indications in the early chapters of *Romans* which reveal
that aspects of Paul's thought about the Law still trouble him.
Despite his massive affirmation that all men are under the power
of sin, all have sinned (3.9-18), Paul himself has mentioned
God's righteous judgment upon both Jews and Greeks who do

good, and who will be judged according to their works (2.6-11), and has taken account of the Gentiles who do what the Law requires even thought they do not have the Law (2.13-16): doers of the Law will be justified (2.13). He acknowledges the value of circumcision for those who obey the law. Those who keep the law, whether they be circumcised or not, are the real Jews and have true circumcision. "He is a Jew who is one inwardly, and real circumcision is a matter of the heart, spiritual and not literal" (2.29; cf. vv. 25-28). The Jews have an advantage in having been entrusted with the oracles of God [all of the words of God, including the Law] (cf. 3.1-2). When Paul asks, "What if some were unfaithful?" (3.3), one can only judge that implicitly he considers that *not all* were unfaithful.

For anyone who has pondered these elements of Paul's thought, the following summary statements can hardly fail to be puzzling: "Now we know that whatever the law says it speaks to those who are under the law, so that every mouth may be stopped, and the whole world may be held accountable to God. For no human being will be justified by works of the law, since through the law comes knowledge of sin" (3.19-20). "For the law brings wrath, but where there is no law there is no transgression" (4.15). "... sin indeed was in the world before the law was given, but sin is not counted where there is no law" (5.13). "Law came in, to increase the trespass; ..." (5.20). "For sin will have no dominion over you, since you are not under the law but under grace" (6.14). Apparently for Paul too they were puzzling, and apparently he was driven by his own further questions to face the role of the Law squarely, and to attempt to answer them adequately. He does so finally in chapter seven, where he deals with dying to the law as one of the effects of our dying with Christ.

In my effort to set forth Paul's thought on the Law, I shall not deal with dying to the Law (Gal 2.19; Rom 7.1-6): for this is part of Christian experience, and I shall consider it later. I am concerned here with Paul's thought regarding the role of the Law before Christ. I shall combine elements taken from his treatments in *Galatians* and *Romans*. In my presentation of these elements I shall set forth first what Paul regards as the positive aspect of the Law: its dignity and value; then, the negative aspects of the role of the Law[26].

---

[26] Once again, for an excellent, concise treatment of both exegesis and Pauline theology, see Fitzmyer's commentaries on Gal and Rom in JBC, already

(a) Positive. The Law is part of the oracles of God with which the Jews have been entrusted: having it is an advantage (cf. Rom 3.1-2). The Law is holy, and the commandment is holy and just and good (7.12-13). The Law is spiritual (πνευματικός) as opposed to carnal, sold into slavery to sin (7.14). What Paul means by "spiritual" here must be sensed by a double contrast. On the one hand, the Law is not spiritual as pertaining to the the new life of the Spirit (or the "newness of the Spirit") of which he wrote in 7.6; it is not the law of the Spirit of life in Christ Jesus, the Spirit of God, of which he will write in 8.2,14. On the other hand, it is opposed to what is carnal (subject to the weakness of the flesh), slave of sin or concupiscence. In what sense, then, is it spiritual? It seems that first it is of divine origin, coming from God and meant to lead men to God. Second, it is directed to the spirit in man: πνεῦμα, that aspect of the whole of human being which "... suggests the knowing and willing self of man and as such reveals him to be particularly apt to receive the Spirit of God...." [27]. Instruction in the Law enables the Jew to know God's will and approve what is excellent (cf. 2.18). In his inner self ("according to the inner man") the Jew delights in the law of God (7.22).

One verse more than any other, in my judgment, suggests the enigma of Paul's attitude toward the Law. It comes in *Galatians*, after his most polemic arguments against the Law. It is in the fifth chapter, in which the word "law" occurs five times, always denoting the Law, the Mosaic law. In four instances (5.3, 4, 18, 23) Paul continues to write of the Law as he has in the whole course of his polemic. This is the enigmatic verse: "For the whole law is fulfilled in one word, "You shall love your neighbor as yourself" (Gal 5.14). Ironically this verse is embedded in one of the many passages in which Paul sets forth the code of Christian conduct (5.1 – 6.10), and shortly after he exhorts: "Bear one another's burdens, and so fulfill the law of Christ" (6.2). When Paul belittles the Law and exhorts the Galatians to stand fast in the freedom bestowed by Christ, and not submit again to the yoke of slavery, he is not writing only of ritual and cultic prescriptions. Here in *Galatians* he can sum up the Law in terms of love of one's neighbor [28]. In *Romans*, his example of a

---

cited above, and his "Pauline Theology," JBC, II, 79:105-123. For my own earlier treatment of Paul's conception of the role of the law, in the context of a cluster of related problems, see *The Mystery*, pp. 291-313.

[27] FITZMYER, "Pauline Theology," JBC, II, 79:121, p. 821.

[28] See FITZMYER, "Galatians", 30, p. 245 on summaries of the Law which

requirement of the Law is not some burdensome ritual or cultic observance, but one of the great moral commandments: "You shall not covet" (7.7). Why do I say that Gal 5.14 is enigmatic? It suggests one of the problems which Paul never mentions, but of which he could hardly have been unaware: that of the relation of the great commandments of the Law to the law of Christ: the code of Christian conduct. I shall return to this later, in reflecting on Paul's doctrine on the Law, and in dealing with the Christian code.

Certain other aspects of the Law as Paul deals with it, though they could hardly be classed with those which I have mentioned thus far as pertaining to the excellence of the Law, still must be regarded as positive, pertaining to any law which is of divine origin. God will render to every man according to his works (Rom 2.6), and in the context this means for the Jew works by which he obeys the Law (cf. 2.12-13, 17-29). "Circumcision indeed is of value if you obey the law" (2.25). The Law, therefore, involves obligation: every one who receives circumcision is bound to keep the whole law (cf. Gal 5.3). Obligation of itself is not a yoke of slavery: Paul will explain how it is that the Law, of itself good, comes to function as an instrument of Sin; the new law of freedom itself involves obligation, as Paul's many exhortations to Christian conduct make clear. What he sets forth in such "exhortations" is not distinct from his "doctrine": it is part of the total gospel, and life according to our basic commitment to Christian life is not optional, but obligatory.

One element of Paul's teaching on the Law seems to me to be ambivalent: it bears on both the positive and the negative aspects of the Law. I shall treat it here in so far as it seems to me to pertain to the former, and I shall return to consider it in the account of the latter. The text which is most challenging is this: "Why then the law? It was added because of transgressions...." (Gal 3.19). There are related texts in *Romans*: "Now we know that whatever the law says it speaks to those who are under the law, so that every mouth may be stopped, and the whole world may be held accountable to God. For no human being will be justified by works of the law, since through the law comes knowledge of sin" (Rom 3.19-20). "For the law brings wrath,

---

Paul might have had in mind: Lev 19.18, a rabbinical summary, or Christ's (Mt 7,12; Mk 12.31 par.). If Paul is referring to Jesus' teaching, the formulation in Mt. 22,34-40, together with Mt 7.12, is closest. Stangely, as Fitzmyer points out, neither here nor in Rom 13.8-10 does Paul mention the love of God.

but where there is no law there is no transgression" (4.15);
"... sin indeed was in the world before the law was given, but sin
is not counted where there is no law" (5.13). "Law came in, to
increase the trespass; but where sin increased, grace abounded all
the more, ..." (5.20).

What is the meaning of these texts, and what possible
positive aspect of the Law can they bring out? Perhaps we may
approach an understanding of Paul's meaning if we take together
the first and last of these texts: the Law was added *because of*
transgressions; Law came in to *increase* the *trespass*, but where
sin increased, grace abounded all the more.

I should say first that the meaning certainly is not the
purpose of the Law: it is unintelligible that Paul should hold that
God gave the Law *in order to* transform sin into trespass, or to
increase trespass [29]. Second, the meaning certainly is not *because
of past* transgressions: according to Paul, there was no
transgression before the Law.

There is, I believe, one hint of a partial explanation: in Rom
5.20 Paul glides from *trespass* to *sin*. There is at least one
instance, then, in which Paul's technical distinction between sin
and transgression does not hold [30]. Such a gliding from
transgression to *sin* can contribute to understanding the whole set
of texts which I have quoted.

I suggest, however, that the explanation of Paul's meaning
may be found rather in a characteristic of his thought and style.
Paul's thought is often elliptical. Here I should say that it is both
elliptical and "proleptic": skipping steps in what should have been
a more carefully worked out thought, and leaping ahead. What
would seem to be a reasonable conjectural "fleshing out" of
Paul's elliptical-proleptic thought and expression? I propose
the following. The Law was given because of sins, in the history
of a sinful mankind. Its purpose was to prevent sin, to curb it, by
bringing out clearly its malice and forbidding it. The Law both
spelled out the evil of sin, and forbade it, thus making it formally
transgression, with the added formal malice of a violation of a
God-given command. What was the effect? Because the Law
could give a further knowledge of sin, and add the obligation of

---

[29] The meaning is not, therefore, that which is given by BAG, for the word
χάριν as used here: "to bring them about".

[30] The word in the text is παράπτωμα. In Paul's usage, παράπτωμα and
παράβασις are interchangeable, and whether they be translated *transgression*,
trespass, or *offense*, they mean sin considered formally as the violation of a
precept or commandment.

obedience to God's command, but could not *give life* (cf. Gal 2.21;
3.21), could not give power to avoid sin, the Law had the effect of
transforming sin into transgression, of multiplying sin which was
now formally transgression, and making all who were under the
Law accountable to God.

Even when Paul's thought is "expanded" in such a way, it
leaves further questions for us, if not for Paul. It is perfectly true
that Paul did not use the later theological distinction between
God's positive and permissive will. If we use the distinction now
to set elements of Paul's thought in an intelligible framework,
admittedly we are going beyond Paul. But we are going beyond
Paul even when we attempt to supply the missing steps in his
frequently elliptical thought. In what follows, then, I am not
under the illusion of proposing a Pauline explanation: I am
attempting as a theologian to suggest an intelligible structure
which is post-Pauline in its conceptual resources, but which may
suggest reasonable answers to quite reasonable non-Pauline
further questions.

The explanation accounts not only for the texts explicitly
concerning the Law, which I have cited, but also for such texts as
these: "The scripture consigned all things to sin, that what was
promised to faith in Jesus Christ might be given to those who
believe" (Gal 3.22); "...God has consigned all men to
disobedience that he may have mercy upon all" (Rom 11.32).

What, then, can we understand to be God's purpose in giving
the Law? In view of Paul's extremely scanty account of salvation
history, of the Mosaic covenant, and of the prophets' continual
pleadings with a sinful people to return to fidelity to their God, we
cannot have recourse to a richer Old Testament theology: that too
would be non-Pauline. What, then, can we propose as an
explanation of his puzzling statements? God permitted evil for a
greater good. His *purpose* in giving the law was to hold his
people to fidelity under the covenant, to prevent sin, to curb sin,
proleptically called transgression by Paul. This is the positive
aspect of the Law, its purpose in accord with its origin in God, its
excellence, the holiness and goodness of its commandments. The
result, fully known to God, and permitted for a greater good, was
this: with pride in their knowledge of the Law as a kind of
wisdom, with a full sense of the malice of sin as a formal violation
of God's command, and of the curse which transgressions would
bring upon them, in their weakness they fell into slavery to sin
now known in its full malice. This God permitted until, under the
curse of the Law, with a sense of their utter helplessness, of their

need of mercy, forgiveness, redemption, deliverance, men would be open at last to rely not on their own righteousness, but on the God of the promise, now revealed to be a God of mercy, forgiveness, deliverance: and they would *believe* and receive a righteousness which is pure gift.

Finally we must credit the Law with its providential roles in relation to Christ. First, Paul acknowledges, without explaining how, that the law and the prophets bear witness to the righteousness of God through faith in Jesus Christ for all who believe (cf. Rom 3.21-22). Second, humble as its role was, the Law was our custodian until Christ came (cf. Gal 3.23-24; 4.1-7).

(b) Negative. The tragedy of the law, its failure and service of sin, and Paul's severe judgment of the law are all rooted in its limitations and its weakness. We can understand this only if we recall Paul's general principle:

> ... [God] will render to every man according to his works: to those who by patience in well-doing seek for glory and honor and immortality, he will give eternal life; but for those who are factious and do not obey the truth, but obey wickedness, there will be wrath and fury. There will be tribulation and distress for every human being who does evil, the Jew first and also the Greek, but glory and honor and peace for every one who does good, the Jew first and also the Greek. For God shows no partiality. All who have sinned without the law will also perish without the law, and all who have sinned under the law will be judged by the law. For it is not the hearers of the law who are righteous before God, but the doers of the law who will be justified.... (Rom 2.6-13).

> I testify again to every man who receives circumcision that he is bound to keep the whole law (Gal 5.3).

Measured by this norm, the Law is limited and weak simply because it does not enable men and women to keep the law. The negative judgment of the Law, therefore, is based on a consideration which spells out its weakness and its tragic role.

I should say that the basic limitation of the Law is that it is a written code, contrasted with the new life of the Spirit (Rom 7.6), the law of the Spirit of life in Christ Jesus: "... for the written code kills, but the Spirit gives life" (2 Cor 3.6)[31]. Beyond Paul's

---

[31] FITZMYER, "Romans", 72, p. 312, points out that 2 Cor 3.6ff is an excellent commentary on Rom 7.6. I should say that 2 Cor 3.6 bears directly on the matter.

explicit thought, but implicit in his contrast of the two laws, the written code is weak because it is extrinsic to man. It informs, but does not empower. One could object that it is intrinsic in so far as it gives knowledge. Still I should say it is extrinsic in the more important sense that it does not give the life and power which would enable a man or woman to observe the law.

The Law cannot make alive (Gal 2.21; 3.21). "He who through faith is righteous shall live" [or: "The righteous lives from faith"] [32]; but the Law does not rest on faith (Gal 3.11-12): the Law is not *from* faith. Rather, the man who seeks a righteousness based on [or "from"] the Law and his own works according to the Law seeks what would be due to him, not what would be the free gift, given because of ["from"] faith in the promise. "He who does them [the works of the Law] shall live by them" (Gal 3.12: cf. Lev 18.5; Rom 10.5). In fact, however, those who have been circumcised do not themselves keep the Law (cf. Gal 6.13).

A man is not justified, made righteous, from works of the Law (cf. Gal 2.16; 3.11). The promise to Abraham and to his descendants did not come through the Law, but through the righteousness of faith (Rom 4.13). It is not from works of the Law, but from hearing with faith [or: from the obedience of faith] that the Spirit was given to the Galatians, and miracles worked among them (cf. Gal 3.2, 5). The inheritance is not from the Law, but from the promise and the righteousness of faith (cf. Gal 3.18; Rom 4.13-4). Though Moses wrote "...that the man who practices the righteousness which is based on the law [which is *from* the law] shall live by it" (Rom 10.5 [33]), the Law could not enable the Jews to fulfill the just requirement of the Law (cf. Rom 8.3-4).

Limited, imperfect as it was, the Law could have only a temporary role in the history of salvation. Given four hundred and thirty years after the promise to Abraham, unable to annul that promise (cf. Gal 3.17, 19), the Law had a temporary function. In Paul's ambivalent expression, the Law "...was added because of transgressions, till the offspring should come to whom the promise had been made; ...." (Gal 3.19). I have attempted to discern the positive aspect of the phrase "because of

---

[32] Cf. Hab 2.4; Rom 1.17.

[33] "You shall therefore keep my statutes and my ordinances, by doing which a man shall live: I am the LORD" (Lev 18.5). Cf. Dt. 4.1; 5.33; 6.17-18, 24-25; and especially 30.15-20.

transgressions'' (above, pp. 238-241). The negative aspect, far more prominent, is touched upon in several of Paul's statements about the Law in *Galatians* and *Romans,* and then treated more fully in his ample dramatic portrayal in Rom 7. I shall consider here the elements of Paul's earlier partial answers to the question: "Why then the law?" (Gal 3.19). Who is the offspring, until whose coming the Law was to function? In the context of *Galatians* obviously the offspring is Christ, and those who are in Christ and of Christ (cf. 3.16, 26-29). Until the coming of Christ and of faith in Christ, the Jews were confined under the Law, kept in restraint by a Law which was their custodian, guardian, trustee (3.23-24; 4.1-6, 8; cf. vv. 21-31). Though they were heirs (4.1-3), sons of Abraham if they were men of faith (3.7-9), until Christ came they were as children, no better than slaves (4.1-3). Their condition was futile, tragic, because the Law gave them knowledge of sin (Rom 3.20) by its explicit prohibition (cf. Rom 7.7), and increased the gravity of sin by making it formally a transgression of God's commandment. So the result of the coming of the Law was an increase of trespass: now it was not only Adam who had trespassed, but all Jews who sinned under the law, with the knowledge that their sin was a violation of God's command (cf. 5.20). Bound by the Law, sinning under the Law, Jews were accountable to God (3.19). The Law brought wrath (4.15) and the curse upon all who were under the Law, relied on it, and yet by virtue of the Law itself could not do what the Law prescribed (cf. Gal 3.10-11).

Paul's major effort to clarify the role of the Law in *Romans* 7 is one of the most enigmatic passages in the Bible. The occasion of Paul's reflection is his treatment of our justification through faith in Jesus Christ and baptism, and its two effects: death to sin (6.1-2, 6-23) and death to the Law (7.1-4, 6). I shall treat both of these effects later. They pertain to justification through faith. Mention of death to the Law, however, prods Paul once more to face the question of the role of the Law in the life of the Jew prior to his faith in Christ. The immediate occasion is Paul's statement: "While we were living in the flesh, our sinful passions, aroused by the law, were at work in our members to bear fruit for death. But now we are discharged from the law, dead to that which held us captive, so that we serve not under the old written code but in the new life of the Spirit" (7.5-6). The further question is inevitable: what is the relation between our sinful passions and the Law? Here Paul faces the real problem, quickly shifting from the first person plural to the singular, and in so doing setting another perennial conundrum for the exegetes.

I shall proceed in this way. First I shall quote the whole text in the RSV version for easy reference. Then I shall propose an interpretation of the "I", which I think is the key to the understanding of the whole passage. Finally I shall fit the elements of Paul's thought into the intelligible structure suggestd by the interpretation of the 'I'' and of the other forces at play.

> [7] What then shall we say? That the law is sin? By no means! Yet, if it had not been for the law, I should not have known sin. I should not have known what it is to covet if the law had not said, 'You shall not covet.' [8] But sin, finding opportunity in the commandment, wrought in me all kinds of covetousness. Apart from the law sin lies dead. [9] I was once alive apart from the law, but when the commandment came, sin revived and I died; [10] the very commandment which promised life proved to be death for me. [11] For sin, finding opportunity in the commandment, deceived me and by it killed me. [12] So the law is holy, and the commandment is holy and good.
> [13] Did that which is good, then, bring death to me? By no means! It was sin, working death in me through what is good, in order that sin might be shown to be sin, and through the commandment might become sinful beyond measure. [14] We know that the law is spiritual; but I am carnal, sold under sin. [15] I do not understand my own actions. For I do not do what I want, but I do the very thing I hate. [16] Now if I do what I do not want, I agree that the law is good. [17] So then it is no longer I that do it, but sin which dwells within me. [18] For I know that nothing good dwells within me, that is, in my flesh. I can will what is right, but I cannot do it. [19] For I do not do the good I want, but the evil I do not want is what I do. [20] Now if I do what I do not want, it is no longer I that do it, but sin which dwells within me.
> [21] So I find it to be a law that when I want to do right, evil lies close at hand. [22] For I delight in the law of God, in my inmost self, [23] but I see in my members another law at war the law of my mind and making me captive to the law of sin which dwells in my members. [24] Wretched man that I am! Who will deliver me from this body of death? [25] Thanks be to God through Jesus Christ our Lord! So, then, I of myself serve the law of God with my mind, but with my flesh I serve the law of sin (Rom 7.7-25).

First, then, who is this "I"? [34] I should say that it is no one in particular, considered in full concrete existence. It is not Paul

---

[34] For a brief account of opinions, see FITZMYER, "Romans," JBC, II, 53:74-75, p. 312.

himself as he was prior to his conversion: the account here simply does not fit what Paul testified to concerning his own life as a Jew (cf. Phil 3.4-6; Gal 1.13-14). It is not Paul as he is living in Christ: what he says here of this "I" would be unintelligible as pertaining to the Paul of Gal 2.19-21, to the Paul whose whole account of the fulness of life in Christ must be regarded as grounded in his own personal experience, or to the Paul who not only writes that his spiritual children imitate him (1 Th 1.6), but exhorts them to be imitators of him (2 Th 3.7, 9; 1 Cor 4.16; 11.1).

It is not Adam, for whom the "law" would be the precept given him by God. There is simply no ground for supposing that Adam, prior to sin, was tugged by sinful passions. We cannot blithely suppose that Paul had St. Thomas' highly developed concepts of original justice and original sin, but neither can we foist upon Paul—without a shred of evidence—a conception which would have been contrary to late dogmatic and theological developments [35].

It is not any particular Jew, nor all Jews under the Law and prior to faith in Christ, for the account abstracts from extremely important factors in the full life of at least some believing Jews, especially faith in the promise to Abraham, and trust in the mercy of their God, who repeatedly calls to repentance and promises purification.

It is not any other Christian, Jew or Gentile, who senses a division within himself or herself. Powerful as this passage may be to express symbolically some aspects of the struggle to live according to the law of Christ despite the pull of passion and lapse into sin, such an interpretation would be a pure appropriation, not an exegesis of Paul.

Who or what, then is this "I"? It is, I think, a sort of Jewish "Everyman", vaguely and abstractly sketched. It is "I" *of myself*, rent by two conflicting elements within "me", at times seemingly a spectator of the inner conflict, more often identifying "myself" with the nobler, once momentarily identifying "myself" with what is base within me, but quickly adding the correction: "... within me, that is, in my flesh" (18).

Paul's "anthropology" is extremely sketchy here. The "higher" element is vaguely conceived. It is at play in what "I"

---

[35] For one example of the theology involved, far from our present concern, one could see my early work, *Grace and Original Justice According to St. Thomas* (*Analecta Gregoriana*, 75, Rome: Gregorian University Press, 1955).

want, what I *hate*, what I *do not want* (15, 16, 18, 19, 21): it embraces what we should call *will* (18). It includes my "mind", by which I agree that the law is good (judge it to be good), delight in it, so that it is "the law of my mind" (16, 22, 23, 25). "I" am somehow identified with what I want, with my inmost self [the inner man], with my mind, or the law of my mind (15-17, 19-20). Consequently, "...if I do what I do not want, it is no longer I that do it, but sin which dwells within me" (20).

"I", vaguely abstractly portrayed, sense the play of three forces which prevail over me, make me sin, bring me to do what is sinful beyond measure. One is Sin, conceived as a great personified force, outside me and yet somehow within me. Another is my "flesh"[36], my "self" as dominated by sinful passions, and so, in this context, equivalently an "enemy within me", a force which is at once the effect of sin and a power compelling me to sin despite my mind, my will, my inmost self. The third force is the Law. In my own usage here, as distinct from quotations from the RSV, I have capitalized *law*, where, with many exegetes, I take it to mean the Mosaic law[37]. Most of Paul's uses of the word *law* in Rom 7 have this denotation: vv. 1-9, 12, 14, 16, 22, 25b. Besides these instances of Paul's use of *law* as Mosaic Law, we must take note of an equivalent: the "commandment" (ἐντολή), in vv. 9-13. *Law* in v. 21 can be understood as a pattern which "I" observe in my action. *Another law* in my members, in 23a, is at war with the *law of my mind* (23b) and makes me captive to the *law of sin*, which dwells in my members (23cd). "I" *of myself* serve the *law of God* with my mind, but with my flesh "I" serve the *law of sin*. How are we to understand these "laws" in vv. 23-25. The other law in my members may be for Paul the drive of passions in the flesh, a tendency to evil which is at once the effect of sin and an agent of sin, making "me" captive to the law of sin. Or it may be simply the law of sin. Sin, as a personified force, has its own "law": it can hardly be defined except in negative terms, as contrary to what is commanded by God and recognized by "me" as good and holy. I doubt that Paul would have been aware of such a fine distinction. The law of sin itself dwells in "my" members, "my" flesh. The *law of my mind* is the norm of conduct which "I"

---

[36] For a brief account of Paul's anthropology, his rather vague conception of human being, see FITZMYER, "Pauline Theology," JBC, II, 79:117-123, pp. 820-821.

[37] See FITZMYER, "Romans," JBC, II, 53:71, 73, pp. 311-312.

recognize with my mind to be right, good, holy, and which is commanded by God in the whole of the Mosaic Law. The *law of God*, in the context, is the Mosaic Law.

What, then, is the role of the Law? Because of "my" weakness, Sin, as a great personified force, active in the world and dwelling in my flesh, my members weakened by sin and tending to sin, instrumentalizes the Law. "I" *of myself* am weak. What I would so as simply evil, sinful, is now formally a transgression, disobedience of God's explicit commandment, violation of the covenant, offense against God. Sin reigned in the world before the Law, because men and women were weakened, and Sin dwelt in their members, their flesh as subject to Sin. When the Law was given, making sin known more explicitly, and known too as being formally a violation of God's commandment, the supreme victory of Sin was possible. Sure of its victory over weakened, carnal man, Sin could now use the Law to make explicit how evil sin was, to flaunt its sinful character, to become sinful beyond measure: not only sin, but formally a violation of God's commandment.

In this situation, "I" *of myself* am wretched (v. 24). Only God through Jesus Christ our Lord can deliver "me" from this "body of death".

What, then, has Paul achieved in his major effort to show the limitations, the utter inadequacy, of the Law and the works of the Law? By a severely abstract portrayal of the Jew under the Law, recognizing the goodness and holiness of the Law, and striving in vain *of himself* to achieve *his own* righteousness, he brings his polemic against justification from works of the Law to its peak. The Law of itself, and works of the law of themselves, and the Jew striving of himself to fulfill the Law and achieve his own righteousness, are utterly futile.

Given the severely abstract nature of Paul's whole portrayal, three elements in the whole account remain especially obscure. The first is Paul's statement in v. 9: "'I' was once alive ..." As I interpret the whole passage, this is not autobiographical: it is futile to seek to explain it as referring to some phase of Paul's own life, or indeed of the life of any other Jew. Seemingly the only explanation is the abstract, almost spectral, character of the "I" in Paul's portrayal. Second, verses 16-20, in my judgment, remain obscure. There is not question of Paul's denying responsibility for sin in the full concrete life of any man or woman. Surely later theologians have recognized factors which diminish the power of will, and so diminish responsibility, in many circumstances. In Paul's account, however, what he says here seems to be a function of the play of abstract forces. *In so far* as the play of these forces alone is considered, what Paul says is intelligible. Finally, his conclusion in v. 25bc suggests what later thinkers would call a "split personality". Once again, the "I" is not a person in full concrete existence, in the totality and unity of his human being, and under the influence of God's grace.

My interpretation of Paul's full-dress account of the role of the Law may seem to be severely critical. It is not. I believe that such an interpretation makes Paul's account intelligible. Moreover, by a profound reflection which is—ironically—both severely abstract and deeply intuitive, Paul has reached not just a peak of his polemic against all temptation to judaize, but a profound insight into the weakness and absolute helplessness of any Jew who would attempt of himself, and purely by works of the Law performed *without faith*, without God's merciful love and pure gift, to achieve *his own* righteousness. I believe that this is borne out in Paul's account of the tragedy of his fellow Israelites of his own day who had refused to believe in Jesus Christ, and to accept God's righteousness: the righteousness which is from God, from faith. I shall return to this later. It is, so to speak, a post-Christian phenomenon. I have been concerned here with the role of the Law in the period prior to God's revelation in and through Christ.

(7) *The zero point.* In Paul's thought concerning the history of mankind before Christ, he fixes the zero point of the human situation. In my treatment of this theme I shall proceed as follows: (a) Paul's massive negative judgment; (b) some apparent conflicts between this judgment and other elements of Paul's thought; (c) a determination of the basic truth, and a resolution of apparent conflicts. This resolution goes beyond Paul's explicit thought, and comes only in the continuing reflection in the life of the Church.

(a) Paul's massive judgment is formulated only gradually in a series of statements which have a cumulative effect, and which must be held together. (i) All men, both Jews and Greeks, are under the power of sin (Rom 3.9, a statement which Paul supports by chain of texts from Scripture in vv. 10-18). (ii) All have sinned and fall short of the glory of God (Rom 3.23). What Paul means here by falling short of the glory of God can be determined only in the context of his thought on light, glory, and likeness, which I shall treat later. For the moment I say only that it does not mean lacking a share in that sensibly perceptible radiance which symbolized God's presence and majesty and power in the

Old Testament. As I have noted in reflecting on God's self-manifestation in the fulfillment realized in Jesus, Paul shifts from the sensibly perceptible symbol to the symbolized reality, and he interiorizes the "light" (see above, pp. 224-226). All men sinned (Rom 5.12). Jews who sinned are under the curse of the Law (cf. Gal 3.10). Gentiles who sin are condemned, for they have the requirement of the law written on their hearts, and their conscience accuses them (cf. Rom 2.6-16): God will render to every man according to his works (Rom 2.6). Scripture consigned all things to sin (Gal 3.22). God has consigned all men to disobedience, that he may have mercy upon all (Rom 11.32). (iii) All died through one man's trespass, for the judgment following one man's trespass brought condemnation [to all]: death reigned through one man, because of one man's trespass (cf. Rom 5.15-17). The whole world is held accountable to God (cf. Rom 3.19). For the Jew, sinning under the Law, he is accountable because he is obliged to keep the whole Law. Implicitly, for the Gentile, not under the Law, but having the requirement of the Law written on his heart, he is accountable for sinning against his conscience. (iv) We were helpless, ungodly, enemies [of God] (Rom 5.6, 10).

(b) Apparent conflicts. If we examine carefully some details of Paul's review of Gentile and Jew in his account of mankind before Christ, we find some apparent conflicts with his massive judgment of condemnation. (i) First, regarding the "Greeks" or Gentiles, God's wrath is revealed [by the manner of his punishment] against all ungodliness and wickedness of *men who* suppress the truth (Rom 1.18); the judgment of God rightly falls upon *those who* do such things (2.2; cf. 2.3): none of these statements are made about all Gentiles; they concern *those who* act thus. Implicitly *not all* do so, and *not all* are condemned and punished. (ii) God will render to every man according to his works (2.6-16): clearly Paul reckons with both Gentile and Jew who do good, and who will receive eternal life (vv. 7, 10); the doers of the Law will be justified (v. 13). Clearly in this account not all are under the power of sin, not all are condemned. (iii) With regard to the Jews, Paul's long, incoherent sentence begins: "But *if* you call yourself a Jew..." (Rom 2.17), and seemingly should have continued "... and do these very things [or some equivalent formulation]." Instead, he breaks after v. 20, and asks a number of questions about inconsistency of teaching and action. The thrust of the whole address to the Jews, however, is that *those who* act thus will be condemned. Implicitly *not all*

Jews do so. Moreover Paul adds that circumcision is of value *if*
the Jew obeys the Law (2.25), and what he states about the real
Jew and real circumcision can most reasonably be understood in
the context to regard both Jew and Gentile who keep the Law
(2.26-29). (iv) Unmentioned by Paul, but leaping to the mind
of any reader who is familiar with the Scripture, is the question
about righteous, holy men and women who lived under the Law:
how does Paul's massive condemnation fit them?

(c) A determination of the basic truth, and a resolution of the
apparent conflicts. Like some other human authors of the Bible,
notably John, Paul makes some stark statements which, as they
stand, seem irreconcilable. He does not make distinctions and
refinements which will come later in the reflection of Christian
thinkers. We must hold all of his statements in the tension in
which they stand in his thought. Resolution of the tension can
come only by a process of distinction and amplification which go
beyond Paul's explicit teaching, but which pertain to the total
process of reflection and further understanding which come in the
life of the Church illumined by the Holy Spirit. I shall note later
another instance of such a tension in Paul's thought, regarding the
roles of faith and baptism in justification. Paul and his fellow
inspired authors have a unique role in passing on God's revelation.
Yet God's self-manifestation is not locked for ever in the
evidently inadequate symbols of his human authors: the total
process goes on in the life of the Church until the end of time [38].

All have sinned. By one man's disobedience, first of all, all
were made sinners, in some mysterious way which Paul does not
indicate, and which centuries of Christian thought, in the development of dogma and of theology, will seek to elaborate in the teaching of original sin [39]. Moreover, all [who lived to be capable of
sinning personally: another qualification which lies beyond Paul's
thought] sinned personally. This seems to many recent and contemporaneous exegetes to be the most reasonable interpretation
of Paul's statement in Rom 5.12: "...because all men sinned" [40].

---

[38] See *Basics*, chapters V and VI, pp. 119-220; chapter VIII, esp. pp.
256-257; and chapter IX, pp. 258-302.

[39] Concerning what later would be called original sin, and also personal sin,
I simply note another truth of faith which only gradually came to explicit
formulation in the teaching and theology of the Church regarding the
Immaculate Conception and the sinlessness of the Blessed Virgin Mary.

[40] See FITZMYER, "Romans," JBC, II, 53:39, p. 301, and 53:57, pp. 307-308.
This is one of the questions on which I reserve judgment, for it would involve a
discussion which would be a long deviation from my present line of consideration,
and in any case would not settle the matter. It is not necessary here.

However one interprets Rom 5.12-21, in Paul's conception all men after Adam's first sin, whether by the effects of that sin alone, or by the additional effects of their personal sins, are under the power of sin. The weakness of sinful flesh is both the effect of sin and the ally of Sin. *Of ourselves,* without the pure grace, the gift, of God, we are helpless to achieve righteousness before God. This is the *zero point* from which every man and woman begins. Absolute bedrock is our realization of this truth, of our utter helplessness and need of God's deliverance.

None of the apparent conflicts which I have noted above weaken Paul's massive affirmation. The resolution of the difficulties regarding Gentiles and Jews who did keep the Law, and the holy men and women of the Old Testament, lies beyond Paul's explicit thought. It can be worked out consistently with his teaching on justification by faith. *Of themselves* they could not achieve *their own* righteousness. Those who were righteous were so by the pure gift of God: their righteousness was *from faith.* For those under the Law, this faith was explicitly in the promise to Abraham and the Fathers. Their performance of the works of the Law was life-giving because it was animated by that faith. For those who lived good lives outside the Law, the power to do so was God's gift, given in the hidden ways of his grace. For all, Jew and Gentile alike, all true righteousness, all fulness of life, is a righteousness which is *from God,* a pure gift, somehow *from faith* in Jesus Christ, the sole savior and reconciler, the sole mediator of all grace. A beautiful statement of this basic truth, with a recognition of the many ways of God's grace, and the variety of relations to Christ, explicit or implicit, was made by the Church in the Second Vatican Council[41].

One important consideration remains. The "zero point" is not a merely historical situation, reached once for all in the history of mankind. It is the starting point for every man and woman from the moment of the first sin. Moreover, in the life of every man and woman it marks not merely the moment at which life begins, but a radical weakness and helplessness and absolute dependence on God's grace which is a constant factor in our existence. It is true that it has a special gravity and poignancy in the extreme situation of the man or woman who has sinned

---

[41] Vatican Council II, *Dogmatic Constitution on the Church* ("Lumen gentium"), chapter II, "The People of God", esp. nn. 13-16, in Walter M. Abbot, S.J., *The Documents of Vatican II* (N.Y.: c. America Press, 1966), pp. 30-35.

seriously. Yet it is a constant factor in our life, a constant basic truth concerning our life. Constantly, whether we are living in God's grace or in the depths of sin, *of ourselves* we are under the power of sin, enemies of God, helpless, absolutely dependent on his grace. In our own awareness of our situation, and our understanding of the basic truth concerning ourselves before God, our realization of our radical weakness and dependence is the constant bedrock of all spiritual life. All righteousness, all fulness of life, is rooted in God's love, his free gift. Even when we can discern many signs that we are living in him, we can look at the man or woman who seems to be a wretched sinner, and say with the saint: "There, but for the grace of God, go I."

(8) *Second formulation of the thesis*:

> But now the righteousness of God has been manifested apart from law, although the law and the prophets bear witness to it, the righteousness of God through faith in Jesus Christ for all who believe. For there is no distinction; since all have sinned and fall short of the glory of God, they are justified by his grace as a gift, through the redemption which is in Christ Jesus, whom God put forward as an expiation by his blood, to be received by faith. This was to show God's righteousness, because in his divine forbearance he had passed over former sins; it was to prove at the present time that he himself is righteous, and that he justifies him who has faith in Jesus. Then what becomes of our boasting? It is excluded. On what principle? On the principle of works? No, but on the principle of faith. For we hold that a man is justified by faith apart from works of law. Or is God the God of Jews only? Is he not the God of Gentiles also? Yes, of Gentiles also, since God is one; and he will justify the circumcised on the ground of their faith, and the uncircumcised through their faith. Do we then overthrow the law by this faith? By no means! On the contrary, we uphold the law (Rom 3.21-31).

Having presented Paul's two formulations of his thesis in *Romans*, I should like to contrast them with the brief early formulation in *Galatians*: "We ourselves, who are Jews by birth and not Gentile sinners, yet who know that a man is not justified by works of the law but through faith in Jesus Christ, even we have believed in Christ Jesus, in order to be justified by faith in Christ, and not by works of the law, because by works of the law shall no one be justified" (2.15-16).

Here Paul states his thesis in a polemical letter intended to prevent the Galatians' yielding to the insistence of judaizers.

The thesis itself is embedded in Paul's account of his confrontation with Cephas (Peter) and other Jewish Christians. Addressing the Galatians, Paul uses two arguments. The first is direct and forceful: a reminder, in the form of a rhetorical question, that the Galatians themselves experienced their own reception of the Spirit not from works of the law, but from hearing with faith 3.2-5). The second is a complex chain of arguments from Scripture (3.6 – 4.31): a line of argument which is subtle, sinuous, tortuous. With rabbinic logic Paul develops his case in a manner which must have been far more familiar to the Jewish Christian advocates of judaizing than to Galatian converts of Gentile background. It is a labored argument, not altogether satisfying. I shall not discuss it in detail [42].

Far from the rabbinic logic of *Galatians*, the two formulations and the development of *Romans* propose a profound, richly theological teaching. The thesis formulated in *Galatians* (2.15-16) is echoed in Rom 3.28, but it is only part of a far more ample development. *Romans*, from 3.21 to 15.13, is the perfect counterpart to Paul's massive statement of our utter helplessness under the power of sin, unable to justify ourselves by works of the law (3.9, 21, 23). It is a message of hope for all who will believe in Jesus Christ.

(9) *God's righteousness.* Paul begins not with man's righteousness or justification or becoming or being made righteous, upright, "just", whether by works of the law or by faith; but with God's righteousness. We can fix fairly well the meanings of the adjective δίκαιος (upright, just, righteous), or the noun δικαιοσύνη (uprightness, righteousness, justice) as they are used regarding men or women. *Upright, just, righteous* mean being in conformity with the laws of God and man [43]: in short, being as one ought to be; and the nouns have corresponding meanings. When, however, we apply such words to God, we must make some adjustments, and at best we can attempt to "purify" or "rectify" human symbols, so that they may be less

---

[42] For a brief commentary, see FITZMYER, "The Letter to the Galatians," JBC, II, 49:20-28, pp. 241-244. In no sense is *Galatians* a sort of preliminary outline of *Romans*, as Fitzmyer points out, *ibid.*, 8, p. 237. I cannot agree with him when he holds that "...the résumé of Paul's gospel in Gal 2:15-21 is almost an outline of Rom 1-8, with the same positive progress of thought" (*ibid.*). One will look in vain in Gal 2.15-21 for most of Rom 1-8. There are points touched in both, but *Romans* simply bursts the résumé in Gal 2.15-21.

[43] See BAG.

inappropriate than they would be without such purification. There
is no external norm to which God "conforms". He *is*. When we
attempt to spell out aspects of his fulness of being, we make
human efforts to conceive and express ways in which he is as he
ought to be: true to himself as God. He is the fulness of being
and good, of wisdom and power. He is "just" on the analogy of
a just judge, both when he rewards and when he punishes (see,
for example, Rom 3.3-7 on God's faithfulness, justice, and
truthfulness).

But beyond such analogies from human qualities, there is a
further revelation of an aspect of God's love and mercy which
reveals deeper mysteries ("deeper" in the sense that they lie
beyond all natural human thought of God, and of the ways in
which he is true to himself). Radically there is the mystery of
God's love by which he freely chooses men and women as the
recipients of his special favors, his grace, his free gift, and his
mercy when they have sinned. Thus, to gain some insight into
the mystery of God's righteousness as Paul conceives it, we must
take into account Paul's tormented meditation on the tragedy and
the eventual hope for his brethren, his kinsmen by race, the
Israelites (Rom 9-11). When God freely chooses and calls and
has mercy and saves a remnant not on the basis of works but by
grace, his free gift (compare 9.6-13, 22-29; 11.1-6,
29-36), he is *just*: he is as he should be, true to himself, faithful.
He *is* in accordance with his own eternal design of love, free choice
and grace, promise and fulfillment.

Within the mystery of election, promise, and gift, we may
distinguish two phases of the revelation of God's righteousness.
The first is involved in God's promise: he will be *faithful*. In this
first phase there is no suggestion of later sin on the part of the
recipient of the promise, or of mercy and forgiveness on God's
part. Such is the case in the promise to Abraham. There is no
suggestion of Abraham's having sinned, and of his receiving God's
mercy and forgiveness. In Paul's account, God simply promised:
"I have made you the father of many nations" (Rom 4.17: cf. Gen
17.4-6); "So [as numerous as the stars] shall your descendants
be" (Rom 4.18: cf. Gen 15.5). As for Abraham, '... in the
presence of the God in whom he believed, who gives life to the
dead and calls into existence the things that do not exist...''
(4.17), he believed then in the *promise*. "He did not weaken in
faith when he considered his own body, which was as good as
dead because he was about a hundred years old, or when he
considered the barrenness of Sarah's womb. No distrust made

him waver concerning the promise of God, but he grew strong in his faith as he gave glory to God, fully convinced that God was able to do what he had promised. That is why his faith was 'reckoned to him as righteousness'" (4.19-22). Two things are implicit here, and both bear on my interpretation of what I have called the first phase of the revelation of God's righteousness within the mystery of election and promise. First, Abraham clearly believed not only that God was *able* to do what he had promised, but also that he *surely would* do it: he would be *faithful* to his promise. Second, Paul does not mention here explicitly God's righteousness: it is implicit, as is Abraham's belief in God's *fidelity*. Once God promises, he is not only *able* to give life to the dead, but he *will* do so: he is faithful to his promise. All depends on Abraham's faith. Once God promises, *fidelity* to his promise is an aspect of his righteousness, his being true to himself. Before the promise, Abraham could know that God can give life to the dead. After the promise, he believes that God will.

The second stage of this line of revelation of God's righteousness is that of the redemption which is in Christ Jesus, "... whom God put forward as an expiation by his blood, to be received by faith. This was to show God's righteousness, because in his divine forbearance he had passed over former sins; it was to prove at the present time that *he himself is righteous* and that he justifies him who has faith in Jesus" (Rom 3.25-26). I have italicized the significant element in this text. The righteousness of God which is manifested (Rom 3.21-22) is not simply the righteousness [of men] that *comes from God* (cf. Rom 10.3). It is God's righteousness, consisting in his divine forbearance, passing over sins, justifying by his grace as a gift (3.24). God acted to prove that *he himself is righteous* and that he justifies him who has faith in Jesus.

There is an analogy between the two stages of this revelation of God. In the first, Abraham knows him as the God who gives life to the dead and calls into existence the things that do not exist (Rom 4.17). In the second, we were dead and have been made alive together with Christ; and in Christ we are a new creation. God has called into existence what did not exist: "And you, who were *dead* in trespasses and the uncircumcision of your flesh, God *made alive* together with him, having forgiven us all our trespasses, ..." (Col 2.13). "For neither circumcision counts for anything, nor uncircumcision, but a *new creation*" Gal 6.15). "Therefore, if any one is in Christ, he is a *new creation*; ..." (2.

Cor 5.17). "For by grace you have been saved through faith; and this is not your own doing, it is the gift of God—not because of works, lest any man should boast. For we are *his workmanship, created* in Christ Jesus for good works, ..." (Eph 2.8-10).

(10) *Man's righteousness.* I am concerned here with man in his relationship with God. A man is righteous when he is "right with God": acknowledging God for what he is, letting God be God in his life. In any stage of man's knowledge of God this would involve recognizing the divine "qualities" which can be known: God's absolute excellence and dominion, his wisdom, goodness, power, holiness. When God has revealed the mystery of his election and his promise, the man who has received such a revelation is right with God when he *believes*: accepts God's revelation of himself, trusts God, entrusts himself to him, and hopes firmly that he will receive the promised good. I should distinguish between a basic righteousness and a further righteousness; and within each I should draw another distinction corresponding to the two stages of the revelation of God within the mystery of election and promise.

Basic righteousness for Abraham was simply *believing* in the God who had revealed himself: in his promise, in his power to fulfill the promise, and in his fidelity. Basic righteousness for us is believing his proof of forgiveness in Christ: in his fulfillment of the promise in raising Jesus from the dead, in the power by which he raised Jesus and can raise us from the death of sin, in his offer of righteousness to all who will believe and thus be justified, in the whole of the gospel, the whole of the good news, which is the power of God for those who believe. For Abraham and for us, analogously according to our different situations, *faith* is reckoned as righteousness.

With regard to further righteousness in the case of Abraham, admittedly in Paul's account there is only the hint which may be detected in one verse: "No distrust made him waver concerning the promise of God, but he grew strong in his faith as he gave glory to God, ..." (Rom 4.20). Implicitly it was not simply the basic act of belief which was reckoned to him as righteousness: he *continued* to believe, giving glory to God. Beyond Paul's account of Abraham, it is clear that Abraham was "right with God" not merely in his initial faith, but in the pattern of his continuing action. "...I have singled him [Abraham] out to command his sons and his household after him to maintain the way of Yahweh by just and upright living. In this way Yahweh will carry out for Abraham what he has promised him" (Gen 18.19: JB). Again, the importance of Abraham's obedience regarding the sacrifice of Isaac is stressed: "... I swear by my own self—it is Yahweh who speaks—because you have done this, because you have not refused me your son, your only son, I will shower blessings on you, I will make your descendants as many as the stars of heaven and the grains of sand on the seashore. Your descendants shall gain possesion of the gates of their enemies. All the nations of the earth shall bless themselves by your descendants, as a reward for your obedience" (Gen 22.15-18: JB). The Priestly account of the covenant with Abraham lays even heavier stress on Abraham's action as the condition of both the divine promise and its fulfillment (Gen 17.1-2, 9-14; 26.3b-5).

As for our further righteousness, or a continuation in a righteous life, without using the word "righteousness" very often, Paul clearly insists on a code of Christian conduct. Only if we continue to live as he exhorts us shall we be "right with God". I shall treat this code later. For the present, it is enough to point out a few texts. Having died to sin, we cannot continue to live in it (cf. Rom 6.2). "Do not yield your members to sin as instruments of wickedness, but yield yourselves to God as men who have been brought from death to life, and your members to God as instruments of righteousness" (6.13; cf. vv. 16-23)[44].

(11) *Hearing, preaching, and hearing the word.* Ironically, it may seem, I present this element in a dialectical form. Absolutely first in our fulfillment is hearing the word of revelation, God's word: that is true of Jeremiah, of Paul, and of Paul's hearers. The speaking of the word is itself a gift: whether on God's part in the original revelation, or on the prophet's or apostle's part in acting as God's spokesman. In every case it is a gift, a grace. Corresponding to every speaking of the word is the hearing, a grace first for the spokesman in his own personal experience, and then for his or her hearers. The message comes in a word: it is heard. Repeatedly Paul writes of this element in the original experience of the Christians whom he addresses in various churches (e.g. 1 Th 1.5; 2.13; Gal 3.2). Paul's mission was to preach (1 Cor 1.17; cf. 2.1-5). In a classic formula Paul indicates the place of hearing in the complex beginning of the fulfillment for any man or woman: "... faith comes from what is heard, and what is heard comes by the preaching of Christ" (Rom 10.17; cf. vv. 14-21).

---

[44] Compare the treatment of new creation as process. *Basics*, pp. 156-172.

(12) *Receiving the Spirit.* Obviously the Spirit and the manifold gift of the Spirit is a constant in the whole process of fulfillment, and I shall return later to consider it more amply. It is important, however, to note here in particular the role of the Spirit at the very outset of the process. I return to one of the texts cited in the preceding section: "For we know, brethren beloved by God, that he has chosen you; for our gospel came to you not only in word, but also in power and in the Holy Spirit and with full conviction...." (1 Th 1.4-5). Note the proof for Paul that God has *chosen* them: the other elements of the total experience of hearing the word. Seeking an order of intelligible priority, I should list them thus: the gift of the Holy Spirit, the power which the word had because of the action of the Spirit within them, and the full conviction. I think that from the context the immediate sense of Paul's words is this: he preached his gospel not only in word, but in power, in the Holy Spirit, and with conviction. This seem to me clear from what immediately follows: "... You know what kind of men we proved to be among you for your sake" (1 Th 1.5). Yet here as often Paul is cryptic and elliptical. He seems to me to affirm that both his preaching and their hearing were accompanied by, or marked by, these other elements. It is the gift of the Spirit to them, its power in them, and the full conviction of their response in the Spirit which are the sign that God has chosen them.

This interpretation of Paul's words here is confirmed, I believe, by other references to the beginnings of the new life. Paul asks the Galatians: "... Did you receive the Spirit by works of the law, or by hearing with faith?" (Gal 3.2). The answer to his rhetorical question is obvious, and Paul's first argument against the judaizers is taken from the Galatians' own experience. When Paul had preached ("publicly protrayed") Jesus as crucified, they received the Spirit, not by [*from*] works of the law, but by [*from*] "hearing with faith". The gift of the Spirit is linked with their total experience of believing. Paul very probably is referring to a total gift: of the Spirit himself, and of the extraordinary gifts which accompanied and symbolized their conversion experience [45]. Going beyond Paul in the effort to establish an intelligible order of priority, I should say the gift of the Spirit is first: by the action of the Spirit within them the word came with power and they believed. If they received the extraordinary gifts, charisms in the

---

[45] See JOSEPH A. FITZMYER, "The Letter to the Galatians," JBC, II, 49:20, p. 241.

special sense of the word, these were symbolic of the total experience, as in the experiences narrated in Acts 2.4; 10.44-47; 11.15-18.

As there is a complementarity and a certain tension between Paul's teaching regarding the roles of faith and baptism in the beginnings of Christian life, so there is a corresponding complementarity of the roles attributed to the Spirit in both faith and baptism. I shall return to consider the role of the Spirit in baptism.

(13) *Love, grace, belief, and rightness.* At this point we are ready to consider the radical, basic human response: a response *to* God's word to man at the zero point, a response made *by* the grace of the Spirit working within us. Most readers, I suspect, would have expected me to entitle this section "Justification by faith", or at least "faith and righteousness", or some similar formulation. Such, in fact, was my intention; for we have become accustomed to the variations of Paul's summary statement of his "thesis":

> ... a man is not justified by [from] works of the law but through faith in Jesus Christ.... (Gal 2.16)
> ... "He who through [from] faith is righteous shall live" (Rom 1.17)
> ... a man is justified by faith apart from works of the law (Rom 3.28).

Why, then, have I chosen instead the title which I have given? First, it is to avoid the danger of locking Paul's teaching in formulae which, detached from their context in the whole of his thought, have a long, at times bitterly controversial, history in Christian interpretation. I shall attempt to suggest the context, the whole within which variations of Paul's "thesis" have their meaning.

Second, I deliberately chose the term *rightness,* in preference to *righteousness.* Both are equally good English words, but the latter, the common choice of translators in the texts which concern us, is laden with repugnant connotations, by association with "self-righteousness". *Righteous* and *righteousness,* like "piety" have acquired an unpleasant flavor, and they hardly serve aptly to designate noble and beautiful realities. I confess that in the development which follows I keep the word *righteousness,* where it figures in a translation which I am quoting, or where I discuss the context of such texts as they have been translated

commonly.   Yet, when I come to my own treatment at the proper
place in this section, I shall hold steadfastly to *right* and *rightness*.

Third, my choice of *belief* instead of *faith* may be at least
equally surprising.   I shall explain it below.

(a) The context.   If we look at the classic texts in which these
formulae are embedded, we find Paul's mention of the power
of God, and his righteousness (Rom 1.16-17).   In his full
statement in Rom 3.21-31, several elements are essential to his
thought: the righteousness of God, manifested now apart from
the law, yet witnessed to by the law and the prophets; justification
by his grace as a gift, through the redemption which is in Christ
Jesus, whom God put forward as an expiation by his blood, to be
received by faith [or literally, with the JB, following the Greek
word order more closely: whom God put forward as (or: destined
to be) a propitiatory through faith by his blood], to show God's
righteousness, because in his divine forbearance he had passed
over former sins; it was to prove at the present time that he
himself is righteous and that he justifies him who has faith in
Jesus.

Complementing and enriching the context given by these
texts of *Romans* are the great passages of *Ephesians*, 1.3-14
and 2.4-10.   Having treated the first text above (pp. 105-108)
as one of the great "prologues", I shall merely single out here
elements which are of chief importance for our present purpose.
Consistently with my choice in my full treatment of the text, I
shall quote elements here as they are drawn from Marcus Barth's
translation in the AB, italicizing especially significant words and
phrases.   [God] has *blessed us in Christ* with the full spiritual
blessing of the heavens (3).   Before the foundation of the world
he has *chosen* us in Christ *to live by love ... holy and blameless
before him* (4).   He has *predesignated* us through Christ *to
become his children according to his favorable decision* (5) so
that the glory of his *grace* be praised which in his beloved son he
has *poured out upon us* (6).   Through [the shedding of] his
blood we possess *freedom* in him, *forgiveness* of our lapses (7).
Such are the riches of his *grace* which he has *lavished upon us*
(8).   He has made known to us the secret of his *decision...* (9)....
As resolved by him who carries out all things after his will and
decision, we [Jews] were first designated and appropriated in the
Messiah (11).   We, the first to set our hope upon the Messiah,
were to become a *praise of God's glory* (12).   You [Gentiles] too
are [included] in him.   For you have *heard the true word*, the
message that saves you.   And after you came to *faith*, you, too,

have been *sealed with his seal*, the *promised Holy Spirit* (13). He is the *guarantee* of what we *shall inherit* [to vouch for] the *liberation* of *God's own people, to the praise of his glory* (14). I point out one variant in the interpretation underlying the RSV translation of verse 4: "He *destined us in love...*" This involves a change in the sense suggested by Paul's word order in the Greek, where "in love" closes the clause. In any case, as the editors of JB point out in their note, " 'Love' here is primarily the love God has for us, and that leads him to 'choose' us and call us to be 'holy'..., but does not exclude our love for God that results from and is a response to his own love for us, cf. Rm 5:5".

I quote the second text according to the JB:

> But God *loved* us with *so much love* that he was *generous* with his *mercy*: when we were *dead* through our sins, he *brought us to life* with Christ—it is *through grace* that you have been *saved*—and *raised us up with him* and *gave us a place with him in heaven, in Christ Jesus.*
> This was to show for all ages to come, through his *goodness towards us in Christ Jesus,* how *infinitely rich* he is in *grace.* Because it is by *grace* that you have been *saved, through faith; not by anything of your own,* but *by a gift from God; not by anything that you have done,* so that *nobody can claim the credit.* We are *God's work of art, created in Christ Jesus* to live the good life as from the beginning he had meant us to live it (Eph 2.4-10).

Some other major texts add to Paul's full context. One follows his great passage on life in the Spirit, after he has affirmed that the Spirit intercedes for us according to the will of God: "We know that in everything God works for good with those who *love* him, who are *called according to his purpose.* For those whom he *foreknew* he also *predestined* to be *conformed to the image of his Son,* in order that he might be the first-born among many brethren. And those whom he predestined he also *called*; and those whom he called he also *justified*; and those whom he justified he also *glorified*" (Rom 8.28-30). In his ecstatic conclusion to the chapter Paul adds these elements pertaining to our theme: we are God's *elect* [or *chosen ones*]; it is God who *justifies* (v. 33); nothing will separate us from the *love of Christ,* the *love of God in Christ Jesus our Lord* (cf. vv. 35-39).

In his reflection on the mystery of Israel, painful yet hopeful, Paul returns again to themes which bear on our total context. The word of God has not failed. "... For not all who are descended from Israel belong to Israel, and not all are *children of*

Abraham because they are his descendants; .... it is not the
children of the flesh who are the *children of God*, but the
children of the promise...'' (9.6-8). And those are children
of the promise whom God *chooses, calls,* upon whom he has
mercy, whom he has *prepared beforehand for glory,* not only
from the Jews but also from the Gentiles (cf. 9.9-26). Only a
remnant of Israel will be saved (cf. 9.27). At the present time
there is a *remnant, chosen* by *grace.* ''... But if it is by *grace,*
it is no longer on the basis of *works* [*from* works]; otherwise
grace would no longer be grace'' (11.5-6). It is the mystery
of God's choice, his irrevocable gifts and call, his mercy, which
lie in the depth of the riches of the wisdom and knowledge of
God, his unsearchable judgments, his inscrutable ways (cf.
11.28-36).

What are we to conclude from this review of texts in which I
have singled out a bewildering cluster of elements which
somehow pertain to the total context within which Paul's ''thesis''
can be understood? Let us recall what may be regarded as Paul's
formulation of the thesis within Rom 3.21-31: ''... he [God]
himself is righteous and ... he justifies him who has faith in
Jesus'' (v. 26). Cutting through to what I have proposed in
dealing with God's righteousness (above, pp. 253-256) and
man's righteousness (above, pp. 256-257), I should re-
formulate the thesis thus: God is *right,* and he *makes right* the
man who believes in Jesus Christ. God is *right*: he is the kind of
God which he should be, faithful to what he has revealed to us
about himself. Man is *right* when he is as God reveals that he can
and should be. Somehow *belief* figures between the two. All of
the elements of the context spell out what kind of God he has
revealed himself to be, what we are to be according to his purpose
for us, and what is the role of belief in the realization of God's
purpose in us.

What, then, has God revealed of himself? I shall attempt
merely to list the elements in what, from a human point of view,
seems to be an intelligible order, grouping small clusters which
are intimately related, or which may be regarded as aspects of a
single divine attribute or action. Later, in the course of my
development of this whole section, I shall deal with love and grace
in some detail. These, then, are the elements: wisdom,
knowledge/foreknowledge, unsearchable judgments, inscrutable
ways; goodness, love, grace; choice/election, favorable decision,
purpose, predestination, call, promise; mercy, expiation by the
blood of Jesus, forgiveness.

What is revealed as pertaining to man's *rightness*? I should distinguish two clusters, one concerning the immediate effects of God's action in us, the other concerning the process which begins with what I have called "basic righteousness" and should continue through life and into eternity [46].

Basic rightness involves belief; justification/being made right; being saved, by grace, by the message; being brought to life; being raised with and in Christ; receiving the graces lavished upon us, God's gifts, all spiritual blessings; being forgiven; freedom; being sealed with God's seal, the Holy Spirit, who is a guarantee of our inheritance; belonging to God's people; being his work, created in Jesus Christ.

The further process includes loving God and living by love; living the good life as from the beginning he meant us to live it; being conformed to the image of his Son; becoming a praise of God's glory; final salvation; and a place in heaven in Christ Jesus.

(b) Love. As it pertains to God's *rightness, love* in the texts concerning our present theme clearly designates God's love of us. God's love has an absolute priority in our understanding of all of his actions on our behalf, and all of the gifts which we receive from him: all proceed from his love of us. Variations on his love are his grace and kindness toward us (cf. Eph 2.7). It is God's love for us which is signified in Rom 5.8 and Eph 2.4. Eph 1.4 may be understood as designating primarily God's love for us, but including our love for him.

Our own rightness is first and foremost the effect of God's love for us. It is by the love, favor, gift received from him that we can believe (cf. Eph 6.23). In many of Paul's expressions concerning the love of God or of Christ, the genitive is what Zerwick aptly called a "general genitive" [47], and the full sense of the expressions cannot be held if we pronounce it as either subjective or objective: that is, God's love of us, or our love of God. The phrases are pregnant, full of meaning, holding both relationships in the vain attempt to capture and express something of the reality which defies all conceptualization. Examples of such expressions are found in 2 Th 3.5; 2 Cor 5.14; 13.13; Rom 5.5; 8.35, 39; Eph 1.4 (?); 3.17, 19; 5.2. Similarly "the God of love and of peace" (2 Cor 13.11), may be taken as

---

[46] On basic righteousness and further righteousness see above, pp. 256-257.

[47] MAXIMILIAN ZERWICK, S.J., *Graecitas Biblica*[4] (Rome: Pontifical Biblical Institute, 1960) pp. 12-14.

meaning the God who is love and the God from whom we have love (of him and of one another).

(c) Grace. Every Pauline letter includes the prayer for grace and peace in the opening greeting, and many in the closing blessing[48]. In instances of Paul's usage which concern us here, *grace* (χάρις) has two meanings: God's love, favor, benevolence; and in us the grace, favor, gift, blessing received, often linked with *gift* (χάρισμα, δόμα, δωρεά)[49]. The two meanings are inseparable aspects of one mystery. Often it is best to regard the word as embracing both[50]. Sometimes the emphasis is clearly on the grace received, though one can never be oblivious of its source in God's favor[51]. This favor is itself an aspect of his love, and so with love it must be given priority in the mystery of the whole process of faith and being made right, in the full sense which I shall indicate.

(d) Belief. I shall treat belief in two parts: first, what is proposed for belief; second, the act, its structure, and its roles.

[1] What is proposed for belief? Briefly, it is the gospel, the word: God's gospel, not man's (cf. 1 Th 2.2-8, 9, 13; Rom 1.1). Paul received it through a revelation of Jesus Christ (Gal 1.11-12, 15-16). Hence it can come not only in word, but also in power and in the Holy Spirit and with full conviction (cf. 1 Th 1.5-8). It is one gospel: there is no other (cf. Gal 1.6-9). It must be preached, for faith comes from what is heard, and what is heard comes by the preaching of Christ (cf. Rom 10.14-8). Finally, it is the whole gospel, not just what is sometimes distinguished as the doctrinal portions as opposed to the moral or hortatory. There are, surely, passages in which Paul exhorts and appeals. There are also passages in which he settles particular points of discipline and order in a community. But the Christian code of conduct itself is part of Paul's teaching, part of a coherent whole, as I shall note later. Except where Paul notes otherwise (e.g. in 1 Cor 7.25-40), or where Paul's teaching represents an

---

[48] I find a striking parallel in what may be regarded as John's bracketing of his Gospel: in the prologue, "...grace upon grace .... grace and truth came through Jesus Christ" (1.16-17); and in Jesus' greeting-blessing in his appearance to the apostles. "Peace be with you" (20.19, 21).

[49] Cf. BAG on these words.

[50] Cf. 2 Th 1.12; 2.16; 1 Cor 15.10; 2 Cor 6.1; 8,1; 9.14; 12.9; Gal 1.6, 15; 2.21; Rom 3.24; 4.16; 5.15, 17, 20, 21; 6.1, 14, 15; 11.5-6; Eph 1.6, 7; 2.5, 7, 8; 3.2; 4.7; Phil 1,7; Col 1.6.

[51] Cf. 1 Cor 1.4; 3.10; 15.10; 2 Cor 1.12; 4.15(?); 8.7, 19; 9.8; Gal 2.9; Rom 1.5; 5.2; 12.3, 6; 15.15; Eph 4.7.

aspect of the culture rather than an absolute commandment of God, Paul's code of conduct is itself part of God's revelation, part of Paul's gospel.

Since, with the exceptions which I have noted, Paul's gospel is the whole of his teaching, it can be held in its entirety only by gathering what he proposes in various places in his letters, in a great variety of forms. Though lines of division here cannot be drawn sharply, I should distinguish roughly three classes of texts: mere or less full summaries, brief essential formulae, and particular statements occurring in a variety of contexts.

There is no single great summary: Paul did not write a treatise embracing the whole of his teaching. Hence one can only consider a series of complementary partial summaries. I should single out these passage as particularly important: Gal 4.4-7; 1 Cor 15.1-7 and 12-28; Rom 1.1-5; 1.6-11; a full treatment of life in the Spirit, Rom 8; the most complete of all in Eph 1.3-14 and 18–2.22; and Col 1.12-14, 15-29.

From among Paul's brief essential formulae I should note these:

> ... if you confess with your lips that Jesus is Lord and believe in your heart that God raised him from the dead, you will be saved (Rom 10.9).
> ... since we believe that Jesus died and rose again, even so, through Jesus, God will bring with him those who have fallen asleep (1 Th 4.14).
> ... [our faith] will be reckoned [as righteousness] to us who believe in him that raised from the dead Jesus our Lord, who was put to death for our trespasses and raised for our justification (Rom 4.24-25).
> ... God has not destined us for wrath, but to obtain salvation through our Lord Jesus Christ, who died for us so that whether we wake or sleep we might live with him (1 Th 5.9-10).
> ... we preach Christ crucified, a stumbling block to Jews and folly to Gentiles, but to those who are called, both Jews and Greeks, Christ the power of God and the wisdom of God (1 Cor 1.23-24). Cf. Gal 3.1.
> ... he who raised the Lord Jesus will raise us also with Jesus and bring us with you into his presence (2 Cor 4.14; cf. 1.9-10).
> ... the mystery, Christ, ... that is, how the Gentiles are fellow heirs, members of the same body, and partakers of the promise in Christ Jesus through the gospel (Eph 3.4-6).
> ... this mystery, which is Christ in you, the hope of glory (Col 1.27).
> ... God's mystery, Christ, in whom are hid all the treasures of wisdom and knowledge (Col 2.2-3).

If then you have been raised with Christ, seek the things that are above, where Christ is, seated at the right hand of God. Set your minds on things that are above, not on things that are on earth. For you have died, and your life is hid with Christ in God. When Christ who is our life appears, then you also will appear with him in glory (Col 3.1-4).

With regard to particular statements, fragmentary allusions to elements of the whole gospel, it is needless to attempt to list them: they occur on almost every page of Paul's writings, as I shall have occasion to note particularly concerning some of his formulations of the Christian code.

[2] The act, its structure, and its roles. Considering Paul's central "thesis", we face crucial questions here considering *believe* and *belief/faith,* as we shall see in the following sub-section concerning *make right, right,* and *rightness.* I wish to make clear some of my own convictions regarding method in these considerations of Paul's text. In my judgment, it is essential, but not sufficient, to have some awareness of the fluidity of the Greek language which Paul used and which he adapted as well as he could to fashion his own unique, personal linguistic symbol. It is essential to have some sense of New Testament Greek as somehow distinctive. In particular, in what concerns us, it is important to consider reliable treatments of the syntax of cases and of prepositions[52]. Such treatments, however, are not sufficient. Paul, like any author who has a distinctive thought in which he is grappling with a unique reality, has a distinctive style within the generally fluid language which he adapts. Pauline words and syntax have their meaning only in the context of his thought. Writing from a unique personal experience and understanding of a transcendent Reality, he fashions a total linguistic symbol which represents a Reality and a complex of relationships which have no exact counterpart in the symbolisms and the symbolized realities of any other writer. His thought and language are distinctively Christian and uniquely Pauline. It is indispensable, therefore, to pay very careful attention to his key words, his principal operative words, in their context.

---

[52] I rely here on BDF for a general introduction to New Testament Greek in its setting (§§ 1-7, pp. 1-6) and the syntax of the cases and of the prepositions particularly (§§ 143-240, pp. 79-125); MAXIMILIAN ZERWICK, *Graecitas Biblica*[4] (Rome: Pontifical Biblical Institute, 1960) for cases and prepositions (§§ 25-135, pp. 9-44); and for treatment of particular words, BAG and FRANCISCUS ZORELL, *Lexicon Graecum Novi Testamenti*[2] (Paris: Lethielleux, 1931).

Though I have divided closely related matters into two sections, *belief* and *rightness,* they are intimately related in Paul's thought and in the principal texts which we must examine. I shall proceed, consequently, in what seems to me to be the only feasible way: by an examination of the principal texts first. Then, on the basis of the evidence gathered from these texts, I shall attempt to give an orderly account of belief in this section, and of rightness in the next. To the evidence of the principal texts I shall add citations of the remaining Pauline texts bearing on either or both.

> [15] We, being Jews by nature [birth] and not sinners from the Gentiles, [16] knowing that a man is not made right [or: pronounced right] from works of the Law, but through belief of Jesus Christ, we too believed in Christ, to be made right from belief of Christ and not from works of the Law, since from works of the Law no one is made right. [17] If, seeking to be made right in Christ we ourselves too were found to be sinners, would indeed Christ be a minister of sin? Absurd! [18] For, if I rebuilt what I had torn down, I would prove myself a transgressor. [19] For through the Law I died to the Law, that I might live to God. I was crucified with Christ. [20] I live, no longer I, but Christ lives in me. The life I live in the flesh I live in belief of the Son of God, who loved me and gave himself up for me. [21] I do not set aside [nullify] the grace of God. For, if rightness were [had] through the Law, Christ would have died in vain (Gal 2.15-21) [53].

Paul, Peter, and the other Jews with him, *knew* that a man is *made right* [or *righted*; or, allowing for another interpretation, *pronounced right*] not *from works* of the Law, but *through belief of Jesus Christ.* Hence they *believed in Christ,* to be *made right from belief of Christ,* and *not from works of the Law.* They believed: what they knew concerned the supreme importance of that *act.* Once for all they believed in Christ. The *belief from* or *through* which they were made right is the noun corresponding to

---

[53] As always, translators go their several ways, and never is this more frustrating than in the variety of opinions by which they diminish the riches of the most pregnant, most crucial words of the author. Here I take my own responsibility for my translation, trying to hold as close to, and as much of the sense of, the Greek as possible. Notably here I use *belief,* not *faith.* It has not only the advantage of the parallel with the cognate Greek words for *believe* and *belief,* but also that of rendering easily Paul's "objective" genitive, belief *of* Jesus Christ, and thus eliminating the need of one option.

that basic, initial, decisive act of believing. Even in this brief text,
Greek constructions to express *to whom* the act is directed vary: it
is belief *of* Jesus Christ ("objective" genitive); they believed *in*
Christ Jesus (εἰς with the accusative Christ Jesus, as if the term of
an act which is a movement, a commitment, a thrust). Similarly
the relationship of *being made right* (twice in v. 16) to *belief* is
expressed as being *through* or *from*. As we shall see, the latter is
Paul's common expression, in contrast with *from* works of the
Law [54].

Paul died to the Law in accordance with the very purpose of
the Law, which in a sense was to bring about its own end. It
imposed a curse from which Christ redeemed us (cf. Gal
4.10-14). Later Paul adds two further figures which suggest
the transitoriness of the reign of the Law: its role as custodian or
pedagogue (Gal 3.23 – 4.3), and Christ's being the *end* of the
Law: to him it was directed, and by him terminated (cf. Rom
10.4). By his act of belief, committing himself to Christ and
uniting himself with Christ (and, as Paul will add later, by
baptism: Gal 3.26-29; Rom 6.3-11) Paul was crucified with
Christ, fixed to the cross with him in the very act in which he
removed the curse of the Law and brought the reign of the Law to
an end. Christ now *lives* in Paul: Paul lives *in* belief [or *by* belief]
of the Son of God. Here again, it is belief *of* the Son ("objective"
genitive). Here, however, I should say that *belief* designates not
the original decisive act, but Paul's continuing life of belief: belief
is a continuing disposition ("virtue" in terms of later theology), a
constant part of his life, a stimulus to what in Paul's intense
response must have been frequent full explicit acts of belief.

Turning upon the Galatians, Paul asks two rhetorical
questions regarding their own experience. "Was it *from works
of the Law* that you received the Spirit, or *from belief of what you
heard*?" "Does he who supplies the Spirit to you and works
miracles among you [do so] *from works of the Law* or *from belief*

---

[54] Verses 17-18 are obscure, and have been interpreted variously: cf.
Fitzmyer, "Galatians," JBC, II, 49:19, p. 241. I suggest a plausible
interpretation as follows. If, being in Christ (taking ἐν Χριστῷ not as
instrumental, but as expressing our being in him after having believed) we
sought to be made right (as the judaizers advocated), we would be sinners, but
Christ would not be the minister or agent of our sin. By trying to rebuild what
we had torn down by believing in Christ, by trying again to live according to the
Law, we would prove ourselves to have been transgressors by seeking any other
rightness than from the Law. This interpretation flows naturally into what Paul
says in vv. 19-20. Moreover, it seems to me to be confirmed by Paul's
argument in Gal 5.1-12.

of what you heard?" (Gal 3.2, 5)[55]. In accordance with the suggestion which I have made in the note, my alternative—and preferred—translation in both verses is this: *"from the obedience of belief."* Worthy of note here are the consequences of belief: the gift of the Spirit, and the miracles worked among them. Gradually in Paul's thought a cluster of "consequences" of believing join the centre-piece: *rightness* or *being made right.*

After his argument from the Galatians' own experience, Paul draws on his great Scriptural argument, both here and in *Romans.*

> [6] ... Abraham *"believed* God [or, in God], and [his having believed, or his belief] was accredited to him as *rightness."* [7] You know, then, surely that *those who are* [right] *from belief* are sons of Abraham. [8] And Scripture, foreseeing that *from belief* God would *make* the Gentiles *right,* proclaimed to Abraham in advance the Good News that "In you all the Gentiles shall be blessed". [9] Thus *those who are from belief* are blessed along with the believing Abraham. [10] For all who are *from works of the Law* are under a curse; for it is written, "Cursed is everyone who does not persevere in doing everything that is written in the Book of the Law." [11] It is clear that by the Law no one is made right before God, for "He who *from belief is right* shall live." [12] The Law on the other hand is not *from belief,* but "The man who practices them [the precepts of the Law] will live by them." [13] Christ redeemed us from the curse of the Law, having become a curse for us, for it is written, "Cursed be everyone who is hanged on a tree," [14] so that the blessing of Abraham might come to the Gentiles in Christ Jesus, so that we might *receive the promised Spirit through belief'*....
> [22] Scripture imprisoned all under the power of sin, so that what was promised *from belief of Jesus Christ* might be given to the *believing.*

---

[55] The second question is obviously elliptical. I have added the minimum to complete the sense, retaining the contrasting *from ... from,* parallel with v. 2. A nicer set of questions concerns the phrase ἐξ ἀκοῆς πίστεως. ἀκοή can mean hearing or listening; or in this case what is heard: the preaching; or, metaphorically, obedience. Zorell, in his *Lexicon.* and Zerwick, in his *Analysis Philologica N. T. Graeci*[2] (Rome: Pontifical Biblical Institute, 1960) take it as *obedience to the faith preached.* That introduces a sense of *faith* which seems foreign to the context. I suggest another interpretation: from the *obedience of belief. Belief* thus is not an objective genitive, but explanatory (epexegetical): belief itself is an obedience, a response to the call to believe in the word, a hearing-listening-receiving-responding-believing. In this interpretation there is a parallel with εἰς ὑποκοὴν πίστεως (Rom 1.5), "to bring about the obedience of belief," where Zerwick, *op. cit.,* admits that belief may be an explanatory genitive.

²³ Before the coming of *belief*, we were held in custody under the Law, confined until the coming belief should be revealed. ²⁴ Thus the Law was our custodian until Christ [came], that we might be made right *from belief*. ²⁵ Now that *belief* has come, we are no longer under a custodian. ²⁶ For you are all *sons of God through belief*, in Christ Jesus.... (Gal 3.6-26). ⁵ By the Spirit, *from belief*, we await the *hope* of *rightness*. ⁶ For in Christ Jesus neither circumcision nor uncircumcision counts for anything, but *belief working through love* (Gal 5.5-6).

Reading the translations which I have made is like riding a rocky road in a cart with wooden wheels and no springs. It is hardly "English" in spots. Yet I should have had to make it rougher and rockier to give a fair impression of what it is to read Paul's Greek at some of the points which are most crucial for our consideration. As far as possible, I have held to a constant version of some of the important, rigidly constant Pauline formulae. I shall return later to discuss some of these, the challenges they pose to any translator, and their significance in Paul's thought. Having established my preference for the rendition of *believe* and *belief*, I trust that for the most part the sense of these words as they occur in these texts is clear. There is one exception, to which I turn now, for it concerns a problematic use of the word *belief* in *Galatians*.

What is the meaning of the word in these expressions: "Before the coming of *belief*' (3.23) and "Now that *belief* has come" (3.25)? BAG, in their account of the meanings which πίστις has, hold on the one hand that in Gal 3.7-26 it means true piety, genuine religion; and on the other, that perhaps in Gal 3.23-25 it means body of faith or belief, doctrine; thus it represents an objectivizing of the belief concept. I should say that the word presents no real problem here: Paul is speaking of before and after the coming of the era in which men *believed*, before *belief* of Jesus Christ.

Having devoted considerable attention to most of the principal texts of *Romans* which bear on belief and rightness from belief[56], I shall not examine them again in their entirety. Regarding the texts which I have just translated and discussed as a sufficient specimen of passages in which Paul writes of believing and belief, I turn now to consider some important aspects of Paul's thought concerning them in all of the letters.

---

[56] Above, especially in sections 1, 2, 5, 8, 10, pp. 228-229, 233-235, 252-253, 256-257.

In what follows I shall approach a grasp of the meaning of *believe* and *belief* by considering the act in its total field, in the fanning out of those relationships by which it can somehow be defined. I shall proceed as follows: the words as referring to a past, initial, decisive act, or to a present act or disposition to act; to whom the act is directed; what [or who] is the "object" of the act; through or from whom or what is the act performed; what are the consequences of the act. Holding together the answers to these questions, we may attempt to fix the meaning.

[a] The distinction between the past, initial, decisive act of belief, and a present act or continuing disposition to act in the life of the believer.

First, the verb *believe* frequently, and most significantly, clearly expresses the past, initial, decisive act. I say "most significantly" because this act is the absolute beginning of the human response. It is *from* this act somehow that a man or woman is *righted* (*made right*), and hence *is right* before God. Outstanding examples, involving the aorist tense, either participle or indicative or subjunctive are these: Abraham *believed* (Gal 3.6); Peter, Paul, and the other disciples *believed* (Gal 2.16)[57].

On the contrary, forms of the present indicative or participle express a present act or disposition in the continuing life of the believer. In Rom 4.24 "to us *believing* in the one who raised Jesus" seems to refer to our present believing, which will be accredited to us as rightness. Again, "if we died with Christ, we believe that we shall also live with him" (Rom 6.8). Paul prays for the Ephesians that they may know the hope to which God has called them, and the greatness of his power regarding us who believe ["the believing"] (Eph 1.19). In a context in which he prays for the Philippians' steadfastness, he tells them that they have been given the grace not only to believe in Christ, but also to suffer for him: evidently in their continuing life in him (Phil 1.29)[58].

In some instances it is questionable whether the present tense refers to a dimension of the initial experience, or to an act or disposition in the continuing life of faith[59]. In others, finally, the

---

[57] For other examples see 2 Th 1.10; Eph 1.13; 1 Cor 3.5; 15.2; Rom 4.3, 17, 18; 10.9; 13.11.

[58] For other examples see 1 Th 1.7; 2.10, 13; 4.14; 1 Cor 1.21; 14.22: 2 Cor 4.13.

[59] Gal 3.22; Rom 1.16; 4.11; 10.4.

verb in the aorist, present, or even future, figures in the
enunciation of a general principle concerning believing [60].

Obviously the significance of the classification lies in the
distinction between belief as the initial act and belief as an act or
disposition to act in the continuing life of believing: belief is not
merely a decisive act which is performed once for all, but also an
important factor in the process of Christian living.

Occurring more frequently than the verb, the noun *belief*
always has its meaning, directly or ultimately, in relation to an *act*
of believing. Generally from the context one can judge that it
refers to either the initial, decisive act of believing, or to an act or
disposition to act in the continuing life of the Christian.

Here are some examples in which *belief* clearly means the
initial, decisive act. Peter, Paul, and the others know "... a man
is not made right from works of the Law, but *from belief of Jesus
Christ...*" and they believed in Christ Jesus in order to "... be
made right *from belief of Christ* and not from works of the
Law..." (Gal 2.16). The Galatians received the Spirit and had
miracles performed among them, not from works of the Law, but
from the obedience of belief (cf. Gal 3.2,5; see note 55 above).
They are all sons of God *through belief*, in Christ Jesus [61] (Gal
3.26). "Now, apart from the Law, God's rightness has been
manifested, [though it was] witnessed to by the Law and the
prophets, God's rightness *through belief of Jesus Christ*, to all the
believing..." (Rom 3.21-22). God himself is *right*, and he
rights the man [who is] *from belief of Jesus* (cf. Rom 3.26).
Abraham received circumcision as a sign, a seal of the *rightness of
belief* (Rom 4.11). Not through the Law did the promise and the
inheritance come to Abraham and his seed, but *through the
rightness of belief* [62] (4.13). For this reason the promise is *from
belief*, that it may rest on *grace* (cf. Rom 4.16). *Made right* (or
"*righted*") *from belief* we have peace with God (Rom 5.1). "By
grace you have been saved *through belief*: this is not from you,
but God's gift" (Eph 2.8). Paul's yearning is to be found in
Christ, not having his own rightness, the rightness from the Law,
but [the rightness] *through belief of Christ*, the rightness from
God, *depending on belief* (Phil 3.9). "In him too you were
circumcised... with the circumcision of Christ, in whom too you

---

[60] Rom 4.5; 9.33; 10.10, 11, 14.

[61] I shall return to this verse later in treating baptism.

[62] In the context I take *belief* here as an explanatory (epexegetical) genitive.
See Rom 4.13, and note 55 above. His *belief was* [was put to his account as, or
accredited to him as] *rightness*. Here, his *rightness* is the *rightness of belief*.

were raised together with him *through belief* in the power of the God who raised him from the dead ... (God 2.11-12)[63].

There is a special set of texts concerning the initial act of belief, marked by a distinctively Pauline expression, whose unique sense can be gathered only from the context of Paul's thought. First, with regard to the context, one can note readily that Paul's most frequent phrase to characterize being made right, being right, or rightness, is the simple prepositional phrase *from belief* (ἐκ πίστεως), with or without indication of the person to whom the act of belief is directed, or of that which is believed. It is to convey the persistency of Paul's use of this phrase that I have deliberately and consistently turned his Greek into the English *from belief.*

There are four examples of the construction to which I refer. "You know that *the from belief* (οἱ ἐκ πίστεως), these are sons of Abraham" (Gal 3.7). Again, "...so that *the from belief* are blessed together with the believing Abraham" (Gal 3.9). In Paul's second formulation of his thesis in *Romans,* God's action was to be a proof of his own rightness at the present time, to [make clear] that he himself is right and making right [righting] *the from belief of Jesus* (Rom 3.26). Finally, "...it is for this reason [that the promise is] from belief, that it may rest on grace, that it be guaranteed to all his seed, not only to *the* [seed] *from the* Law, but also to *the* [seed] *from Abraham's belief...*" (Rom 4.16). In the first three instances especially we have a prepositional phrase following a definite article. If one looks to the shape of the expression, one can find here a construction which is classical. It is an eliptical expression, which may designate one or more by their place of origin[64]. In my judgment, Paul's use of the expression has a unique sense determined by the context of his thought. I take it as his shorthand phrase for "those who *from belief* [are *right*, or have been *righted* or *made right*]". He has another phrase which is close in meaning: *the rightness from belief* (ἡ ἐκ πίστεως δικαιοσύνη: Rom 10.6). Finally, Paul twice quotes *Habakkuk* 2.4 (Gal 3.11; Rom 1.17) in a statement which can be taken in two

---

[63] I shall return to this text too in dealing with baptism. For my analysis of the structure of the text and my interpretation developed at some length, see *The Mystery*, pp. 217-220.

[64] Cf. LSJ, ὁ, ἡ, τό, B.II.3. ZORELL, *op. cit.*, ἐκ, VI.c, followed by ZERWICK, *Graecitas Biblica*, 134, p. 44, points out that Paul uses ἐκ with the genitive to designate what characterizes a person or persons. I do not think that this quite hits the mark.

ways: "The righteous man finds life through faith" (JB), or "He who through faith is righteous shall live" (RSV). It seems to me that the whole Pauline context favors the latter interpretation as *Paul's* understanding of the text. Consistently with my effort to sacrifice smooth English to a formula which lays bare the structure of Paul's thought, I should turn it thus: "The man [who] *from belief* [is] *right* will live."

What is the point of this whole exercise? It is simply to bring out that Paul continually uses *from belief* to express by the preposition and genitive a unique, vague relationship of origin, a relationship beyond sharp conceptualization: *being righted* or *made right*, and *rightness* are somehow *from belief*. We can approach that degree of understanding which is attainable through exegesis and biblical theology only by holding all that Paul affirms. Ultimately we can come to a deeper understanding, further defying conceptualization, *by believing*, in our own experience of *belief*. Toward the end of my long treatment of Paul I shall return to reflect on the roles of belief. It will remain for the next volume of this work to attempt to point to the way of experiencing God in belief [65].

These are, in my judgment, the more significant texts in which *belief* indicates a present act or disposition to act in the continuing life of the Christian. Paul witnesses to his own past experience and present life: "...through the Law I died to the Law, that I might live to God. I was crucified with Christ. I live, no longer I, but Christ lives in me. The life I live in the flesh I live *in belief* [or: *by belief*] of the Son of God, who loved me and gave himself up for me" (Gal 2.19-20). I should say that *belief* here has a full, pregnant meaning: it is by virtue of his initial act of belief *and* his present conviction and frequent explicit act of belief that he lives now in Christ, or rather Christ in him. Initial act, continuing disposition, and repeated explicit act are in continuity, as we shall reflect later in considering the structure and the roles of belief in Christian life.

Similar reflections bear upon Paul's affirmation of the grounds for his solemn warning to Galatians tempted to judaize (Gal 5.1-4): "For by the Spirit, *from belief*, we *wait* for the *hope* of *rightness*, for in Christ Jesus neither circumcision nor

---

[65] Other texts in which, in my judgment, *belief* designates the initial act are these: 1 Cor 2.5; Gal 2.20 (?): I shall treat this text in the next section; Gal 3.8, 14, 22; 5.5 (?): again, I shall discuss this text in the next section; Rom 1.5, 17 *from belief to belief* (?): see the next section; 3.28, 30 (twice); 4.12; 5.2 (variant text); 9.30, 32; 16.26 (cf. 1.5).

uncircumcision avails anything, but *belief* working through love"
(5.5-6). It is significant that *now, from belief*, we await the
hope of rightness, which can mean here definitive rightness at the
coming of Christ, as *salvation* often has that meaning in Paul.
Moreover, what *counts* is belief *working through love*: *belief*
which is not just a past act, performed once for all, but an active
principle, a constant source of action, in Christian life. Here, as in
Gal 2.20, belief as initial act and as constant principle of action are
in continuity, as I shall reflect later.

Belief is one of the fruits of the Spirit in full, continuing
Christian life (cf. Gal 5.22). In the gospel, God's rightness is
revealed *from belief to belief* (Rom 1.17). This verse, in
particular the pair of phrases *from belief to belief*, has been
interpreted in many ways in the long history of exegesis [66]. It is
reasonable to interpret *from belief to belief*, as I have suggested
in Gal 2.20 and 5.5-6, consistently with the continuity of initial
and continuing faith in the process of Christian life.

Even in Paul's interpretation of Abraham's belief, one detects
not merely the initial act, but continuing belief. He did not
weaken in belief, no distrust made him waver, but he grew strong
in belief (cf. Rom 4.18-20). And *this* is why his belief was
accredited to him as rightness (4.22).

Philippians is particularly rich for our present concern with
the continuing role of faith in Christian life. What Paul says here
concerning faith, his own and that of the Philippians, must be held
in the context.

First, consider Paul's witness to his own experience.

> [3] For we are the true circumcision, who worship God in spirit, and
> glory in Christ Jesus, and put no confidence in the flesh. [4] Though
> I myself have reason for confidence in the flesh also. If any other
> man thinks he has reason for confidence in the flesh, I have more:
> [5] circumcised on the eighth day, of the people of Israel, of the tribe
> of Benjamin, a Hebrew born of Hebrews: as to the law a Pharisee,
> [6] as to zeal a persecutor of the church, as to righteousness under
> the law blameless. [7] But whatever gain I had, I counted as loss for
> the sake of Christ. [8] Indeed I count everything as loss because of
> the surpassing worth of knowing Christ Jesus my Lord' For his
> sake I have suffered the loss of all things, and count them as
> refuse, in order that I may gain Christ, [9] and be found in him, not
> having a righteousness of my own, based on the law, but that
> which is through *faith in Christ* [*belief of Christ*], the

---

[66] See FITZMYER, "Romans", JBC, II, 53:21, pp. 295-296, for a sketch of
opinions and his interpretation.

righteousness from God that *depends on faith*; [10] that I may know
him and the power of his resurrection, and may share his
sufferings, becoming like him in his death, [11] that if possible I may
attain the resurrection from the dead. [12] Not that I have already
obtained this or am already perfect; but I press on to make it my
own, because Christ has made me his own. [13] Brethren, I do not
consider that I have made it my own; but one thing I do, forgetting
what lies behind and straining forward to what lies ahead, [14] I
press on toward the goal for the prize of the upward call of God in
Christ Jesus (3.3-14).

Paul's whole account of his own life and conversion bring out two
things clearly: his conversion from a striving for his own
righteousness *from the Law* to that which is *through belief of
Jesus*, the *rightness from God*, [based] *on belief*; his *continued*
striving to attain this still distant goal. *Belief* certainly is a
constant factor in that striving.

Both in his rejoicing over the Philippians' life and in his
exhortation to constancy and progress, the continuing role of
belief is prominent, sometimes implicitly, sometimes explicitly.

Implicitly, in my judgment, Paul refers to their initial and
continuing belief in the good work begun in them, and to be
brought to completion (1.6, 9-11). He is convinced that he shall
remain with them and continue with them for their progress and
joy in belief (1.25). He exhorts them to a manner of life worthy
of the gospel, standing firm in one spirit, striving side by side for
the belief of the gospel: for it has been granted to them that for
the sake of Christ they should not only believe in him, but also
suffer for his sake (1.27-30). They are to *work out* their
salvation with fear and trembling: God is at work in them both to
will and to work for his good pleasure (2.12-13). Paul's figure
of being poured out as a libation upon the sacrificial offering of
their belief, obscure as it is, surely refers to their continuing belief
(2.17).

Finally, without entering into the many problems of
interpretation of *Ephesians*, I suggest that Paul has in mind not
only that act by which they first believed (1.13), but also their
continuing belief. In Christ they are holy and believing
("faithful"), as he greets them at the opening of the letter. Above
all his prayer for them regards a belief which is part of that
growth and enrichment for which he asks: "... that according to
the riches of his glory he may grant you to be strengthened in the
inner man, and that Christ may dwell in your hearts *through
belief*; and that you, being rooted and grounded in love, may

have power to comprehend with all the saints what is the breadth and length and height and depth, and to know the love of Christ which surpasses knowledge, that you may be filled with all the fulness of God" (3.16-19). I shall have to return to this text later. For the moment it is enough to cite that somehow, in a knowledge and total experience which shatters all conceptualization, continuing belief surely is part of the mystery[67].

[b] To whom the act is directed. Except for the few texts concerning Abraham's believing in *God* (Gal 3.6; Rom 4.3, 17) and in the formulation of the general principle explaining his act (Rom 4.5), in the vast majority of cases the act expressed by either the verb or the noun regards Christ Jesus, Jesus, Christ, Jesus Christ, the Son of God[68]. Once the noun regards simply God (1 Th 1.8), Once the verb (Rom 4.24) and once the noun (Col 2.12) regards God, but in connection with his action in raising Jesus from the dead.

As for suggestions of the relationships Paul meant to convey by his uses of cases and prepositions, these texts in themselves contribute little. First, cases governed by the verb *believe*: in the instance of Abraham's believing, the dative is used twice explicitly (Gal 3.6; Rom 4.3) and once implicitly where it is attracted into the genitive (Rom 4.17). Concerning Christian believing there is only one implicit instance (taking "confess" as parallel to and equivalent to "believe") in which "Lord Jesus" is not "the Lord Jesus" as object, but rather "that Jesus is the Lord" (Rom 10.9). This, then, is a proposition which is believed, and I shall treat it in the following section: "Who or what is believed". As for cases governed by the noun *belief*, one instance regards Christian belief in God (Col 2.12); and several, Christian belief in Christ (Gal 2.16, 20; 3.22; Rom 3.22, 26; Phil 3.9; Eph 3.12). In all instances the case is the genitive, the "objective" genitive, which I shall discuss later.

As for prepositional phrases modifying the verb *believe*, one instance concerning Abraham's believing (in a general principle

---

[67] I shall not give the long list of other texts in which I judge *belief* to designate present belief or the continuing disposition to believe in the process of Christian life. Most, but not all, remaining instances of the use of belief belong to this class. Nor shall I separate and explain the relatively few instances in which, for example, *belief* figures in the formulation of what could be called a general principle, as in Rom 4.5.

[68] Gal 2.16, 20; 3.22; Rom 3.22, 26; and implicitly in Rom 9.33; 10.11, 14; Eph 1.13, 15; 3.12; Phil 1.29; Col 1.4; 2.5.

explaining his belief) is ἐπί with the accusative (Rom 4.5). Christian believing directed to God is expressed once by ἐπί and the accusative (Rom 4.24); directed to Christ, by εἰς and the accusative (Gal 2.16; Phil 1.29), by ἐπί and the dative [in a text of Isaiah applied to Christ] (Rom 9.33; 10.11), and by ἐν and the dative (Eph 1.13). The noun *belief*, directed to God, occurs once modified by πρός and the accusative (1 Th 1.8); directed to Christ, modified by ἐν and the dative (Eph 1.15; Col 1.4), and by εἰς and the accusative (Col 2.5).

For the moment I leave these data. Of themselves, they contribute little to our grasp of Paul's meaning of *believe* and *belief*. Yet, as I shall reflect later, they are not without significance, not without their meaning as symbolic elements in the whole of Paul's thought. To some it may seem that I am overlooking a convenient, and perhaps for some satisfying, shortcut to the meaning of *believe* and *belief*: consulting classic dictionaries and grammars of the New Testament for the meaning of the verb and the noun, and for the relationships suggested by the cases and the prepositional phrases. As I have indicated at the outset of my treatment of the act of belief, its structure, and its roles (above, pp. 266), I recognize the importance of such works. Yet I insist that Paul's meaning can be gathered only gradually from a careful consideration of the total context of his thought: every symbolic element has its full meaning only as it is set in the whole complex symbol; and I regard the whole of Paul's works as the complex symbol by which he attempted to image and represent the whole of his world, subjective and objective, to communicate the imaged reality, and to evoke in us the total response which is within our personal potential. Thus far we have taken only the first steps in the approach to a grasp of Paul's meaning.

[c] Who or what is believed. Here again I limit the data to what can be gathered from texts in which explicitly or implicitly (from the immediate context) Paul uses *believe* or *belief*. There are two clusters of texts containing either closely related words or formulae expressing the object of belief in the broadest terms, or particular truths. Besides these, in numerous places Paul ·uses *believe* or *belief* absolutely, without indication of what is believed.

In general terms, *what* is believed is the word of God (1 Th 2.13); the witness: that is, that to which Paul or other Apostles bear witness (2 Th 1.10); the gospel: explicitly so called (Rom 10.16; Phil 1.27), or implicitly alluded to in a variety of expressions (1 Cor 15.1-2; 15.11; Rom 1.16; 10.8; 10.12; Eph 1.13; Col 2.7); the truth (2 Th 2.13).

These are the particular truths: one regarding Abraham: his becoming the father of many nations (Rom 4.18); Jesus died and rose (1 Th 4.14); he who raised the Lord Jesus will raise us also with Jesus (2 Cor 4.13-14: immediately the object of *knowing*, but in the context obviously what we believe and of what we speak); we shall live with him (Rom 6.8); God raised him from the dead (Rom 10.9); Jesus is Lord (Rom 10.9); Jesus Christ is in you (2 Cor 13.5); the expiation put forth by Christ's blood (Rom 3.25); God's rightness (Rom 3.21-26).

Texts in which *believe* or *belief* are used absolutely are too numerous to list. In general one could say that in early texts they are forerunners to explicit elaboration of the object of belief; in later texts they are summary allusions to what has been explicitly formulated.

Again for the moment I simply present the data. Later, reflecting on the full context of Paul's thought, I shall indicate how the very objects of our faith contribute to our determining the meaning of *believe* and *belief* for Paul.

[d] Through whom or what, or from whom or what, belief comes. This title is awkward; yet what is involved here is a vast range of divine and human factors, to all of whom belief is somehow due, yet in widest range of degrees and manners. My order here may be bewildering. Yet I have a certain reason for it. I range from specially designated persons and their actions, to the various formulations of the divine power which penetrates their actions and makes them effective, to a final human role in the continuing life of the Church.

First, Paul and Apollos (1 Cor 3.5-9) and the other Apostles and specially designated witnesses are servants or ministers through whom we believe.

Their action is preaching (1 Th 1.5), giving witness (2 Th 1.10), announcing the gospel unashamed (cf. Rom 1.16), speaking the word concerning Christ, that through preaching the word may be heard, and from hearing faith may come (cf. Rom 10.8, 14-17), teaching (cf. Col 2.7).

The gospel is the word of God: He or it is at work in us (cf. 1 Th 2.13, where the relative pronoun may refer to God or to the word: ultimately the meaning is the same, for He is at work in us through his word). To the Thessalonians Paul writes: "... our gospel came to you not only in word, but also in power and in the Holy Spirit and with full conviction" (1 Th 1.5). He reminds the Corinthians: "... my speech and my message were not in plausible words of wisdom, but in demonstration of the Spirit and power, that your faith might not rest in the wisdom of men but in the power of God" (1 Cor 2.4-5).   In the continuing life of the believers, "through the Spirit, by faith, we wait for the hope of righteousness" (Gal 5.5).   Again, the role of the Spirit is prominent in Paul's prayer for the Ephesians' progress: "... that he [the Father] may grant you to be strengthened with might through his Spirit in the inner man, and that Christ may dwell in your hearts through faith..." (Eph 3.16-17: cf. vv. 14-21). Without the Spirit we cannot make our most basic acts of belief: "Jesus is Lord" and "Abba! Father!" (cf. 1 Cor 12.3; Gal 4.6; Rom 8.15-16).   Belief is one of the fruits of the Spirit (Gal 5.22).   Finally, "... by grace you have been saved through faith; and this is not your own doing, it is the gift of God—not because of works, lest any man should boast" (Eph 2.8-9).

In the continuing life of the Church, belief comes to us somehow through one another: one person's belief, or the belief of one community, somehow mediates the belief of others (cf. Rom 1.12; 1 Th 1.7-10; 3.7-10)[69].

[e] What comes from belief.   I have noted above the frequent recurrence of the simple phrase *from belief*, and in my stark translations I have sought to give a sense of the prominence of that simple expression in the Greek.   It is the vaguest of expressions of some sort of origin.   When we gather from Paul's letters the many "effects" which somehow come from belief, we gain a rich increment to our fund of relationships of the act of belief.   Here again I have sought to introduce some order, which I hope will seem rational.

[i] By belief we are sons and daughters of Abraham (Gal 3.7-9; Rom 4.11-18), and as his descendants we are heirs to the promised blessings.   What the promised blessings are, far beyond Abraham's dreams, is spelled out gradually by Paul.

[ii] Expiation (Rom 3.25) and forgiveness of our sins (Rom 3.25; 4.7-8).   This is part of the mystery of fulfillment which could not be foreseen in the promise as Abraham must have understood it.   In the mystery of a sinful mankind, weak and helpless, unable of our own powers to be *right* with God, fulfillment, for those men and women chosen by God in the mystery of his love, begins with receiving by belief the expiation which God put forth by the blood of Christ, redemption in Christ Jesus, and the forgiveness of our sins (Rom 3.21-26).

---

[69] This is part of the mystery of mutual mediation of grace which I have called "the dialectic of charisms": see *Basics*, pp. 198-212.

Believing in him, we will not be put to shame (cf. Rom 9.33; 10.11).

[iii] Conversion. Paul ses the word "turn" or "convert" in a sense pertinent to our theme only once, yet it is noteworthy, for in the context it clearly expresses one of the results of the Thessalonians' belief: "For not only has the word of the Lord sounded forth from you in Macedonia and Achaia, but your faith in God has gone forth everywhere, so that we need not say anything. For they themselves report concerning us what a welcome we had among you, and how you turned to God from idols to serve a living and true God" (1 Th 1.8-9).

[iv] Being righted, with all that it involves. To express the great event, Paul multiplies his figures, bringing out the many facets of an extremely complex experience. From belief we are righted, made right, are right with God, have the rightness which is from God (cf. Gal. 2.16; and concerning both Abraham and us, Gal 3.6-10; Rom 3.21-26, 28, 30; concerning Abraham 4.3, 5, 9; 4.24; 5.1; 9.30, 32; 10.4, 6-10). We are saved (cf. 2 Th 2.13; 1 Cor 1.21; Rom 1.16; 10.9-10). We are crucified with Christ and die to the Law (Gal 2.19-20). We are raised with Christ (Eph 2.6; Col 2.12), made alive (Eph 2.1-5), live to God (Gal 2.19). We are his workmanship, created for good works, which God prepared beforehand, that we should walk in them (Eph 2.10). Hence Paul thanks God for the Thessalonians' work of belief (1 Th 1.3) and prays that God may make them "...worthy of his call, and may fulfill every good resolve and work of faith by his power, ..." (2 Th 1.11). And to the Galatians he can affirm: "...in Christ Jesus neither circumcision nor uncircumcision is of any avail, but faith working through love" (Gal 5.6). As for Paul, it is no longer he who lives, but Christ who lives in him; "...the life I live in the flesh I live in belief of the Son of God, who loved me and gave himself up for me" (Gal 2.20). To the Romans he writes: "...if we have died with Christ, we believe that we shall also live with him... So you...must consider yourselves dead to sin and alive to God in Christ Jesus" (Rom 6.8, 11). For the Ephesians he prays "...that Christ may dwell in your hearts through faith..." (Eph 3.17). From belief, through belief, the Galatians have received the Spirit: Christ redeemed us from the curse of the Law, that in Christ Jesus the blessing of Abraham might come upon the Gentiles. that we might receive the promise of the Spirit [the Spirit who *is* the promised blessing] through belief (cf. Gal 3.2, 13-14). The Ephesians, having heard the word of truth, the gospel of their salvation, and having believed in

him, "... were sealed with the promised Holy Spirit, which is the
guarantee of our inheritance until we acquire possession of it
[or, with NEB: "... and that Spirit is the pledge that we shall
enter upon our heritage, when God has redeemed what is his
own ..."] to the praise of his glory [or: to his praise and glory]"
(Eph 1.13-14).   Through belief we are sons of God (Gal 3.26).
"The proof that you are sons is that God has sent the Spirit of
his Son into our hearts: the Spirit that cries, 'Abba, Father', and
it is this that makes you a son, you are not a slave any more; and
if God has made you son, then he has made you heir" (Gal
4.6-7: JB).

   [v] Having been righted, in the continuing life which is from
belief, we should experience many further consequences.
Prominent among them are a deepening wisdom and knowledge.
Though we walk by belief, not by sight (2 Cor 5.7); though our
knowledge is imperfect:

> ... as for knowledge, it will pass away.   For our knowledge is
> imperfect and our prophecy is imperfect; but when the perfect
> comes, the imperfect will pass away.   When I was a child, I spoke
> like a child, I thought like a child, I reasoned like a child; when I
> became a man I gave up childish ways.   For now we see in a
> mirror dimly, but then face to face.   Now I know in part; then I
> shall understand fully, even as I have been fully understood.   So
> faith, hope, love abide, these three; but the greatest of these is love
> (1 Cor 13.8-13)

yet in the fulness of continuing life which is from belief Paul
affirms a rich, paradoxical wisdom: folly to the wise of this world,
yet Christ crucified, the power of God and the wisdom of God for
those who believe.   It is a secret and hidden wisdom, which God
decreed before the ages for our glorification, a wisdom revealed
through the Spirit, not taught by human wisdom but by the
Spirit, spiritual truth imparted to those who possess the Spirit: to
the unspiritual it is folly (cf. 1 Cor 1.18—2.16).   In two prayers
Paul asks for this wisdom for the Ephesians:

> For this reason, because I have heard of your faith in the Lord
> Jesus and your love toward all the saints, I do not cease to give
> thanks for you, remembering you in my prayers, that the God of
> our Lord Jesus Christ, the Father of glory, may give you a spirit of
> wisdom and of revelation in the knowledge of him, having the
> eyes of your hearts enlightened, that you may know what is the
> hope to which he has called you, what are the riches of his glorious
> inheritance in the saints, and what is the immeasurable greatness of

his power in us who believe, [a power which we can judge] according to the working of his great might which he accomplished in Christ when he raised him from the dead and made him sit at his right hand in the heavenly places, ... (Eph 1.15-20).

... that according to the riches of his glory he may grant you to be strengthened with might through his Spirit in the inner man, and that Christ may dwell in your hearts through faith; that you, being rooted and grounded in love, may have power to comprehend with all the saints what is the breadth and length and height and depth, to know the love of Christ which surpasses knowledge, and you may be filled with all the fulness of God (Eph 3.16-19).

These texts defy sharp conceptualization. Belief, love, wisdom, knowledge, power, a massive sense of breadth and length and height and depth, a knowing of the love of Christ which is beyond knowing, and a being filled with the utter fulness of God—all this shatters any sharp conceptualization of the "cognitive dimension" of belief, yet establishes beyond challenge that somehow in the total concrete experience of Christian life there is a wisdom and a knowledge which are from belief.

I note more briefly many other blessings which somehow are from belief: joy and peace (Rom 15.13; Phil 1.25); love of one another (2 Th 1.3); strength and steadfastness symbolized by belief as a shield or breastplate (Rom 11.20; 1 Th 5.8; Eph 6.16); boldness and confidence in our access to God (Eph 3.12).

Besides that expression of the concrete fulness of the life which is from belief (in Paul's prayer, Eph 3.14-21), we have Paul's witness to his own aspiration;

... But because of Christ, I have come to consider all these advantages that I had as disadvantages. Not only that, but I believe nothing can happen that will outweigh the supreme advantage of knowing Christ Jesus my Lord. For him I have accepted the loss of everything, and I look on everything as so much rubbish if only I can have Christ and be given a place in him. I am no longer trying for perfection by my own efforts, the perfection that comes from the Law, but I want only the perfection that comes through faith in Christ, and is from God and based on faith. All I want is to know Christ and the power of his resurrection and to share his sufferings by reproducing the pattern of his death. That is the way I can hope to take my place in the resurrection of the dead. Not that I have become perfect yet; I have not yet won, but I am still running, trying to capture the prize for which Christ Jesus captured me. I can assure you my brothers,

I am far from thinking that I have already won. All I can say is
that I forget the past and I strain ahead for what is still to come; I
am racing for the finish, for the prize to which God calls us
upwards to receive in Christ Jesus (Phil 3.7-14: JB).

Finally, in that concrete fulness of life which is somehow
from belief, I should note that marvelous blend of present
realization and hope of final fulfillment. We have been raised
with Christ, yet we live in hope of our own final resurrection (cf.
1 Th 4.14; 2 Cor 4.13-14; 1 Cor 15.12-19). We have been
righted: we have that rightness from belief which is from God,
pure gift; yet we live in hope of attaining definitive, final
rightness (cf. Gal 5.5; Phil 3.9). We have been saved, yet we
look to, and must live in a manner becoming, that salvation
which is nearer to us now than when we believed (Rom 13.11).
We look to the glorification of the Lord Jesus in us, and ours in
him: "To this end we always pray for you, that God may make
you worthy of his call, and may fulfill every good resolve and
work of faith by his power, so that the name of our Lord Jesus
may be glorified in you, and you in him, according to the grace
of our God and the Lord Jesus Christ" (2 Th 1.11-12).
Essential to the grace by which we live is this hope which is a
living force in our lives, and which makes our lives not a surd but
a mystery: "If for this life only we have hoped in Christ, we are
of all men most to be pitied" (1 Cor 15.19).

I entitled this section "The act, its structure, and its roles,"
and, consistently with my theory of symbolizing and symbols, I
maintain that we can approach an understanding of the meaning
of *believe* and *belief* only as we fix more and more of the
relationships in the total field in which the act may be understood.
I have dealt with all of the principal data which I judge to be
significant in the texts which explicitly or implicitly (from the
immediate context) concern the act. One might expect
reasonably, therefore, that at this point I should undertake to
formulate the structure, roles. and meaning of *believe* and *belief*.
Yet, for reasons which to me are compelling, I must defer that
effort to my final reflections on Paul. The reason is simply this:
texts concerning *believe* and *belief* open upon many elements of
fulfillment in us which Paul develops more fully elsewhere. Since
all such development somehow concerns all of what is somehow
from belief, I shall trace Paul's more ample treatment of these
elements, and then return at the end to reflect on the structure,
roles, and meaning of *belief*.

One task still remains, however, before I leave the cluster of closely-related elements which I presented above: (13) *Love, grace, belief, and rightness* (above, p. 259). Though in the many pages already devoted to this theme I have written much about *being righted, made right, right,* and *rightness,* I must gather the elements and formulate what must be said about rightness.

[e] Rightness. My treatment of *rightness* in Paul's thought will be similar in ways to my treatment of *belief.* In this sub-section, I shall consider all texts bearing upon the meaning of six related words in Paul's vocabulary, a meaning determined from the context, the immediate context in which the words appear. In so far as I limit myself here to the texts in which the words themselves appear, I shall be holding myself to the object of representative works of biblical scholars in their consideration of righteousness and justification[70]. Anyone who reads their works, however, will soon be aware of the intrusion of terminology which is not Pauline, and which represents the scholars' own confessional, and at times perhaps vaguely conscious philosophical, backgrounds. Examples are *forensic, ethical, moral.* I shall deal with Paul's vocabulary and with the texts involved against the ground of my own theological and philosophical thought. Here, as in the whole of my recent work, I am doing a work of personal reflection, and personal, creative theological thought. As I have maintained elsewhere, the only verification of such thought is its coherence, intelligibility, and resonance in the reader: this *fits.*

In subsequent sections of this chapter, I shall be going beyond texts which deal directly with *rightness,* considering all that pertains to fulfillment in us. All this too is from *belief,* and spells out more of what Paul means by *rightness*: what it means to be *right with God,* or *right in relation to God,* in Christian life. Hence, as with *belief,* so with *rightness,* only in my closing reflections on the full field of relationships, shall I attempt to define them.

[l] Pauline vocabulary. There are three words of primary importance in Paul's writings, and three of secondary importance.

---

[70] For representative studies in full N.T. theological dictionaries, see G. SCHRENK, δίκη, δίκαιος, etc., in KITTEL, TDNT, II, pp. 178-225; C. BROWN, "Righteousness, Justification," in BROWN DNTT, III, pp. 352-377. For a Lutheran contribution to the United States Lutheran—Roman Catholic Dialogue, see JOHN REUMANN, *"Righteousness" in the New Testament,* with responses by JOSEPH A. FITZMYER and JEROME QUINN (Philadelphia: Fortress Press—New York/Ramsey: Paulist Press, 1982).

I shall not give a full account of their meanings in other literature, which can be found amply treated in the works to which I have referred, and briefly in BAG. I shall give my own judgment of the meanings of the words as Paul uses them, a judgment which clearly involves a kind of reflection which is not limited to what can be found in standard treatments, and which I propose entirely on my own responsibility, as I do my translations of the words.

[a] δίκαιος. This is, I should say, the basic word, but of the three principal words it occurs least frequently in Paul: twelve times, seven in *Romans*. It is an adjective, and in the Pauline usage which concerns us it is said principally of man, and means *right in relation to God*, with various nuances of the relationship. Said of God, it is used only once by Paul (Rom 3.26); once it is said of the Law, as being from God (Rom 7.12). It can hardly refer to God as a just and righteous *judge*. I have attempted to work out its meaning in the context of Paul's thought concerning God's *righteousness* or *rightness* (above, pp. 303-305), and I shall return to that in a moment. If, however, you ask me point-blank what *right* means as said of God, my answer is this: (1) obviously it does *not* mean that God is right as being in conformity with some norm of rightness: there is no norm external to God by which he could be judged; (2) implicit in the context of Paul's thought is that God is *right* because he is true to himself, not in any sense men might have of what God ought to be, but in the sense that he is consistent with himself as he himself has revealed himself to be. He *is* in accordance with his own revelation of his eternal love and loving design for us, his free choice, grace, promise, fidelity, mercy, and fulfillment of promise.

[b] δικαίως. This is a rare, secondary word in Paul, simply the adverb, *rightly*, with a sense corresponding to the adjective, and applied twice to human conduct (1 Th 2.10; 1 Cor 15.34).

[c] δικαιοσύνη. This is the second, and most frequently occurring, of Paul's principal words. It is the abstract noun, usually translated *righteousness* or *uprightness*; my translation is simply *rightness*, with meanings corresponding to the adjective. In Paul's usage it is attributed to men, who have a *rightness from God*, a pure gift, somehow *from belief*; it is contrasted with the vainly sought *rightness from works of the law*; it is also attributed to God, with nuances according to the context. By far the greatest number of instances of Paul's use of the word are in *Romans*.

[d] δικαιόω. This is the third of Paul's principal words, and its interpretation is crucial. The possible meanings (given the very form of the Greek verb) are two: *to judge* (someone) *to be right*; or *make right, to right*. Since in our whole context there is question of being *right in relation to God*, only God can be the subject of the verb in the active voice: only God can know and judge man's rightness; and, in a sense of the word which obviously goes beyond any parallel in purely human usage in other literature, only God can *right* a man, can *make right*. In the passive voice, man is *judged* (by God) *to be right*, or *righted, made right* by God. The verb occurs almost exclusively in *Galatians* (8 times) and *Romans* (15)[71].

[e] δικαίωμα. In Paul's usage, the word means *precept, command, requirement* [what God deems right and commands] (Rom 1.32; 2.26; 8.4); *right action* [in obedience to the command]; in one instance (Rom 5.16) it has a meaning equivalent to δικαίωσις, the last word which we shall consider.

[f] δικαίωσις. In two instances (Rom 4.25; 5.18) this noun means either the action or the result of the action of *judging* (someone) *to be right* or *making right*. The meanings parallel those of the verb δικαιόω. As one would expect, BAG give only the first meaning: *justification, vindication, acquittal* [in the "forensic" sense].

[2] God is *right*, and *rights/makes right*. Paul's strongest statements come in his great formulation of his "thesis" in Rom 3.21-31. God *is* right (3.26), and his *rightness* is shown forth in his forbearance and forgiveness of sins (3.25-26)[72]. God's

---

[71] BAG do not indicate *make upright* as a meaning of this verb as referring to God's activity. They do not give any explicit meaning, and one can only presume that they mean implicitly that it has meanings corresponding to those which they give for the passive voice as referring to men in Paul's usage: *be acquitted, be pronounced and treated as righteous* and thereby become δίκαιος, receive the divine gift of δικαιοσύνη, as a theological [technical term] *be justified*. They add: "... For the view (held since Chrysostom) that δ. in these and other pass. means 'make upright' [see Goodspeed] ... " To say the least, this is giving short shrift to an interpretation current for sixteen centuries. ZORELL, *Lexicon*, acknowledges the possible meaning *make right* (*justum reddo*), on the analogy of *to blind, to free*. I readily admit that in his argumentation for the meaning *make right*, especially in Paul, ZORELL resorts to dogmatic and theological language. Still one must face the possibility, and perhaps acknowledge the reasonableness, of this meaning in Paul, even though, as Zorell points out, there could be no instance of such a use of the word in profane literature, for the simple reason that in the natural order no one can make another *right* (upright, righteous).

[72] See also Rom 3.5: our wickedness shows God's rightness (his right, just judgment); and the citation of Ps 112.9: his rightness endures for ever.

rightness in Rom 1.17 and 3.21 can mean either his own rightness or the rightness which is from God, or more probably *both* in a pregnant sense of the phrase, brought out especially in 3.21-26. God's decree is right (Rom 1.32): its rightness is expressed in the very word δικαίωμα (see above, Paul's vocabulary). The Law and the commandment, because they are God's, are holy, right, and good (Rom 7.12). God is declared or acknowledged to be right (Rom 3.4).

God *rights* or *makes right* by grace, as a gift, through redemption in Christ Jesus (Rom 3.24). He rights the [one who is] *from belief* (3.26); man is righted [by God] by belief, apart from works of the Law (3.28). "We know that for those who love God [he] makes all things work together for [their] good, for those called according to his purpose. For those whom he foreknew he also predestined to be conformed to the image of his Son, in order that he might be the first-born among many brethren. And those whom He predestined he also called; and those whom he called he also *righted*; and those whom he *righted* he also glorified" (Rom 8.28-30)[73].

I have begun this subsection by affirming that God *is right* and *rights* or *makes right*. Obviously he also *judges* a man or woman to be right, or condemns as guilty; and God's judgment is right: just and true. I do not intend to go through the dialectic of opinions advanced in more than four centuries of controversy concerning "righteousness" and "justification": whether God only judges, declares, pronounces a person to be right, or also makes him or her right, giving a rightness which is surely pure gift, yet is real, intrinsic, not merely somehow attributed, imputed, extrinsic[74]. Nor do I intend to disregard the matter.

---

[73] Once again, I explain my retention of the single word *right* as both adjective and verb. In prefering *right* and *rightness* to *righteous* and *righteousness*, as I have explained, I wish to use equally good English words unspoiled by the distasteful connotations of the latter pair. Using *right* as adjective and verb, I avoid *just* and *justify*, as also in using *righting* or *making right* I avoid *justification*, because *just*, *justify*, and *justification* have come to be taken spontaneously in a sense far too narrow to be apt to convey the full sense of the words as used generally in translation of biblical terminology; moreover they are only slightly less spoiled by their connotations in common English usage. I have no intention of re-translating the Bible! I use these rather unfamiliar words in the deliberate attempt to call attention to the sense of Paul's Greek. Having done this, I am resigned to acknowledging that translators' common choices—and those of authors of dictionaries of biblical Greek and New Testament theology—will prevail.

[74] For the wide variety of views in this matter see the works cited in note 70, p. 285.

This seems to be the best place for some reflections bearing upon it.

The notion of a judicial or "forensic" justification is drawn by analogy from authoritative judgment of a man's or woman's standing in relation to human law. When a person is accused of having violated the law, the person or persons authorized to judge on the basis of evidence pronounce the person innocent or guilty. The judgment is always fallible; yet when it is given according to honest evaluation of the evidence, it is just. It is extremely important to recognize, however, that the judgment of judge, jury, or whatever sort of tribunal may be authorized in a given society, does not *make* a man or woman innocent or guilty. If a man is judged rightly to be innocent or guilty, the rightness of the judgment is grounded on the prior fact: the man *is* innocent or guilty. To the extent of the accuracy of the judgment, the judge recognizes the reality of innocence or guilt. No one is made innocent or guilty by the judgment itself.

When there is question of our standing in relation to God, he alone can judge: we are forbidden to judge. Before God, in relation to God, we are right when we stand in the relationship in which we should stand with God. For us that means being what we should be in accordance with God's revelation of himself, and of his plan for us. In turn, we are right in relation to other men and women also according to the mystery of relationships grounded upon his plan for all of us.

We can *be right* only by the gift of God: our rightness is rooted in God's love, free choice, call. In Paul's teaching, we are right only from belief, and belief itself is possible only within the realm of grace, pure gift. Only God can *right* us. Only God can judge us to be right, or condemn us for not being right: only God can read the human heart. God's judgment is infallibly true and just. Hence his judging us to be right is inseparable from our truly being right: obviously with a rightness grounded upon, and continually worked out within, the mystery of his continuing love, grace, pure gift. That is the mystery of God's continual operation within us, and of our action sustained and penetrated by Him working within us.

Both making man right and judging him to be right, therefore, pertain to God alone. We are in the realm of mystery, beyond any parallel in purely natural human actions and relationships. Paul's way of accentuating this mystery is his depiction of the failure of all mankind, Jew and Gentile, to achieve a rightness by their own resources, their own works, whether in accordance with the Law or outside the Law. At the zero point (above, pp. 248-252) our weakness and utter helplessness is manifest. At the zero point God's rightness is revealed (Rom 3.21-26).

[3] Abraham. [a] The principle. "Now to one who works, his wages are not reckoned as a gift, but as his due. And to one who does not work but believes him who rights the ungodly, his belief is reckoned as rightness" (Rom 4.4-5). Applied to Abraham, this principle means that "... if Abraham was righted from works. he has something to boast about, but not before God" (4.2).

[b] The initial, decisive act. "For what does the scripture say? 'Abraham *believed* God, and it [his *believing*, his act of *belief*] was reckoned to him as *rightness*'" (Rom 4.3; Gal 3.6). The figure "reckoned to him as *rightness*" is taken from accounting. It does not mean that it was put down to his credit *as if* it were rightness. For Abraham, to *believe* was *right*, his *belief* was *rightness*[75] (see also 4.9). Circumcision was a sign, a seal, of the *rightness of belief* (4.11): the genitive *of belief* I take as explanatory. His was the rightness of belief, consisting in belief: belief was rightness.

[c] Continuing belief, growing strong in belief. Though Paul is extremely abstractive in his treatment of Abraham, and he uses Gen 15.6 as his decisive "proof text", one can detect a subtle distinction between Abraham's initial, decisive act, and his hoping against hope, not weakening in belief, not wavering because of any distrust, but growing strong in his belief as he gave glory to God, fully convinced that God was able to do what he had promised: *that is why* his belief was "reckoned to him as rightness" (Rom 4.18-22). It was *right* for him to continue to believe, to grow in belief: *this* was reckoned to him as *rightness*.

[4] The Law and rightness. Having given a fairly ample treatment of the Law (above, pp. 235-248), I shall not attempt to give here even a brief recapitulation. I simply register its relevance here in a consideration of rightness: rightness is *not* from works of the Law.

[5] Rightness from God, through Christ, from/through belief of Jesus Christ.

---

[75] See BAG, λογίζομαι, 1, a; and εἰς, 8: predicate nominative replaced by εἰς with the accusative.

[a] The rightness now revealed apart from the Law is from God (above, pp. 287-290): Rom 1.17; 3.21-22; 2 Cor 5.21; Phil 3.9.

[b] It is through Christ. It is through the redemption in Christ Jesus, whom God put forth as an expiation by his blood (Rom 3.24-25). It is through our Lord Jesus Christ that we were righted from belief and have peace with God (5.1). Righted by his blood we shall be saved from God's wrath (5.9). Paul develops this theme especially in his contrast between Adam and Christ (5.15-21). It is implicit in the obscure text in Rom 10.6-7: "But the rightness from belief says, Do not say in your heart, 'Who will ascend into heaven?' (that is, to bring Christ down) or 'Who will descend into the abyss?' (that is, to bring Christ up from the dead)": Christ has come, died, risen, and we need only *believe*. "[God] is the source of your life in Christ Jesus, whom God has made our wisdom, our rightness and sanctification and redemption; ..." (1 Cor 1.30). "For our sake [God] made him to be sin who knew no sin, so that in him we might become the rightness of God" (2 Cor 5.21).

[c] We are right, have rightness from/through belief. One can distinguish a number of phases in Paul's development of this thesis. First, implicitly, on the analogy of Abraham, our belief itself *is* rightness (cf. Rom 4.11, 25).

Second, we are right, or have rightness from/through our *initial act* of *belief* (Rom 1.17; 3.28, 30; 5.1), *belief of Jesus Christ* (Gal 2.16; Rom 3.22, 26; 10.9). As I have noted above concerning belief (pp. 280-282), rightness is intimately linked with a cluster of consequences of our initial act of belief[76].

Third, our righting and rightness are part of the continuing process of Christian life, as is our believing (see above, on belief as a present act or disposition to act in the continuing Christian life, pp. 271-277; and on the consequences of belief in that continuing process, pp. 282-285). One of the principal texts is doubly interesting, for the insistence on rightness in continuing Christian life follows one of Paul's capital texts on the effects of baptism, to which we shall turn in the next section. As a consequence of our having been baptized into Christ, into his death, by which he died once for all to sin, we too are dead to sin, alive to God in Christ Jesus (cf. Rom 6.1-11). "Do not yield your members to sin as instruments of wickedness, but yield yourselves to God as men who have been brought from death to

---

[76] See, for example, 1 Cor 1,30; Rom 5.17, 18, 21; 14.17; Eph 4.24; 5.9.

life, and your members to God as instruments of rightness" (Rom
6.13; cf. vv. 15-23; 8.3-4, 9-11)[77].

Finally, "...by the Spirit, from belief, we await the *hope of
rightness*" (Gal 5.5): though in this letter Paul does not speak of
Christ's coming, clearly here he is writing of the hope of final,
definitive rightness: that at the end we *be right* with God, and *be
judged to be right.*

[d] The role of baptism. Two texts regarding rightness serve
as transitions to our next theme: the role of baptism in our
fulfillment. The first is that which I have already cited: Rom 6:
our obligation to live lives of rightness is a consequence of our
baptism. The second is implicitly, but I should say obviously, a
baptismal text, in which *being righted* is linked with two other
figures by which Paul seeks to express the concrete reality of our
experience of the beginning of life in Christ: "...you were
washed, you were sanctified, you were righted in the name of the
Lord Jesus Christ and in the Spirit of our God" (1 Cor 6.11).

(14) *Baptism.* I shall consider briefly here some aspects of
Paul's teaching on baptism. Less prominent than belief and
rightness from belief, baptism nonetheless is extremely
important. Like faith, baptism is somehow a source of our life
in Christ, and it opens upon the themes which will be developed
in subsequent sections of this chapter. Moreover, the texts on
baptism suggest a certain tension between the roles of faith and
baptism, and I shall return to consider this among other
relationships in my closing reflections on the roles of faith and
the full sense of rightness in Paul's gospel. I shall limit this
treatment to three themes: (a) who acts in baptism; (b) what are
its effects; (c) what are the resulting relationships of the
baptized.

(a) Who acts? In Paul, as in other New Testament writers,
attention is directed principally not to the person who performs
the symbolic action, not to the role of the Church, but to the
action of Father, Son, and Holy Spirit.

In the New Testament there are a few texts which can be
called trinitarian in their presentation of baptism. Most explicit
are Mt 28.19 and a text in a letter which most scholars do not
recognize as authentically Pauline: Tit 3.4-7. Only one text

---

[77] See also Eph 4.22-24; 5.6-10, esp. v. 9; 6.14; Col 4.1-5; 1 Th 2.10
(concerning Paul's conduct); Phil 1.9-11; 4.8; 1 Cor 15.30-34; 2 Cor 6.7, 14;
9.10. For the same sense of process in a closely-related consequence of the
total reality of our being righted or made right, see my treatment of "The New
Creation as Process," in *Basics*, pp. 156-172.

within the Pauline corpus can be taken as implicitly trinitarian if it is considered in its context: "For just as the body is one and has many members, and all the members of the body, though many, are one body, so it is with Christ. For by one Spirit we were all baptized into one body—Jews or Greeks, slaves or free—and all were made to drink of one Spirit" (1 Cor 12.12-13). "By one Spirit" (ἐν ἑνὶ πνεύματι) may be understood in a sort of transcendent instrumental sense, or may mean "by the power of one Spirit." In any case the action of baptizing is that of the Spirit. On the other hand, "were made to drink of one Spirit" seems to me to suggest another agent, perhaps God (the Father). Christ in this text is the term of the action: we were baptized into one body, the body of Christ (12.27). In the context too, Jesus is honored by a confession inspired by the Spirit: "No one can say 'Jesus is Lord' except by the Holy Spirit'" (12.3). The context contains too a classic trinitarian formula: "Now there are varieties of gifts, but the same Spirit; and there are varieties of service, but the same Lord; and there are varieties of working, but it is the same God who inspires them all in every one" (12.4-6). However the differentiation of the roles of the Spirit and of the Lord be understood, one thing is clear: the initiative is God's. The Spirit is the Spirit of God (12.3). Though gifts are given through the Spirit or according to the same Spirit (12.8), by the same Spirit, the one Spirit (12.9), by one and the same Spirit who apportions to each one individually as he wills (12.11), still it is God who inspires them all in every one, and it is God who has appointed the members of the body of Christ to their functions (12.27-30), as he arranged the organs of the natural body (12.18, 24).

Two texts which probably are baptismal bring out the role of God, the Father: "...it is God who strengthens us together with you as Christ's, and who anointed us, and sealed us, and gave us his Spirit in our hearts as a pledge" (2 Cor 1.21-22)[78] and "In

---

[78] "I do not follow the RSV here. Four actions are ascribed to God, all of them grounds for confidence in Paul's constancy and sincerity: (1) God is now strengthening both Paul and the Corinthians, not 'in Christ' (RSV) but 'to Christ' or 'unto Christ': the sense probably is that he is confirming them in their consecration to Christ, as belonging to Christ; (2) he also anointed and (3) sealed them, and (4) gave the Spirit in their hearts as a pledge of the future. RSV translates (2) as 'has commissioned us', taking one of the options for the meaning of 'anointed', which may be either the anointing of all Christians in baptism or in the gift of the Spirit, or the anointing in the commissioning of Paul to his apostolic office. Since the other three actions regard both Paul and the Corinthians, it seems more probable that in all four Paul is indicating their common guarantee of constancy. Cf. NEB." (*The Mystery*, p. 209, note 9).

him [Christ] you also, who have heard the word of truth, the gospel of your salvation, and have believed in him, were sealed with the promised Holy Spirit, which is the guarantee of our inheritance until we acquire possession of it, to the praise of his glory" [or, with NEB: "... and that Spirit is the pledge that we shall enter upon our heritage, when God has redeemed what is his own, to his praise and glory"] (Eph 1.13-14).

The texts are obscure, and any interpretation is at best probable or plausible. I still find the exegesis of De la Potterie reasonable. He marks a parallelism of three elements in the texts:

2 Cor 1.21-22	Eph 1.13
(1) he anointed us	(1) having heard ... believed
(2) sealed us	(2) you were sealed
(3) gave us his Spirit in our hearts as a pledge	(3) with the promised Holy Spirit, which is the pledge

In his interpretation, the anointing is an anointing with *faith*, prior to baptism. The *sealing* seems to have been baptism, so called by analogy with circumcision. Circumcision was a sign or seal of the rightness which Abraham had from belief (Rom 4.11). Baptism is a spiritual circumcision (cf. Col 2.11; Phil 3.3 [79]: in baptism God sealed their faith.

The only clearly baptismal text in which Christ's action is indicated is Eph. 5.25: "... Christ loved the church and gave himself up for her, that he might sanctify her, having cleansed her by the washing of water with a word." Christ's role (though not explicitly his action), together with that of the Spirit, is clear in 1 Cor 6.11: "... you were washed, you were sanctified, you were righted in the name of the Lord Jesus Christ and in the Spirit of our God." The phrases "in the name of the Lord Jesus Christ" and "in the Spirit ..." are parallel, and seem to indicate the power and action of Jesus and the Spirit.

(b) What are the effects of baptism? Most prominent, I should say is this: we are *in Christ, one with Christ*. Two texts are remarkable precisely because they come in the midst of Paul's strongest insistence on the importance of faith: in *Galatians* and in *Romans*.

---

[79] I. DE LA POTTERIE, S.J., "L'onction du chrétien par la foi," *Biblica* 40 (1959) 12-69, also published now in S. LYONNET and I. DE LA POTTERIE, *La vie selon l'Esprit* (Paris: Les Éditions du Cerf, 1965) pp. 107-167.

You are all sons of God through belief, *in Christ Jesus*. For as
many of you as were baptized into Christ have put on Christ.
There is neither Jew nor Greek, there is neither slave nor free,
there is neither male nor female; for you all one in Christ Jesus.
And if you are Christ's, then you are Abraham's offspring, heirs
according to the promise (Gal 3.26-29).

The text begins as one might expect in the context of Paul's
teaching on belief. Then quite unexpectedly the phrase which I
have italicized seems to have triggered Paul's teaching on
baptism. I have preserved the word order of the Greek, setting
off "in Christ Jesus" by a comma. The meaning is not, more
probably, "through belief in Jesus Christ". Rather, Paul is
saying that through belief we are sons of God, adding "in Christ
Jesus" consistently with his teaching, to explain that it is in him
that we are sons. But then the phrase seems to have suggested a
further question: but *how* are we *in Christ Jesus*? Happily that
question occasioned one of Paul's principal texts on baptism. He
multiplies his efforts to express the effects of baptism: we have
been baptized *into* Christ: union with Christ, insertion somehow
into him, "putting on" Christ, being Christ's, all of us together
being *one* in Christ Jesus, without any significant differences: not
one "thing", but as if one person, suggested by the masculine
singular "one". Further effects are being Abraham's offspring,
heirs according to the promise: a significant addition, coming as it
does after Paul's attributing these same effects to belief; as indeed
he attributed his own intimate oneness of life in Christ to belief
(cf. Gal 2.20).

What shall we say then? Are we to continue in sin that grace may
abound? By no means! How can we who died to sin still live in it?
Do you not know that all of us who have been baptized into Christ
Jesus were baptized into his death? We were buried therefore
with him by baptism into death, so that as Christ was raised from
the dead by the glory of the Father, we too might walk in newness
of life. For if we have been united with him in a death like his, we
shall certainly be united with him in a resurrection like his. We
know that our old self was crucified with him so that the sinful
body might be destroyed, and we might no longer be enslaved to
sin. For he who has died is freed from sin. But if we have died
with Christ, we believe that we shall also live with him. For we
know that Christ being raised from the dead will never die again;
death no longer has dominion over him. The death he died he
died to sin, once for all, but the life he lives he lives to God. So
you also must consider yourselves dead to sin and alive to God in
Christ Jesus (Rom 6.1-11).

The text goes beyond *Galatians* 3.26-29 by probing the mystery of our oneness with Christ, and by bringing out other consequences.   *Baptize* etymologically means dip, immerse, plunge into (water, for instance).   Here the prevailing symbolism is that of death: plunged into Christ symbolically by a ritual action similar to his death, we are one with him in the very mystery of his death.   United with him in that mystery, we remain united with him, and so share in his resurrection, and in his complete break with sin [80].

In my judgment, the text which brings out most sharply the symbolism of baptism and the sense in which we are *in Christ* is *Colossians* 2.11-13, which I translate in sense lines thus:

> [11] *in whom* [Christ] also you were circumcised,
> with a circumcision
> done without hands,
> by putting off the body of flesh,
> by the circumcision of *Christ*,
> [12] buried *with him* in baptism,
> *in whom* also you were raised
> through faith in the working of God,
> who raised *him* from the dead.
> [13] And you,
> who were dead in trespasses
> and the uncircumcision of your flesh,
> God made alive together *with him*,
> having forgiven us all our trespasses, ...

The crucial point in this text is the reference of the relative pronoun in verse 12b: does it refer to *baptism*, which is closer to it in the sentence, or to *Christ*; should we translate *in which* [baptism] or *in whom* [Christ]? Despite the nearness of *baptism*, I judge that the whole structure of the immediate text, and the context of Col 1.2 – 2.15 favors taking the pronoun as referring to Christ, and translating as I have.

The structure of the immediate context stands out clearly in the parallism of the key words:

> [6] in him
> [7] in him
> [8] according to ...
> according to ...

---

[80] In this brief account I cannot go into details of the obscurity of Paul's text, especially in verse 5, which almost certainly is elliptical, and certainly is obscure. I have dealt with the matter in an earlier work, *The Mystery*, pp. 211-215.

and not according to Christ
[9] in him
[10] in him
[11] in whom too
    [12] with him in baptism
in whom [or in which] too
    [13] with him
[15] in him.

In the context of 1.2–2.15 *in* is used eighteen times with *Christ, him, whom.* Moreover in seven other instances other prepositions (διά through, εἰς for, κατά according to, and σύν with) are used with *him, his blood, Christ.* The whole structure of the immediate text and context favor the choice which I have made. Moreover, an objection against the awkwardness of doubling our relationship to Christ (the preposition expressing our being raised *in* him, and the compound verb indicating *with* him) has little force concerning Pauline usage. Struggling with inadequate linguistic resources to express our multiple relationship with Christ, Paul would not have been bothered by such niceties. Moreover, apart from such a general observation on Paul's style, two passages of *Ephesians* witness to the same doubling of relationships: God raised us *with* Christ and made us sit *with* Christ *in* Christ (Eph 2.6); *in* Christ you are built into a temple *with* [Christ] (2.21).

Why do I say that this text is the sharpest both for the explicit symbolism of baptism in Paul's thought, and for the sense in which we are in Christ?

First, with regard to the symbolism of baptism, Gal 3.27 yields no more than being somehow plunged into Christ, with the resulting putting on Christ and the further development of our oneness in Christ. In Rom 6.3-5, baptism symbolizes death and burial. By analogy with the real death and resurrection of Jesus, we undergo a symbolic death in baptism, and as a consequence ("we shall" in verse 5 referring not to our future resurrection in glory, but to the logical consequence) we shall be, or we are, like him in his resurrection by analogy, in the sense that we walk in newness of life now. There is a further implicit reference to our future resurrection in verses 5 and 8: we shall be united with him in a resurrection like his; we shall live with him. Nothing suggests a twofold symbolism of the rite of baptism: death and rising. Nor is there any explicit mention of our being raised in the moment of baptism. On the analogy with Christ's resurrection, we are to walk now in newness of life, and we shall share in his resurrection. Given the sophism which Paul is refuting in the whole text (cf. v. 1), the whole emphasis in *Romans* 6 is on death to sin, and walking in newness of life.

What, then, is to be said of *Colossians* by contrast? *If* one were to take the interpretation of the relative pronoun in verse 12b which I have rejected, taking it to refer to baptism, *then* Paul would suggest a twofold symbolism of the rite: burial (death) in the immersion, and being raised in the symbolic emersion. This would be the sole text in which Paul's symbolism of baptism would be twofold: immersion-death and emersion-resurrection. If my interpretation stands, the direct symbolism of baptism is burial-death. In later patristic interpretation of the rite of baptism the twofold symbolism is found. I should say that it is not Pauline.

On the other hand, the text in *Colossians* does express most sharply the sense in which, as a consequence of baptism, we are in Christ, one with Christ. Because we undergo in baptism a ritual, symbolic death with Christ, we are raised in and with him because we undergo symbolic death with *belief* in the working of God, who raised him from the dead.

What is the point of all this? It is simply a matter of taking individual texts for what they contribute to a complex Pauline concept of our being raised in and with Christ. From different texts we can gather four phases of our being raised. (1) Radically, God raised us with Christ (Eph. 2.4-7). (2) At the moment of our baptism he raised us in and with Christ (Col 2.12). (3) *Now*, having been buried with him by baptism into death, on the analogy of Christ's resurrection we walk in newness of life (Rom 6.4). (4) We will share finally in Christ's resurrection (cf. 1 Cor 15.12-56).

Briefly, these are other effects of baptism: union with all who have been baptized into Christ (cf. Gal 2.27-28; 1 Cor 12.12-13, 27); being Abraham's offspring and heirs to the promise (Gal 3.29); being washed, sanctified (or consecrated), and righted (1 Cor 6.11). If 1 Cor 12.13, 2 Cor 1.21-22, and Eph 1.13 are taken as baptismal texts (see above, pp. 292-294), then the Spirit is given in baptism.

(c) Relationships resulting from baptism. We are related to the Father, to Christ, and to the Spirit, with relationships varying according to their roles in baptism. Implicitly they are relationships of the New Covenant (cf. 2 Cor 3). We are related to one another according to our gifts and functions in the body of Christ. We are committed to a new way of life, a life in the

Spirit, a Christian code of conduct, grounded upon aspects of the Mystery, as we shall see in a subsequent section.

(15) *New creation*. I merely mention briefly here another figure by which Paul expresses the mystery of the fulfillment of the promise in us [81]. Paul concludes his argument in *Galatians* with one of three of his statements of what really counts: "For neither circumcision counts for anything, nor uncircumcision, but a new creation" (6.15; for his other partially parallel affirmations, see Gal 5.6 and 1 Cor 7.19). To the Corinthians he writes: "... if any one is in Christ, he is a new creation; the old has passed away, behold, the new has come" (2 Cor 5.17). He expands, and perhaps varies the concept, in *Ephesians*:

> For by grace you have been saved through faith; and this is not your own doing, it is the gift of God; not because of works, lest any man should boast. For we are his workmanship, created in Christ Jesus for good works, which God prepared beforehand, that we should walk in them.
> Therefore remember that at one time you Gentiles in the flesh, called the uncircumcision by what is called the circumcision, which is made in the flesh by hands—remember that you were at that time separated from Christ, alienated from the commonwealth of Israel, and strangers to the covenants of promise, having no hope and without God in the world.
> But now in Christ Jesus you who once were far off have been brought near in the blood of Christ. For he is our peace, who has made us both one, and has broken down the dividing walls of hostility, by abolishing in his flesh the law of commandments and ordinances, that he might create in himself one new man in place of two, so making peace, and might reconcile us both to God in one body through the cross, thereby bringing the hostility to an end. And he came and preached peace to you who were far off and peace to those who were near; for through him we both have access in one Spirit to the Father.
> So then you are no longer strangers and sojourners, but you are fellow citizens with the saints and members of the household of God, built upon the foundation of the apostles and prophets, Christ Jesus himself being the cornerstone. in whom the whole structure is joined together and grows into a holy temple in the Lord; in whom you also are built [or with JB: are being built] into it for a dwelling place of God in the Spirit (Eph 2.8-22).

---

[81] I have treated the theme fairly fully elsewhere: "The New Creation as Process," in *Basics*, pp. 156-172.

(16) *Living in Christ.* Two sets of data are important for us: Paul's witness to his own unique experience of living in Christ; and elements of his gospel which bear directly on aspects of our living in Christ.

First, then, Paul testifies to his own profound sense of his living in Christ: "I have been crucified with Christ; it is no longer I who live, but Christ who lives in me; and the life I now live in the flesh I live by faith in the Son of God, who loved me and gave himself for me" (Gal 2.20). His coming to the Corinthians and professing that he knew nothing among them except Jesus Christ and him crucified (1 Cor 2.2) is consistent with his own glorying only in the cross of our Lord Jesus Christ, by which the world had been crucified to him, and he to the world (Gal 6.14), and with his obscure witness to bearing on his body the marks of Jesus (Gal 6.17). "For me to live is Christ, and to die is gain. If it is to be life in the flesh, that means fruitful labor for me. Yet which I shall choose I cannot tell. My desire is to depart and be with Christ, for that is far better. But to remain in the flesh is more necessary on your account" (Phil 1.21-24). Finally Paul reveals the depths of his own conversion, and his aspiration to gain Christ and be found in him, to know him and the power of his resurrection, to share his sufferings in the hope of attaining the resurrection from the dead; he has not yet obtained it, nor is he perfect, but he presses on to make it his own, because Christ Jesus has made him his own [or: to *seize* it, because I was *seized* by Christ] (cf. Phil 3.7-16).

Second, Paul strives to make his readers and us understand dimensions of the mystery of our living in Christ. Our bodies are members of Christ (1 Cor 6.15): Paul cites this mystery as a motive for shunning immorality, making the members of Christ members of a prostitute (vv. 13-20); but it is a basic truth which should give us a sense of our being in Christ, intimately united with Christ, members of his body, with all that this mystery should evoke in our full response to the gift given us. He tells the Corinthians that he has betrothed them to Christ as a pure bride to her one husband (2 Cor 11.2), and he holds up the mystery of Christ's spousal love of his church as the model for husbands' love of their wives (Eph 5.25-33): *we* are of that Church, Christ's own flesh, members of his body (cf. vv. 28-32).

Paul challenges the Corinthians: "Examine yourselves, to see whether you are holding to your faith. Test yourselves. Do you not realize that Jesus Christ is in you ..." (2 Cor 13.5). How can they test themselves, how can they realize that Jesus Christ is in them? Paul's words here seem unintelligible unless we understand that he means that the Corinthians should have an experiential knowledge of Jesus' presence within them, a living sense of his presence. The mystery, he tells the Colossians, is *Christ in you* (Col 1.27). They are to live in Christ, rooted and built up in him and established in the faith, as they were taught (Col 2.6-7).

Paul's prayer for the Ephesians is clear proof that in God's plan and by his power they too have the potential for the most profound experience of living in Christ and having him live in them, of coming to an experiential knowledge and a love which are beyond knowledge, beyond all human conceptualization:

> For this reason I bow my knees before the Father, from whom every family in heaven and on earth is named. that according to the riches of his glory he may grant you to be strengthened with might through his power in the inner man, and that Christ may dwell in your hearts through faith; that you, being rooted and grounded in love, may have power to comprehend with all the saints what is the breadth and length and height and depth, and to know the love of Christ which surpasses knowledge, that you may be filled with all the fulness of God.
>
> Now to him who by the power at work in us is able to do far more abundantly than all that we ask or think, to him be glory in the church and in Christ Jesus to all generations, for ever and ever. Amen (Eph 3.14-21).

What is the meaning of these texts for us? Obviously, they are a witness to extraordinary graces given to Paul, to an experience of Christ, of living in Christ, which are within the human potential by the grace of Christ, the power of the Spirit. But they mean more than that. The dimensions of the mystery of our being in Christ, and the object of Paul's prayer for all of the Ephesians—and beyond them for all of us who believe, all who are called to believe—are a challenge to us. It is not enough to read the texts, and with the help of exegetes and biblical theologians come to an understanding of the meaning of the words. Paul's words come from a profound personal experience and a profound sense of the potential of all who live in Christ. We cannot have Paul's experience by reading about it. We cannot begin to understand what Paul is praying for, for the Ephesians and for us, until we begin to respond to Christ living in us. In believing and knowing him present within us by belief, in loving him and knowing him in the very shape of the experience of loving him, in an ever deepening mutual knowledge and love, we shall begin to understand what Paul is writing about, and what, through Paul, God is calling us to.

(17) *Suffering, weakness, and power.* Part of the mystery of living in Christ is the paradoxical blend of weakness, suffering, and power. Paul bears witness to this repeatedly concerning his own experience, and he insists often on the role of suffering and affliction in the lives of all who receive the word and live in Christ. This is part of God's plan, for by his grace in our very suffering and weakness we are strong: all that is achieved in us is due not to human wisdom and power, but solely to the power of God.

There is no need to insist on Paul's witness to his own sufferings, or to quote texts familiar to all who have read him [82]. His sufferings for Christ are his boast; they are his credentials, proof of the genuineness of his apostolate. By them he fills up, completes what is lacking in Christ's afflictions for the sake of his body, the church (Col 1.24). Though his words are cryptic, his meaning surely is not that Christ did not suffer all that was needed for our redemption, but rather that those who would follow him and live in him must take up their cross, share in his sufferings, in the hope of sharing in his resurrection, in eternal life.

Not only for Paul, but for all who receive the word, affliction and suffering is part of the mystery of their lives (cf. 1 Th 1.6; 2.14; 2 Th 1.4). "For it has been granted to you that for the sake of Christ you should not only believe in him but also suffer for his sake, engaged in the same conflict which you saw and now hear to be mine" (Phil 1.29-30). Paul feels deep affection for the Philippians because they are partakers with him of grace, both in his imprisonment and in the defense and confirmation of the gospel, for what has happened to him has served to advance the gospel (Phil 1.7, 12-14).

Paul can speak in the first person plural when he speaks of rejoicing in suffering, and of the role of suffering: "...we rejoice in our hope of sharing the glory of God. More than that, we rejoice in our sufferings, knowing that suffering produces endurance, and endurance produces character, and character produces hope, and hope does not disappoint us, because God's

---

[82] The principal texts are these: 1 Cor 4.9-12; 2 Cor 1.4-11; 4.7–5.5; 6.3-10; and 11.23–12.5. See also 1 Th 3.3-4; Gal 6.14, 17; 1 Cor 15.31; 2 Cor 7.5; Phil 1.12; 3.10-11.

love has been poured into our hearts through the Holy Spirit which has been given to us" (Rom 5.2-5). "When we cry, 'Abba! Father!' it is the Spirit himself bearing witness with our spirit that we are children of God, and if children, then heirs, heirs of God and fellow heirs with Christ, provided we suffer with him in order that we may also be glorified with him. I consider that the sufferings of this present time are not worth comparing with the glory that is to be revealed to us" (Rom 8.15-17).

Quite apart from the hope of a share in glory, there is a deep paradox of the demonstration of God's power in weakness and suffering. In general, this is the mystery of the means which God chose to bring us to belief and salvation.

> For the word of the cross is folly to those who are perishing, but to us who are being saved it is the power of God. ... For since, in the wisdom of God, the world did not know God through wisdom, it pleased God through the folly of what we preach to save those who believe. For Jews demand signs and Greeks seek wisdom, but we preach Christ crucified, a stumbling block to Jews and folly to Gentiles, but to those who are called, both Jews and Greeks, Christ the power of God and the wisdom of God. For the foolishness of God is wiser than men, and the weakness of God is stronger than men" (1 Cor 1.18-25).

Thus, among the Corinthians themselves, God chose those who in the eyes of the world were low, not the noble or the wise (cf. 1 Cor 1.26-31). Paul's preaching among them was not a demonstration of human wisdom and eloquence, but simply the message of Jesus Christ crucified. He came among them "... in much fear and trembling; and my speech and my message were not in plausible words of wisdom, but in demonstration of the Spirit and power, that your faith might not rest in the wisdom of men but in the power of God" (1 Cor 2.3-5).

Further, Paul witnesses to this mystery in his own unique personal vocation.

> But we have this treasure in earthen vessels, to show that the transcendent power belongs to God and not to us. We are afflicted in every way, but not crushed; perplexed, but not forsaken; always carrying in the body the death of Jesus, so that the life of Jesus may also be manifested in our bodies. For while we live we are always being given up to death for Jesus' sake, so that the life of Jesus may be manifested in our mortal flesh. So death is at work in us, but life in you (2 Cor 4.7-11).

After telling of the visions and revelations which God had given him, Paul adds: "And to keep me from being too elated by the abundance of revelations, a thorn was given me in the flesh, a messenger of Satan, to harass me, to keep me from being too elated. Three times I besought the Lord about this, that it should leave me; but he said to me, 'My grace is sufficient for you, for my power is made perfect in weakness.' I will all the more gladly boast of my weaknesses, that the power of Christ may rest upon me. For the sake of Christ, then, I am content with weaknesses, insults, hardships, persecutions, and calamities; for when I am weak, then I am strong" (2 Cor 12.7-10). To the Philippians he writes, "I know how to be abased, and I know how to abound; in any and all circumstances I have learned the secret of facing plenty and hunger, abundance and want. I can do all things in him who strengthens me" (Phil 4.12-13).

(18) *Living in the Spirit.* I have anticipated a portion of what could be called a Pauline theology of the Spirit: the presence and operation of the Spirit in the preaching and hearing of the word (above, pp. 258-259). Here I shall present the principal lines of his further thought.

(a) The gift of the Spirit. God has given us his Spirit in our hearts as a guarantee of our inheritance (cf. 2 Cor 1.22; Eph 1.13-14; 1 Th 4.8). He has sealed us with the promised Holy Spirit, and Paul's figure of sealing may be taken as signifying baptism, on the analogy of circumcision, or as the Spirit himself as a seal in our hearts, imprinted in baptism (see above, pp. 293-294). We are temples of God, of his Spirit, who dwells in us:

> Do you not know that you are God's temple and that God's Spirit dwells in you? If any one destroys God's temple, God will destroy him. For God's temple is holy, and that temple you are (1 Cor 3.16-17).
> Do you not know that your body is a temple of the Holy Spirit within you, which you have from God? You are not your own; you were bought with a price. So glorify God in your body (1 Cor 6.19-20; cf. Eph 2.19-22).
> But you are not in the flesh, you are in the Spirit, if the Spirit of God really dwells in you. Any one who does not have the Spirit of Christ does not belong to him. But if Christ is in you, although your bodies are dead because of sin, your spirits are alive because of rightness. If the Spirit of him who raised Jesus from the dead dwells in you, he who raised Christ Jesus from the dead will give life to your mortal bodies also through his Spirit which dwells in you (Rom 8.9-11).

(b) The Spirit's gifts.   In this section I am not limiting myself to what Paul explicitly calls "gifts": χαρίσματα.   Yet surely the unique wisdom which we have from the Spirit, and prayer proceeding from the Spirit must be regarded as gifts.   For this reason I include them under the general heading of gifts.

First, then, from the Spirit we have a unique wisdom:

> Yet among the mature we do impart wisdom, although it is not a wisdom of this age or of the rulers of this age, who are doomed to pass away.   But we impart a secret and hidden wisdom of God, which God decreed before the ages for our glorification.   None of the rulers of this age understood this; for if they had, they would not have crucified the Lord of glory.   But, as it is written,
>
> > "What no eye has seen, nor ear heard,
> > nor the heart of man conceived,
> > what God has prepared for those who love him" [cf. Is. 64.4]
>
> God has revealed to us through the Spirit.   For the Spirit searches everything, even the depths of God.   For what person knows a man's thoughts except the spirit of the man which is in him? So also no one comprehends the thoughts of God except the Spirit of God.   Now we have received not the spirit of the world, but the Spirit of God, that we might understand the gifts bestowed on us by God.   And we impart this in words not taught by human wisdom but taught by the Spirit, interpreting spiritual things to those who possess the Spirit.   The unspiritual man does not receive the gifts of the Spirit of God, for they are folly to him, and he is not able to understand them because they are spiritually discerned.   The spiritual man judges all things, but is himself to be judged by no one.   "For who has known the mind of the Lord so as to instruct him?" [cf. Is 40.13]   But we have the mind of Christ (1 Cor 2.6-16; cf. Eph 1.17-23).

Second, the Spirit teaches us how to pray.   It is he who moves us to call on the Father as our own.   "When we cry 'Abba! Father!' it is the Spirit himself bearing witness with our spirit that we are children of God, and if children, then heirs, heirs of God and fellow heirs with Christ, provided we suffer with him in order that we may also be glorified with him" (Rom 8.15-17; cf. Gal 4.6).   It is only by the Holy Spirit that we can say: "Jesus is Lord" (1 Cor 12.3).   "Likewise the Spirit helps us in our weakness; for we do not know how to pray as we ought, but the Spirit himself intercedes for us with sighs too deep for words. And he who searches the hearts of men knows what is in the mind of the Spirit, because the Spirit intercedes for the saints according to the will of God" (Rom 8.26-27).   Thanks to the

Spirit, "...we are the true circumcision, who worship God in spirit [or, with many variant readings: by the Spirit of God]" Phil 3.3). Through Christ we have access in one Spirit to the Father (cf. Eph 2.18).

Further, it is by the power of the Holy Spirit (a power given to us) that we may abound in hope (cf. Rom 15.13). It is through God's Spirit that we are to be strengthened, empowered, so that Christ may live in our hearts through faith, according to Paul's prayer for the Ephesians (cf. Eph 3.14-21), a prayer in which the blend of power, belief, love, and knowledge surpassing all knowledge reveals Paul's massive sense of the fulness of Christian experience which defies all conceptualization.

If we take *gift* as used by Paul in the broad sense, surely the most precious of all is love, as Paul teaches in 1 Cor 13, significantly inserted in the midst of his teaching regarding "charisms", gifts in a special sense. Again in *Romans*, after another classic text on "charisms" (12.3-8), Paul insists on love, and its implications in the lives of Christians (12.9-21), and shortly later adds: "Owe no one anything, except to love one another; for he who loves his neighbor has fulfilled the law. The commandments...are summed up in this sentence, You shall love your neighbor as yourself.' Love does no wrong to a neighbor; therefore love is the fulfilling of the law" (13.8-10).

In the special sense of gift, Paul teaches the roles of those gifts of the Spirit which were prominent in the life of the early Church, and which characterize a richness of the lives of many Christians today[83].

One rich Pauline text remains to be considered:

> Therefore, since we are justified by faith, we have peace with God through our Lord Jesus Christ. Through him we have obtained access to this grace in which we stand, and we rejoice in our hope of sharing the glory of God. More than that, we rejoice in our sufferings, knowing that suffering produces endurance, and endurance produces character, and character produces hope, and hope does not disappoint us, because *God's love has been poured into our hearts through the Holy Spirit which has been given to us* (Rom 5.1-5).

---

[83] For my own treatment of these gifts, see *Basics*, pp. 172-188. For a full treatment by a theologian who writes from experience of the role of these gifts in the renewal of the Church, see FRANCIS A. SULLIVAN, S.J., *Charisms and Charismatic Renewal. A Biblical and Theological Study*. (Ann Arbor, Michigan: Servant Books, c. 1982).

What is the meaning of this text, especially the portion which I have italicized, giving the reason why hope does not disappoint us? First, *God's love*, if we consider the following verses (6-11), seems to mean most obviously God's love for us: Paul shows how God demonstrated his love for us.

Yet Paul's proof that our hope does not disappoint us is not simply a statement of truths which we believe. His thought here seems to me to be full of meaning, and to suggest a proof from our experience: we *know* that our hope is not deceptive. How do we *know* that? We have *experienced* the gift of the Spirit, the working of the Spirit within us, the God-given love which is the most precious gift, or fruit, of the Spirit. Is this stretching Paul's meaning? I do not think so. Surely one could hold that this is not the immediate "literal" sense of verse 5. Yet Paul's words here seem to be pregnant, and his symbolism suggests all of the reverberation of the love poured into our hearts through the Holy Spirit which has been given to us.

(c) Living according to the Spirit. I gather here a number of related elements of Paul's teaching: living according to the Spirit, walking by the Spirit, experiencing the fruits of the Spirit.

> But I say, walk by the Spirit, and do not gratify the desires of the flesh. For the desires of the flesh are against the Spirit, and the desires of the Spirit are against the flesh ... Now the works of the flesh are plain: immorality, impurity, licentiousness, idolatry, sorcery, enmity, strife, jealousy, anger, selfishness, dissension, party spirit, envy, drunkenness, carousing, and the like ... But the fruit of the Spirit is love, joy, peace, patience, kindness, goodness, faithfulness, gentleness, self-control; against such there is no law. And those who belong to Christ Jesus have crucified the flesh with its passions and desires. If we live by the Spirit, let us also walk by the Spirit ... (Gal 5.16-25; cf. 6.7-8).

> ... the law of the Spirit of life in Christ Jesus has set me free from the law of sin and death. For God has done what the law, weakened by the flesh, could not do: sending his own Son in the likeness of sinful flesh and for sin, he condemned sin in the flesh, in order that the just requirement of the law might be fulfilled in us, who walk not according to the flesh but according to the Spirit. For those who live according to the flesh set their minds on the things of the flesh, but those who live according to the Spirit set their minds on the things of the Spirit. To set the mind on the flesh is death, but to set the mind on the Spirit is life and peace. For the mind that is set on the flesh is hostile to God; it does not submit to God's law, indeed it cannot; and those who are in the flesh cannot please God.

But you are not in the flesh, you are in the Spirit, if the Spirit of God really dwells in you. Any one who does not have the Spirit of Christ does not belong to him. But if Christ is in you, although your bodies are dead because of sin, your spirits are alive because of righteousness. If the Spirit of him who raised Jesus from the dead dwells in you, he who raised Christ Jesus from the dead will give life to your mortal bodies also through his Spirit which dwells in you.

So, then, brethren, we are debtors, not to the flesh, to live according to the flesh—for if you live according to the flesh you will die, but if by the Spirit you put to death the deeds of the body you will live. For all who are led by the Spirit of God are sons of God... (Rom 8.2-14).

How was the just requirement of the law fulfilled in us (8.3-4)? There are two parts of Paul's answer to that question: Jesus' condemning sin in the flesh, and, as a consequence of the gift which we have received, our walking according to the Spirit.

To the list of the "fruits" of the Spirit we might add here freedom from the yoke of a law which could not be kept, a yoke of slavery (cf. Gal 4.21-31; 5.1-6, 13, 18; Rom 7.6; 8.1-2, 15). We are under a new covenant: "... not in a written code but in the Spirit; for the written code kills, but the Spirit gives life. ... Now the Lord is the Spirit, and where the Spirit of the Lord is, there is freedom..." (2 Cor 3.6, 17). Yet our freedom is not license, nor to be used as an opportunity for the flesh, as Paul makes clear in the very context of his exaltation of freedom (cf. Gal 5.13-15), and as he emphasizes in his many exhortations to live according to the Christian code, as we shall consider later.

Finally I should point out one more fruit of the Spirit: a sense of fellowship from and in the Spirit: "So if there is any encouragement in Christ, any incentive of love, any participation in the Spirit [or: fellowship from and in the Spirit], any affection and sympathy, complete my joy by being of the same mind, having the same love, being in full accord and of one mind..." (Phil 2.1-2).

(d) Experience of the Spirit. According to varying contexts, Paul witnesses to his own experience of the Spirit, to that which he shares with others, and to that which is common to all who live in the Spirit, according to the Spirit. I make that distinction only to recognize the differences of experience according to explicit attribution to Paul himself or to himself and others, or to all. If we look to the aspects of experience of the Holy Spirit as dimensions of the fulfillment of the promise in us, the differences are insignificant. Whether it is a question of Paul, or of the Galatians, or of all who live in the Spirit, every aspect of experience of the Spirit pertains to the potential of all: all are aspects of the mystery of the fulfillment in us. Personally we may not have had some of the experiences which Paul mentions. Yet his testimony should open our minds, by the action of the very word as a vehicle of grace, to our own potential.

Paul is aware, he *knows*, that his speech and his message had their efficacy because they were a demonstration of the Spirit and power (cf. 1 Cor 2.4). He is fully conscious of possessing and imparting a wisdom which God has revealed to him through the Spirit: taught by the Spirit, he interprets spiritual truths to those who possess the Spirit (cf. 1 Cor 2.6-16). And Paul and the spiritual men and women who understand this wisdom are aware of discerning spiritual truths by the Spirit whom they possess. They judge, and are to be judged by no one (who does not have the Spirit). *We*, Paul and the spiritual men and women who understand by the Spirit, have the mind of Christ (cf. 1 Cor 2.14-16). To the unspiritual, that may sound like an arrogant claim. For the spiritual, who receive Paul's words as bearers of grace, and who recognize in Paul an authentic witness, an apostle whose credentials cannot be disregarded, he is a credible witness. Even when he gives his personal judgment, as distinct from a command revealed by the Lord (cf. 1 Cor 7.25-38), he writes: "And I think that I have the Spirit of God" (v. 40).

Refuting any charge of vacillation in his conduct, Paul appeals to the assurance of constancy which he and the Corinthians have in common: God has established them together in Christ, has anointed them, has sealed them, and given them his Spirit as a pledge (cf. 2 Cor 1.21-22). These are part of their experience of the Spirit: no other interpretation of Paul's words here would be intelligible. Again, in his description of his experience of afflictions, part of Paul's conscious experience is "...purity, knowledge, forbearance, kindness, *the Holy Spirit*, genuine love, truthful speech, and the *power of God...*" (2 Cor 6.6-7). When he begins his meditation on the mystery of Israel, he testifies: "I am speaking the truth in Christ, I am not lying; my conscience bears me witness in the Holy Spirit, that I have great sorrow and unceasing anguish in my heart..." (Rom 9.1-2).

Paul not only witnesses to his own experience, but appeals to the experience of others, and teaches aspects of the whole mystery which clearly can be understood only in terms of experience of all who live in the Spirit. His argument from the experience of the

Galatians is clear (Gal 3.2-5). His teaching regarding the
Spirit as the one who cries within us, "Abba! Father!" and thus
shows that we are sons (Gal 4.6-7) is true not only of the
Galatians but of all who by belief are sons and daughters of the
Father (cf. Rom 8.14-17). Through the *Spirit*, from *belief*, we
await the *hope* of rightness (Gal 5.5): living from belief, we are
conscious not only of believing, and of hoping, but also of being
moved to both by the Spirit. We are to walk by the Spirit,
distinguish desires of the flesh from those of the Spirit, be led by
the Spirit, and experience the fruits of the Spirit (Gal 5.16-18,
22-23, 25; cf. Rom 8.4-16). If the Spirit of Christ really
dwells in us, then we are not in the flesh but in the Spirit, we
belong to Christ, our spirits are alive because of rightness, and
we are sure that God who raised Christ Jesus from the dead will
give life to our mortal bodies through his Spirit which dwells in
us (cf. Rom 8.9-11). Such assurances, guarantees, make sense
only if we can know from experience that the Spirit of God really
dwells in us, that we have the Spirit of Christ. Having the first
fruits of the Spirit, we *hope*: waiting for adoption as sons, for
the redemption of our bodies [in the final revelation which, with
all creation, we await (cf. Rom 8.18-25)]. "Likewise the
Spirit helps us in our weakness; for we do not know how to pray
as we ought, but the Spirit himself intercedes for us with sighs
too deep for words. And he who searches the hearts of men
knows what is the mind of the Spirit, because the Spirit
intercedes for the saints according to the will of God" (Rom
8.26-27). Again, Paul's teaching here cannot be understood of
some intercession which occurs "outside" us: it makes sense
only in terms of an experience of prayer in which, by faith, we
are conscious of the action of the Spirit within us.

Having heard the word of truth, and having believed, we
were sealed with the promised Holy Spirit: the guarantee of our
inheritance (Eph 1.13-14): again, as surely as hearing and
believing are conscious acts, so too, by belief, is our experience of
the Holy Spirit within us as a guarantee. Paul's prayer for
wisdom, revelation, knowledge—ineffable knowledge which is
beyond knowledge—is a prayer for gifts which we are to have
through God's Spirit strengthening our inner selves (cf. Eph
1.15 – 2.22; 3.14-21). We are to lead a life worthy of our
calling, with a sense of, and desire to maintain, the unity of the
Spirit in the bond of peace, to live according to the variety of
graces, gifts, given to every one, according to a way of life which
will not grieve the Holy Spirit, in whom we were sealed for the

day of redemption (cf. Eph 4). We are to be "... filled with the Spirit, addressing one another in psalms and hymns and spiritual songs, singing and making melody to the Lord with all your heart, always and for everything giving thanks in the name of our Lord Jesus Christ to God the Father" (Eph 5.18-20).

(e) Personal relationship to the Spirit. Does Paul witness to his own sense of personal relationship to the Holy Spirit, or teach that such a relationship should be part of our conscious lives as we come to a fulness of life in the Spirit? I should say that only one plea suggests it: "... do not grieve the Holy Spirit of God ..." (Eph 4.30). What we have in Paul is not explicit teaching concerning such personal relationship, but rather a gospel which sets forth the roles of Father, Son, and Holy Spirit in such a way as to evoke a personal response to Them inevitable in the continuing experience of Christians.

(19) *Sons and daughters of the Father.* I begin with Paul's two references to what evidently he takes for granted as a common Christian experience, personal experience, of the Father: in prayer we call upon him, "Father!" (cf. Gal 4.6; Rom 8.15). This is not prayer like many of Paul's, that God be praised, or that God bless those to whom he is writing. In such cases we have a report of the content of Paul's prayer, but not the actual words of Paul himself addressing God, the Father, in an I-Thou relationship. When we call upon God, "Father!", we are addressing the Father directly, in a full second-personal act [84]: we are not professing to others that God is our Father, nor are we telling others that we pray to him as Father. We are making a full personal response to him. This is the only form of full conscious act in which we make our full response to the revealing and saving God, Father, Jesus, and Holy Spirit. To God, who in the first person reveals the name which says all that can be said about himself: "I am," we make our full response: "You are!" To Jesus, who in John's gospel seems to claim the divine name, "I am," and who, in the apostolic preaching and in Paul's gospel, was given the divine name, "Lord", we reply in full second-personal relationship by addressing him: "You are!" or "Jesus, you are the Lord!"

What is the meaning of that name, or those names, as we use them in addressing the Father or Jesus? What is the reverberation of those names in us? The answer is unique for

---

[84] For the differentiation of acts: first-, second-, and third-personal, see *Man the Symbolizer,* pp. 126-132.

every man or woman, and depends on the degree to which God's full revelation is grasped and evokes a personal response. What *can* that name "Father" mean to us, as we utter it from our grasp of the whole of Paul's gospel? It can have a meaning which corresponds to our knowledge of the Father's roles in our lives and fulfillment. I can only trace here some of the principal lines of that gospel in so far as it regards the role of the Father, and should evoke in us a personal response which recognizes and is a full response to what we know by faith to be his role in us.

(a) Source of all blessings. I cite two capital texts, which I shall not quote: we have considered them often: Rom 8.28-30 and Eph 1.3-14. Texts too numerous to list fill in the details of the blessings, graces, gifts [85]. The mystery, the Master plan, is God's (see above, pp. 210-212). Christ crucified is the wisdom and power of God (1 Cor 1.21-25). The gospel which Paul preaches is the power of God for salvation to every one who has faith (Rom 1.16). In the whole work of our redemption by Christ, God shows his love (Rom 5.8), and his love is poured into our hearts by the Spirit which has been given to us (Rom 5.5).

(b) At work in Christ. "...God was in Christ, reconciling the world to himself..." (2 Cor 5.19; cf. vv. 17-21).

(c) He raised Christ and will raise us (Gal 1.1; 2 Cor 13.4; Rom 6.4, 8; 8.11; 1 Th 4.14; 1 Cor 6.14; 15.51; 2 Cor 1.9-10; 4.14).

(d) His creation. We are a new creation (Gal 6.15; 2 Cor 5.17), God's workmanship, created in Christ Jesus (Eph 2.10).

(e) He dwells in us as in his temple (1 Cor 3.9, 16-17; cf. 6.19-20; 2 Cor 6.16; Eph 2.19-22).

(f) He is at work in us. He began a good work in us and will bring it to completion at the day of Jesus Christ (Phil 1.6). He is at work in us, both to will and to work for his good pleasure (Phil 2.13). In Christ we are being built into a holy temple, a dwelling place of God in the Spirit (Eph 2.22). It is God who gives growth (1 Cor 3.6; Col 2.19), who comforts (2 Cor 1.3-7; 7.4, 6-7, 13; 2 Th 2.16-17), who strengthens (2 Cor 1.21-22; Eph 3.14-21).

(g) Fulfillment. For us personally, God's work in us comes to term in the rightness of God, from God (2 Cor 5.21); in love: God's love of us and our God-given love of him, from which

---

[85] Here are some, for those who wish to fill out details: 1 Cor 1.23, 30; 3.6; 12.4; 2 Cor 13.4; Rom 1.16; 3.21-31; 7.25; 11.33; Col 2.19; Eph 2.8, 10. I omit from this list those texts which I shall cite or quote in my following summary account of the Father's roles, and of the relationships which result.

nothing can separate us (cf. Rom 8.31-39); in spiritual worship (Rom 12.1); in being filled with all the fulness of God (Eph 3.17-21); in being changed into his likeness from one degree of glory to another (2 Cor 3.18); in peace with God (Rom 5.1; Phil 4.7, 9). Universally, the end will come

> ... when he [Christ] delivers the kingdom to God the Father after destroying every rule and every authority and power. For he must reign until he has put all his enemies under his feet. The last enemy to be destroyed is death. "For God has put all things in subjection under his feet" [cf. Ps 8.6). But when it says, "All things are put in subjection under him," it is plain that he is excepted who put all things under him. When all things are subjected to him, then the Son himself will also be subjected to him who put all things under him, that God may be everything to every one (1 Cor 15.24-28) [86].

(h) Finally, what is God's purpose in all? In his great «prologue», Eph 1.3-14, Paul terminates three phases of his thanksgiving for all of the blessings which God had blessed us with in Christ. With slight variations they express the purpose of all: "*to the praise of the glory of his grace*, with which he has graced us the Beloved" (v. 6); "that we be *to the praise of his glory*, we who first hoped in Christ" (v. 12); "who [the promised Holy Spirit] is the first instalment [as a pledge] of our inheritance until we acquire possession of it [or, with NEB: "the pledge that we shall enter upon our heritage, when God has redeemed what is his own], *to the praise of his glory*" (v. 14). It is not that we shall contribute to, much less establish, the infinite glory which is his eternally, but that gradually, "... being changed into his likeness from one degree of glory to another..." (2 Cor 3.18), being renewed in the spirit of our minds, and putting on "... the new nature, created according to [the likeness of] God in true rightness and holiness" (Eph 4.23-24) we shall *be* a manifestation and praise of the glory of God. We shall be for eternity *right* with God, as we should be according to his eternal plan for us. Changed gradually into the image or likeness of Christ, who is the image or likeness of God (Col 1,15), we shall show forth the image or likeness of God, for the praise of his glory.

---

[86] For a brief statement of basically the same truth, see 1 Cor 3.21-23: "So let no one boast of men. For all things are yours, whether Paul or Apollos or Cephas or the world or life or death or the present or the future, all are yours; and you are Christ's; and Christ is God's."

(20) Love. Though I have mentioned love many times in various contexts, it calls for explicit treatment, for it is the most important element of our full response, of fulfillment accomplished in us.

(a) Paul's praise of love. I cite three texts in ascending order of importance. "For the whole law is fulfilled in one word, 'You shall love your neighbor as yourself'" (Gal 5.14). "Owe no one anything except to love one another; for he who loves his neighbor has fulfilled the law. The commandments, ... are summed up in this sentence, 'You shall love your neighbor as yourself.' Love does no wrong to a neighbor; therefore love is the fulfilling of the law" (Rom 13.8-10). Paul's greatest praise of love and of the beautiful qualities of a life of love is one of the most beautiful pages in the Bible:

> If I speak in the tongues of men and of angels, but have not love, I am a noisy gong or a clanging cymbal. And if I have prophetic powers, and understand all mysteries and all knowledge, and I have all faith, so as to remove mountains, but have not love, I am nothing. If I give away all I have, and if I deliver my body to be burned, but have not love, I gain nothing.
> Love is patient and kind; love is not jealous or boastful; it is not arrogant or rude. Love does not insist on its own way; it is not irritable or resentful; it does not rejoice at wrong, but rejoices in the right. Love bears all things, believes all things, hopes all things, endures all things.
> Love never ends; as for prophecies, they will pass away; as for tongues, they will cease; as for knowledge, it will pass away...
> So faith, hope, love abide, these three; but the greatest of these is love (1 Cor 13.1-8, 13).

There is an anomaly in Paul's praise of love as the greatest of the commandments, as the sum of all: he omits mention of the love of God. The explanation lies the context, in the immediate concern which occasions his teaching: there is always a question of our conduct in relation to others [87].

---

[87] To clarify two matters which could puzzle some, I repeat what I have written earlier concerning 1 Cor 1.13. "... Two questions remain, ... what sort of faith is involved in v. 13; in what sense faith and hope remain [10]. It seems that faith here is not the charismatic intensity of faith, as in v. 2 and also in 12.9. Faith here is the basic gift given to all who are in Christ. The one truth which Paul holds emphatically here is the excellence of love, better than all other gifts" (Basics, p. 185). Note 10 on the same page: "This latter question poses a problem only if the translation of μένει in the RSV, and similar versions in NEB,

(b) Paul's love. Again and again Paul mentions his love for those to whom he writes in the churches which he established. His most personal revelation of his feelings comes in *Philippians*: "It is right for me to feel thus about you all, because I hold you in my heart, for you are all partakers with me of grace, both in my imprisonment and in the defense and confirmation of the gospel. For God is my witness, how I yearn for you all with the affection of Christ Jesus" (1.7-8). He seeks in various ways to find analogies of his love in the feeling of a nurse (1 Th 2.7-8), in the travail of a mother (Gal 4.19), in the love of a father (1 Cor 4.14-16; 1 Th 2.11). There is a pathos in the anguish of his love (2 Cor 2.4), and even more in the feeling that his love is unrequited, and in his appeal for a return of love (2 Cor 6.11-13; 7.2-3).

(c) Our love. [1] Of God and of the Lord Jesus. Having observed Paul's omission of the love of God in his reference to love as the sum and fulfillment of the commandments, I can point here only to texts which at best could be taken as uncertain, or as including the love for God in a full, pregnant sense of the word *love*. One text probably refers to love for the Lord Jesus: "... I hear of your love and of the faith which you have toward the Lord Jesus and all the saints, ..." (Philem 1.5). *Faith* surely must regard Jesus. Does *love* too? The matter is obscure. In what follows Paul writes of Philemon's love for the saints, appeals for a love of Onesimus [88]. God's love poured into our hearts (Rom 5.5) could be taken in a full, pregnant sense: God's love for us, our God-given love for him, and our love for one another. Similarly, in Rom 8.35, 39, "the love of Christ" and "the love of God in Christ Jesus our Lord" can be taken in the full sense: their love of us, and our love of them (cf. also 2 Cor 5.14; Eph 3.17-19; 1 Th 1.3).

[2] Of one another. Paul's teaching on our love of one another and of all men is full, and beautiful in its delicate elaboration of all that a life of such love involves in our manner of dealing with one another. As for the range of our love, Paul

---

JB, and others is to be taken in the sense of lasting forever. More probably, in my opinion, there is no real problem here; JB in its note suggests an alternative: 'In short, then, we are left with three things.' In other words, having compared love with the special gifts, there remains the question regarding the relative value of these three."

[88] FITZMYER, "Philemon," JBC, I, 54:9, p. 333 notes the obscurity of the verse and refers to C. F. D. MOULE, *Colossians and Philemon*, pp. 142-143 for various interpretations.

insists most often on love for all the saints: love within the community of believers. Yet he extends our love to all men (1 Th 3.12). In many ways he teaches what a life of love means, the way in which we are to deal with one another. Thus many of the texts which formulate a code of Christian conduct are intimately connected with his teaching on love, from which such conduct must spring. Through love we are to be servants of one another, not biting and devouring one another (Gal 5.13-15). The great praise of love in 1 Cor 13 is also the most beautiful description of the qualities of those who love: qualities which without question are rooted in love, for love is the subject, as if personifed as the one acting. When one has caused us pain, we are to forgive and comfort him and reaffirm our love of him (2 Cor 2.5-7). In *Romans*, as in 1 Cor 13, after Paul has taught the variety of special gifts in the one body (12.3-8), he goes on to love, and his long code of conduct (12.9–13.10) elaborates the way of life which is consistent with genuine love (12.9), the love which does no wrong to a neighbor, and so fulfills the law. One of the beautifully delicate ways in which we are to show love is to avoid injuring our weaker brother or sister: at times when according to our own conscience we are free to act in a way which we know is right, we are to refrain from doing so, lest we be a stumbling block or hindrance for one who would not understand our action, and would suffer spiritual harm (cf. Rom 14.13–15.3). One of Paul's most beautiful exhortations to a life which is consistent with our having died and been raised with Christ (Col 3.1–4.5) reaches its peak in vv. 12-14, concluding: "... And above all these put on love, which binds everything together in perfect harmony" (v. 14). To the Philippians, for whom he felt a special love, he appeals for unity of spirit, mind, love (Phil 1.27–2.11).

Finally, I call attention to an aspect of the role of love which is extremely subtle and profound, and which can be understood only from experience: the link between love and a cluster of closely related aspects of fulfillment in us: faith, wisdom, revelation in the knowledge of God (Eph 1.15-23 especially, but continuing through chapter 2); love and a grasp of the breadth, length, height, and depth: a knowledge beyond knowledge, a sense of being filled with the utter fulness of God (Eph 3.17-19); love, knowledge, and discernment (Phil 1.9-11). There is a profound knowledge of God and of the mystery of our life in him, a delicate discernment of what is excellent, a massive knowledge beyond knowledge: shattering all conceptual knowledge. It can be reached only in that massive, intuitive, mystical if you will, knowledge which is in our sense of the very shape of the experience of loving Him/Them.

(d) A triad. Within Paul's full teaching on love, we may distinguish three quite distinct elements.

[1] What we *are* by *faith, baptism,* and the *Eucharist:* we are one by all that we share as consequences of the three. From belief [by faith] we *are* sons and daughters of Abraham, heirs to the promised good (Rom 4.11-18; Gal 3.7-9). We *are* sons and daughters of God (Gal 3.26). We *are* a new creation (Eph 2.8-22). We *are* living in Christ (cf. Gal 2.20; and, above, pp. 300-302). We *are* one new man, created by Christ, fellow-citizens with the saints and members of the household of God (Eph 2.11-22). We *are* temples of God, of the Spirit (1 Cor 3.16-17; 6.19-20).

By baptism we *are* one with Christ, and *one together in Christ* (Gal 3.26-29; 1 Cor 1.10-16). We have been *sealed* and *given the Spirit* as a pledge (2 Cor 1.21-22; Eph 1.13-14). We are *one* in our relationships to Father, Son, and Spirit, in accordance with their roles in baptism, and *one* in our relationships with one another (see above, pp. 292-299).

Through the Eucharist we *are* one body, members of a single body (1 Cor 10.16-17; cf. 12.4-27).

Through all three, whose effects in us at times cannot be distinguished in Paul's teaching, we *are one:* having in common all these aspects of the life which has been given to us (cf. 1 Cor 12.4-27; Rom 12.4-5).

[2] What we *are to become: one* in actually living a life of mutual love. Much of Paul's teaching regards this ideal.

[3] *Witness to experience* of mutual love, of fellowship. Here we may distinguish between Paul's witness to his own experience, and his witness to the experience of others. A constant element of Paul's personal experience is the loving concern for those to whom he writes, and his joy in the blessings which they have received: the beginning of every letter expresses a variation of such feelings. He is comforted and rejoices at the news of the Thessalonians' faith and love (1 Th 3.6-10). He desires mutual encouragement (Rom 1.8-12). He feels a special love and affection for the Philippians (Phil 1.3-8; 4.1,10-18). He longs to be with those whom he loves (Rom 1.11-12; 1 Th 3.10; Phil 1.8). He is consoled by their love for him (Phil 4.10-14).

Paul also writes of what he knows of others' experience of love and fellowship. He knows what was the effect he had on the Thessalonians (1 Th 1.4-6); the influence which they had on others (1 Th 1.7-10), and similarly that which the Romans had on others (Rom 1.8). He writes of the mutual encouragement experienced by the Corinthians and himself (2 Cor 1.4-7), and by the Thessalonians among themselves (1 Th 5.11); and of the love which the Colossians have for all the saints (Col 1.4). The Philippians especially had had the experience of fellowship with Paul, as partakers of his gospel (Phil 1.5; 4.3), and in their loving concern for Paul and their sharing in his trouble (Phil 4.10-14).

(21) *Hope.* One of God's gifts to us, part of our fulfillment in "the time between" Christ's resurrection and our own, is hope. Paul exhorts to, and rejoices in, steadfastness of hope (1 Th 1.3), holding fast, standing firm (1 Cor 15.1-2) being immovable in hope (1 Cor 15.58), unshaken (2 Cor 1.7), not losing heart (2 Cor 4.16), being of good courage (2 Cor 5.6, 8). He rejoices in his own afflictions (see above, pp. 302-304), and gives thanks for and boasts of the Thessalonians' steadfastness and faith in all the afflictions and persecutions which they are bearing (2 Th 1.3-4), as they wait for God's Son from heaven, and their deliverance (cf. 1 Th 1.10).

What is the mystery of this hope? What is the meaning of Christian hope for Paul? As always, the full sense of Paul's words can be gathered only from the context of his thought and teaching; and the uniqueness of Christian hope as Paul understands it, emerges from the cluster of elements of the full concrete Christian experience.

Christian hope is not any expectation, or mingling of desire, trust, and expectation of a promised good which is as yet unseen, unattained. It is not just the pure, unwavering trust of Abraham, which in a sense was more remarkable: for Abraham had nothing to go on but the promise given by the God who could give life to the dead, and call into existence things that did not exist (cf. Rom 4.17-21). Christian hope is expectation and desire and trust grounded on the promise, but in the unique situation of our life in the time between fulfillment in Christ and our own final fulfillment, our hope is full of conviction, strong, grounded upon our experience of partial fulfillment of the promise. We *know* by faith that God has raised Christ and will raise us (cf. 1 Cor 15.20-28; see above, p. 265). We look to our own resurrection. For those who believed and have died, we do not grieve as others who have no hope (cf. 1 Th 4.13). It is our hope alone which makes sense of the kind of lives which we are called to live: "If for this life only we have hoped in Christ, we are of all men most to be pitied" (1 Cor 15.19). It is in the hope of the resurrection, grounded on God's raising Jesus from the dead, that Paul dies daily: this alone makes sense of the way in which he lives: "If the dead are not raised at all... Why am I in peril every hour? I protest, brethren, by my pride in you which I have in Christ Jesus our Lord, I die every day! What do I gain if, humanly speaking, I fought with beasts at Ephesus? If the dead are not raised, 'Let us eat and drink, for tomorrow we die'" (1 Cor 15.29-32). We know that our work is not in vain (1 Cor 15.58). We rely on God, who raises the dead (2 Cor 1.8-10), who has delivered us, and will deliver.

It is not just our faith in God's having raised Jesus, and so having fulfilled his promise in the most unexpected way, which grounds our hope. We have conviction and strength grounded also in our own experience of his partial fulfillment of the promise is us. Paul builds up to this in his powerful witness in *Romans:*

> Therefore, since we have been made right from belief, we have peace with God through our Lord Jesus Christ. Through him we have access to this grace in which we *stand*, and we *rejoice* in our *hope* of sharing the glory of God. More than that, we *rejoice* in our sufferings, knowing that suffering produces *endurance*, and endurance produces *character*[89], and character produces *hope*, and hope *does not disappoint us, because God's love has been poured into our hearts through the Holy Spirit which has been given to us* (Rom 5.1-5).

Clearly Paul indicates a process resulting in hope as a strength and steadfastness. The stages of that process are not those of some sort of growth of which a person would not be conscious. There is question here of conscious growth and gathering of strength from the experience of suffering, enduring, passing the test of trial and affliction, and coming to a mature sense of one's strength. It is, however, in the whole context of Paul's thought and of Christian belief, not a growth and maturing and perfecting which are due to human effort, and grounded in human power: all is gift. All is from belief. All pertains to the *rightness* which is from belief, and which is in process. Even to this point in the text, then, there is question of a strength gradually developed in a process of a fully conscious life. Beyond that, the final stage of

---

[89] δοκιμή: cf. BAG: "the quality of being approved," hence *character*. The related verb, δοκιμάζω means *put to the test, prove by testing, accept as proved* [having been proved by the test].

the argument is all-important: we *know* that our hope does not, will not, disappoint us, precisely because we have experience of the love of God [a love God-given and directed to God and to others whom we love in God] poured into our hearts by the Holy Spirit who has been given to us. For Paul, not only our *love* is a gift of which we are conscious, but the gift of the Holy Spirit too: we are *aware* of the Spirit which has been given. His thought here is linked with the argument by which he seeks to convince the Corinthians of his constancy: "The one who strengthens us together with you [assuring us that we belong to Christ[90]], and has anointed us, is God, who also sealed us and gave the first portion of the gift of the Spirit in our hearts" (2 Cor 1.21-22).

For Paul surely both the love which we experience, and the Spirit within us as the source of that love, are parts of conscious Christian experience. How else would they function as guarantees, as assurances that our hope does not disappoint us, will not disappoint. The sense fully elaborated perhaps is this: our hope does not *delude* us, and will not disappoint us, for the reason which Paul gives.

Our hope, therefore, does not rest solely on belief in the promise: it is grounded upon experience of partial fulfillment of the promise. Paul and his fellow Christians have experience of enduring affliction and persecution by the strength which God gives them. "For we do not want you to be ignorant, brethren, of the affliction we experienced in Asia; for we were so utterly, unbearably crushed that we despaired of life itself. Why, we felt that we had received the sentence of death; but that was to make us rely not on ourselves but on God who raises the dead; he delivered us from so deadly a peril, and he will deliver us; on him we have set our hope that he will deliver us again (2 Cor 1.8-10; cf. 4.7–5.5). Hope, then, is grounded upon experience of God's grace, a God-given power, part of the mystery of Christian power and strength in weakness (cf. 2 Cor 12.7-10, and above, pp. 302-304).

---

[90] A literal translation would be: "The [one] strengthening us with you to/into/unto Christ ... " I think that the preposition εἰς retains something of its primitive sense of movement to or into. We were baptized *into* Christ: hence we are one with him (cf. Gal 3.27-29). "Strengthening" here seems to be elliptical or pregnant in meaning: God strengthens us with the assurance that we stand in Christ [cf. JB]: we have been plunged into Christ, are one with him, stand in him. Both Paul and the Corinthians in common have this awareness, as also of their having been anointed and given the partial gift, the first portion of the gift, the first instalment of the gift, of the Spirit.

(22) *The Christian code of conduct.* Paul's gospel is not simply his great thesis of being made right not from works of the Law, but from belief; and of a rightness which is pure gift, grace: *if* we take that thesis to refer simply to *belief* as an initial, decisive act, and to *being made right* or *rightness* as simply from that initial act of belief. One cannot read the whole of Paul without encountering an overwhelming mass of evidence that such a reduction of Paul's gospel to a thesis understood in that narrow sense would be a falsification of that gospel, a reduction which would be truly a mutilation.

Two elements of our consideration of "Love, grace, belief, and rightness" (above, pp. 259-292, surely ample within the limits of this work) suggest that there is much more to be considered.

First, belief itself is not merely an initial, decisive act which suffices once for all: surely it is decisive, and of primary importance; but Paul gives clear witness to belief as a present act and a disposition to act in the continuing life of the one living in Christ, in the Spirit. I have treated the initial act (pp. 271-274) and also the present act and disposition to act (pp. 274-277). Moreover, rightness is not only from the initial act of belief, but also from continuing belief (above, pp. 291-292).

Second, as I have set forth (pp. 264-266), if we ask *what* is proposed for belief, the full answer is the *whole* gospel preached by Paul. A great part of that gospel is devoted to Paul's teaching concerning what we can call the Christian code of life. The many passages which I shall indicate cannot be set aside as "hortatory" as distinct from "doctrinal". First, clearly they are set forth as part of the mystery, and they present a way of life which is motivated by aspects of the mystery: they constitute a distinctively Christian code, with a motivation which is unique, and which gives Christian conduct a unique character. Second, if one were to regard Paul's "doctrine" as his thesis taken in the narrowest sense, and excluding the relevance of *all* works for salvation, then his many passages which urge and spell out details of a Christian code of conduct as significant for our salvation and final judgment· would be absolutely incoherent, in conflict with his "doctrine". We must consider now those texts on Christian conduct.

(a) Judgment according to works. The basic principle in this whole matter is formulated by Paul in his review of the history of a sinful mankind, Jews and Gentiles: "... on the day of wrath when God's righteous judgment will be revealed ... he will render to every man according to his works ... For God shows no partiality'' (Rom 2.5-6, 11); ''... it is not the hearers of the law who are righteous before God, but the doers of the law who will be justified ... on that day, when *according to my gospel*, God judges the secrets of men by Christ Jesus'' (Rom 2.13, 16). That principle is never revoked. Neither Gentile nor Jew was able to keep the law by his or her own power: all sinned, all were under the power of sin (cf. Rom 3.9-20). But Paul clearly teaches the consequences of God's making us right from belief, not from works of the Law: ''... God has done what the law, weakened by the flesh, could not do: sending his own Son in the likeness of sinful flesh and for sin, he condemned sin in the flesh, in order that the just requirement of the law might be fulfilled in us, who walk not according to the flesh but according to the Spirit...'' (Rom 8.3-4). Made right by God from belief, with a rightness which is pure gift, we must walk according to the Spirit, live by the Spirit, put to death the deeds of the flesh: for if we live according to the flesh we will die, but if by the Spirit we put to death the deeds of the body we shall live (cf. Rom 8.5-13).

Paul prays: ''... may the Lord make you *increase and abound in love* to one another and to all men, as we do to you, so that he may establish your hearts unblamable in holiness before our God and Father, at the coming of our Lord Jesus with all his saints'' (1 Th 3.12-13). We must *live* to *please* God (1 Th 4.1). God has not destined us for wrath, but to obtain salvation through our Lord Jesus Christ (1 Th 5.9). We must live according to the scripture (1 Cor 4.6), keep the commandments (1 Cor 7.19). As we sow, so shall we reap (cf. 2 Cor 9.6). We are to walk in newness of life (cf. Rom 6.4). We are to sin no longer, but yield ourselves and our members to God as instruments of righteousness (cf. Rom 6.12-14), obedient from the heart to the standard of teaching to which we were committed (v. 17), yielding our members to righteousness for sanctification (cf. vv. 19, 22). We are ''[God's] workmanship, created in Christ Jesus *for good works*, which God prepared beforehand, *that we should walk in them*'' (Eph 2.10). Paul begs the Ephesians to lead a life worthy of the calling to which they have been called (Eph 4.1), and he continues to elaborate the manner of the life which they must lead (4.2-3, 17 – 6.20). He prays that the Colossians may be filled with the knowledge of his will in all spiritual wisdom and understanding, ''... to lead a life worthy of the Lord, fully pleasing to him, bearing fruit in every good work...'' (Col 1.10). Christ has reconciled them in his body of flesh by his death, in order to present them ''... holy and blameless and irreproachable before him, provided that you continue in the faith, stable and steadfast, not shifting from the hope of the gospel which you heard..." (1.22-23). Having risen with Christ they are to seek the things that are above, to set their minds on things that are above, not on things that are on earth (3.1-2); and Paul instructs them in detail concerning the way in which they are to live (3.5–4.6). "Whatever your task, work heartily, as serving the Lord and not men, knowing that from the Lord you will receive the inheritance as your reward; you are serving the Lord Christ. For the wrongdoer will be paid back for the wrong he has done, and there is no partiality" (3.23-25).

Paul prays for the Philippians: "...that your love may abound more and more, with knowledge and discernment, so that you may approve what is excellent, and may be pure and blameless for the day of Christ, filled with the fruits of righteousness which come through Jesus Christ, to the glory and praise of God" (Phil 1.9-10). They are to imitate Paul (3.17). "Finally, brethren, whatever is true, whatever is honorable, whatever is just, whatever is pure, whatever is lovely, whatever is gracious, if there is any excellence, if there is anything worthy of praise, think about these things. What you have learned and received and heard and seen in me, *do*; and the God of peace will be with you" (4.8-9).

Surely it is only in and through Christ, only by the Father who sanctifies us (1 Th 5.23) and who is at work in us, both to will and to work for his good pleasure (Phil 2.13), and in the Spirit, without whom we cannot even say "Jesus is Lord" (1 Cor 12.3), and who moves us to cry "Abba! Father! (Gal 4.6; Rom 8.15), that we can act so as to please God. Yet we are to *obey*, and to *work out our own salvation* with fear and trembling (cf. Phil 2.12).

(b) Holiness. One could sum up Paul's teaching concerning our task and our way in this one word: all else spells out its implications: "...this is the will of God, your *sanctification* [*holiness*] (1 Th 4.3): both the process and the term of the process of becoming holy. There is an analogy here with the new creation: we are a new creation, and yet we are in the process of being created [91]. Like the Corinthians, we were washed, we were sanctified, we were justified (cf. 1 Cor 6.11): yet clearly Paul teaches the process by which we are to *be made holy, become holy* (cf. the context: 1 Th 4.1-12, one of Paul's many for-

---

[91] I merely cite again "The New Creation as Process", in *Basics*, pp. 156-172.

mulations of the code. "Since we have these promises, beloved, let us *cleanse ourselves* of every defilement of body and spirit, and *make holiness perfect* in the fear of God" (2 Cor 7.1).

(c) The code. I shall not quote texts, much less attempt a synthesis of Paul's moral teaching, his code of Christian conduct. The texts are numerous, many of them long. As I have pointed out (above, p. 264), there are portions of these texts which are exhortation, and others in which Paul is giving his own personal opinion, or a solution based on the culture of the time or place. Yet the vast majority of the contents of these texts are part of his gospel: part of the Mystery, part of what it means to live in Christ[92].

One element of Paul's code deserves special consideration, for it corresponds to an element of Jesus' teaching which he emphasized in the gospel accounts. It is forgiveness. It is Matthew who highlights the importance of forgiveness. Only in Matthew does Jesus add a commentary on one petition of the prayer he has taught: "For if you forgive men their trespasses, your heavenly Father also will forgive you; but if you do not forgive men their trespasses, neither will your Father forgive your trespasses" (Mt 6.14-15)[93]. Only Matthew has the parable of the unforgiving servant (18.23-35), by which Jesus reinforces his answer to Peter on forgiving his brother who has sinned against him (18.21-22).

Paul's teaching is notable too for significant links of his terminology, suggesting a profound meaning. The first instance is Paul's teaching to the Corinthians:

> But if any one has caused pain, he has caused it not to me, but in some measure—not to put it too severely—to you all. For such a one this punishment by the majority is enough; so you should rather turn to *forgive* and comfort him, or he may be overwhelmed by excessive sorrow. So I beg you to reaffirm your *love* for him. For this is why I wrote, that I might test you and know whether you are obedient in everything. Any one whom you *forgive*, I also *forgive*. What I have *forgiven*, if I have *forgiven* anything, has been for your sake in the presence of Christ, ... (2 Cor 2.5-10).

[92] These are the texts, long and short: 1 Th 4.3-8, 11; 5.5-11, 12-22; 2 Th 3.6-15; Gal 5.13–6.10; 1 Cor 1.10-17; 3.1-15; 5.1–8.13; 10–11; 2 Cor 6.14–7.1; 8.1–9.15; Rom 6.4-23; 12.1–15.13; Eph 4.1–6.20; Phil 2.1-18; 3.17–4.1; 4.4-9; Col 2.20–4.6.

[93] Mark has a partial parallel in Jesus' teaching on prayer in another situation (Mk 11.25).

Paul's verb here is χαρίζομαι, which, as I indicated has not only an interesting set of meanings and applications, but also interesting and suggestive links with other words prominent in his vocabulary. Χαρίζομαι is linked immediately with χάρις: in the sense of favor or grace received (cf. BAG). The verb χαρίζομαι means (1) give freely or graciously as a favor; (2) give = remit, forgive, pardon (BAG). In Paul's usage, God both *gives* (Rom 8.32; 1 Cor 2.12; Gal 3.18; Phil 1.29; 2.9) and *forgives* (Eph 4.32; Col 2.13; 3.13). With regard to our conduct, he uses the word only with the meaning *forgive* (2 Cor 2.7-10 [four times]; 12.13; Eph 4.32; Col 3.13). Two texts are especially important, for they point out the parallellism of God's forgiving and ours: "...and be kind to one another, tenderhearted, forgiving one another, as God in Christ forgave you" (Eph 4.32); "Put on then, as God's chosen ones, holy and beloved, compassion, kindness, lowliness, meekness, and patience, forbearing one another and, if one has a complaint against another, forgiving each other; as the Lord has forgiven you, so you also must forgive. And above all these put on love, which binds everythings together in harmony" (Col 3.12-14).

Beyond what strikes me as an interesting link in Paul's terminology, I find the suggestion of a profound meaning. God's *favor* or *grace* or *gift* received, and his *giving* are mentioned by Paul in a context in which he writes of God's *love*, the source of all giving, and of all favor, grace, or gift received. The most striking example is *Romans* 8.31-39. There is more than a casual linguistic link too between his *giving* and his *forgiving*, expressed by the same verb: his forgiving is a second giving, a second gracing, a re-gracing. We were *saved* by *grace*, through belief: this is not our own doing, but the *gift* of God. Out of the great *love* with which he loved us, *when we were dead in our trespasses*, he made us alive together with Christ (cf. Eph 2.4-5, 8). All had sinned and had fallen short of the glory of God. They were *made right* by his *grace* as a *gift*, through the redemption which is in Christ Jesus. God showed his rightness, because in his divine forbearance he had passed over former sins (cf. Rom 3.21-26). Having given up [delivered, handed over] his own Son, he will give us [grace us with] all things. Nothing, then, shall separate us from the love of Christ, the love of God: their love for us, and our God-given love for them (cf. Rom 8.31-39).

There are two stages, then, in the understanding of our complete dependence upon God's love and free gift. First, all is gift. Paul asks the proud and arrogant Corinthians: "What have you that you did not receive? If then you received it, why do you boast as if it were not a gift?" (1 Cor 4.7)[94]. But deeper than that, what God has given us out of love he has given by forgiving: his giving is a second giving, his gracing a second gracing, a re-gracing of those who by sin had forfeited his first gift. All, then, is not only gift, but doubly gift. With a sense of the double gratuity of our gift, we in turn should forgive; reaffirm our love by forgiving those who have pained us, giving freely of what we ourselves have freely received in the mystery of God's second giving, his forgiving. In forgiving, we are giving not of what is ours by right, but what is God's: his second gift to us.

(d) Motivation. Some of Paul's formulations of the Christian code can resemble other ancient ethical teachings or lists of duties. I am not interested here in going into such parallels. What is far more profound and significant in Paul's code of conduct, his "ethical" or "moral" teaching, is the unique motivation which transforms it. I say *motivation* in the singular, for the many motives which can be distinguished, and which I shall in fact distinguish and arrange in an order which seems reasonable, are all aspects of the one Mystery. What I point out here is intimately related to what I have developed above: living in Christ, living in the Spirit, and sons and daughters of the Father. What is *right* conduct for us is grounded in the unique Mystery in which we share: what we *are* in the Father, in Christ, in the Spirit; what we are consequently in relation to one another; what we recognize as the unique transcendent value at the core of our own being and that of our fellow Christians, and as the unique potential dignity and value of all men and women who radically have been saved in Christ, and can come to a fulness of life in him. We live in a unique transcendent interpersonal world, in our relationships with Father, Jesus, and the Spirit, and in our relationships with one another. This world for us is most precious, counts most, is most *real*. We are called upon to recognize the Mystery in one another, and to act in relation to Father, Jesus, and the Spirit, and in relation to one another, in accordance with that Mystery. This is what specifies Christian conduct, and what makes it unique. What, then, are some of the principal aspects of that Mystery which we can distinguish, and of

---

[94] There is a parallel thought, though expressed in other terminology, in Jesus' instructions to the Apostles as he sends them out on a mission: "You received as a gift (δωρεάν), give as a gift" (Mt 10.8).

which we can and should be aware as we live as Christians? I shall list them, and cite the texts which are relevant. Before doing so, I call attention to a significant feature of this whole consideration. I am not merely listing aspects of the Mystery which are to be found in what some would distinguish as Paul's "doctrinal" portions of the letters involved. These texts are embedded in his moral teaching, and from their very position their function is clear: they are clearly and directly proposed as motives for the conduct which is itself part of Paul's gospel. I shall merely list the motives and cite the texts. Given the vastness of Paul's moral teaching. I must leave it to the reader to consider both the list of texts which I gave in note 92, and the texts which I shall cite here.

[1] You are not your own; you were bought with a price (1 Cor 6.19-20; 7.23).

[2] We who are many are one body (1 Cor 10.14-17), members of one body (1 Cor 12.12-13).

[3] We are to lead a life worthy of Christ. There can be no fellowship of rightness and iniquity, of light and darkness, of Christ and Belial (2 Cor 6.14-15). We were betrothed to Christ as a pure bride to her one husband (2 Cor 11.2). If we live, we live to the Lord, and if we die, we die to the Lord; so then, whether we live or whether we die, we are the Lord's (Rom 14.8). We are to please not ourselves, but our neighbor for his good, for Christ did not please himself (cf. Rom 15.1-3). We must live a life worthy of our calling, eager to maintain the unity of the Spirit in the bond of peace (cf. Eph 4.1-6). We must live as we have learned Christ, as we heard about him and were taught in him, as the truth is in Jesus (cf. Eph 4.20-21). Husbands are to love their wives as Christ loved the Church (cf. Eph 5.25-33). Lead a life worthy of the Lord (cf. Col 1.10). Raised with Christ, seek the things that are above, where Christ is (cf. Col 3.1). Let your manner of life be worthy of the gospel of Christ (Phil 1.27). Model your mind, your way of thinking, on Christ Jesus' (cf. Phil 2.5). We are temples of the Holy Spirit (1 Cor 6.19), of the living God (2 Cor 6.16-18). We must prove by our lives that our love is genuine, according to the example of Christ (cf. 2 Cor 8.8-9; cf. Phlm. 9).

(23) *Likeness, glory, light.* I am concerned here with these three intertwining themes in so far as they regard fulfillment in us now, in the period between Christ's glorification and our own final share in his glory, in the process which tends toward that final glory. I shall proceed in this order: (a) principal texts

regarding us; (b) the analogy with Christ; (c) a cluster of symbols; (d) a comment on *Romans* 3.23.

(a) Capital texts regarding us.

[1] Rom 8.29-30: For those whom he foreknew he also *predestined* to be *likenesses* of [similar in form to] *the image* [or *likeness*]: his Son, in order that he might be the first-born among many brethren. And those whom he predestined, he also *called*; and those whom he called he also *righted* [*made right*]; and those whom he righted he also *glorified* (ἐδόξασεν).

In translating "the image [or likeness]: his Son", I take "of his Son" as an explanatory genitive: we are to become like [similar in form to] his Son, who *is* the *image/likeness* (cf. Col 1.15, and above, pp. 257-258)[95].

What is the meaning of *glorified* in this text? Like the other four verbs in these two verses, this is in the aorist tense in the Greek. Three problems, of different orders, can be raised. (1) The kind of action and the temporal sense of the Greek aorist indicative. This is strictly a matter of the syntax of the New Testament Greek verb[96]. In the instance with which we are concerned, in which God is the subject, such a problem is taken up into the second problem, properly theological. (2) The deeper theological problem regards the utter inadequacy of all human languages to express God's *action*. This is not my concern here, for it pertains to the problem of human speech about God, which I shall consider in the third volume of this work. (3) The third concerns not the action itself, but the effect of the action: does the glorification occur during the life of the Christian "on earth", or only "at the last day"? This is our question here, and the answer can be given from the context of Paul's thought, gathered from the other texts which we must consider.

[2] 2 Cor 3.7–4.6. This is by far the most important text for our intertwining themes of likeness, glory, and light. I shall give my own translation of the Greek, done with an eye upon the RSV, NEB, and JB, and incorporating bits taken from them. My principal concern in holding as closely as possible to the Greek is to

---

[95] NEB comes close to this: "be shaped to the likeness of his Son." JB has "to become true images of his Son". The Son is the image of God. We are to be like him, imperfectly to be sure. As man in the beginning was created in God's image, after God's likeness (cf. Gen 1.26-27), analogously in the mystery of the new creation, we are to be in the image of his Son, who is his image.

[96] See BDF, § 318, pp. 166-167; and § 332, p. 171; and ZERWICK, *Graecitas Biblica*[4] (Rome: Pontifical Biblical Institute, 1960) §§ 240-255, pp. 74-79.

translate the most important Greek words always with the same English word. In order of diminishing importance they are these: δόξα: glory; δοξάζω: glorify; διακονία: ministry. I do this especially to bring out the prominence of *glory* through the text. In my judgment, the key to understanding this text is the subtle shifts in the sense of *glory* and *light*, which I shall point out and comment on later.

> [7] If the ministry of death, [the ministry of a dispensation] carved in letters on stone, came in *glory*,
>> so that the sons of Israel could not look upon Moses' face because of the *glory* of his face, [a glory which was] fading,
>
> [8] how much more will the ministry of the Spirit be in *glory*?
> [9] For if the ministry of condemnation was *glory* [accompanied by glory],
> much more does the ministry of rightness abound in *glory*.
> [10] For what had been *glorified* is [now] not *glorified* in this respect: because of [or: in comparison with] the surpassing *glory*;
> [11] For if the fading was through *glory* [was a ministry fading in glory],
> much more is the permanent in *glory*.
> [12] Having such a hope, we have great confidence,
>> [13] and are not like Moses, who put a veil over his face, so that the sons of Israel might not look upon the end of that which was fading.
>> [14] But their minds were hardened; for to this day, when they read the old covenant, that same veil remains unlifted, because only through Christ is it taken away.
>> [15] Yes, to this day, whenever Moses is read a veil lies over their minds;
>
> [16] but when one turns to the Lord the veil is removed.
> [17] Now the Lord is the Spirit,
> and where the Spirit of the Lord is, there is freedom.
> [18] And all of us, with unveiled face,
>> beholding the *glory* of the Lord,
>> are transformed into the same *image/likeness* [that is, his image]
>> from *glory* to *glory*,
>> by the Spirit of the Lord.

> [1] Therefore, having this ministry by the mercy of God, we do not lose heart, ...
> [3] And if our gospel is veiled, it is veiled for those who are perishing,
>> [4] in whom the god of this world has blinded the minds
>> of the unbelieving,
>> so that they might not see the *light* of the gospel
>> of the *glory* of Christ,
>> who is the *image* of God.

⁵ For we preach not ourselves, but Jesus Christ the Lord, and ourselves as servants for Jesus' sake.

⁶ For it is the God who said, "Out of darkness let *light shine*," who has *shone in our hearts*,

to give the *light* of the *knowledge* of the *glory* of God in the face of Christ.

Some further details in the context are noteworthy, for they are related to elements of other texts bearing on our themes. (1) Paul has this treasure in an earthen vessel, to show that the transcendent power belongs to God, not to him (4.7). (2) In all of his afflictions, Paul attests, he is "... always carrying in the body the death of Jesus, so that the *life* of Jesus may also be *manifested* in our bodies. For while we live we are always being given up to death for Jesus' sake, so that the *life* of Jesus may be *manifested* in our mortal flesh. So death is at work in us, but *life in you*" (4.10-12). (3) Paul knows "... that he who raised the Lord Jesus will raise us also with Jesus and bring us with you into his presence" (4.14). (4) "For it is all for your sake, so that as grace extends to more and more people it may increase thanksgiving, to the *glory* of God" (4.15). (5) "So we do not lose heart. Though our outer nature is wasting away, our *inner nature is being renewed* every day. For this slight momentary affliction is preparing for us an eternal *weight of glory* beyond all comparison" (4.16-17).

[3] A cluster of texts from *Ephesians*:

1.16-23. [Paul prays]
that God may give you a spirit of *wisdom* and *revelation* in *knowledge of him* (17)
having the eyes of your hearts *enlightened*, that you may *know* what is the *hope* to which he has called you,
what are the *riches of his glorious inheritance* in the saints (18)
and what is the *immeasurable greatness of his power in us who believe*,
[which you can judge] according to the *working* of his *great might* which he accomplished in Christ when he raised him from the dead and made him sit at his right hand in the heavenly places... (19-20).

2.1-10.
[We were dead through trespasses and sins (1-3).]
God, rich in *mercy*, because of the great *love* with which he loved us, *made us alive together with Christ* (5), and *raised us up with [him]*,

and *made us sit with [him] in the heavenly places in Christ Jesus* (6),

in order to *show* in future ages the *surpassing wealth* of his *grace* in kindness toward us in Christ Jesus (7).

For by *grace* you have been saved *through faith*; and this is not your own doing, it is the *gift* of God—not because of works, lest any man should boast (8).

For we are *his workmanship, created in Christ Jesus for good works*, which God prepared beforehand, that we should walk in them (10).

3.14-21. [Paul prays:]
that according to the wealth of his *glory*
he may grant you to be *strengthened inwardly* with *power* (16),
so that *Christ may live in your hearts through faith*;
[that you] *rooted in love* and *founded on love* (17), may have *power* to *grasp* with all the saints what is the *breadth and length and height and depth* (18), and to *know* the *love of Christ surpassing knowledge*, so that you may be *filled with all the fulness of God* (19).

To him who is able, according to the power at work in us, to do much more than we ask or imagine (20), to him be the *glory* in the Church and in Christ Jesus to all generations, for ever and ever. Amen. (21)

[4] Two texts from *Colossians*:

2.11-13.
In whom [Christ] also you were circumcised, ... (11)
    buried with him in baptism,
in whom also you were raised
    through faith in the working [active power] of God,
    who raised him from the dead (12).
And you,
    who were dead in trespasses
    and the uncircumcision of your flesh,
God made alive together with him,
    having forgiven us all our trespasses (13), ...[97]

3.1-4: "If then you have been raised with Christ, seek the things that are above, where Christ is seated at the right hand of God. Set your minds on things that are above, not on things that are on earth. For you have *died*, and your *life* is *hid with Christ in God*. When Christ who is our life appears, then *you also will appear with him in glory*."

---

[97] See above, pp. 296-298.

[5] A cluster of texts on *light*:

> Rom 13.12: ... put on the armor of *light*.

> 2 Cor 6.14-16:
> ... what partnership have *rightness* and iniquity
> ... what fellowship has *light* with darkness? (14)
> What accord has *Christ* with Belial?
> Or what has a *believer* in common with an unbeliever? (15)
> What agreement has the *temple of God* with idols?   For we
> are the temple of the living God; ... (16).

> Eph 5.8-14:
> ... once you were darkness, now you are *light* in the Lord;
> walk as children of *light* (8)
> (for the fruit of *light* is found in all that is good and right and
> true (9), ...
> Therefore it is said,
>   "Awake, O sleeper, and arise from the dead,
>   and Christ will give you *light*" (14).

> Phil 2.15-16:
> that you may be *blameless* and *innocent*,
> *children of God without blemish* in the midst of a crooked
> and perverse generation,
> *among whom you shine* as *lights* in the world,
> *holding fast the word of life*, ...

> Col 1.12: [the Father] ... has qualified us to share in the
> inheritance of the saints in *light*.

> 1 Th 5.5: "For you are all sons of *light* and sons of the day;
> we are not of the night or darkness.

(b) Aspects of an analogy with Christ.   Before attempting to
reflect on Paul's thought concerning likeness, glory, and light as
they are aspects of the fulfillment of the promise in us, I wish to
point out some aspects of an analogy with Christ which help to
understand Paul's thought concerning us.

Treating fulfillment of the promise in Christ, I distinguished
four aspects of his existence: (a) as he is in the form of God;
(b) as he was during his earthly existence; (c) as he is in glory
from the moment of his resurrection; (d) as he will be at the last
day.   What is pertinent to our present theme is a certain analogy
between fulfillment in us now and Christ's condition in the second
and third aspects of his existence.

Christ is the *image*, the *likeness*, of God (cf. Col 1.15). As I
have written above (pp. 217-218), what is said of Christ in the
immediate context seems most reasonably to refer to him as he is
in the form of God; yet analogously he is the image of God also as
man, in the second, third, and fourth aspects of his existence. The
analogy between Christ and us now regards his being image as
man in the second and third aspects of his existence. Being flesh
eternally the image of God, he came in the likeness of sinful flesh
(Rom 8.3: the word is ὁμοίωμα, likeness, not εἰκών, image as in
Col 1.15): he was like us, not our *image*.

In what sense was he God's image in the likeness of sinful
flesh? Paul's gospel does not recount the public life of Jesus.
There is, consequently, nothing corresponding to John's account
of the *glory* of the Son, gradually shown forth in his signs, his
works, and fully accomplished in his "hour" [98]. There is one hint
in Paul's broad statement: "... All this is from God, who through
Christ reconciled us to himself and gave us the ministry of
reconciliation; that is, God was in Christ reconciling the world to
himself..." (2 Cor 5.18-19). Yet it was in the form of sinful
flesh, in which he was sent for sin, and to condemn sin in the
flesh, that Christ died for us, and by Christ's dying for us sinners
God showed *his* love for us. I have pointed out the paradox of
this text (Rom 5.6-8) [99]. One would have expected Paul to say
that Christ showed *his own* love for us. He did surely. But the
implicit meaning of Paul's cryptic, elliptical statement seems most
reasonably to be this: Christ is the image of God, the perfect
revelation of the Father even in his being in the likeness of sinful
flesh. It is in this condition that he made his supreme act of love
for us. That love is the image of God's.

With regard to the third aspect of Christ's existence, again I
can do no more than indicate what seems to be implicit in Paul's
thought. If Christ is the image of the invisible God both as divine
and as man, and if implicitly he is God's image even in the
likeness of sinful flesh, then all the more must Christ in his glory
be the image of God also in his glorified human being.
Admittedly this is a tenuous line of thought, and I present it as
such. Yet it seems necessary to regard it as implicit if we are to
understand in what sense we are being changed into his likeness
(cf. 2 Cor 3.18): necessarily into the image of the God-*man*
immediately.

---

[98] See above, ch. VI, pp. 182-183.
[99] Above, pp. 221-222.

What, then, is to be said concerning Christ's *glory*? First, it is curious that Paul never uses the word *glorify* (δοξάζω) to express God's action in raising and exalting Jesus. He expresses that action in other ways, as I have set forth above (pp. 220-221). He does write of Christ's *glory*, always with reference to the risen Son of God in power [100]. With regard to the sense of *glory*, as Paul uses the word concerning both Christ and us, I have pointed out a subtle shift in the meaning of the word in his usage (above, pp. 224-226), and I shall return to it when I discuss his meaning in using the word concerning us.

I point out a few scattered references to Christ's *light* and *power*. Paul never affirms that Christ *is* the light. Yet we are now light in the Lord (Eph 5.8); and, in the words of an unidentified quotation, Christ will shine on us [give us light] (Eph 5.14). In an obscure expression, Jesus was set up as Son of God in power *from/by* (temporally or causally) his resurrection (Rom 1.4) [101]. Paul desires to know Christ and the *power* of his resurrection (Phil 3.10). The gospel is the *power* of God for salvation to every one who has faith (Rom 1.16). Earlier Paul identified that gospel as the word of the cross (1 Cor 1.18): to those who are being saved it is the *power* of God. What Paul preaches is Christ crucified: to those who are called, Christ the power of God and the wisdom of God (1 Cor 1.23-24). As I observed above concerning God's power (p. 223), *power* here must be understood in a sense which transcends all concepts of power within the range of natural human knowledge. The power which is Christ's, and which we experience, is a power in a mysterious higher realm of reality.

(c) A cluster of symbols. I had intended to work out at this point a synthesis of Paul's thought concerning the themes likeness, glory, and light as aspects of fulfillment of the promise in us. Upon reflection I decided that there can be no such synthesis. A synthesis would be the result of the elaboration of an intelligible structure in prevalently conceptual symbols. It would call for fairly sharply fixed relationships conceptualized, and a certain order and progression of thought. Such a synthesis, it seems to me now, could hardly be faithful to Paul's thought. What we encounter in the texts which I selected and presented above is

---

[100] See 2 Th 1.9; 2.14; 1 Cor 2.8; 2 Cor 3.18; 4.4, 6; Col 1.11 (Christ or God?); 1.27 (obliquely: "the glory of this mystery, which is Christ in you ...").

[101] For a brief presentation of the problems of the expression see FITZMYER, "Romans," JBC, II, 53:16, pp. 294-295.

rather a cluster of symbols, a blending and intertwining of highly intuitive symbols, multiple and varied in their suggestive power and in their interrelationships. Obviously to give any account of such symbolism involves some initial grouping of symbols. Yet one must return to consider their blending in a complex intuitive symbolism which suggests the inconceivable richness and complexity of the concrete reality which Paul is contemplating. I shall proceed in that manner: presenting some groups of symbols which in some respects at least are closely linked, and then reflecting upon their blending and their multiple inter-relationships.

[1] Image or likeness: the master symbol, or dominant symbol. As I read Paul, this is the dominant symbol in this sense: all others somehow contribute to suggesting as fully as Paul can what is implied in our being concretely in the image and likeness of Christ. Now, as we are by grace in this life, we are like him. Paradoxically we are like him both as he was in the form of a servant, and as he is as the Son of God in power. Hence I attempted to work out the tenuous account of how implicitly at least Christ is the image of the invisible God, and somehow is in glory, in both the second and the third aspects of his existence.

We are to be like him as he was in the form of a servant: we are to think as Christ thought in the mystery of his abasement: "In your minds you must be the same as Christ Jesus:

> His state was divine,
> yet he did not cling
> to his equality with God
> but emptied himself
> to assume the condition of a slave,
> and became as men are;
> and being as men are,
> he was humbler yet,
> even to accepting death,
> death on a cross" (Phil 2.5-8: JB).

In the context Paul cites Christ Jesus' self-effacement as a model for us in our treatment of one another (vv. 1-4). Yet we must be rooted in him and like him as he is now, risen and seated at the right hand of God. Paul spells out what this means, first in his general appeal to seek the things that are above (Col 3.1-4), and then in the details of a Christian way of life consistent with having been raised with Christ (Col 3.5—4.6). The notion of coming to a fulness of likeness to Christ is implicit in coming to maturity in him (cf. Col 1.28), and in that culmination of the process for which Paul prays: being filled with all the fulness of God (Eph 3.19: cf. vv. 14-21).

[2] Symbols which suggest primarily a cognitive aspect of our being in Christ, but which in the context are inseparable from many others suggesting non-cognitive aspects: light in our hearts, faith, knowledge, wisdom, revelation, and finally two which shatter all conceptualization: knowing the love of Christ which surpasses knowledge, and grasping or comprehending with all the saints the breadth and the length, the height and the depth—the ineffable fulness.

[3] Intertwined symbols which, seemingly non-cognitive, express aspects of our total life in Christ without which we cannot advance in faith, knowledge, wisdom: strength, power, love, knowledge of love in the very experience of loving, and finally light, which is linked with many others: (a) it is parallel with rightness, Christ, belief, being the temple of the living God (cf. 2 Cor 6.14-16); (b) being light in the Lord, we must *walk* as children of light (Eph 5.8); the *fruits* of light are all that is good and right and true (Eph 5.9), being blameless and innocent, without blemish, holding fast to the word of life (cf. Phil 2.15-16); (c) not only being illumined. but shining as lights in the world (*ibid.*).

[4] Glory. The key to the understanding of what Paul writes about glory and light in our fulfillment is that subtle transformation of the meanings of both words, a transformation which is clear in the capital text 2 Cor 3.7 – 4.6. I have discussed this transformation above (pp. 224-226). Essentially it is a shift from symbol to symbolized reality. *Glory* in the Old Testament was a visibly perceptible luminous splendor, symbol of the presence, power, majesty, sublimity of God. *Light* was also that light which figures in visual perception. Paul transforms both, as they regard God, and as they regard Christ, and as they regard us. Jesus was raised by the glory of God, by the power of God: and *glory* here is not visibly luminous splendor, but the very majesty, power, sublimity of God. Christ is in glory, but nowhere in Paul is there the suggestion of Christ's luminous splendor, visible for us. *Glory* is now the very symbolized reality: the divine excellence. *Light* is the interior light, the light shining in our hearts, the light of the Gospel: light only for those who have been enlightened interiorly and who believe. In two verses Paul expresses the mysterious fusion of *glory* and *light* as they

refer to God and Christ (2 Cor 4.4, 6: see above, p. 226); and as they refer to us, in the same text, 3.18.

What, then, is our glory, as the promise is fulfilled in us now? It is a participation in Christ and in God which we know only by faith, the light of God which illumines us interiorly. It is an excellence, a real enrichment and heightening of our being which is hidden completely from those who do not believe, and is a mystery known by a veiled unveiling only to those who also believe.

We are alive in and with Christ, having been brought to life from the death of sin. Ours is a glory which is a reality despite our weakness and affliction and the wasting away of our outer nature: our inner nature is being renewed every day. Yet somehow we are a mystery to be probed. Somehow the life of Jesus is manifested in our mortal bodies. In us now, despite all external appearance, there is the glory of the Mystery: Christ in us. We know the hope of the riches of God's glorious inheritance in the saints, to be judged by his active power in raising Christ from the dead and making him sit at his right hand in the heavenly places. We ourselves have been raised in and with him, and somehow now in a mysterious participation in anticipation we too are seated with him in the heavenly places. We are in process, advancing from glory to glory, as we tend to that final fulfillment which will come in our own resurrection, to the eternal *weight of glory* beyond all comparison (2 Cor 4.17): a curious expression in which Paul reverts knowingly or unknowingly to what some modern scholars regard as the primitive concept at the root of the Hebrew notion of glory: weight or heaviness.

Clearly, then, there is a link between *glory* and *image* or *likeness*: as we advance from glory to glory, from one degree to another in a participation of the glory, the life and majesty and excellence of Christ and of God, we become more like the Son, who is the image of God the Father.

The sense of the analogy with Christ also becomes clear. We are like him somehow as he was in the form of a servant. Like Paul, we in our afflictions are always carrying in our bodies the death of Jesus, we are being given up to death for Jesus' sake, death is at work in us (cf. 2 Cor 4.10-12). Though we have died with Christ, we must continue to put to death what is earthly in us (cf. Col 3.3, 5, 8). We are in process. We share in his life and his glory, but what we share is hidden. So Christ, who *is* eternally in the form of God, during his abasement in the form of a servant, had a glory which was hidden. We are like him as the

Son of God in power from the moment of his resurrection, for all of our life in him, all of our glory, is a participation of the glory which is his from that moment. Our life is *hidden* in Christ, but it is truly *life* in him. What we *are* will appear when we appear with him in glory (cf. Col 3.1-4).

Finally, sharing in the life and excellence of Christ and of God, living our response to the blessings which God has given us in Christ, *we* are glorified, and we *give glory to God*: we share in the goodness of God, and in our sharing we manifest the goodness of God. All is for the praise of his glory (cf. Eph 1.3-14).

(d) A comment on *Romans* 3.23: "... all have sinned and fall short of the glory of God, ..." I return to this text now to offer an interpretation which I reserved when I dealt with the text earlier (p. 248). In the light of my treatment of glory, I should say that Paul's meaning in Rom 3.23 is twofold. In Paul's massive judgment of all mankind, all fall short of that share in God's glory which could have been theirs, had they not sinned as they did: in the case of the great mass of mankind, by suppressing the truth, knowing God but not honoring him as God nor giving him thanks, exchanging the glory of the immortal God for images resembling mortal man or birds or animals or reptiles (Rom 1.18-23); in the case of the Jews, priding themselves on their possession of the law, and seeking a rightness not from belief, but from their own works of the law. First, then, all lack the gift of glory which would have been theirs. Second, all failed to give glory to God, as they might have, had they accepted God's gift, shared his goodness, and shown it forth for the praise of his glory.

(24) *Mission and witness.* In the mystery of fulfillment in us, mission and witness are most conspicuous in the unique vocation of Paul himself. Yet a Jeremiah in the Old Testament or a Paul in the New reveals a dimension which in many degrees and countless ways is part of the human potential in God's plan. To a certain extent Paul makes this explicit in what he writes of others who in various ways were his fellow workers, partakers or partners in his apostleship. Without quoting the many long and beautiful texts in which Paul blends details of his gospel, defense of his apostleship, and witness to his personal experience of the life of an apostle, I shall distinguish aspects of his message and cite some of the most important texts, familiar to all readers of Paul.

(a) Paul's sense of his own mission and call to witness.

[1] Most of Paul's letters open with his declaration of his title: he is an apostle, sent as a spokesman for God and Jesus

Christ. That declaration is not just a literary device. It sets the tone, the situation, the world into which we are entering as we begin to hear or read his letter. This is the proclamation of the gospel, not Paul's, not from man, but from God. As we hear or read these words, we receive God's word to us. Paul himself is keenly aware, and we are to be aware, of the function of his word, which comes with Spirit and power.

[2] At times Paul vigorously defends his apostleship: not from any merely human desire to vindicate himself against the accusations of others, or their odious comparisons with other apostles, but to make clear from his credentials that this gospel is God's word, the only gospel, to be received as such. It is in his letter to the Galatians and both letters to the Corinthians especially that Paul defends himself and his gospel: Gal 1.6 – 2.21; 6.17; 1 Cor 9.1-27; 2 Cor 1.15 – 2.4; 2.15 – 6.10; 10.1 – 13.4.

[3] Often Paul reveals intimate details of what his apostleship meant to him. He has a deep conviction of his mission to preach (1 Cor 1.17; 9.16: "...Woe to me if I do not preach the gospel!"), of his privileged mission to reveal the Mystery (cf. Col 1.24-29; Eph 3.1-13). He knows that he is passing on a tradition (1 Cor 15.1-11). He senses the power of the Spirit in his words (1 Th 1.5; cf. Rom 1.16-17). He is aware of his role as an exemplar (1 Th 1.5-6; 1 Cor 4.1-4), imitated (1 Th 1.6) and to be imitated (2 Th 3.7, 9; 1 Cor 4.16; 11.1). He speaks with courage (1 Th 2.2), without flattery or greed (1 Th 2.5). He feels a nurse's gentleness (1 Th 2.7), the anguish of a mother in travail (Gal 4.19), fear and trembling (1 Cor 2.3), yet a sense that he has received a wisdom from the Spirit, which he imparts to those who have the Spirit (1 Cor 2.6-14), a conviction that he has the mind of Christ (1 Cor 2.16), a relationship of father to those whom he has begotten in Christ Jesus through the gospel (1 Cor 4.15), a full awareness of the role of his suffering, affliction, weakness, being fool for Christ's sake, making himself all things to all men (cf. 1 Cor 4.9-13; 9.19-27). He reveals to the Philippians his deep affection for them: "For God is my witness, how I yearn for you all with the affection of Christ Jesus" (Phil 1.8), and how he was touched by their concern for him (4.10-14). One chapter must be read in its entirety for a unique revelation of Paul's inner life: 2 Cor 5.

[4] Finally I should point out an important aspect of Paul's apostolic experience: his sense of sharing his apostleship with

others. He mentions his co-workers, for example Apollos (cf.
1 Cor 3.5-9; 4.1-6). One could draw up a list of those
whom he regarded individually as sharing in his mission in some
way. Most striking, perhaps, is his sense of the role of the whole
bodies of believers in the churches whom Paul addresses. Here
again it is the Philippians who are outstanding (Phil 1.3-7;
4.10-19).

(b) Our mission and call to witness. This is the other side of
the coin of fellowship in the apostleship. It is illustrated in the
role of the Thessalonians (1 Th 1.6-10). In this fellowship Paul
witnesses to what I have called the dialectic of charisms [102], that
interplay of the roles of the apostle and of the children he has
begotten in Christ. Paul's impact on the Thessalonians is evident.
In turn, they are his "glory and joy" (1 Th 2.20). Paul's role and
that of the Thessalonians are complementary: they comfort him
and give him joy; he in turn prays earnestly that he may again see
them face to face and supply what is lacking in their faith (1 Th
3.9-10). Here again the most striking witness to a mutual
influence and enrichment is that which Paul gives regarding his
experience and that of the Philippians (Phil 4).

(25) *Reflections on belief and rightness.* I have
distinguished between an initial act of belief and a continuing role
of belief in the total process of living in Christ (above, pp.
271-277); and also between an initial or basic rightness and a
continuing development or process of rightness (above, pp.
256-257, 285-292). Now, in the light of our treatment of
fulfillment of the promise in us according to Paul, we may reflect
fruitfully on the roles of belief and the full sense of rightness.

(a) Belief. When we believe a person, our act has many
dimensions. We put credence in him or her; we accept the truth
of what is said or promised and we ourselves affirm it; we trust
the one who speaks or promises; we entrust ourselves to him or
her. All of these dimensions enter into our belief in God who
reveals and promises: we enter into a complex transcendent
interpersonal relationship. Within the limits of human speech
Paul expresses himself with the variety of cases and of
prepositional phrases at his disposal, and one can suspect his
feeling of frustration at the inadequacy of the linguistic and
conceptual resources which he can command and adapt. Our
belief in the God of Christian revelation is a multiple belief, a

---

[102] See *Basics*, pp. 198-212.

many-faceted belief in Father, Jesus Christ, and the Spirit dwelling within us and enlightening and moving us.

What do we believe? The whole gospel, which can be summed up in Jesus Christ: it is Jesus Christ whom Paul preaches. We believe *in* Jesus Christ. Our belief is *of* Jesus Christ: he is the sum of "what" we believe. So we have the irony of the expression belief *of* Jesus Christ, in which the "objective" genitive names a Person, not an object. We believe Christ.

From beginning to end, our act of belief has many dimensions. It has an important cognitive dimension: it is linked with knowledge, wisdom, revelation, discernment; it opens to us a new world of transcendent Reality. Yet it is not merely cognitive: it involves emotion, will, motor action in our total response to the revealing and promising God and his promise. In its cognitive dimension, until we die, belief has a role analogous with the natural role of intellect: penetrating all of our conscious life in the new higher realm which we have entered. Only in the light of revelation and by our belief can we be aware of, and discern and differentiate, all the dimensions of our experience of living in Christ: emotive, volitional. and motor. It permeates all, for only because we believe the whole gospel are we able to recognize the dimensions of our full response. We believe the whole gospel: all that Paul teaches as he develops all aspects of life in Christ and its implications. Ultimately we come full cycle: we believe not a set of propositions, but Jesus Christ, the full Reality of Christ and of the Mystery of Christ in us.

(b) Rightness. In the full sense, rightness is all that is involved in our being right with God, in right relation to Father, Jesus, and the Spirit: being as He/They will us to be from eternity. To believe in our initial act of belief is *right*, and our initial or basic rightness is from belief. To continue to respond fully to every aspect of the Mystery of our life in Christ is *right*. Our rightness, then, is a process, as we "... are being changed into his [Christ's] likeness from glory to glory [from one degree of glory to another]" (2 Cor 3.18). Our ideal goal is likeness to the Son, likeness to Christ, who *is* the Image. Our rightness, then, like what we believe, cannot be summed up in a set of propositions about us. Rather, it is the total reality of Christ in us, or our living in him. It is our *being right*, being as God eternally designs us to be in Christ (cf. Eph 1.3-14). It is the fulness of our glory: our share in, and manifestation of, the goodness of God. As such it is to the praise of his glory (Eph 1.6, 12, 14).

(26) *What God reveals of himself in us.* We can gather here in a few words the sum of all that we have seen of Paul's conception of fulfillment in us, and hold the answer to the question concerning God's self-revelation in us. To the extent that we respond fully to God's grace, his free gift, advancing from glory to glory, we become like Christ, who is the image of the Father. In the likeness of Christ, we are a manifestation of the kind of God who has graced and gifted us. We share in his goodness, we show it forth, we are living symbols, evoking in others a sense of a Mystery to be probed, a Mystery to which hopefully they too will respond, evoking a praise of the God whose master plan is worked out in us. We *are* to the praise of his glory.

FURTHER PROMISE

I shall not separate here what pertains to Jesus from what pertains to us, for both are blended in Paul's account of the final fulfillment. Moreover, what is involved is not just the final fulfillment of the promise, but also the final execution of the threat. Throughout this volume I have stressed promise and fulfillment, yet, as I noted at the outset, there is not a simple dialectic of promise, fulfillment, further promise, and final fulfillment. The dialectic of salvation history is contrapuntal: of promise and fulfillment, of threat and punishment [103]. I shall distinguish stages in Paul's account of what will come at the last day.

(1) *Jesus' coming.* Paul's most graphic portrayal of the coming is given ironically in his warning to the Thessalonians not to be shaken by any false report that the day of the Lord has come. He tells what will be involved in the approach to that event, and what Jesus will do. As one might expect, Paul's account of events which transcend all experience and all imagination takes on cosmic, apocalyptic dimensions (cf. 2 Th 2.1-11). Usually his mention of the coming is in simple and sober language regarding this aspect of our hope (cf. 1 Th 5.23-24; 1 Cor 1.7-9; 11.26; Phil 1.6).

(2) *Judgment.* Often Paul writes of both aspects of the judgment: reward and punishment (2 Th 1.5-10; Gal 6.8-9; Rom 2.5-11; and 2 Cor 5.1-10, with a stress on our hope).

---

[103] See above, pp. 50-51.

At times he regards only the judgment bringing reward (1 Cor 1.7-9; 4.5; 9.24-25).

(3) *Resurrection.* This is the most prominent element in Paul's teaching regarding our future hope (1 Th 4.13-18; 1 Cor 6.14; 2 Cor 4.13-14; Rom 6.8 [probably referring to our final resurrection]; Phil 3.11). In the course of his most extended teaching on the resurrection of the dead (1 Cor 15.12-58) Paul is not content to reply to a foolish question with his initial "You foolish man!" (v. 35). He goes on to give a highly imaginative account of the resurrection (vv. 36-55). Here, as in a more modest degree in 1 Th 4.13-18) imagination becomes bolder as the reality is more remote from all experience in this life.

(4) *A cluster of symbols representing aspects of the final fulfillment.* Salvation—definitive salvation—will be ours (cf. 1 Th 5.9; Rom 5.9-10; 13.11). The reward for rightness will be eternal life (cf. Rom 5.20-21; 6.22). When the perfect comes, the imperfect (our present knowledge) will pass away: we shall see face to face; love will remain: it never ends (cf. 1 Cor 13.8-13). God will bring his good work in us to completion (Phil 1.6; cf. vv. 10-11). Most prominent is eternal glory, a glory to be revealed in us, in which all creation will somehow share (cf. Rom 8.18-25; and simpler mentions of our own glory: Rom 5.2; 8.30 [taking *glorified* as designating the whole process terminating in final glory]; Phil 3.21). "When Christ our life appears, then you also will appear with him in glory" (Col 3.4). The mystery is "... Christ in you, the hope of glory" (Col 1.27). We shall have a heavenly dwelling, and be at home with God (cf. 2 Cor 5.1-10). We have a hope laid up in heaven (Col 1.5); we wait for the hope of rightness (Gal 5.5), our inheritance, of which the Spirit is a pledge (Eph 1.13-14). Paul presses on for the prize (Phil 3.14; cf. 1 Cor 9.24-27). God "... raised us up with him [Christ], and made us sit with him in the heavenly places in Christ Jesus, that in the coming ages he might show the immeasurable riches of his kindness toward us in Christ Jesus" (Eph 2.6-7). Our "... commonwealth is in heaven, and from it we await a Savior, the Lord Jesus Christ, who will change our lowly body to be like his glorious body, by the power which enables him even to subject all things to himself" (Phil 3.20-21).

(5) *Details of Paul's hope.* Even as he accepted remaining in the flesh for the sake of the Philippians, Paul's desire was "... to depart and be with Christ" (Phil 1.23). He desires that they be blameless and innocent, holding fast the word of life, "... so that in the day of Christ I may be proud that I did not run in vain or

labor in vain" (Phil 2.14-16). Similarly he tells the Thessalonians: "For what is our hope or joy or crown of boasting before our Lord Jesus at his coming: Is it not you? For you are our glory and joy" (1 Th 2.19-20).

(6) *The end:*

But in fact Christ has been raised from the dead, the first fruits of those who have fallen asleep. For as by a man came death, by a man has come also the resurrection of the dead. For as in Adam all die, so also in Christ shall all be made alive. But each in his own order: Christ the first fruits, then at his coming those who belong to Christ. Then comes the end, when he delivers the kingdom to God the Father after destroying every rule and every authority and power. For he must reign until he has put all his enemies under his feet. The last enemy to be destroyed is death. "For God has put all things in subjection under his feet." But when it says, "All things are put in subjection under him," it is plain that he is excepted who put all things under him. When all things are subjected to him, then the Son himself will also be subjected to him who put all things under him, that God may be everything to every one (1 Cor 15.20-28).

CHAPTER VIII

FURTHER WITNESS

I gather here some elements of *1 Peter*, *Hebrews*, and *Apocalypse* which are significant for complementary aspects of fulfillment of the promise in both Jesus and us. My treatment of these works, therefore, is very limited, much as they would deserve more ample consideration. They are important for my theme in this work, and I shall concentrate on those elements which enrich notably our understanding of Jesus and his role, and of dimensions of our present life and hope of final fulfillment. Happily these works have more in common than merely being "further witness". As we shall see, they have a certain affinity, and they complement one another in their treatment of the themes which I have selected for consideration.

1 PETER[1]

The principal complementary contribution of this letter, with regard to both Jesus and us, is its stress on priesthood and sacrifice.

With regard to Jesus, the note is struck in the greeting: "To the exiles of the Dispersion... chosen and destined by God the Father and sanctified by the Spirit for obedience to Jesus Christ and for *sprinkling with his blood*" (1.2). The implicit allusion to the sacrificial rite of covenant ratification in *Exodus* is highly suggestive: "... And Moses took the blood and threw it on the people, and said, 'Behold the blood of the covenant which the LORD has made with you...'" (24.8). That sprinkling with blood, and the covenant which it ratified, were types, figures foreshadowing the New Covenant ratified by the sacrificial death of Jesus. We "... were ransomed... with the precious blood of Christ, like that of a lamb without blemish or spot" (1.18-19).

---

[1] For a bibliography, introduction, and commentary see J. FITZMYER, "The First Epistle of Peter," JBC, II, 58, pp. 362-368.

He is the living stone, the cornerstone, of the spiritual house into which we, as living stones, are being built (2.4-8). Mixing his figures, Peter seems to glide into the notion of our being built into him as priest, to be a holy priesthood, whose spiritual sacrifices are acceptable to God through Jesus Christ (2.4-5). In his exhortation to suffer patiently for doing right, Peter not only holds up the example of Christ, who suffered for us (2.20-21), but clearly alludes to Christ's fulfillment of the figure of the Suffering Servant and his sacrificial suffering (2.22-24: cf. Is 53.4-12).

With regard to us, the most significant contribution of this letter is that of our own priestly and sacrificial character. In the context of the letter, our being sanctified by the Spirit and destined for sprinkling with the blood of Jesus Christ (1.2) and our being called to holiness (1.15-16) take on special meaning. As living stones, we are being built into a spiritual house (temple), to be a holy priesthood, to offer spiritual sacrifices acceptable to God through Jesus Christ. We "...are a chosen race, a royal priesthood, a holy nation, God's own people, that you may declare the wonderful deeds of him who called you out of darkness into his marvelous light. Once you were not people but now you are God's people; once you had not received mercy but now you have received mercy" (2.9-10). As a people we fulfill the type, the figure, of the Old Covenant: Israel as the people of God. And, in a transcendent manner in Christ, as a people we are destined to the worship of God and witness to his deeds.

I should single out some other details of this letter which enrich the conception of fulfillment in us. First, there is a precious explicit mention of our unique *love* of Jesus Christ: "Without having seen him you love him; though you do not now see him you believe in him and rejoice with unutterable and exalted joy" (1.8). Second, besides all of the examples of a Christian reading of Old Testament texts, and the implicit references to fulfillment in Christ, one strikes me as richly human and touching:

The prophets who prophesied of the grace that was to be yours searched and inquired about this salvation; they inquired what person or time was indicated by the Spirit of Christ within them when predicting the sufferings of Christ and the subsequent glory. It was revealed to them that they were serving not themselves but you, in the things which have now been announced to you by those who preached the good news to you through the Holy Spirit

sent from heaven, things into which angels long to look
(1.10-12).

In a letter which is recognized commonly as being intimately
linked with early baptismal liturgy[2], one passage particularly,
obscure as it is, highlights a dimension of baptism which is
important:

> That water is a type of the baptism which saves you now, and
> which is not the washing off of physical dirt but a *pledge* made to
> God *from* a good conscience, through the resurrection of Jesus
> Christ, ... (3.21: JB).
> Baptism, which corresponds to this, now saves you, not as a
> removal of dirt from the body, but as an *appeal* to God *for* a clear
> conscience. through the resurrection of Jesus Christ, ... (RSV).
> This water prefigured baptism through which you are now
> brought to safety. Baptism is not the washing away of bodily
> pollution, but the *appeal* made to God *by* a good conscience; and it
> brings salvation through the resurrection of Jesus Christ, ... (NEB).

Peter here is making the point of the role of baptism as antitype
(fulfillment) to the water of the flood as type, a tenuous enough
link. I am not concerned here with the obscure relationship
between being saved *from* the water of the flood and being saved
by the water of baptism. Nor am I concerned with the merits of
the translations except for their renditions of the words which I
have italicized. The key word here, occurring only once in the
New Testament, is ἐπερώτημα. Judging from the arguments
advanced by Selwyn and others, I regard the JB translation here
far more plausible. There are persuasive arguments for
regarding the word as a legal term, the equivalent of the Latin
stipulatio, stipulation, which was crucial in the clause of a contract
containing the formal question and consent of the contracting
parties. It echoes the stipulations of the covenant form traced in
the Old Testament. It is echoed in Tertullian's conception of
baptism on the analogy of the Roman military oath, and in
ancient and renewed baptism liturgy, in the renewal of the
baptismal promises in the Easter vigil[3].

---

[2] For an idea of the range of opinions in this matter, see FITZMYER, *op. cit.*,
4, p. 363.
[3] For the basic treatment, see EDWARD GORDON SELWYN, *The First Epistle of
St. Peter*[2] (London: Macmillan & Co., 1947, reprinted 1964) pp. 205-206. See
also JOSEPH CREHAN, S.J., *Early Christian Baptism and the Creed* (London: Burns

Preferable as *pledge* seems to be in this text, either translation suffices for the point which I wish to make here. Peter's "...gaze is fixed not on baptism as a past saving event, but on our present commitment, our future task, and the salvation still to be obtained. Baptism saves through the resurrection of Jesus Christ, but the central statement concerning baptism as an appeal or pledge looks to the present and the future...." [4]

Finally, prominent in 1 *Peter* is exhortation to endure trials as a test of the genuineness of our faith (1.6-7, 9). We are to suffer for doing right, imitating Christ (cf. 2.11-12, 19-25; 3.13-18; 4.1, 12-19).

HEBREWS

Considering Heb 1.1–4.13 above (pp. 108-110) as one of the great prologues which give profound theological answers to the question regarding Jesus: "Who *is* he?", I dwelt on the mystery of his divine sonship and his messiahship. Yet the "prologue" opened upon the mystery of his priesthood and sacrifice, and of the new and better Covenant which he mediated. It is to the cluster of themes, priesthood, sacrifice, covenant, that I turn now. They complement our knowledge of the mystery of Jesus himself, and of our own lives.

Though *Hebrews* has an admirable structure, and careful attention to that structure is essential to any full exegesis and commentary [5], one can gather and synthesize profitably elements which recur, and which contribute richly to our general theme of promise and fulfillment. With such a very limited scope, I propose to treat these prominent elements: (1) regarding Jesus,

---

Oates & Washbourne, 1950) pp. 10-12, 102-103, 110. BAG give as meanings of ἐπερώτημα (1) question; (2) request, appeal, or pledge, and for the latter refer to LSJ where evidence is cited of the equivalent of the Latin *stipulatio*, which means a promise given on demand; an engagement, agreement, bargain, covenant, stipulation, contract (cf. CHARLTON T. LEWIS and CHARLES SHORT, *A Latin Dictionary* (Oxford: Clarendon Press, 1879, printing of 1958). On Covenant in the ancient world and in the Old Testament, see DENNIS J. McCARTHY, S.J., *Treaty and Covenant*... New edition completely rewritten (Rome: Biblical Institute Press, 1978). For the stipulations in the O.T. covenant form, see pp. 170-172.

[4] *The Mystery*, pp. 229-230.

[5] See ALBERT VANHOYE, S.J., *La Structure Littéraire de l'Épitre aux Hébreux²*. Préface du R. P. STANISLAS LYONNET, S.J. (Paris: Desclée De Brouwer, 1976). Father Lyonnet's preface is notable.

his character as priest "for us"; the uniqueness of his priesthood, sacrifice, and covenant; and the manner in which his glorification is integrated into the mystery of his priesthood and sacrifice; (2) regarding us, several truths which ground the repeated exhortations which the author directs to his immediate addressees.

(1) *Regarding Jesus.* (a) Complementing other New Testament portrayals of Jesus, *Hebrews* brings out beautifully how Jesus is a priest *for us*:

> For it was fitting that he, for whom and by whom all things exist, in bringing many sons to glory, should make the pioneer of their salvation perfect through suffering. For he who sanctifies and those who are sanctified have all one origin. That is why he is not ashamed to call them brethren....
> Since therefore the children share in flesh and blood, he himself likewise partook of the same nature, that through death he might destroy him who has the power of death, that is, the devil, and deliver all those who through fear of death were subject to lifelong bondage. For surely it is not with angels that he is concerned but with the descendants of Abraham. Therefore he had to be made like his brethren in every respect, so that he might become a merciful and faithful high priest in the service of God, to make expiation for the sins of the people. For because he himself has suffered and been tempted, he is able to help those who are tempted (2.10-11, 14-18).

> For we have not a high priest who is unable to sympathize with our weaknesses, but one who in every respect has been tempted as we are, yet without sinning (4.15).

Jesus has this in common with all high priests appointed to act on behalf of men: "He can deal gently with the ignorant and wayward, since he himself is beset with weakness" (5.2). So,

> In the days of his flesh, Jesus offered up prayers and supplications with loud cries and tears, to him who was able to save him from death, and he was heard for his godly fear. Although he was a Son, he learned obedience through what he suffered; and being made perfect he became the source of eternal salvation to all who obey him, ... (5.7-9).

He "... has gone as a forerunner on our behalf..." (6.20).

(b) Priesthood, sacrifice, and covenant. In a unique reading of Ps 110.4, the author sees in God's words Jesus' appointment to a unique priesthood: "Thou art a priest for ever, after the order

of Melchizedek'' (5.5). In the course of his long contrast between
the Levitical priesthood and this new priesthood (7.1-28), the
author returns to the full text of Ps 110.4 to mark another
difference between them: the Levitical priests took office without
an oath; this priesthood is confirmed by a divine oath: "The Lord
has sworn and will not change his mind, 'Thou are a priest for
ever'" (7.21).

In an argument which is spread through much of the book,
the author demonstrates the excellence of Jesus' priesthood, as
contrasted with the Levitical, which for brevity I shall indicate as
"old" and "new". The old was by carnal descent (7.16; cf. vv.
11, 14); the new, God's Son, appointed by God (5.5-6; 7.17,
21; cf. the tenuous argument on Melchizedek, 7.1-17). The
old could not attain perfection (7.11), but was weak and useless
(7.18); the new introduces a better hope, through which we
draw near to God (7.19), made a purification for sins (1.3);
priests of the old took office without an oath; the new priest was
addressed by God in an oath (7.20-21); priests of the old were
many, because they were mortal (7.23); Jesus "...holds his
priesthood permanently, because he continues for ever.
Consequently he is able for all time to save those who draw near
to God through him, since he always lives to make intercession
for them" (7.24-25). The old, high priests chosen from
among men, had to offer sacrifice for their own sins as well as
for those of the people (cf. 5.1, 3). Jesus is "...a high priest,
holy, blameless, unstained, separated from sinners, exalted
above the heavens. He has no need, like those high priests, to
offer sacrifices daily, first for his own sins and then for those of
the people; he did this once for all when he offered up himself.
Indeed, the law appoints men in their weakness as high priests,
but the word of the oath, which came later than the law,
appoints a Son who has been made perfect for ever"
(7.26-28). The old served a copy and shadow of the heavenly
sanctuary (8.5); the new high priest is seated at the right hand of
the throne of Majesty in heaven, a minister in the sanctuary and
the true tent which is set up not by man but by the Lord
(8.1-2). The old served a faulty, obsolete covenant (8.7-9;
13); the new has obtained a ministry which is as much more
excellent than the old as the covenant which he mediates is
better, enacted on better promises (8.6, 10-12). Again and
again the author insists on the excellence of the new covenant:
9.15; 12.24; 13.20. A change in the priesthood necessarily
entails a change in the law (cf. 7.12).

Comparison of priesthoods and covenants leads to a comparison of the sacrifices by which they were ratified. The old was ratified by the blood of calves and goats (9.18-22); its sacrifices could not perfect the conscience of the worshiper (cf. 9.9); its priest stood at his service daily, offering repeatedly the same sacrifices, which can never take away sins (10.11). Now Christ has entered into heaven itself, to appear in the presence of God on our behalf once for all at the end of the age to put away sin by the sacrifice of himself (cf. 9.24-26). He offered his own blood, thus securing an eternal redemption (9.12):

> For if the sprinkling of defiled persons with the blood of goats and bulls and with the ashes of a heifer sanctifies for the purification of the flesh, how much more shall the blood of Christ, who through the eternal Spirit offered himself without blemish to God, purify your conscience from dead works to serve the living God. Therefore he is the mediator of a new covenant, so that those who are called may receive the promised eternal inheritance, since a death has occurred which redeems them from the transgressions under the first covenant (9.11-15).

> For it is impossible that the blood of bulls and goats should take away sins. Consequently, when Christ came into the world, he said,
> > "Sacrifices and offerings thou hast not desired,
> > but a body thou hast prepared for me;
> > in burnt offerings and sin offerings thou hast taken no pleasure.
> > Then I said, 'Lo, I have come to do thy will, O God,'
> > as it is written of me in the roll of the book."....
> He abolishes the first in order to establish the second. And by that will we have been sanctified through the offering of the body of Jesus Christ once for all.... when Christ had offered for all time a single sacrifice for sins, he sat down at the right hand of God, then to wait until his enemies should be made a stool for his feet. For by a single offering he has perfected for all time those who are sanctified. And the Holy Spirit also bears witness to us; for after saying,
> > "This is the covenant that I will make with them
> > after those days, says the Lord:
> > I will put my laws on their hearts,
> >   and write them on their minds,"
> then he adds,
> > "I will remember their sins and their misdeeds no more."
> Where there is forgiveness of these, there is no longer any offering for sin (10.4-7, 9-10, 12-18).

(c) Sacrifice and glorification. Unique as he is in his treatment of Jesus' priesthood, sacrifice, and mediation of a new covenant, the author of *Hebrews* is perhaps more remarkable in his integration of Jesus' glorification into the total mystery of his sacrifice and heavenly ministry. Perhaps one could speak more properly of a sort of dialectic or interplay of elements which is unique in the theology of this writer. I shall distinguish two sets of elements of his teaching: [1] general statements about Jesus' glorification; [2] stages in a unique theological conception.

[1] General statements:

> When he had made purification for sins, he sat down at the right hand of the Majesty on high, having become as much superior to angels as the name he has obtained is more excellent than theirs (1.3-4).
> For it was not to angels that God subjected the world to come, of which we are speaking. It has been testified somewhere,
>> "What is man that thou art mindful of him,
>> or the son of man, that thou carest for him?
>> Thou didst make him for a little while
>>   lower than the angels,
>> thou hast crowned him with glory and honor,
>> putting everything in subjection under his feet."
> Now in putting everything in subjection to him, he left nothing outside his control. As it is, we do not yet see everything in subjection to him. But we see Jesus, who for a little while was made lower than angels, crowned with glory and honor because of the suffering of death, so that by the grace of God he might taste death for every one (2.5-9).
> ...Jesus the pioneer and perfecter of our faith, who for the joy that was set before him endured the cross, despising the shame, and is seated at the right hand of the throne of God (12.2).

These statements regarding Jesus' glorification fit easily into the pattern of other New Testament writings.

[2] Stages in a unique theological conception. First, *Hebrews* makes only one mention of the resurrection, of Jesus' rising or being raised, and it comes only in a subordinate clause in the closing blessing, in a formulation which is linked with the central theme of the book: "Now may the God of peace who *brought back again from the dead our Lord Jesus... by the blood of the eternal covenant....*" (13.20). For the rest, what in other New Testament witness regards the resurrection is conceived of as a stage in the culmination of Jesus' sacrifice: on the analogy of the high priest entering once yearly into the earthly Holy of Holies to

complete his sacrifice by offering blood for himself and the sins of
the people (9.1-10), Jesus "...entered once for all into the Holy
Place [heaven: cf. 9.24], taking not the blood of goats and calves
but his own blood, thus securing an eternal redemption" (9.12).
The sacrifice is not consummated on the cross, but Jesus enters
heaven (cf. 4.14) to complete his sacrifice with the offering of his
blood. Then, when he had offered for all time a single sacrifice
for sins, "...he sat down at the right hand of God, then to wait
until his enemies should be made a stool for his feet"
(10.12-13). He is in honor and glory at the right hand of God,
though not all is subject to him as yet. His ministry is
consummated, therefore, in heaven, and yet it does not end with
the offering of his blood and his sitting in honor at the right hand
of God. He "...holds his priesthood permanently, because he
continues for ever. Consequently he is able for all time to save
those who draw near to God through him, since he always lives to
make intercession for them" (7.24-25).

(2) *Regarding us.* I should single out four elements which
regard the author's addressees, and eventually us. Two, dealing
with antecedents, are treated briefly. Two deal with the author's
urgent present concern: his fellow-believers' present disposition,
and action consistent with it.

(a) God's call, and Christ's radical act on our behalf. We
share in a heavenly call (3.1). By his action as our great high
priest Jesus delivered us (2.15), purified us (1.3; 9.14), redeemed
us (cf. 9.12), sanctified us. These effects of Jesus' action pertain
to what theologians later would call "objective redemption": the
redemption or salvation accomplished radically by his action, but
still to be appropriated by men and women personally in the
course of time.

(b) The beginnings of personal belief and share in Christ. It
is only obliquely and in passing that the author refers to what I
have called the initial, radical act of personal faith, in treating
Paul's thought[6]. We share in Christ (3.14): only implicit in this
statement is the fact that at some point in our lives we *came* to
share in Christ; the author's concern here is holding firm to the
end. We have believed (4.3). The actions involved in the
foundations lie behind: repentance, faith, ablutions, and laying on
of hands, being enlightened, tasting the heavenly gift, becoming
partakers of the Holy Spirit, tasting the goodness of the word of

---

[6] See above, pp. 271-277.

God and the powers of the age to come (cf. 6.1-2, 4-5). We
have received the knowledge of the truth (10.26), have been
enlightened (10.32).

(c) Our present disposition: faith, confidence, and perseverance.

[1] Faith and confidence. Moving to the heart of the matter,
I turn first to the capital text: "Now faith is the assurance of
things hoped for, the conviction of things not seen" (11.1)[7]. The
two key words in the Greek text are ὑπόστασις and ἔλεγχος. The
former has a wide range of meanings in classical Greek [8]. For the
five instances in which it occurs in the New Testament, BAG give
two meanings: (1) substantial nature, essence, actual being,
reality; (2) confidence, conviction, assurance, steadfastness. They
apply the first to Heb 1.3; the second to 2 Cor 9.4; 11.17 and Heb
3.14; 11.1. ἔλεγχος, more remote from its origins in early Greek,
is given by BAG as having three meanings: (1) proof, proving; (2)
conviction (of a sinner); (3) reproof, censure, correction. Its
meaning in Heb 11.1, the sole instance in the New Testament,
seems to be derived from the first meaning: corresponding to a
proof or proving is the inner conviction of the person satisfied
with the proof. I should say that the verse involves a double
parallelism: of the nouns, and of the their corresponding objective
genitives, rendered by the prepositional phrases in translation.
Assurance and conviction are aspects of the abiding personal
disposition, as they are of the initial act of faith. Hoped for and
unseen are aspects of the reality which is part of what is believed,
both in the initial act and in the continuing disposition.
Consistently with the whole thrust of the author's argument, and
with the long list of illustrious examples given in chapter eleven,
faith is abiding personal assurance and conviction, holding firmly
to things hoped for, as yet unseen.

It strikes me that by a strange irony the word ὑπόστασις,
which seems originally to have meant *standing under*, as an act,
and then in the course of use *foundation*, and which passed
through a long history of philosophical and post-philosophical
usage as *substance* (with who knows how many different shades
of meaning, and degrees of sharpness or vagueness of conception)
here comes full cycle as it is applied to a transcendent new world.
Faith, both as initial act and as abiding disposition, regards things

---

[7] For an excellent concise treatment of this verse, and of its various interpretations, see MYLES M. BOURKE, "The Epistle to the Hebrews," JBC, II,
61:62, p. 401.

[8] Cf. LSJ.

hoped for, as yet unseen, and is the foundation, base, under-
pinning, bedrock of all Christian living.

[2] Perseverance. Much of *Hebrews* is exhortation, for the
author's purpose seems clearly not to elaborate a theological
treatise for its own sake, or simply for teaching, but to save his
fellow-believers from falling away. Commentators outline the
book differently, as one would expect[9]. Though the author
blends rich theology and fervent exhortation, and grounds his
exhortation on the reality of the world which we know by faith, I
should say that the following portions of the work are
predominantly hortatory: 2.14; 3.1 – 4.16; 5.11 – 6.20; 10.19-
39; 11.1 – 13.22.

I shall not attempt to detail the exhortation or the doctrinal
motivation. I do consider that the whole of *Hebrews*, with its
distinctive theology and its urgent exhortation, is a rich
complement to other New Testament writings. In its entirety it
contributes profound insights into the Christian Mystery, and into
those aspects of Christian living, of trial and temptation and near
despair which necessitate a profound meditation upon our many
motives for belief, confidence, and perseverance.

The long exhortation grounded on the examples of great men
and women of the Old Testament is a striking example of Christian
reading of the Bible. In the midst of his long recital, the author
gives an example of what I have called elsewhere "a remarkable bit
of phenomenology before its time" (above, p. 280):

> These all died in faith, not having received what was promised, but
> having seen it and greeted it from afar, and having acknowledged
> that they were strangers and exiles on the earth. For people who
> speak thus make it clear that they are seeking a homeland. If they
> had been thinking of that land from which they had gone out, they
> would have had the opportunity to return. But, as it is, they
> deserve a better country, that is, a heavenly one. Therefore God is
> not ashamed to be called their God, for he has prepared for them a
> city (11.13-16).

And he concludes:

> And all these, though well attested by their faith, did not receive
> what was promised, since God had foreseen something better for
> us, that apart from us they should not be made perfect
> (11.39-40).

---

[9] Two examples are the work of Vanhoye which I have cited, and the
outline given by Bourke in the brief commentary in JBC, 6, pp. 282-283.

As a Christian reading of the Bible goes beyond the mind and the intention of the human author of an earlier age, and reads God's meaning as it is projected by the whole of the Bible, somewhat similarly I should grant readily that the author of *Hebrews* reads into the minds of these great men and women of the past thoughts which they could never have formulated thus. In doing this, he is like Peter, interpreting the minds of the prophets (1 Pt 1.10-12). Both go far beyond what we could possibly verify. Yet both express a deep truth: the beauty and the pathos of those ancient men and women on the one hand, and the humiliating riches for which God has destined us on the other. Both deepen our insight into the great Reality, the Mystery. Both should draw us to the full response to God's gift to us.

(d) The action to which we are called. I am dealing here with parts of the exhortation: the action to which the author calls his fellow-believers and us, action which is a response to those aspects of the Mystery which he develops in his rich theology of Jesus' priesthood, sacrifice, covenant, and of the reality of our present situation.

Holding firm in our faith, we are to enter into the rest which God prepared for those who would believe, and not fall away in disobedience (cf. 3.7 – 4.11).

> Since then we have a great high priest who has passed through the heavens, Jesus, the Son of God, let us hold fast our confession .... Let us then with confidence draw near to the throne of grace, that we may receive mercy and find grace to help in time of need (4. 14, 16).

> Therefore, brethren, since we have confidence to enter the sanctuary by the blood of Jesus, by the new and living way which he opened for us through the curtain, that is, through his flesh, and since we have a great priest over the house of God, let us draw near with a true heart in full assurance of faith, with our hearts sprinkled clean from an evil conscience and our bodies washed with pure water. Let us hold fast the confession of our hope without wavering, for he who promised is faithful; and let us consider how to stir one another to love and good works, not neglecting to meet together, as is the habit of some, but encouraging one another, and all the more as you see the Day drawing near (10.19-25).

> For you have not come to what may be touched, a blazing fire, and darkness, and gloom, and a tempest, and the sound of a trumpet, and a voice whose words made the hearers entreat that no further messages be spoken to them .... But you have come to Mount Zion and to the city of the living God, the heavenly Jerusalem, and

to innumerable angels in festal gathering, and to the assembly of the first-born who are enrolled in heaven, and to a judge who is God of all, and to the spirits of just men made perfect, and to Jesus, the mediator of a new covenant, and to the sprinkled blood that speaks more graciously than the blood of Abel (12.18-19, 22-24).

We are to "... offer to God acceptable worship, with reverence and awe; for our God is a consuming fire" (12.28-29). Through him [Jesus] then let us continually offer up a sacrifice of praise, that is, the fruit of lips that acknowledge his name. Do not neglect to do good and to share what you have, for such sacrifices are pleasing to God" (13.15-16).

What strikes me in the texts which I have quoted here is that the *action* to which we are called corresponds to that of Jesus our high priest. It is a blend of worship, sacrifice, and of obedience. The distinctive note of *Hebrews* in its treatment of Jesus is his unique priesthood, sacrifice, and covenant. Yet, in abolishing the old sacrifices and offering the new: his own body, his blood, himself, Jesus is presented as saying: "... 'Lo, I have come to do thy will, O God,' as it is written of me in the roll of the book" (10.7: cf. Ps 40.7-8: 39.8-9 in the LXX). So too, we are to worship, to enter into the sanctuary; yet our worship involves obedience. We are the people of God, with a new priesthood, a new covenant, a new law. We are set aside for the worship of God, and obedience is itself part of that worship.

APOCALYPSE

This closing book of the Bible is a revelation which *God* gave: a revelation of Jesus Christ, given through God's angel and John to the seven churches, of what must take place soon. The *seven* churches seem symbolic of the universal church: the revelation is for all. It is a revelation of what must take place *soon*. Yet it is not a cosmography and detailed prediction of events easily to be identified and a timetable of their occurrence. Thrusting beyond all human experience into an unknown future and a fulfillment which transcends all human imagination and conception, *Apocalypse*, like all apocalyptic literature, is fashioned in powerful intuitive symbols, by which it makes a massive impact and evokes a massive total response to a transcendent Reality.

Five complex symbols or clusters of symbols strike me as dominant. They strike me as rich complements to our whole account of promise and fulfillment.

(1) *God.* God, who gives this revelation, dominates it, and a multiple symbolism suggests powerfully his absolute transcendence, and his lordship over the whole of world process culminating in this prophetic vision of its culmination.

(a) The names. He is "who is and who was and who is to come" (1.4: cf. in whole or in part the name as given in 1.8; 4.8; 11.17; 16.5). Translations of the name (roughly the same in RSV, JB, and NEB) smooth over the roughness of the Greek[10]. The formula as it stands here bears the influence of rabbinical exegesis of "I am" (Ex 3.14) and translations of the divine name in the LXX. Significantly we come full cycle to the divine name "I am". The force of the name is heightened by the characterization of the beast: it "... was, and is not, and is to ascend ... and go to perdition ... was and is not and is to come ... was and is not, ... and goes to perdition" (17.8, 11).

Other names and titles are "the Alpha and the Omega" (1.8), repeated with additions: "the beginning and the end" (21.6), "the first and the last, the beginning and the end" (22.13); the Almighty (1.8); the living God (7.2; cf. 4.9-10; 10.6; 15.7); the Holy (16.5). He created heaven and what is in it, the earth and what is in it, and the sea and what is in it (10.6: cf. 4.11).

(b) Two unique symbols express the degree of awe which his presence inspires: the open door (4.1) and silence in heaven for about half an hour (8.1).

(c) His majesty and supremacy are symbolized particularly by the repeated description of him as the one seated on the throne (4.2 and throughout the book).

(d) In the terrible play of forces depicted, God has absolute control. It is his secret purposes which are revealed in the opening of the scrolls, and by his will that the forces are released (5 ff.) and that harm is done (cf. 7.3). The kingdom is his (11.15-19; 12.10).

---

[10] ὁ ὢν καὶ ὁ ἦν καὶ ὁ ἐρχόμενος. If one were to attempt to match in English the violence done to the Greek, it would be possible in part by some such rendition: "the being [taken as participle expressing being, existing without qualification], the 'was-ing' [an imperfect indicative taken as a participle expressing being in the past], the coming". One cannot reproduce in English the anomaly of nominatives used in place of genitives as objects of ἀπὸ, *from.* For the latter, see BDF, § 143; for the former, BAG, on εἰμί, I.1.

(e) In words that echo the covenant formula, he will dwell with them, and they shall be his people (cf. 21.3-8).

(f) In the new heaven and the new earth (21.1), in the holy city, the new Jerusalem coming down out of heaven (21.2, 10-21) there is no temple: no symbol of God's presence: "... for its temple is the Lord God the Almighty and the Lamb. And the city has no need of sun or moon to shine upon it, for the glory of God is its light, and its lamp is the Lamb" (21.22-23).

(2) *Jesus Christ.* (a) Images. Two major images recur: "one like a son of man" and the Lamb; a third is the one sitting on a white horse.

> ...I saw seven golden lampstands, and in the midst of the lampstands one like a son of man, clothed with a long robe and with a girdle around his breast; his head and his hair were white as white wool, white as snow; his eyes were like a flame of fire, his feet were like burnished bronze, refined as in a furnace, and his voice was like the sound of many waters; in his right hand he held seven stars, from his mouth issued a sharp two-edged sword, and his face was like the sun shining in full strength. When I saw him, I fell at his feet as though dead. But he laid his right hand upon me, saying, "Fear not, I am the first and the last, and the living one; I died, and behold I am alive for evermore, and I have the keys of Death and Hades (1.12-18).

> Then I looked, and lo, a white cloud, and seated on the cloud one like a son of man, with a golden crown on his head, and a sharp sickle in his hand (14.14).

Details of the two portrayals blend to characterize this fulfillment of the apocalyptic vision of Daniel in a figure who has symbols of divine attributes, of a conqueror, and of an eschatological judge (cf. Dan 7.9-14; 10.4-11; Mk 14.62).

The second image portrayed, and then prevailing throughout the book is that of the Lamb:

> And between the throne and the four living creatures and among the elders, I saw a Lamb standing, as though it had been slain, with seven horns and with seven eyes, which are the seven spirits of God sent out into all the earth; and he went and took the scroll from the right hand of him who was seated on the throne. And when he had taken the scroll, the four living creatures and the twenty-four elders fell down before the Lamb, each holding a harp, and with golden bowls full of incense, which are the prayers of the saints; and they sang a new song, saying,

> "Worthy are thou to take the scroll
> and to open its seals,
> for thou wast slain and by thy blood
> didst ransom men for God
> from every tribe and tongue and
> people and nation,
> and hast made them a kingdom and
> priests to our God,
> and they shall reign on earth"...

"Worthy is the Lamb who was slain, to receive power and wealth and wisdom and might and honor and glory and blessing!" And I heard every creature in heaven and on earth and under the earth and in the sea, and all therein, saying, "To him who sits upon the throne and to the Lamb be blessing and honor and glory and might for ever and ever!" And the four living creatures said, "Amen!" and the elders fell down and worshipped (5.6-14).

Two details of the symbolism are especially significant: the Lamb who had been slain is *standing*: risen, victorious; he is worshipped along with the One seated on the throne. Both as *standing*, victorious over death, and as implicitly divine, he gives assurance of final victory in the impending struggles.

The third image is the rider on the white horse. He may be the same as the rider in 6.2, who "... had a bow; and a crown was given to him, and he went out conquering and to conquer." In any case, the rider in 19.11-16 is clearly Christ, and the symbol is rich in detail. I shall not quote the text here, but shall indicate details of the imagery in the following sections.

(b) Titles, names, attributes. He is "... Jesus Christ the faithful witness, the first-born of the dead, and the ruler of kings on earth (1.5). He is "... the first and the last, and the living one; ..." (1.17-18); "the holy one, the true one, who has the key of David, who opens and no one shall shut, who shuts and no one opens" (3.7); "the Lion of the tribe of Judah, the Root of David" (5.5); "the Lamb standing" (5.6); "shepherd" (7.17); "Lord of lords and King of kings" (17.14; cf. 19.16; cf. 11.15: the kingdom is of our Lord and of his Christ); "Faithful and True" (19.11); "... he has a name inscribed which no one knows but himself" (19.12); "... the name by which he is called is The Word of God" (19.13).

(c) Victory achieved before the end: the effects of his victory. He "... has conquered, so that he can open the scroll and its seven seals" (5.5). Though he was slain, he is standing (cf. 5.6). Hence is he celebrated in a new song:

> "Worthy art thou to take the scroll
>   and to open its seals,
> for thou wast slain and by thy blood
>   didst ransom men for God
> from every tribe and tongue and people and nation,
> and hast made them a kingdom and priests to our God,
> and they shall reign on earth" (5.9-10).

Already he is worthy "... to receive power and wealth and wisdom and might and honor and glory and blessing" (5.12); and he is worshiped together with the one who sits on the throne (5.13-14). Those who are clothed in white robes (7.9, 13) "... are they who have come out of the great tribulation; they have washed their robes and made them white in the blood of the Lamb" (7.14). The Lamb in the midst of the throne will be their shepherd and he will guide them to springs of living water (7.17). After the passing of the second woe, "... there were loud voices in heaven, saying, 'The kingdom of the world has become the kingdom of our Lord and of his Christ, and he shall reign for ever and ever'" (11.15; cf. vv. 17-19). After Michael's defeat of the dragon, called the Devil and Satan, and his angels, there was a loud voice in heaven, saying, "Now the salvation and the power and the kingdom of our God and the authority of his Christ have come, for the accuser of our brethren has been thrown down, who accuses them day and night before our God. And they have conquered him by the blood of the Lamb and by the word of their testimony, for they loved not their lives even unto death..." (12.10-11).

(d) Final victory. After a succession of violent conflicts and outpourings of the wrath of God (15-16), judgment and fall of Babylon [Rome], victory over the beast and the false prophet, and first and final victory over the Devil (Satan)—all portrayed by symbolism of the greatest physical violence—there is, it seems to me, a powerful contrasting symbolism in the final victory. It is simply by word: what is written in the book of life. Beyond all physical power, all physical violence, is the transcendent power of the word of God.

(e) Marriage of the Lamb and consummation. In a strangely incoherent account, the marriage of the Lamb is announced as having come (19.6-9) prior to the last triumphs. In fact it comes with the coming of a new heaven and a new earth, and the descent of the holy city, the new Jerusalem, the Bride, the wife of the Lamb; and the description of the new Jerusalem and of the

life and worship of the blessed are merged (21.1 – 22.5). Here
again, after the most extravagant symbolism expressing the
beauty of the city, the transcendent wonder is achieved by the
elimination of all symbolism. There is no temple, symbol of the
divine presence: its temple is the Lord God the Almighty and the
Lamb. There is no sun or moon or light of lamp: the glory of
God is its light, and its lamp is the Lamb; the Lord God will be
their light (21.22-23; 22.5).

(3) *The contrapuntal dialectic.* I am concerned here with
clusters and at times swirling masses of symbols which portray the
awesome interplay of cosmic and metacosmic forces "now" and to
the end. Significantly the author presents himself as "... your
brother, who share with you the tribulation and the kingdom and
the patient endurance ..." (1.9): a strange sequence. One might
have expected him to reverse the order of the first two things
which they share. In any case, with these words he somehow
sounds the theme of this book. First in the letters to the seven
churches (the universal church) he bears word of the blend of
praise and blame, of promise and threat, and the call to hold fast,
to conquer, and to be rewarded. Then, in the greater part of the
book, the eschatological and apocalyptic visions, the scale of the
conflict is amplified beyond imagination. I shall not go into
detail: to a certain extent I have done so in the preceding section.
Rather I suggest what seems to me to be the meaning and the
scope of the whole symbolism. I think that is is this: "the
breadth and the length, the height and the depth" of the Reality,
the "world", the universe of being in which we *are*, in which
salvation history is in process. Supreme is the figure of God, the
one seated on the throne, whose will prevails over all opposition.
Great protagonist is the Lamb, who has conquered and will
conquer, has been slain and is standing. It is the vision of them,
and of those who have already conquered by the blood of the
Lamb, which is to give us courage and strength. The forces at
play are more than cosmic: they transcend the physical universe
and all human power. Successions of the most vivid symbolisms
represent both the consummation of evil and the deployment of
even greater violence by God and the Lamb in conquering them.
Yet somehow all this symbolism, in my judgment, palls and cloys.
Far more powerful, far more suggestive of the wonderful Reality,
are the open door, the silence for a half hour, the word of
judgment in which the victory is consummated. Far more
powerful than all the vivid symbolisms representing the marvels
of the new Jerusalem is the surpassing of symbols: there will be

no temple, no sun or moon or lamp: God is the temple, God is the light.

(4) *Worship.* One of the principal purposes of the book, as I read it, is to emphasize worship. The opening vision of the glory of God and of the Lamb portrays the heavenly scene, with a superabundance of vivid symbols, and exuberant hymns of praise. Those ransomed for God by the blood of the Lamb have been made a kingdom of priests to our God, and they shall reign on earth (cf. 5.9-11). Yet I am struck by three anomalies. First, though the Lamb was slain, and conquered, and those who are ransomed have been ransomed by the blood of the Lamb, it is difficult to establish that Jesus Christ, the Lamb, is himself a priest: victim yes implicitly, but not priest[11]. Second, the book gives no sense of the communion of saints, of continuity and community of the church on earth and the ransomed in heaven. Third, for all the riches of symbolism, the book strikes me as coldly impersonal. We are given the account of visions of a great mass of worshipers, sealed with the seal of the living God, washed in the blood of the Lamb, white-robed, worshiping in unison, falling down in adoration and singing stylized hymns of praise.

(5) *Absolute transcendence.* In two stages the book suggests the absolute transcendence of the consummation, an absolute heterogeneity and discontinuity with earthly reality. The first is the symbolism by which both forces, of good and evil, exceed all limits of human experience on earth: a symbolism of terror and wonder which surpass all imagination and understanding. The second is the stage of the consummation itself, in which the new heaven and the new earth, the new Jerusalem descending from heaven, exceed all symbolism. God and the Lamb are its temple and its light.

COMPARISON AND CONTRAST

At the outset of this chapter I wrote that happily the three books treated here have more in common than being "Further

---

[11] The matter is obscure, and exegetes differ. See ALBERT VANHOYE, S.J., *Prêtres anciens prêtre nouveau selon le N. T.* (Paris: Éditions du Seuil, 1980) esp. pp. 309-320; UGO VANNI, S.J., "Il simbolismo nell'Apocalisse," *Gregorianum* 61 (1980), esp. pp. 477, 495. Arguments to establish that Christ is the high priest of the N. T. according to Ap involve deciphering arcane symbolism, and leave me unconvinced.

Witness''. All of them have this in common: they serve to complement the conceptions of fulfillment of the promise set forth in the other biblical theologies of the New Testament which I have considered. In doing so, however, they also complement one another, for they differ greatly among themselves. I shall compare and contrast their treatment of three themes.

First, priesthood and sacrifice. 1 *Peter* stresses both Christ's priesthood and ours. We are a royal priesthood, to offer spiritual sacrifices through Jesus Christ. *Hebrews* develops the richest and most distinctive theology of Christ's high priesthood and of the consummation of his sacrifice by the offering of his own blood in the heavenly sanctuary, where he remains priest for ever, making intercession for us. Moreover *Hebrews* brings out most beautifully how he is a priest *for us*, is in solidarity with us, sharing our weakness, and having compassion. Having *such* a priest, we are inspired to hold fast our confession, to draw near with confidence, to enter into the sanctuary by the blood of Jesus. In *Apocalypse*, those ransomed by the blood of the Lamb have been made a kingdom of priests; but, though the Lamb implicitly is a sacrificial victim, no mention is made of his being a priest.

Second, heavenly liturgy. In *Hebrews* Christ's sacrifice is consummated in heaven, and our worship is in continuity with his. *Apocalypse* repeatedly portrays the worship offered to God and to the Lamb; yet there is no clear suggestion of a priestly role of Christ, nor of any real continuity of our worship with theirs. Consequently, *Hebrews* can enrich our Eucharist; *Apocalypse* can enrich us with a deep sense of the transcendent world in which we are and in which we worship, but it suggests nothing concerning our worship, in particular our Eucharist, as the unique saving sacrifice of Christ.

Third, trials and endurance. All three books stress trial, and exhort to endurance and conquering. Yet they do so in very different ways, and, I should say, with varying efficacy. Warmest, most personal and compassionate, and most effective in my judgment is *Hebrews*. 1 *Peter* is unique in recognizing love of Jesus Christ as a motive; yet the argument that it is better to suffer for doing right than for doing wrong is, in my judgment, a bit thin. In *Apocalypse* one must distinguish between the letters to the churches and the eschatological-apocalyptic visions. In the former, there is a certain compassion, but on the whole I should say the tone is cold and impersonal, and the letters measure out praise and blame and the rather stiff exhortation to conquer and be rewarded. In the visions, which should strengthen us in trials by giving us a sense of the cosmic struggle in which we are living, the account of the vision of the Lamb and of the ransomed portrays them *there*, far remote from the reality of our lives, and I should say that only a profound personal appropriation in Christian experience could give *Apocalypse* a resonance and an efficacy in our lives.

CHAPTER IX

OPEN-ENDED PROMISE, FAITH, AND FULFILLMENT

I am near the end of the first phase of my Telling. The moment to pause has not yet come, for this chapter itself is part of the phase, which will end only when I shall have reflected upon my telling in this phase, and the meaning of what I have told. Without this reflection it would be impossible for you or for me to understand what I have been doing, and what we, hopefully, have been sharing; where I am or shall be, and you too, in as many different, uniquely personal ways as you are; and where I am to go and what I am to do, and hopefully you too, again all of us in our uniquely personal ways. For the promise is open-ended, and the belief, and the fulfillment, and so too the telling, which for every one of us will end only with death or the decline of powers.

I propose reflections: not a synthesis, not *a* biblical theology, not a conclusion. I shall come to a moment of pause in writing, but, God willing, not in living: in continuing total personal experience of the Mystery, in continuing response, and, within that response, in a continuing intellectual effort to elaborate the intelligible structure of the total experience, and of the experienced God.

What have I done? I have worked out a series of essays in biblical theology. I have explored our remaining traces of the personal worlds, subjective and objective, of the many writers whom God inspired to contribute to his book, to the elaboration of his great Symbol, the Bible. Every one of those writers has left the fragmentary witness to his world, the fragmentary account of what he has been able to grasp of the great Reality which the whole Bible, precious as it is, symbolizes inadequately. Sketchily for the clusters of Old Testament writers, more in detail for the New, I have worked out what seemed to me to be an intelligible structure of their thought, and of the Reality to which they witnesssed. What I have done represents the fruit of my own effort to understand. I offer it as one man's contribution, one man's series of guides to a fruitful reading of the Bible.

I do not propose a synthesis, or what might be conceived of as a general biblical theology. Perhaps someone could work out such a synthesis. I do not see that it is feasible, or even desirable. Every human writer of the Bible wrote from his unique point of view, his moment in the total process of a continuing salvation history, his insights and total personal experience of God and of the mystery of his saving action. The personal worlds of so many men, and their unique personal powers of symbolizing, must be respected. Their works cannot be homogenized. There is unity of the Bible, a twofold unity: in the mind of God the Author, and in the living faith of the Church and of the individual believer in the Church[1]. Obviously the two unities, or perhaps more properly the One and the many, are simply incommensurate. At any stage in the life of the individual believer and in the life of the whole Church, we hold the unity of the Bible and of the revealed truth only by holding what has been mediated to us by the individual human writers. And we are open to their mediation of what they have grasped and symbolized only to the extent to which we succeed in entering their personal worlds. We do not blend them. In a total living faith we hold what they witness individually together with what others have witnessed from other points of view. But there must be a moment when we seek truly to concentrate on Matthew, or John, or Paul, and understand what he is telling us within the context of his thought. In this first phase of my Telling, and this first volume, I have limited myself to the task of probing the work of individual writers, especially of the New Testament, and of elaborating an intelligible structure which may enable us to grasp the meaning of elements of their thought. This effort, which involves both exegesis and biblical theology, is indispensable as a preparation and a base for an eventual richer Christian reading of the Bible. Without it, we could engage in a pseudo-Christian flight of fancy and untrammeled subjectivity, cut off in fact from any authentic meaning of the text.

There is, then, an indispensable task, in which we dedicate ourselves in turn to determine the minds of the individual witnesses to the Reality, the Mystery. Yet, ironically, as we read them, we see them performing a function upon the thought of their predecessors, a function which we shall perform in another mode, in that Christian reading of the Bible to which we shall devote ourselves in the next phase of our work. In the Old Testament and more remarkably in the New, the inspired writers,

---

[1] See *Basics*, pp. 130-131.

enlightened by a further revelation and by the illumination of the
Holy Spirit, read a deeper, richer meaning in the words of their
predecessors, a meaning which goes far beyond what the original
author grasped and intended to communicate.

We shall never know in this life what the promise meant
originally to Abraham. In the New Testament account, we find
Jesus himself (Jn 8.56), Paul (Rom 4, esp. vv. 17-22), and the
author of *Hebrews* (11.8-16) reading the mind of Abraham. We
detect a gradual deepening and enrichment of the conception of
the promised good in the course of the Old Testament; yet surely
the fulfillment proclaimed by Peter on Pentecost and after
reversed all Israelite expectations. We shall never know in this
life how David understood the promise made to him, nor what
individual psalmists meant by the deliverance which they hailed,
to be wrought by a king. We do find New Testament writers
reading Old Testament texts as messianic, beyond all judaic
interpretation: they write in the light of a further revelation. We
can only surmise what Jesus meant when he told the Jews that
Moses wrote of him (Jn 5.46), or what texts of Scripture he cited
as he interpreted to the disciples in the scriptures all the things
concerning himself (Lk 24.27, 32). We can come to understand
the New Testament writers' thought only when we consider
within it their own Christian reading of the Scripture.

So much for my task in this first phase, this first volume of
my work. What do I mean by the title of this chapter?

Promise, faith, and fulfillment are all open-ended. We are
in process. Salvation history is process. From God's first word
of promise, through all successive partial fulfillments and further
promises, to the great fulfillment in Jesus Christ, and the further
promises of his Coming, judgment, and final consummation, the
meaning of the promise is continually unfolded. So too, until the
end, is the meaning of our faith and commitment.

In the total process we may distinguish three phases. The
first extends from the first word of promise to fulfillment in the
glorification of Jesus, in which all expectations are reversed. Jesus
transcends all that the Jews could have foreseen, and the reversal
of expectations for many is a stumbling block.

The second extends from the beginning of Jesus' revelation
through his glorification to the end of public revelation. It is a
period of privileged illumination and revelation in the apostolic
age: of a process of illumination and insight and formulation of
the gospel which is normative for all times, for all who will
believe. In this phase we must distinguish the full revelation

which *is* Jesus Christ in the fulness of his reality, in all that he is and does and says, and the many fragmentary revelations given to men and women of this age, and preserved mostly in the inspired works of the New Testament. Precious as these revelations are, and precious and privileged as the inspired works are, they are fragmentary and varied. All are the fruit of efforts to answer the question, "Who *is* he?" and "What is the meaning of it all?" All are cast in divine-human symbols, fragmentary, utterly inadequate, bewildering in their variety.

The third phase is the life of the Church to the end of time. There will be no further public revelation. The gospel, the good news has been proclaimed. We have believed, and we *hold* that gospel: *all* of it, in its bewildering variety and frustrating obscurity. The Holy Spirit dwells in us, in the Church, and illumines us. In our daily personal experience and the shared experience of the living community of believers through the centuries the promise continues to be fulfilled, and by the light of the Holy Spirit we gain deeper insight into the meaning of the promise, and into the meaning of the commitment which we have made by believing. We gain deeper insight into the meaning of the gospel, the Word. For the Word concerns God, Father, Jesus, and Holy Spirit; the eternal master plan for our life in them; the gradual unfolding of revelation and realization of the promise; fulfillment in Jesus Christ; and continuing fulfillment as the saving action comes to term in us, and will continue to the end of time. For the fulness of life in Christ is shared in all the unique ways of personal vocation, and in all of them facets of the Mystery are discovered. To the extent to which we let God be God in our lives, let his grace come to fulfillment in our full personal response, we manifest something of the fulness of Christ, something of the meaning of the Word.

Promise and fulfillment are open-ended: in continual fulfillment more of the meaning of the promise becomes manifest. And the further promises concerning the last things are a thrust into the unknown: beyond all human experience, imagination, understanding, and conception, they are cast in symbolism which culminates in apocalyptic, and which will fill men and women with wonder until the vision comes.

Faith is open-ended. When we believe in Christ, we believe the truth of the unseen of which he told, trust him and his Father, entrust ourselves to them, commit ourselves to a way of life which is our only hope. We never know fully the implications of that commitment: daily we learn more of what it involves.

Within the kingdom, we live our unique personal vocations,
infinitely varied, continually developing, ever surprising. For the
man and woman who marry, what does their mutual
commitment—for them now part of their way of life in
Them—what does that commitment mean in the moment of
mutual giving and taking? What will it mean, beyond all
imagination, as the days and years pass? And for every couple the
pattern varies, the meaning is different. For the young man who
answers the call to the priesthood, and commits himself as he
receives the precious gift, what does his commitment mean, how
does the meaning unfold as the days and years pass? And so for
the young man or woman who makes a commitment to a way of
life, of greater love, of sacrifice, in a vocation which is always
personal, always unique, the same question recurs. Whatever the
variation of our commitment within a life of faith, personal
vocation holds surprises as God's masterplan is worked out in our
lives.

There is a twofold application of the principle of
open-ended promise, faith, and fulfillment. First, it is a law
which we discover as we probe the history of salvation as it is
recorded in the Bible. To that discovery I have dedicated my
effort in this volume. Second, it is a law which we must keep in
mind as we seek to deepen our experience of God, and our
knowledge of the God whom we experience.

And here I pause, for we are at the threshold of another
volume.

ABBREVIATIONS

Books of the Bible

Old Testament

Gn or Gen	Genesis	Ct	Canticle of Canticles
Ex	Exodus	Wis	Wisdom
Lv	Leviticus	Sir	Sirach (Ecclesiasticus)
Nm	Numbers	Is	Isaiah
Dt	Deuteronomy	Jer	Jeremiah
Jos	Joshua	Lam	Lamentations
Jgs	Judges	Bar	Baruch
Ru	Ruth	Ez	Ezekiel
1 Sm	1 Samuel	Dn	Daniel
2 Sm	2 Samuel	Hos	Hosea
1 Kgs	1 Kings	Jl	Joel
2 Kgs	2 Kings	Am	Amos
1 Chr	1 Chronicles	Ob	Obadiah
2 Chr	2 Chronicles	Jon	Jonah
Ezr	Ezra	Mi	Micah
Neh	Nehemia	Na	Nahum
Tb	Tobit	Hab	Habakkuk
Jdt	Judith	Zeph	Zephania
Est	Esther	Hag	Haggai
Jb	Job	Zech	Zechariah
Ps(s)	Psalms	Mal	Malachi
Prv	Proverbs	1 Mc	1 Maccabees
Eccl	Ecclesiastes (Qoheleth)	2 Mc	2 Maccabees

New Testament

Mt	Matthew	Gal	Galatians
Mk	Mark	Eph	Ephesians
Lk	Luke	Phil	Philippians
Jn	John	Col	Colossians
Acts	Acts of the Apostles	1 Th	1 Thessalonians
Rom	Romans	2 Th	2 Thessalonians
1 Cor	1 Corinthians	1 Tm	1 Timothy
2 Cor	2 Corinthians	2 Tm	2 Timothy

Ti	Titus	1 Jn	1 John	
Phlm	Philemon	2 Jn	2 John	
Heb	·Hebrews	3 Jn	3 John	
Jas	James	Jude	Jude	
1 Pt	1 Peter	Ap	Apocalypse	
2 Pt	2 Peter			

Other Works

AB   Anchor Bible

BAG   *A Greek-English Lexicon of the New Testament...* by William F. Arndt and F. Wilbur Gingrich. Chicago: University of Chicago Press—London: Cambridge University Press, c. 1957.

BDF   *A Greek Grammar of the New Testament...*, A revision of F. Blass and A. Debrunner... translated and edited by Robert W. Funk. Cambridge: University Press—Chicago: Chicago University Press, 1961.

Basics   W. A. Van Roo, S.J., *Basics of a Roman Catholic Theology* (see bibliography).

BZ   *Biblische Zeitschrift.*

DNTTh   *The New International Dictionary of New Testament Theology.* 3 volumes. Edited by Colin Brown. Exeter: Paternoster Press, c. 1975, 1976, 1978.

Goodspeed   *The Complete Bible. An American Translation*, translated by J. M. Powis Smith... and Edgar Goodspeed. Chicago: University of Chicago Press, 1939.

JB   *The Jerusalem Bible.* London: Darton, Longman & Todd, 1966.

JBC   *The Jerome Biblical Commentary.* 2 volumes. London: Chapman, 1969—Englewood Cliffs, N.J.: Prentice–Hall, c. 1968.

Knox   *The New Testament.* Translated by Ronald A. Knox. New York: Sheed & Ward, 1944.

LSJ   *Greek-English Lexicon.* H. G. Liddell, Robert Scott, new edition by H. S. Jones. Oxford: Clarendon Press, 1940.

LXX   *Septuaginta.* Ed. quarta. Edidit Alfred Rahlfs. New York: American Bible Society, c. 1935.

MS   W. A. Van Roo, S.J., *Man the Symbolizer* (see bibliography).

NEB   *The New American Bible.* Washington: Confraternity of Christian Doctrine, c. 1971.

RSV   *The Oxford Annotated Bible with the Apocrypha.* Revised Standard Version. New York—Oxford: Oxford University Press, 1965.

Spencer   *The New Testament.* Translated by F. A. Spencer, O.P. New York: Macmillan, 1946.

TDNT   *Theological Dictionary of the New Testament.* 10 volumes. Edited by G. Kittel. Translator and Editor, G. W. Bromily. Grand Rapids, Mich.: Eerdmans, c. 1964-1976.

BIBLIOGRAPHY

ABBOTT, W. M., S.J., *The Documents of Vatican II.* New York: America Press, 1966.

ALAND, K. and others, *The Greek New Testament,* edited by K. A. and others. New York: United Bible Societies, 1966.

BARTH, M., *Ephesians,* AB, vols. 34 and 34A. Garden City, N.Y.: Doubleday, 1974.

BENOIT, P., O.P., review of J. Bonsirven, *Le divorce dans le Nouveau Testament* (Paris, 1948) in *Revue biblique* 58 (1951) pp. 116-118.

BONSIRVEN, J., S.J., *Le divorce dans le Nouveau Testament.* Paris, 1948.

———, "Excerpta fornicationis causa," *Recherches de sciences religieuses* 35 (1948) 442-464.

BOURKE, M. M., "The Epistle to the Hebrews," in JBC, II, pp. 381-403.

BROWN, C., editor DNTT, 3 volumes. Exeter: Paternoster Press, c. 1975, 1976, 1978.

BROWN, R. E., S.S., *The Gospel according to John* I-XII, AB, vol. 29. New York: Doubleday, 1966.

———, *The Birth of the Messiah: A Commentary on the Infancy Narratives in Matthew and Luke.* New York: Doubleday, 1977.

BUZY, D., S.C.J., *Evangile selon Matthieu* in *La Sainte Bible* (Pirot-Clamer). Paris: Letouzey et Ané, 1950.

CREHAN, J., S.J., *Early Christian Baptism and the Creed.* London: Burns Oates & Washbourne, 1950.

DAUBE, D., "The 'I am' of the Messianic Presence," in *The New Testament and Rabbinic Judaism.* London: Athlone, 1956.

DE LA POTTERIE, I., S.J., "L'onction du chrétien par la foi," *Biblica* 40 (1959) 12-69.

ELLIS, P. F., C.SS.R., "1-2 Kings", JBC, I, pp. 179-209.

FITTKAU, G., *Der Begriff des Mysteriums bei Johannes Chrysostomos.* Bonn, 1953.

FITZMYER, J., S.J., "Acts of the Apostles," (with Dillon, R.J.) JBC, II, pp. 165-214.

———, "The Letter to the Galatians," JBC, II, pp. 236-246.

———, "The Letter to the Philippians," JBC, II, pp. 247-253.

———, "The Letter to the Romans," JBC, II, pp. 291-331.

———, "The Letter to Philemon," JBC, II, pp. 332-333.

———, "The First Epistle of Peter," JBC, II, pp. 362-368.

———, "Pauline Theology," JBC, II, pp. 800-827.

———, *The Gospel According to Luke* (I-IX). Introduction, Translation, and Notes. AB, vol. 28. Garden City, N.Y.: Doubleday, 1977.

GAST, F., "Synoptic Problem," JBC, II, 1-6.

GRASSI, J. A., M.M., "The Letter to the Colossians," JBC, II, pp. 334-340.

———, "The Letter to the Ephesians," JBC, II, pp. 341-349.

HASTINGS, J., editor, *Dictionary of the Bible.* New York: Scribner's, 1963.

HUESMAN, J. E., S.J., "Exodus," JBC, I, pp. 47-66.

KEARNEY, P. J., "Joshua," JBC, I, pp. 123-148.

KINGSBURY, J. D., *Matthew: Structure, Christology, Kingdom.* Philadelphia: Fortress Press, 1975.

KNOX, R. A., *The New Testament*. New York: Sheed & Ward, 1944.

LEWIS, C. T. and Short, C., *A Latin Dictionary*. Oxford: Clarendon Press, 1879 (printing of 1958).

LYONNET, S., S.J., preface to Vanhoye, A., S.J., *La Structure Littéraire de l'Epître aux Hébreux*, ed. 2. Paris: Desclée De Brouwer, 1976.

MALLY, E. J., S.J., "The Gospel According to Mark," JBC, II, pp. 21-61.

McCARTHY, D. J., S.J., *Treaty and Covenant* [new edition]. Rome: Biblical Institute Press, 1978.

McKENZIE, J., *Dictionary of the Bible*. Milwaukee: Bruce, 1965.

———, "The Gospel According to Matthew," JBC, II, pp. 62-114.

———, "Aspects of Old Testament Thought," JBC, II, pp. 736-767.

MEIER, J. P., *The Vision of Matthew*. New York: Paulist Press, 1979.

O'ROURKE, J. J., "The Second Letter to the Corinthians," JBC, II, pp. 276-290.

REUMANN, J., *"Righteousness" in the New Testament*, with responses by J. A. Fitzmyer and J. Quinn. Philadelphia: Fortress Press—New York/Ramsey: Paulist Press, 1982.

SCHRENK, G., "δίκη, δίκαιος," etc. in Kittel, TDNT, vol. II, pp. 178-225.

SELWYN, E. G., *The First Epistle of St. Peter*. London: Macmillan, 1947, reprinted 1964.

SHORT, C., [with Lewis, C. T.] *A Latin Dictionary*. Oxford: Clarendon Press, 1879, printing of 1958.

SPICQ, C., O.P., review of J. Bonsirven, *Le divorce dans le Nouveau Testament*, in *Revue des sciences philosophiques et théologiques* 34 (1950) 47-48.

———, *L'Epître aux Hébreux*. 2 vols. Paris: Gabalda, 1952-1953.

STANLEY, D. M., S.J., with BROWN, R. E., S.S., "Aspects of New Testament Thought," JBC, II, 768-799.

STUHLMUELLER, C., C.P., "Post-exilic Period: Spirit, Apocalyptic," JBC, I, 337-343.

SULLIVAN, F. A., S.J., *Charisms and Charismatic Renewal*. A Biblical and Theological Study, Ann Arbor, Mich.: Servant Books, c. 1982.

VANHOYE, A., S.J., *La Structure Littéraire de l'Epître aux Hébreux*, ed. 2. Préface du R. P. St. Lyonnet, S.J. Paris: Desclée De Brouwer, 1976.

———, *Prêtres anciens prêtre nouveau selon le N.T.* Paris: Editions du Seuil, 1980.

VAN ROO, W. A., S.J., *Grace and Original Justice According to St. Thomas* (*Analecta Gregoriana*, 75). Rome: Gregorian University Press, 1955.

———, *De Sacramentis in Genere*. Rome: Gregorian University Press, 1957, 1960, 1962.

———, *The Mystery*. Rome: Gregorian University Press, 1971.

———, *Man the Symbolizer* (*Analecta Gregoriana*, 222). Rome: Gregorian University Press, 1981.

———, *Basics of a Roman Catholic Theology* (*Analecta Gregoriana*, 226). Rome: Gregorian University Press, 1982.

VATICAN COUNCIL II, *Dogmatic Constitution on the Church* (*Lumen gentium*) in W. M. Abbott, S.J., *The Documents of Vatican II*. New York: America Press, 1966, pp. 14-101.

VAWTER, B., C.M., "Introduction to Prophetic Literature," JBC, I, 223-237.

———, "The Gospel According to John," JBC, II, 414-466.

ZERWICK, M., S.J., *Graecitas Biblica*, ed. 4. Rome: Pontifical Biblical Institute, 1960.

ZIMMERMANN, H., "Das absolute 'Ego eimi' als die neutestamentliche Offenbarungsformel," BZ 4 (1960) 54-69, 266-276.

ZORELL, F., S.J., *Lexicon Graecum Novi Testamenti*, ed. 2. Paris: Lethielleux, 1931.

INDEX OF AUTHORS

Bl - Theo / INL

DATE DUE

TIPOGRAFIA POLIGLOTTA DELLA PONTIFICIA UNIVERSITÀ GREGORIANA
PIAZZA DELLA PILOTTA, 4 - ROMA